The
CENTRAL COAST
OF CALIFORNIA
Book

A Complete Guide

Don Fukuda

THE
CENTRAL COAST
OF CALIFORNIA
BOOK

A Complete Guide

CHRISTINA WATERS

&

BUZ BEZORE

Berkshire House Publishers
Stockbridge, Massachusetts

ON THE COVER AND FRONTISPIECE

Front Cover: Background — *Field of California Poppies* by Tony Hertz; Insets — *Mission Carmel* by Shmuel Thaler; *Sandpiper at Sunset* by Tony Hertz; *Waves Crashing on Coastal Rocks* by Shmuel Thaler.
Frontispiece: *Forested slopes and meadows dominate Central Coast bluffs overlooking the ocean beyond* by Don Fukuda.
Back cover: *Cal-Mex Food* by Paul Schraub; *Surfer in Bottle Green Curl* by Dan Coyro; *San Luis Obispo Street Artists* by Tony Hertz.

The Central Coast of California Book: A Complete Guide
Copyright © 1994 by Berkshire House Publishers
Cover and interior photographs © 1994 by credited photographers

Library of Congress Cataloging-in-Publication Data

Waters, Christina.
   The Central Coast of California book : a complete guide / Christina Waters & Buz Bezore.
     p. cm. — (The Great destinations series, ISSN 1056-7968)
   Includes bibliographical references and indexes.
   ISBN 0-936399-51-1 : $16.95.
   1. Pacific Coast (Calif.)—Guidebooks. I. Bezore, Buz. II. Title. III. Series
F859.3.W38   1994
917.94—dc20   93-40275
                                          CIP

ISBN: 0-936399-51-1
ISSN: 1056-7968 (Series)

Editor: Sarah Novak. Managing Editor: Philip Rich. Original design for Great Destinations™ series: Janice Lindstrom. Cover design: Jane McWhorter. Maps: Maia Farrell. Production services by Ripinsky & Company, Connecticut.

Berkshire House books are available at substantial discounts for bulk purchases by corporations and other organizations for promotions and premiums. Special personalized editions can also be produced in large quantities. For more information, contact:

Berkshire House Publishers
Box 297, Stockbridge MA 01262
800-321-8526

Manufactured in the United States of America
First printing 1994
10 9 8 7 6 5 4 3 2 1

No complimentary meals or lodgings were accepted by the authors and reviewers in gathering information for this work.

The <u>GREAT DESTINATIONS</u>™ Series

The Berkshire Book: A Complete Guide
The Santa Fe & Taos Book: A Complete Guide
The Napa & Sonoma Book: A Complete Guide
The Chesapeake Bay Book: A Complete Guide
The Coast of Maine Book: A Complete Guide
The Adirondack Book: A Complete Guide
The Aspen Book: A Complete Guide
The Charleston, Savannah & Coastal Islands Book:
  A Complete Guide
The Gulf Coast of Florida Book: A Complete Guide
The Central Coast of California: A Complete Guide
The Newport & Narragansett Bay Book: A Complete Guide
The Hamptons Book: A Complete Guide

The Great Destinations™ series features regions in the United States rich in natural beauty and culture. Each Great Destinations™ guidebook reviews an extensive selection of lodgings, restaurants, cultural events, historic sites, shops, and recreational opportunities, and outlines the region's natural and social history. Written by resident authors, the guides are a resource for visitor and resident alike. Maps, photographs, directions to and around the region, lists of helpful phone numbers and addresses, and indexes.

Contents

CHAPTER ONE
Of Blue and Golden Dreams
HISTORY
1

CHAPTER TWO
The Freeway and the Right Way
TRANSPORTATION
28

CHAPTER THREE
Coastal Comforts
LODGING
41

CHAPTER FOUR
Preserve and Promote
CULTURE
75

CHAPTER FIVE
Matters of Taste
RESTAURANTS AND FOOD PURVEYORS
117

CHAPTER SIX
Grape Expectations
WINERIES
166

CHAPTER SEVEN
Pump It Up
RECREATION
193

CHAPTER EIGHT
We Want It All
SHOPPING
234

CHAPTER NINE
Nuts and Bolts
INFORMATION
253

Acknowledgments

We were lucky enough to be able to draw on a wealth of expert regional informants whose suggestions, insights, and generous contributions allowed us to present readers with a comprehensive taste of the splendid and varied Central Coast.

As he has always done in projects we've shared, award-winning photographer Shmuel Thaler infuses these pages with the atmospheric images of the Central Coast landscape and with a sense of place. Additional thanks go to lens people Stan Cacitti, Jay Swanson, Paul Schraub, Don Fukuda, Dan Coyro, Tony Hertz, and Kim Reierson, as well as the "map queen," Maia Farrell.

Everywhere we traveled throughout the length of this stretch of California, we met experts on history, local color, restaurants, recreation, attractions, and wines who were generous with their accumulated wisdom.

Providing insightful feedback every step of the way was our seasoned global traveling companion Rosemary Bryan. Rita Bottoms, head of University of California, Santa Cruz' Special Collections, was always forthcoming with background lore on the region's historic flock of artists, writers, and trend-setting dreamers. The careful reading by historian Ross Eric Gibson lent expert credibility to the research-intensive *History* section.

Ed Galsterer helped plug us into the behind-the-scenes history and personalities that shaped much of Santa Barbara's special charm. Seasoned food writers Joe Tarantino (Monterey and Carmel) and Hilary Dole Klein (Santa Barbara) contributed the lion's share of the writing of the *Restaurants* sections for those two areas of the Central Coast.

To the winemakers up and down the Central Coast, we are grateful for sharing their time, information, tasting room enlightenment, and most of all, sensational vintages.

Without the painstaking research and sound judgment of Keri Frankel and Ben Klein (who used the opportunity as a distraction from completing his doctoral dissertation), the *Recreation* section could not have been accomplished. Also, Michael Allen took time out from his quest for the perfect wave to fill us in on insider surfing details, a portion of the book that also was improved by insights provided by Kim Hall.

For additional up-to-the-minute details, we thank Genial Johnny Simmons, Bill Morem, Bruce Howard, Jeffrey Whitmore, Paul LePort, Jeff Mahoney, and Fred Munroe. And Sean Love came forth with graphs, charts, and information for the *Transportation* section.

Our editor, Sarah Novak, demonstrated the right balance of drill sergeant and emergency room nurse to guarantee the book got to print, and we thank her for using a scalpel rather than a cleaver in her editing. And our hard-working researchers and fact checkers — Suzanne De Long Philis, Leslie Ariel, and Kate Warren — made sure we didn't embarrass ourselves, fact-wise, in print.

Special thanks goes to our colleagues at Metro Newspapers of Silicon Valley and the University of California, Santa Cruz who offered non-stop support during the long months of compiling, organizing, and packaging the ideas, energy, and information that went into this book.

Throughout the writing of this book, we were inspired by the accomplishments of a great interweaving of cultures — the Chumash and Ohlone, the Spanish and Yankee immigrants, and the 20th-century settlers — all of whom at one time or another called the Central Coast home.

We were lucky enough to set off on our many field trips of discovery during what was to prove the most verdant springtime in Central Coast memory. It is to the lupines of Santa Margarita that we dedicate this work.

Introduction

In the 15 years that we have worked and lived together on the Central Coast, we've never taken for granted the sheer beauty of the place we call home. How clever of our great-great-grandparents to have settled in what amounts to one of the natural treasures of the country. We've been fortunate to have our professional lives intersect with our personal interests. In creating countless weekend getaway pieces for a variety of regional publications, we've combed the area, enjoying unforgettable accommodations, sampling cuisine that continues to set trends, and soaking up ambiance that attracts visitors from all over the world.

From our house, we can walk to the beach in under three minutes and thread through atmospheric coastal bluffs and ancient oak groves by the simple act of driving to work. The walk from the parking lot to office affords astonishing views of the shimmering Monterey Bay in the distance through a frame of towering redwood trees. It would be impossible to take all this for granted. Besides, we firmly believe in being tourists in our own home town. When the surf's up, we're there gawking at the hypnotic wave action right along with visitors from New York, Italy, and Australia. Fine fall weather sends us out beachcombing, or wine tasting at some of our favorite wineries.

Not a day goes by that we aren't firmly impressed by the fact that we happen to live in a place that other people covet as a destination. That's another reason that vacations often find us exploring some new nook or cranny of the Central Coast instead of getting on a plane to somewhere else. We already live in one of the most desirable parts of the world. And while we're convinced that it will take a lifetime to explore it all, to savor its richness, we've already begun tasting the best of the region. Frankly, we don't mind sharing it one bit. After all, we can hardly blame visitors smart enough to make our slice of paradise their next vacation spot.

Christina Waters and Buz Bezore
Santa Cruz, California

THE WAY THIS BOOK WORKS

This book is divided into nine chapters. Entries within each chapter are arranged alphabetically under four regional headings: "Santa Cruz Coast," "Monterey Coast," "San Luis Obispo Coast," and "Santa Barbara Coast." Travelers driving along the Central Coast can turn to the section they're interested in — *Lodging*, for example — and look over possible places they may want to stay in towns coming up on their trip. Or, if a single area within the region is the destination, that area can be found in the same location within all of the major sections.

Each chapter has its own introduction designed to orient the reader to the Central Coast possibilities in each major heading. But however you decide to consult the various sections, we recommend that you take a look at the *History* and *Culture* sections, which provide the best overview to the unique personality of the entire region.

Some entries include specific information — telephone numbers, addresses, business hours, and that sort of thing — organized for quick and easy reference in blocks in the left-hand column. All information was re-checked as close to the publication date as possible. But since these details can change frequently, it's a good idea to call ahead to confirm. If you need to write to an inn or museum or any other place listed here, you'll find the zip code in the *Information* chapter.

PRICE CODES

Lodging price codes are based on a per-room rate, double occupancy during summer months. Off-season rates are invariably less expensive. Restaurant price ratings indicate the cost of an individual meal including appetizer, entree and dessert but not cocktails, wine, beverages, tax or tip.

	Lodging	Dining
Inexpensive	Up to $75	Up to $10
Moderate	$75 to $150	$10 to $25
Expensive	$150 to $225	$25 to $40
Very Expensive	$225 or more	$40 or more

The following abbreviations are used for credit card information:

AE — American Express   DC — Diners Card
CB — Carte Blanche   MC — MasterCard
D — Discover Card   V — Visa

The
CENTRAL COAST
OF CALIFORNIA
Book
A Complete Guide

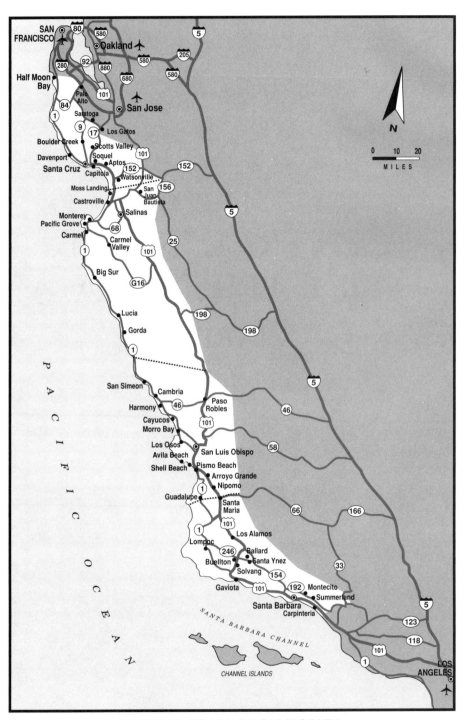

CENTRAL COAST OF CALIFORNIA

CHAPTER ONE

Of Blue and Golden Dreams
HISTORY

Just as the coastline of central California was formed by geologic forces, so in turn did this conjunction of land and sea shape the patterns of life and work for those first lived here, and for those who came to explore and stay. Natural harbors gave safe berth to sailors and settlers alike, just as the rich marine life along the coast provided both sustenance and bounty ripe for commercial development. The fertile land and mild climate invited agricultural endeavors, and the sheltering isolation and splendor of the landscape beckoned to legions of immigrants who would call this stretch of California home.

Covello & Covello

Wealth from the sea: the Central Coast fishing industry was established in the mid-nineteenth century; the Santa Cruz Wharf, circa 1910, was the domain of Italian immigrant fishermen.

NATURAL HISTORY

COASTLINES AND FAULTLINES

More than 100 million years ago, when two great continental land masses collided — a red hot meeting that marked the birth of the infamous San Andreas Fault — coast mountains forced their way up along the length of California. The grinding slow dance of the Pacific and North American tectonic plates pushed the northern ranges up to a height of 5000 feet and moved the edge of the land 100 miles westward (the coast of California once called eastern Nevada home).

Fourteen million years ago, volcanic activity formed the archipelago of the Channel Islands off the Santa Barbara coast. One trace of former molten activity still on dramatic display in the San Luis Obispo area is Morro Rock, a volcanic plug landmark that juts suddenly out of surrounding smooth sand beach.

At Point Conception, halfway between Pismo Beach and Santa Barbara, the northwest shoreline of California takes an abrupt ninety-degree turn, creating south-facing beaches — and highly prized surfing conditions — the length of Santa Barbara County. As late as 5 million years ago, the geologically adolescent mountains of the Santa Lucia range began lifting up out of the shoreline behind Santa Barbara.

Erosion of strata from millions of years ago carved the labyrinthine tide pools of the northern Santa Cruz and Monterey coastlines and the action of wind on sand has produced acres of softly shifting sand dunes along the southern stretches of San Luis Obispo. During the last ice age, glaciers carved channels into the land. When the glaciers eventually melted, the process reversed, flooding the land with lush estuaries and wetlands.

Typical of the northern portion of the Central Coast are large rock outcroppings that protect white sand beaches.

Shmuel Thaler

FLORA AND FAUNA

A long the Central Coast, highly specialized ecological niches — tide pools, estuaries, chaparral, oak woods, redwood forests — flourish in all their rich diversity. The influence of a persistent high-pressure system lying off the

Chaparral-covered mountains run along the entire Central Coast, and some years catch a few inches of snowfall.

Shmuel Thaler

Whole Lotta Shakin' Goin' On

The San Andreas Fault runs halfway up the California coast, from the Gulf of California in the south to just off San Francisco in the north, and has been responsible for earthshaking mischief ranging from the nerve-wracking to the deadly. The shiftings and bucklings of neighboring continental plates that produce this volatile seismic activity were responsible for the 1906 earthquake, which hurled the cultural outpost of San Francisco into international headlines, and for the Loma Prieta quake (7.1 on the Richter Scale) that rearranged private and public property and fortunes along the northern stretches of the Central Coast in 1989.

While countless adjacent faultlines create various seismic disturbances, none has more dramatic impact than the San Andreas, the Pacific side sidling northward past the larger North American plate at the rate of two inches per year. The stress of this enormous though largely invisible encounter builds up and creates ruptures, many as mild as ocean tides; some, however, create temblors of unforgettable impact.

These faultline upsurges, which invariably bring landslides — not to mention gas line and water main breakage — in their wakes, can prove devastating in areas lying on sandy soils, where a liquefaction effect magnifies the impact of the earth's crust slamming down upon the deeper soils below. When a major quake occurs, ensuing shock waves ("aftershocks" to anyone still standing) often serve as deadly collaborators, exponentially enlarging the initial damage.

The miracle is that the Central Coast has preserved as much of its original architectural heritage as it has. Unfortunately, many of its oldest settlements — including almost all the earliest mission complexes — retain only pieces of their original structure, the rest painstakingly recreated in the lull following seismic destruction. Shaken, but not dislodged, Central Coast residents periodically rebuild, invariably accepting earthquakes as a small price to pay, a fair trade, for living in what they consider the most beautiful spot on earth.

coast creates the felicitous, dry summers and mild, wet winters that give the Central Coast a Mediterranean climate unique in the continental United States.

The signature summer fog of the region, responsible in large part for the year-round growing season, brings other rewards besides relief from the heat that sears valleys just ten miles inland. In the mountainous northern Central Coast, it also contributes to the presence of lush ferns and forests of towering redwoods, the *sequoia sempervirens*. Growing up to 325 feet in height and living to great age — some 2000-year-old specimens have been recorded — these astonishing evergreens, whose tough wood is remarkably fire-resistant, attracted ax-wielding hordes of 19th-century loggers, who posed for early cameras on stumps large enough to accommodate a team of horses and wagon.

The heart of the Central Coast is its ranch-land sprawl of chaparral grasslands dotted by enormous Spanish oaks, a zone above and beyond the fog line where wild lilac and manzanita bloom in the summer heat. The state flower, the brilliant orange California poppy, grows abundantly each spring along every roadside, often in the company of broad swaths of purple lupine. By

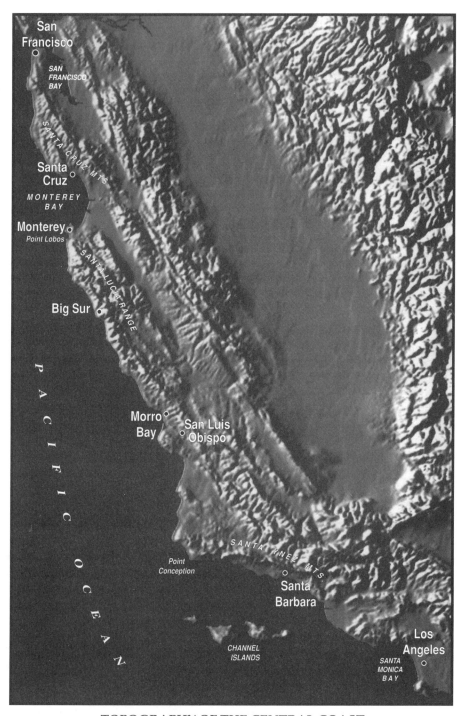

TOPOGRAPHY OF THE CENTRAL COAST

Majestic redwood stands stretch from the summits of coastal ranges to the ocean shore along the Central Coast.

Shmuel Thaler

August, the dried-yellow high grasses gild the hillsides along the entire length of the Coast Highway.

In the dappled woodland sunlight of 1000-feet elevations, oaks coexist with the graceful madrone, whose thin red bark peels off in tightly-rolled curls. In the heat of the afternoon, the heady scent of bay fills the upper canopy, while low to the ground grows the pungent yerba buena — the "good herb" prized by Native Americans and latter-day tea-drinkers alike. Western gray squirrels, raccoons, possums, and skunks share the harvests of acorns and native berries with woodpeckers, all under the surveillance of soaring hawks.

While the grizzly bear disappeared from California early this century, mountain lions, wild boar, and black bear still roam protected areas of the coastal mountains. With little to disturb their solitude, gray fox, mule deer, and coyotes flourish in the brush of steep coastal canyons. Winter ushers in the annual migration of millions of monarch butterflies, who drape their favorite coastal groves of eucalyptus trees with a living fabric of fluorescent orange wings.

Winter also announces the yearly return of gray and humpback whales, an event that brings legions of nature lovers within easy viewing distance of some of the planet's largest mammals. The barnacle-encrusted cetaceans join sea lions, dolphins, salmon, shellfish, and bonito in the region's teeming marine sanctuaries.

Vast expanses of sandy beach give way all along the coast to spectacular tide pools and jagged cliffs. The rocky outcroppings of Año Nuevo and Point Lobos provide safe harbor for the delicate ecology of tide pools and their resident hermit crabs, anemones, star fish, and sand dollars. Majestic underwater kelp forests stretch tendrils up onto the rocks and sand, sharing these harsh and secluded places with elephant seals and sea otters.

Where the Central Coast's many small rivers meander to the sea, wetland estuaries host a plethora of diverse sealife, including oysters, shrimp, and crabs,

Back from the brink of extinc-tion, elephant seals get up close and personal at Año Nuevo breeding grounds.

Shmuel Thaler

all of which feed on the nutrient-rich blend of salt and fresh water. These shell-fish, in turn, attract throngs of harbor seals and sea otters, and scores of fish and bird species. At Elkhorn Slough, where the Salinas River meets Monterey Bay at Moss Landing, tens of thousands of shearwater gulls, white egrets, blue herons, and migratory ducks and geese gather, feed, and nest.

Thanks to a chain of rigorously maintained state parks and beaches, the Central Coast offers nature-loving visitors ample opportunities for wilderness camping, beachcombing, and wildlife observing in accessible, protected environmental preserves.

SOCIAL HISTORY

PARADISE LOST: THE NATIVE CALIFORNIANS

California was the name of a mythical island kingdom, rich in gold and precious stones, described in a long Spanish poem written about 1500. Hernando Cortez is credited with applying the name to the land he encountered in his New World expeditions in the 16th century.

By that time, the Central Coast already was home to several hundreds of thousands of Native Americans. The largest tribes were the Ohlone in the north and the Chumash in the south, nomadic hunter/gatherer peoples who had arrived in the region 3000 years before the Spanish. An easy climate, ample fresh water, and an abundance of edible plants, wild game, and marine life allowed these peaceful Native Californians to exist in harmony with their environment.

From San Francisco Bay south to San Luis Obispo, the Ohlone set up temporary villages of dome-shaped, tule-thatched structures and men-only ceremonial sweat lodges close to springs and rivers along the coast. From the sea, they gathered abalone and oysters; the shells piled up over the years into giant middens, some of which persist to this day. From the forests — which the Ohlone managed through controlled burning — berries and pine nuts were staples of their diet, as were acorns, which they blanched to remove toxins before grinding into an all-purpose meal. The region's huge herds of buffalo, together with quail, deer, elk, and bear, augmented their diet.

South of San Luis Obispo, the Chumash had established active trade links with the tribes of the Channel Islands. The sea provided a wealth of fresh produce: bonito and sardines caught by net, salmon speared by stick, even the occasional whale taken by harpoon. These native peoples were, in turn, to provide the raw material for a religious and territorial conquest that transformed the face of the western frontier forever.

MEN WITH A MISSION: THE SPANISH CONQUEST

Thanks to overblown reports of potential riches and to the discovery of fabulous natural harbors in the area by explorer Juan Rodriguez Cabrillo, Spain laid claim to the entire coast of California in 1542. Once claimed, the land remained largely unexplored for the next 50 years, while Spanish galleons laden with trade goods sailed near the Central Coast on lucrative voyages between colonies in Mexico and Manila.

The need for a convenient port on the California coast prompted new exploration in Alta (upper) California. The search was on for a spot where Spanish ships could take on supplies halfway through the arduous intercontinental trading voyages. Basque mariner Sebastian Vizcaino set out on such a venture in 1602 and discovered Monterey Bay in the process. Naming it after the Viceroy of Mexico, Vizcaino described Monterey in such exaggerated terms that later explorers had some difficulty recognizing it.

When King Charles III took the Spanish throne in 1759, he was determined to strengthen Spanish New World enterprises — both economic and religious — and ordered an expansion of the mission system already present in Baja (lower) California. Taking up the quest was the Spanish governor of Baja California, Gaspar de Portola. In 1769, he led the "Sacred Expedition" to Alta California, accompanied by the *padre presidente* of the Franciscan missionary effort, the indefatigable Padre Junipero Serra.

When the mountains of gold they pursued proved to be fantasy, the colonial powers of New Spain envisioned a different kind of El Dorado — in the form of land, with potential Christian souls in the people who lived on it. Joining forces, the military and the Franciscan clergy set out to found missions and spread the word of Christ, to cultivate the fertile land, and to erect military forts, or *presidios*, which headquartered the soldiers accompanying the monks and protected the newly won territory. Their successes inspired civilian colonists from Mexico, who followed and built pueblo settlements in the shadow of the missions.

Bringing with them herds of cattle — for the beef, leather, and tallow (for soap and candles) industries that thrived for more than a century — Serra and Portola began their conversion of territory and native Indians in San Diego in

*A painting of the original
Santa Cruz Mission.*

Covello & Covello

1769. With Serra remaining in San Diego to found the first Californian mission, Portola continued overland — the first European to do so — through San Luis Obispo and Monterey (whose bay, of course, he failed to recognize), turning around within sight of San Francisco Bay. On a second trip a year later, Portola finally extracted the reality of Monterey Bay from Vizcaino's hyperbole and developed a presidio there.

So the padres and soldiers came, also bringing agriculture, orchards, vineyards, irrigation techniques, the water wheel, horses, written language — and, ultimately, the decimation of native populations who succumbed to mistreatment and European diseases.

THE RANCHO AND THE REPUBLIC

Mexico won its independence from Spain in 1821, and vast holdings once belonging to the Catholic Church were divided into generous land grants. These were deeded to the loyal *Californio* citizens or sold at rock bottom prices to the highest, and most adventurous, bidder. The name of the game was ranching. Family fortunes were made and sustained by herds of cattle whose hides were tanned — by another booming local industry — and sent by ship to destinations around the world. Some of the *ranchos* subsequently became the core of the Central Coast's richest territory, and survive today not only as huge ranches, but also as private farms, golf courses, and state-owned natural park lands.

The Spanish monopoly on trading now at an end, new American entrepreneurs came to this Mexican province to seek their fortunes. Many stayed and married into Californio families. The middle of the 19th century saw an influx of East Coast and European whalers, tanners, dairy farmers, merchants, fur traders, and loggers, exploring the unlimited possibilities of this abundant coast.

This was also a colorful period of Mexican hospitality, of famous week-long fiestas and rodeos at the cattle-wealthy Californios' lavish *casas*. The expansive mood — eloquently evoked in Richard Henry Dana's *Two Years Before the Mast* — was punctuated by the brisk mercantile development and sea trading economy of the English-speaking newcomers.

Rejection of Mexican rule gained momentum during the 1830s, and in the

1840s John C. Fremont — pathfinder, military engineer, and future United States senator — explored Central California on a mission from the U.S. government, which was rapidly developing an interest in the Far West. With the help of Fremont's men — and aided by the underground efforts of wealthy Yankee merchants like Monterey's Thomas Larkin — a peaceful takeover occurred in 1846 at the Sonoma headquarters of Mexican General Mariano Vallejo. There, a makeshift flag bearing the emblem of the territory's mighty grizzly bear proclaimed the end of the Mexican era.

Ultimately, the Bear Republic — itself an unofficial and very short-lived affair — gave way to statehood. A constitutional convention was convened by delegates from all over the state in Monterey in 1849, and in 1850 the sun officially set on Old California one day and rose again the next on the new State of California.

GOLDEN OPPORTUNITIES: THE RUSH WAS ON

The discovery of gold near Sacramento in 1848 ushered in a rush of Americans, Europeans, and Chinese eager to get rich quick in the gold fields of the Sierra Nevada foothills. Raising the temperature of migration, gold fever helped trigger a tidal wave of adventurers to the Central Coast, where the wealth of virgin timber spawned an overnight shipping industry fueled by a sudden rash of sawmills and logging camps. Schools, churches, courthouses, cottages, and mansions sprang up in growing towns along the coast. Though the mines and streams quickly ceased to "pan out" — the expression itself is another legacy of the '49ers — the youthful new population of Americans stayed on to become the business and political leaders of the late 19th and early 20th centuries.

The story of the Central Coast's accelerating fishing industry is a saga of cultural competition. Chinese immigrants, who came to mine gold and build the growing network of railroads, stayed to establish the first fishing industry in a succession of highly lucrative villages hugging the coast. By the mid-1870s, more than 100,000 Chinese had taken up residence in the state, including large settlements in Santa Cruz, Watsonville, and Monterey. By 1890, following an

Quong Chong was a leading Chinese merchant (and proud father) in turn-of-the-century Santa Cruz.

The redwood forests of the Central Coast lured entrepreneurs looking to strike it rich in timber rather than gold in the late 1880s.

Covello & Covello

unfortunate period of vigilante activity against the industrious Asian immigrants (who were willing to work for well below the going wages), the Chinese domination of the maritime wealth was eclipsed by Italians, Portuguese, and Japanese.

CAPTAINS OF INDUSTRY AND THE PURSUIT OF PLEASURE

The new prosperity was supported by a plethora of industries; fortunes boomed in the new communications networks — shipping and the railroad. Once the Golden Spike was driven in Utah in 1869, linking railroads across the continent, settlers rushed to the Far West from all over the country. Charles Nordhoff and other writers composed such glowing accounts of the natural wonders of the Golden State in popular books and magazines that, overnight, California was literally put on the map. The great resorts of the coast thronged with Victorians enamored of salt air vacations, eager to loosen their corsets for a bit of sea bathing.

When Santa Barbara was finally linked to San Francisco by rail in 1901, a growing Central Coast bourgeoisie continued to develop seaside resort attractions. The enduring reputation of the balmy California coast as a resort area *par excellence* was firmly entrenched. Santa Barbara emerged as a bedroom community for the new Hollywood film industry and, along with Santa Cruz, became an open air movie set for a glut of celluloid Westerns, romances, and cliffhangers that filled the nation's nickelodeons.

Entrepreneur Fred Swanton concocted a fabulous Brighton-style resort casino, dance palace and amusement park at the water's edge in Santa Cruz in 1903. A major attraction for legions of tourists from its opening day, the Boardwalk thrives today as the last example of its kind on the California Coast. The turn of the century also saw the germination of efforts to preserve the region's breathtaking natural resources, with the first state redwood park: Big Basin Redwoods in Santa Cruz, purchased with the help of the Sempervirens Club in 1901.

The legendary Fred Swanton built his Santa Cruz pleasure dome to attract tourists from San Francisco.

Covello & Covello

OUT OF THE DUST, INTO THE FUTURE

The rise of the Hollywood movie, which painted California as a land of romantic opportunity, along with the more mundane realities of the Depression, lured yet another wave of eager immigrants to the temperate climes of the Central Coast during the 1930s. They came from America's drought-stricken dust bowl to add their energy and urgency to the creative melting pot. They were the Okies, Arkies, and other heartland refugees who fled foreclosed farms to pick coastal lettuce, work the sardine canneries, and fuel the gritty dramas of John Steinbeck. However, times were tough in California, too. By 1935, almost a fifth of its population was on the dole. But the climate was mild and you might as well go hungry in paradise.

Those who came and hung on during the lean times were rewarded by the full employment of World War II, which brought military bases and the aeronautics industry to eager workers. The opening of the University of California in Santa Barbara just after the war piqued the fortunes of that community, as did the coming of University of California in Santa Cruz to that tiny resort in the mid-'60s.

The post war period witnessed an increase of private building and public ownership along the Central Coast. Enormous military bases built for coastal defense lured related industries to the region and created the growth of entire towns full of families and businesses dependent on the military presence. Meanwhile, a burgeoning state park system that was to become a showcase for the rest of the nation protected huge expanses of native flora and fauna.

ARTISTS, DREAMERS, AND THE AGE OF AQUARIUS

In the years between the two world wars, the scenery and seclusion of the Central Coast was a siren song for literary bohemians, freethinkers, and metaphysical cults. Isadora Duncan, John Steinbeck, Henry Miller, Robinson Jeffers, Jack London, Emil White, and Mark Twain immortalized the liberated lifestyles and meditative splendor they found at the region's secluded canyons, natural springs, and coffeehouses.

If San Francisco was the spiritual headquarters of the Beat Generation, then Big Sur was its vacation hideaway. When quintessential bad boy Jack Kerouac went On the Road, he did it along the coast roads linking San Francisco with Big Sur, where he stopped for a breather in the mountain cabin owned by poet Lawrence Ferlinghetti and penned the book that spawned a generation of rebels without a cause. At Carmel, photographers Ansel Adams and Edward Weston captured the haunting marriage of earth, sky, and sea in black and white images that still define the California coastal magic a full 50 years later. The bewitching landscape and maverick heritage that attracted Robert Louis Stevenson and Richard Henry Dana a century before continued to exert its pull.

Hidden and out of the way, the rugged coast offered a sanctuary for those marching to a different drummer. Theosophists, Zen Buddhists, and naturalists came, stayed, set up salons and meditative retreats, and preached the good life far from the status quo of staid and traditional America.

During the 1960s, consciousnesses expanded up and down the western seaboard and the Central Coast became a nursery for the emerging human potential movement. As the counterculture entered the "new age," the Central Coast led the way with its consciousness-raising centers at Esalen, Tassajara, and Big Sur. The hippies' experimentation with mind-altering drugs gradually gave way to attitude adjustments of non-chemical varieties. And, after being found, the "inner child" needed to be fed — organically. The natural food and organic gardening movement also was nurtured here.

Before they cut their hair and moved on — and quite a few never did — bohemian baby boomers had infused almost every inch of the Central Coast with their attitude of tolerance. After all, people had been "doing their own thing" in the relative inaccessibility of the rugged coastal mountains since the beginning.

The hills and canyons of the Central Coast were — and still are — alive with the truly laid-back and self-sufficient, all seeking an alternative approach to life in Eden. Up and down the coast, the footprints in the sand are more likely to be made by Birkenstocks or thong sandals than anything resembling a leather oxford.

THE NEW COAST GUARDIANS

With consciousness-raising inevitably came new sensitivity to the dynamic between people and plants, so that, by the '70s, the Central Coast boasted a highly vocal population of environmental activists. Beaches were increasingly snapped up by the state for management and protection, and kept clean with a vengeance. Litterers became outcasts and recycling was an unwritten law. With the rise of off-shore drilling along the southern reaches of the Central Coast, environmental protection legislation aggressively signaled concern for the region's natural treasures. The infamous Santa Barbara oil spill of 1969 focused worldwide attention on that city and catalyzed local activists to scrutinize the precarious balance of nature and technology.

The state formed the Coastal Commission in 1976 to monitor development and to maintain and protect the unique biosystems of the coastline. National wildlife sanctuaries were designated to protect rare wildlife habitats along the coast and in the sea, the latest and largest being the Monterey Bay National Marine Sanctuary.

In the short 150 years since the twilight of Junipero Serra's missions, the Central Coast has managed to nurture the past while protecting its privileged resources for the future. Thanks to a prized sense of self-reflectiveness, it still looks and feels remarkably like the very new world it is.

JOURNEY DOWN THE COAST

A drive down the Central Coast is a drive through California's historic past, through layers of distinctive landscapes shaped as much by generations of explorers, ranchers, and pioneers, as by wind and wave. A 300-mile length of spectacular seascapes, towering forests, appealing towns, and atmospheric ranch lands, this region can be best, and most intimately, savored by following the legendary Highway 1. The following section is a brief tour of these coastal pleasures, with more information about what to see and where to stay detailed in the rest of this book.

HALF MOON BAY

Nestled squarely on Highway 1, this hamlet is known to locals as the halfway point between San Francisco and Santa Cruz. The arts and crafts emporium "Spanishtown" pays tribute to the town's nickname circa 1840 when Baja California immigrants claimed this slice of the coast for their own. When Prohibition dried up the nation's official alcohol consumption, Half Moon Bay's many secluded coves harbored rum smugglers who supplied San Francisco with enough spirits to wait out the dry years.

Soothed by prevailing fogs, the hemispherical bay still nurtures the rich fisheries and moist growing season that attracted its Portuguese, Spanish, and Italian settlers in the 19th century. From here fleets plumb the coastal waters for salmon, anchovies, and herring, and surrounding fields boast Christmas tree farms and pumpkins. Artichokes, berries, and brussels sprouts share the hillsides with cattle and sheep; greenhouses supplying cut flowers to the entire state line the highway leading south.

Linked to San Francisco by the little mountain pass of Highway 92, the town of Half Moon Bay is in the process of reinventing itself as a condominium-studded bedroom community for the Greater San Francisco Bay Area.

PESCADERO

Ghosts of Californio ranchers and Japanese fishing pioneers haunt this one-street town, whose name means "fishing place" in Spanish. A gateway to redwood campgrounds, prime surf, and the convoluted stretches of Pescadero State Beach, the town is the setting for houses, barns, and authentic general stores straight out of the frontier West. The top destination here is Duarte's Tavern, populated with real cowboys, migrant workers, and colorful raconteurs.

An idyllic 210-acre expanse of wildlife sanctuary faces Pescadero Beach across Highway 1. On one side of the road waves reverberate against miles of wide tide pools, on the other elegant egrets, mallards, blue herons, and brilliantly colored wood ducks pose and sail blissfully on lagoons threaded by giant cattails. This is a favorite underground playground for northern California's hip young community and has been since the 1960s. Even before the Summer of Love, a young, slender Jerry Garcia regularly jammed with his newly formed Grateful Dead to the roar of huge bonfires on the beach.

AÑO NUEVO AND POINTS SOUTH

In January, when the velvety grasses of the Central Coast's "false spring" add an elegance to the rough-hewn land, this stretch of the coast offers irresistible driving pleasure. The winter months are also famous along the coast for whale-watching and, for those who join the guided tours at Año Nuevo State Reserve, elephant seal mating rituals.

Redwood forests — many protected as part of Big Basin, Castle Rock, and Butano state parks — crown the coastal highlands, which momentarily fan out into verdant crops of artichokes or brussels sprouts before plunging into the sea.

Just north of Davenport, the stately lagoon of Scott Creek hosts Canadian geese, coots, and mallards floating noisily on pools fringed with cattails and tule. Ghostly pampas grass rims the steep ridges behind, and across the road, sandy beaches curve out of sight.

Down the road a piece, Waddell Creek finally spills out into the Pacific after tumbling down from its source high in Big Basin Park. This spot has been claimed by hang gliders and windsurfers. Nearby, waterfowl stake out their plots in saltwater marshes and freshwater lagoons. This is a magic location for year-round beachcombing (look for gnarled driftwood and sea-smoothed rocks).

DAVENPORT

The tiny village of Davenport was, since shortly after the turn of the century, a company town built, owned, and operated by and for the Santa Cruz Portland Cement Company. Everything and everyone in it was white from cement dust — houses, cars, people, and gardens. All of that was cleaned up in the '60s, but, if you squint, your imagination can do the rest. There are still signs of the past in some of the original, identical houses — one of which, the Bath House, turned saloon, then sporting house, is now part of the New Davenport Bed and Breakfast establishment.

Across the street from the bustling Cash Store — a lodging, restaurant, and community core, and global arts and crafts emporium — the whale-watching is as good as it gets. In the mid-19th century, whalers from all over the world came here to fill their ships with precious oil and line their pockets with gold. One of those adventurous souls was Rhode Island's John Davenport, who came in 1850 and ended up running not only a major whaling operation but a lumber wharf as well. (In those days, you were nobody unless you had your own wharf.)

Davenport is charm itself, easily circumnavigated on foot, with glimpses into world-class glassblowing, boat-building, and knife-making studios.

Captain John Davenport and wife Ellen, founders of the 19th-century north Central Coast whaling town that bears their name.

Cruciform from Another Planet

Stretching from Half Moon Bay down through Monterey County, mighty portions of the Central Coast lie cultivated with miles of brussels sprouts, which flourish in the lengthy growing season and cool summer fog of this moist seaside climate. The brussels sprout is a cruciform and a distant relative of the mustard family. Almost extra-terrestrial in appearance, the stalks are studded with miniature cabbage heads, gray-green knobs growing the entire two-foot length. Harvested when the little heads are still tiny and tender, the sprouts provide luxurious eating, simply steamed and bathed in butter, lemon, and vinegar. Though denigrated for its ripe aroma when allowed to grow past maturity, the brussels sprout is an agricultural mainstay once celebrated by its own festival each year at the Santa Cruz Beach Boardwalk.

Grower Steve Bontadelli proudly displays a stalk of brussels sprouts.

SANTA CRUZ

Long one of the state's most appealing seaside resorts, the town of Santa Cruz supports an eclectic population of artists, writers, winemakers, restaurateurs, and rabble-rousers. Originally settled by the Franciscan fathers who established the Mission La Exaltacion de la Santa Cruz in 1791, the area that would become Santa Cruz flourished, ironically, thanks to the very secular residence of the nearby Branciforte Pueblo, the center of town life in Spanish days, then by Mexican land-grant ranchos that followed the pueblo's breakup, and, finally, by American entrepreneurs attracted by the matchless setting of mountains descending into Monterey Bay.

The original mission was destroyed by earthquake — twice — but exists today as a one-third scale replica; the past also lives on in the city's tree-lined streets of impeccable Victorian mansions and classic examples of Craftsman bungalows. The 1989 earthquake — centered a mere eight miles away — felled many of the historic commercial buildings in downtown Santa Cruz, but a rebuilding effort is now nearly complete. A restoration of the 19th-century St. George Hotel now forms the cultural heart of the town.

For well over 100 years, the expansive main beach of Santa Cruz has welcomed visitors, many flocking to the massive amusement park of the Santa Cruz Beach Boardwalk. The Victorian ballroom of the Cocoanut Grove features big name big bands and rock groups. In addition to a colorful assortment of death-defying rides, the Boardwalk is graced with the Giant Dipper — the oldest surviving wooden roller coaster in the country — and an enchanting 1911 carousel bedecked with hand-carved painted horses.

Lined with summer homes and gingerbread Victorian retreats, West Cliff Drive curves along the coast, linking the end of the Santa Cruz Municipal Wharf with the wild cliffs of Natural Bridges State Park a few miles northward. In the middle, just at the point where the sheltered Monterey Bay gives way again to the turbulent Pacific Ocean proper, is Lighthouse Point. On this site, a lighthouse has warned ships at sea of dangerous rock outcroppings since 1869. Today's tiny beacon, built in 1967 to replace the badly undermined original, not only still warns fishing fleets at dawn, but also houses the state's first surfing museum.

Following the uphill curve of High Street past historic Mission Plaza, visitors arrive at the former ranch of lime and cattle potentate Henry Cowell. This splendid 2000-acre site — whose sweeping fields are filled with deer and coyote and framed by thick stands of redwoods — is now the home of the youngest campus of the University of California, a showpiece of contemporary architecture. The original limestone quarry and many of Cowell's lime kilns, barns, and ranch buildings still are scattered scenically throughout the campus. The sweeping view of the entire Monterey Bay from this academic vantage point is worth the drive.

CAPITOLA AND SOQUEL

Once the intersection of 19th century commerce and stage lines, these sister cities face each other across diminutive Soquel Creek, which empties into a broad, sheltered beach at Capitola. Today Capitola-by-the-Sea attracts fami-

Santa Cruz scene: the Central Coast lifestyle is passionately devoted to active (and not so active) outdoor pursuits.

Shmuel Thaler

lies of sunbathers to its sheltered children's beach and shoppers to its galleries, crafts shops, and boutiques. The beach and the shopping area adjoin the Esplanade, with its trendy watering holes and seafood restaurants.

Across the creek and Highway 1, lies sleepy Soquel, founded by Yankee merchants, settled by ambitious loggers, and peopled by generations of cattle ranchers and horse trainers. Country roads lead away from the ocean, up into the Santa Cruz Mountains through pastures, small organic farms, and thriving microwineries. This is also begonia country, where vast fields and nurseries breed the large, luscious blooms sold to dealers and florists around the world. Well-tended and with an abundance of antiques shops, Soquel offers a surprising diversity of fine restaurants all built on the same small scale as the town itself.

RIO DEL MAR AND APTOS

Sugar beet king Claus Spreckels made such a fortune in the fields near Aptos Creek that the imprint of his private polo grounds can still be seen just outside the entrance to 10,000 pristine acres of redwood lands that form the Forest of Nisene Marks. Made infamous in recent years as the epicenter of the Loma Prieta earthquake of 1989, this otherwise undisturbed forest offers hiking and horseback trails extending far into the interior of the coast ranges. The slender stretch of Highway 1 occupied by Aptos Village offers some of the finest dining in the Central Coast.

At the coast, Aptos yields to the seaside community of Rio Del Mar, an attractive amalgam of beach homes abutting a short esplanade and miles of wide beachfront offering camping, barbecuing, and walking for hours. In the middle of Seacliff Beach (a short stroll away) sits the wreck of a World War I cement ship. Accessible by a slender pier, the boat is ideal for surf fishing.

These primarily residential areas offer secluded sunning, surfing and — for the young and hardy — fine swimming conditions in water that remains just a few degrees too cool for most adults without wetsuits. Further south, the state beaches of La Selva, Manresa, and Sunset offer broad expanses of sand and fine swimming conditions.

MOSS LANDING

Marking the midway point of the Monterey Bay, where the Salinas River bisects the low-lying artichoke fields between Santa Cruz and Monterey, Moss Landing is just south of the sensational bird watching of Elkhorn Slough. The slough's 2500 acres of salt marsh and tidal flats not only provide sanctuary for tens of thousands of waterfowl, they also contain plankton rich enough to nurse oyster and shrimp farms supplying Central Coast restaurants.

In 1864, this was a bustling scene. Established as a whaling station by Captain Charles Moss, a busy harbor soon serviced schooners loaded with produce from the Salinas Valley and whaling ships from around the world. Today, Moss Landing is essentially a faded postcard of a fishing village — a collection of piers, docks, and duck-filled lagoons without a town in sight. What Moss Landing does have is scores of antique stores lining the one road that twists through its ramshackle collection of docks.

The drive inland from Moss Landing wanders through a gray-green sea of artichokes as far as the eye can see. In the middle of it all is Castroville, a heartland ranching and agricultural settlement with one foot in the last century. Comprised of a single street and fortified by produce stands, tiny Castroville — ten miles inland from Monterey — proudly calls itself the Artichoke Capital of the World. None dare argue.

MONTEREY

Fifty years after Columbus sailed to the New World, Spanish explorers began bumping into Monterey, first Cabrillo in 1542, then Vizcaino in 1602, and, finally, military commander Portola in 1769. Father Serra joined Portola in Monterey in 1770, and the duo founded the second mission and presidio in the Alta California conquest. The mission, originally built in what is today downtown Monterey, was moved in 1771 to the more fertile fields and abundant fresh water of Carmel, a few miles to the south.

Monterey is an impeccably maintained fabric of historic old sections, waterfront wharves and piers, Cannery Row tourism, and well-groomed conference hotels and seaside lodgings, all ringed by the teeming natural kingdom of Monterey Bay. Fisherman's Wharf — originally built in 1846 and once bursting with international whaling traffic — offers seafood dining and souvenir shopping as well as fine sport fishing amidst the nets, boats, and paraphernalia of today's busy tuna, bonito, and salmon industries. This is a prime vantage point for observing the antics of sea otters and sunning harbor seals.

Global Matters

The artichoke — a Mediterranean native and member of the thistle family — was widely cultivated by Italian immigrants attracted by the climatic and scenic resemblance of the Central Coast to their European homeland. Thriving along the Central Coast — especially in Monterey and Santa Cruz counties — artichoke fields, in some places, stretch down to the very edge of bluffs overlooking the ocean. The distinctive, sea-green plant grows in round "islands" of feathery leaves, crowned by the fat globe that is the edible prize. The ultimate finger food, steamed artichoke leaves are simply pulled off, dipped in a lemon/butter mixture or dragged through garlic-infused mayonnaise and scraped clean of tender meat with the teeth. Nestled in the thistled interior lies the succulent heart, favored by Californians and prepared in myriad ways — from deep fried to candied. Few can resist stopping to buy $1 bags of these locally grown chokes.

Cooled by coastal fog, Castroville is the artichoke capital of the world.

Shmuel Thaler

Starting at the wharf, Monterey's historic district of plazas, streets, and calles is best seen on foot. A walking tour of this "Path of History" takes visitors back through the 18th and 19th centuries.

Poised at the tip of the bay as it begins to yield to the open waters of the Pacific Ocean, the first fort of the Spanish empire in California — the Monterey Presidio — still maintains a military watch over the harbor. From its commanding position, the old bastion marks the beginning of Cannery Row, in its prime a cheek-by-jowl amalgam of sardine canneries and processing plants, colorfully chronicled in the 1940s by John Steinbeck. Today the canneries house galleries, gift shops, wine-tasting rooms, and fine restaurants, or offer their atmospherically ruined foundations to sea gulls and kelp beds.

The centerpiece of this seafront revival is the spectacular Monterey Bay Aquarium, with its innovative natural habitat exhibits — some several stories high and literally carved out of the rock and underwater sanctuaries of the bay itself.

PACIFIC GROVE

Founded in the 1870s as a seaside retreat for the Methodist Church, this quiet gem adjoining the northern edge of Monterey proper boasts incomparable Victorian homes turned into inviting, often luxurious, bed and breakfast accommodations. Long a popular conference site, Pacific Grove houses the landmark Asilomar meeting center, designed by Julia Morgan of Hearst Castle fame.

At Asilomar State Park, sand dunes give way to a wildly dramatic expanse of tide pools and crashing surf on the rocks of Point Pinos — alleged to be the first Central Coast location spied by Cabrillo. The spot still boasts a tiny searchlight of the Point Pinos Lighthouse, which has steered ships away from the treacherous rocks since 1856. Local abalone divers continue to search the waters off the point for the prized sea delicacy.

Each November, the orange and black magic of hundreds of thousands of monarch butterflies fill the trees of the town's main avenue with a glory of quivering color.

PEBBLE BEACH AND 17 MILE DRIVE

Even before Bing Crosby's annual clambake, landed gentry put this region on the map, with its incomparable cliffs, churning surf, and occasional movie crews. Winding between Pacific Grove and Carmel is an extraordinary stretch of road affording fabulous ocean vistas and glimpses of the lifestyles of the rich and famous. Here, some of California's founding families built their own versions of great European country homes, most designed by the leading architects of the early 20th century.

The 5000-acre Del Monte Forest is a sanctuary for the rare Monterey cypress, including that most photographed of Central Coast trees, the Lone Cypress. Its ancestors gave shelter to the landing party headed by Portola during his 1769 exploration of Alta California.

At each turn of this popular drive, some new, yet somehow familiar estate comes into view through the Monterey pines and stone gate houses. Hitchcock's *Rebecca* was among the many Golden Age of Hollywood films set in these monuments to conspicuous, if tasteful, consumption.

In addition to truly spectacular coastal visuals, this area is a testament to lavish country club living. For the $6 toll to drive 17 Mile Drive, visitors can take in the action on some of the world's most famous golf courses with legendary names like Pebble Beach and Spyglass Hill.

CARMEL

Carefully nurtured artistic ambiance and romantic windswept cypresses share Carmel with one of the gems of early Spanish mission architecture. Here, photographer Ansel Adams flourished, Clint Eastwood was elected mayor, and eating on the streets isn't allowed. Neon signs and telephone poles also are banned. Tidy, quaint, and almost impossibly tasteful in its collection of landscaped cottages, elegant lodgings, and upmarket restaurants, diminutive Carmel still exerts an undeniable, if conservative, appeal.

History has left its mark most vividly in the nearby Carmel Mission, established in 1771 by Father Junipero Serra. With its barrel-vaulted ceiling, Moorish tower, and replicated kitchen, sleeping quarters, and refectory, the mission rewards visitors seeking a taste of Spanish occupation in the New World.

Bohemian painters, writers, photographers, and bon vivants flocked here at the turn of the century, attracted by the magnanimous deal of land barons James Devendorf and Frank H. Powers: dirt cheap land to anyone actively engaged in the fine arts. The offer, plus fragrant pine forests at the edge of a serene beach, attracted the likes of Upton Sinclair, Jack London, George Sterling, and Edward Weston, as well as hundreds of their best friends, hangers-on, and lesser-known (though similarly talented) colleagues. Robinson Jeffers found the peaceful inspiration he sought in 1914 when he built his landmark Tor House and Hawk Tower completely of native stone.

The outfall from the Monterey Jazz Festival annually enlivens its streets and the brilliant brass and contrapuntal melodies of the baroque masters fill the town each year during the Carmel Bach Festival. And everybody — tourist and local alike — stops for a cocktail at Clint Eastwood's Hog's Breath watering hole.

CARMEL VALLEY

A cross from the Carmel Mission, Carmel Valley Road threads its way along the tiny Rio Carmel and climbs into the hills. Much of Carmel Valley is owned by the very wealthy — Doris Day maintains a compound here — and has been immaculately groomed into golf courses, country clubs, and plush resorts. In these coast ranges, thriving remnants of the early land-grant ranchos offer perhaps the purest taste of the *Californio* essence still to be found. Orchards of pear, apricot, and walnut line the verdant valley floor, which rises into slopes studded with grazing herds of cattle. Up into chaparral country, Carmel Valley offers prime side road exploration through steep canyons and up onto ridges offering stunning views of the ocean below.

BIG SUR COAST

M ost signs of human habitation disappear abruptly just south of Carmel. For the next 90 miles, the majestic coastal splendor of Big Sur reigns supreme. With few permanent residents and no towns to speak of, this pristine coastline still boasts its unspoiled, breathtaking grandeur. Here, Highway 1 earns its reputation as the most beautiful, if vertiginous, roadway in the country, carved out of sheer cliffs dropping straight into the swirling tide below; spectacular bridges defy gravity to span deep canyons and gorges.

From Bixby Creek, two noteworthy side roads — Palo Colorado, and the Old Coast Road — lead deep into the interior of the coast mountains, through fern canyons, and up to windswept hilltops, affording stunning views of the entire Monterey Bay.

The Ventana Wilderness joins with the Los Padres National Forest at Big Sur, offering close to two million acres of pristine hiking and riding trails, and awe-inspiring forests, beaches, trails, and hilltops, including the southernmost habitat of the giant redwoods. Immediately south of the "town" of Big Sur, lie the beautiful beaches, caves, and cliffs of Pfeiffer Beach. After the day's ritual of beachcombing and hiking, locals come down from the hills for a sunset cocktail at the legendary Nepenthe, a restaurant/arts complex almost 1000 feet directly above the sea. A hangout for local culturati since 1949, Nepenthe has since been joined by other fashionable resort neighbors, including Ventana Inn just across the road.

On each side of the highway continuing southward, state parks, beaches, and forests spill as far as the eye can see, working their way to the very end of Monterey County. Julia Pfeiffer Burns State Park haunts the coast beginning 10 miles south of Nepenthe, its border encircling waterfalls, creek trails, and dizzying ridges. After a dip in the public-access hot springs and tubs at the new-age think tank of nearby Esalen Institute, visitors might continue southward to Sand Dollar Beach and Jade Cove.

Throughout the southern Big Sur area, rugged side roads — many overlaying old ranch trails — lead from the coast through redwoods and chaparral, retracing the steps of early pioneers. One of the loveliest of these, Nacimiento Road, begins south of Lucia and ascends 3000 feet through oak groves and brush-covered ridges. It ends in the isolated setting of Junipero Serra's third mission, the authentically restored Mission San Antonio de Padua, founded in 1771.

Along the Big Sur coastline, Highway 1 offers convenient pull-outs and vista points almost every mile of the way; most travelers find themselves using them frequently. Don't forget the camera and binoculars.

SAN SIMEON

As Monterey County gives way to San Luis Obispo County, the steep and agitated landscape of Big Sur calms down and gradually rambles downhill toward the beginning of superb beach country. The Central Coast's Mediterranean climate becomes more apparent as you head further south, the days upping the temperature a few more degrees, the evenings staying balmier longer.

The most graphic reminder of Old World influence here is that fantasy recreation of the Spanish Renaissance — William Randolph Hearst's La Cuesta Encantada (The Enchanted Hill). Between 1919 and 1947 — on hundreds of thousands of acres of San Simeon land-grant inherited from his indomitable mother Phoebe and senator father George — the newspaper magnate unleashed his fortune and passion for building and collecting. With architect Julia Morgan to shape his pipe dreams, Hearst constructed a tile, marble, wood, and gilt hideaway filled with 37 bedrooms, indoor swimming pools, fountains, gardens, and even a zoo.

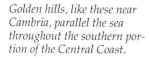

Golden hills, like these near Cambria, parallel the sea throughout the southern portion of the Central Coast.

Visnius

CAMBRIA

South of San Simeon, Highway 1 slides through gentle beach country to the artists' colony of Cambria, which also serves as the lodging center for visitors to the Hearst spread a few miles up the road. Settled in the 1860s by Welsh miners attracted by news of copper and quicksilver prospects, Cambria's lumber industry, dairy farming, and superb swimming beaches have maintained the community's popularity up to the present.

All along this section of coastline, great stands of blue-green eucalyptus dominate the hillsides and saturate the air with a heady, mentholated perfume. Imported from Australia in the last century under the misguided impression that they would provide fast-growing timber for construction, the eucalyptus has long since gone native. Though their lumber proved unsturdy, these distinctive trees persistently caress the entire Central Coast in ranch-land windbreaks and as the region's signature ocean backdrop.

MORRO BAY

Crowned by a formidable volcanic peak, the extensive beaches of this popular playground are home to abundant shellfish and spectacular processions of windswept dunes. A busy fishing port, the bay is one of the major waterfowl habitats in the country. Before it was that, this 12-mile stretch of coast extending from Morro Strand State Beach down to Montaña de Oro State Park was a prized harbor and hub of the shipping industry. By 1879, coastal steamers regularly put in at its sheltering bay. Protected by a slender sandspit of high dunes, the bay is chock-a-block with waterfront development, pleasure and commercial fishing boat docks, and every amenity for visitors drawn to this outdoor sports magnet.

The pinnacle, in every sense, of this portion of the San Luis Obispo coast is dramatic Morro Rock, highest of a dozen volcanic plugs still visible in the area along Highway 1. At almost 600 feet, the miniature Gibraltar commands the entrance to the bay and was formed by the same volcanic uplifts that produced the intricate stratifications of Montaña de Oro State Park's tide pools. Hikers and beachcombers are free to explore the base of the rock, but its upper cliffs and crags — a sanctuary protecting the nests of peregrine falcons — are off limits to humans.

Exposed at low tide, the vast mud flats here provide a smorgasbord of tiny crustacean snacks for 250 species of shorebird. Outstanding variety and quantity of wildlife combine with the recreational possibilities of dunes and surf to make this area a hit with vacationing Californians. Fine camping opportunities abound at Morro Bay State Park, the site of protected heron rookeries high in eucalyptus groves where the stately birds nest for half the year beginning in January.

All You Need to Know About Pismo Clams

An entire culture is devoted to clamming in the sand at low tide, with much debate about the proper technique for digging, the correct clam fork to use, and whether to steam or grill the harvested shellfish. Wily veterans will gladly give advice about any aspect of clamming if approached, but all you really need to know is that the Pismo clam obligingly spends most of its time burrowing less than six inches into the sand. Licenses for clamming are required and are available at every roadside attraction. Areas of state beaches where clamming is off-limits are all clearly marked.

SAN LUIS OBISPO

An eclectic blend of frontier ranching, Spanish mission memories, and Victorian vernacular, this often overlooked community nestles against the velvety Santa Lucia Mountains 10 miles from the ocean. San Luis Obispo was another coastal town that got its start from busy Father Serra, who established his fifth outpost of Christian civilization here among the Chumash Indians in 1772. One of the richest missions in the California chain, Mission San Luis Obispo boasted thousands of cattle, huge wheat harvests, and eight sheep farms on and around its fertile fields. Twenty-five years later, Serra's successor established the chain's sixteenth mission — San Miguel Arcangel — to the northeast. The two Franciscan compounds are nicely preserved examples of the world of the fathers and their ranching abilities, an expertise continued today in the best tradition of hell-for-leather land-grant cattlemen.

Almost 100 years ago, the state of California established a technical college in the rambling ranch lands once cultivated by Spanish settlers. Nowadays, San Luis Obispo maintains its lively pulse thanks to the presence of California State Polytechnic College (affectionately known as Cal Poly) and the post-hippie baby boomers who have settled in and maintained the area's considerable appeal. San Luis also boasts its share of well-preserved adobes and historical buildings. In the heart of the tiny downtown are the mission and its grassy plaza, the two-story Sauer-Adams Adobe, the region's first Episcopal church built in 1867, and the circa 1874 Ah Louis Store — a reminder of the strong Chinese presence during the railroad building period.

SOUTHERN BEACH TOWNS AND DUNES

Tiny secluded coves and bluffs covered with ice plant and coreopsis merge southward into small communities at Avila Beach, Pismo Beach, Grover Beach, and, finally, Guadalupe Dunes Beach. Several piers providing top fishing vantage points extend out into the curve of San Luis Obispo Bay. At Avila Beach — with one of the prettiest beaches imaginable in what seems like an endless procession of the prettiest beaches imaginable — the sybaritic pleasures of mineral springs bathing also beckon.

One giant, 15-mile-long recreation area, the town, beaches, and voluptuous sand dunes of Pismo — named for the mighty clam — seem to exist only for life in the great outdoors. Beach rentals and mobile homes cluster together to form the heart of the town of Pismo Beach, an appropriately ramshackle assortment of lodgings and conveniences saved from the mundane by its voluptuous stretch of sand dunes. Near the Santa Barbara County line are the spectacular 400-foot dunes of Guadalupe Dunes Beach. The mountains of pale soft sand are home to the brown pelican and other curious native fauna.

Increasingly, the dunes of the Nipomo Dunes Preserve south of Pismo Beach are shaken to the raucous sounds of dune buggies, those unlovable all-terrain vehicles with huge tires that usually turn up just over the next sand dune, where you least expect or want them.

Where today's recreational vehicles play, a maverick group of artists, musicians, hedonists, bums, and bohemians who called themselves "Dunites" once roamed. During the 1930s, these alternative lifestylers, for whom clothing was often optional, constructed lean-to huts on the dunes and proceeded to do their thing until the Depression finally reached their piece of coastal paradise. Little remains of their colorful presence, though for the price of a beer, old-timers will oblige with tall tales.

Even before the Dunites, Hollywood mega-producer Cecil B. DeMille spotted the cinematic potential of the mighty Nipomo dunes, and cast them as the Sinai desert in his epic *The Ten Commandments*.

Just north of the Santa Barbara County line, lakes, sand dunes, lagoons, and coastal canyons converge at the campgrounds of Oceano, which also marks an inland twist in Highway 1. Though the highway swings away from the ocean in order to avoid the sensitive missile testing operations of Vandenberg Air Force Base, there is plenty of coastal access to fishing areas and rocky points teeming with shorelife.

SANTA YNEZ VALLEY

Turning right abruptly at Point Conception, the Central Coast heads into the Santa Ynez Mountains at the town of Lompoc, a sprawling land-grant rancho whose latter-day growing fields produce more flower seed than any-where else in the world. During summer and autumn, when the brilliantly pat-terned fields blaze with neon color, it's easy to believe that this town produces almost half of the U.S. annual flower crop.

Hans Christian Andersen would feel right at home in Solvang, a taste of Denmark 10 miles from the coast in the Santa Ynez Valley's prime dairy country. Settled by Danes attracted to pasture lands that mimicked the old country, Solvang defined itself with the establishment of Atterdag College in 1911. This began the perpetuation of Danish folk customs, architecture, and language, making the town a Scandinavian theme park. Though it boasts its own restored Spanish mission and museum — Santa Ines, founded in 1804 as the 19th in the Franciscan chain — Solvang attracts a lion's share of visitors for its half-timbered shops, Old World windmills, thatched roofs, and cob-blestone streets. A monument to all things Danish, Solvang is a shameless tourist trap, its citizens even dressing in traditional garb on weekends and special occasions.

Solvang and Lompoc are also gateways to several dozen wineries tucked into the transverse hillsides and valleys of the Santa Ynez Mountains.

SANTA BARBARA

In addition to sensuous architecture, clusters of attractive, Spanish-style shopping complexes, laid-back wealth, and the ultimate in balmy climates, Santa Barbara is the inspiration for its very own network television soap opera. The town can be summed up in two words: rich and beautiful. Even to Central Coasters spoiled by hundreds of miles of drop-dead gorgeousness, this quin-tessential resort town is the fairest of them all. It's also the most architecturally unified, thanks, ironically, to a disastrous earthquake in 1925 that forced a complete rebuilding of the downtown.

The happy decision was made to evoke the Spanish Renaissance and mis-sion influences of the region in rebuilding the heart of this self-dubbed "Cali-fornia Riviera." The result is a remarkable collection of red tile roofs, rounded windows and colonnades, and bell towers whose pale pink domes echo Spain's architectural debt to the Moors. The soaring rooflines, ornate arch-ways, and Mediterranean curves of Santa Barbara's 1929 County Courthouse have made it the most photographed structure on the Central Coast.

The structure that started it all — Mission Santa Barbara, founded in 1786 — overlooks the city from a matchless setting of gardens, fountains, and stately palms. Continuously in use since its founding, the mission was refurbished and enlarged many times in the late 18th and early 19th centuries, earning the affectionate title of "Queen of the Missions."

While few traces of the mighty 1782 presidio remain visible, the town wisely has preserved 16 blocks of its historic adobes for a display of early California daily life, rivaled only by Monterey. At the edge of the historic district, Stearns

Wharf — the oldest in California and once owned by Hollywood legend Jimmy Cagney — provides visitors and leisure-set natives with spectacular views of mountains, ocean, and the nearby yacht harbor.

Like all rivieras, Santa Barbara boasts flawless sunning and swimming beaches, all protected from rough surf by the Channel Islands 20 miles offshore and facing southward for maximum "rays." Those who aren't soaking up the sun are soaking up the limelight. This area has been home to film stars since the early days of the industry, when Santa Barbara was the first movie capital. Though the movie industry moved south, its major players stayed on to enjoy off-duty seclusion. Resort accommodations for the well-heeled cling to both beachfront and canyons, resplendent with those red tile roofs and artfully appointed with exotic palm trees.

THE GOLD COAST

Draped over the foothills of the Santa Ynez Mountains southeast of Santa Barbara is a well-groomed bedroom retreat for celebrities, millionaires, and movie stars. Montecito ("little mountain" in Spanish) re-mints the term "exclusive" and proudly boasts a fine collection of mansions and manors dating from the 1920s. By that time, the movie industry had boomed to the point that the newly rich actors, producers, and directors yearned, even then, to get away from the urban rat race. If only for the weekend — at first —big stars came in droves to unwind, play, and rendezvous in the seclusion of the seaside enclave.

Secluded inns, resorts, and magnificent gardens tucked into Montecito's pretty country lanes and wooded hills continue to make this area a favorite movie and television star getaway.

Heading south, the cliffs overlooking the ocean continue to boast mansions as big as ocean liners, especially at the aptly named Summerland, a fishing village graced by particularly swimmable surf (no riptides) and textbook beaches. More recently, the unofficial Western White House for the 42nd President of the United States is among the current attractions of Summerland, home of close friends of Bill and Hillary Clinton, television producers Linda Bloodworth-Thomason and Harry Thomason of *Designing Women* and *Evening Shade* fame.

At Carpinteria, named by 18th-century explorer Portola for the expert Chumash Indian carpenters he encountered, the ultimate in user-friendly state beaches offers campsites, trailer hook-ups, grassy picnic areas, and tempting sand dunes. On a more chichi level, well-heeled equestrians from Santa Barbara society laid out the fabled Polo Club during the '30s. Recognized as the "safest beach on the coast" thanks to a sheltering offshore shelf, Carpinteria eventually surrenders to the world-class surfing conditions of Rincon Beach.

CHAPTER TWO

The Freeway and the Right Way
TRANSPORTATION

In the 18th century, the "King's Highway" — El Camino Real, or the royal road — was laid down by the Franciscan fathers and their military protectors. But travel up and down the Central Coast remained an arduous undertaking well into the 19th century. Seasonally impassable roadways and the rugged terrain of the coastal mountains kept townships relatively isolated. Most travel in-

Shmuel Thaler

Big Sur's spectacularly rugged seascape has lured travelers to the Central Coast for generations.

volved lengthy sea journeys. In 1861, a stagecoach line began carrying mail and passengers three times a week from Los Angeles to San Francisco, with a stop in San Luis Obispo. Once the system had been "refined," the journey, including four relays of horses, could be made in just under four days. It wasn't until 1893 that travelers could enjoy the safety and comfort of railroad travel between San Francisco and San Luis Obispo.

In the 1920s and '30s, Works Progress Administration work teams engineered the gravity-defying roads and bridges that increased access to the region. Dynamite, nerves of steel, and fiscal desperation helped chisel a road out of the steep sides of the coast ranges to reveal the thrilling vistas along Highway 1, which runs — with a few minor detours inland — the entire 1100-mile coastline of California. Along the tortuous roadway, the occasional breathtaking bridge — like the Bixby Creek Bridge curving hundreds of feet above a canyon crevasse — symbolizes how much access to the Central Coast depended on backbreaking effort combined with architectural poetry.

Now Highway 101 takes the place of El Camino Real; the coastal mountains are laced with connecting highways that often follow the routes of original stage coach circuits. And Highway 1, the Pacific Coast Highway, is the ultimate visual thoroughfare — the royal road of coastal panoramas.

GETTING TO THE CENTRAL COAST

BY CAR

Unless you're entering the state from due north or due south, all roads to the Central Coast lead west. Out-of-state visitors immediately will encounter the major topographical features of this 1000-mile-long edge of the U.S. — the formidable Sierra Nevada, the broad, flat Central Valley (known as San Juaquin in the north, Imperial in the south) and the slender, but persistent, uplift of the coast ranges. One way or another, all major interstate highways entering California to the coast will take you over these natural landmarks.

Entering the state from Arizona and New Mexico, motorists manage to miss the high Sierra passes by following Interstate 10 through the Mojave Desert to Los Angeles, hooking up there with the Coast Highway for all points north. Travelers from Las Vegas will find Interstate 15 the fastest route to the middle-of-nowhere crossroads of Barstow. From there, Highway 58 heads through the tail end of the Sierras, over the 4000-foot Tehachapi Summit, to connect with Interstate 5.

Visitors driving to the coast from Nevada and Idaho will find Interstate 80 a fabulous passage through the Sierra. It travels through the infamous Donner Pass (7227 feet) before dropping to Sacramento and the San Francisco Bay Area. All of these east-west highways are fast, multi-lane, state-of-the-art thorough-fares. All hook up with mighty Interstate 5, the widest and fastest, if not prettiest, of them all. Interstate 5 — which begins at the Canadian border and stretches to Mexico — provides a straight longwise shot through the center of California. From here, visitors can peel out over the coastal pass of their choice to arrive at seaside destinations from Half Moon Bay all the way down to Santa Barbara.

From San Francisco

It is tempting to approach Santa Cruz and parts south from San Francisco via the corkscrew turns and sweeping vistas of Highway 1. But that would be the farthest thing possible from a shortcut. A better idea — one favored morning and evening by Central Coast commuters — is to take Highway 280 south from San Francisco (always referred to as "The City" by locals) and then cut across the coast ranges via Highway 92, connecting with Highway 1 at Half Moon Bay. A more circuitous shortcut, but one featuring primeval redwood glens and fern canyons, is La Honda Road, which exits Highway 280 farther south and connects eventually with the Coast Highway at Pescadero.

From San Jose

From San Jose, Highway 17 — a daredevil's dream offering 23 miles of non-stop twists and turns — traverses the Santa Cruz Mountains to connect with Highway 1 at Santa Cruz, affording fine views of Loma Prieta Mountain (which lent its name to the 1989 earthquake) and the Monterey Bay. The quickest way into the heart of California's 19th century-ranching landscape lies by way of Highway 101, south from San Francisco to King City, 100 miles down the road. By turning west on rustic Nacimiento Road, adventurous drivers can literally tack the ridges and canyons of the Santa Lucia Mountains, winding through classic cattle country and groves of superb Spanish oaks all the way to the southern Big Sur coast. This challenging back road is well worth the extra time.

From Los Angeles

The place where freeways were born, Los Angeles is a driver's dream — or worst nightmare, depending on your mood and blood sugar level. It is possible to locate the threads through this labyrinth and get to the coast. One obvious route is to head toward the ocean until you find Highway 1 at Santa Monica and then work your way up to the Central Coast. Another possibility is to take the queen of gridlock, Highway 405, until it bumps into Highway 101 northwest of the metropolitan area. Highway 101 connects with the Coast Highway at Ventura, just south of Santa Barbara. Then, you're on your way to the good stuff on the Central Coast.

Bad Road Conditions Hotline

Travelers can call CalTrans Highway Information Network at 800/427-7623 for recorded details of adverse highway conditions, updated as they change. Don't call for anything else — no humans are around.

BY BUS

Any out-of-state or inter-state bus traveler headed for the Central Coast must pass through either of two major hubs, Los Angeles or San Francisco, and connect to buses headed for their destinations. Here are the surest, fastest, and most scenic options available.

Greyhound buses leave San Francisco three times daily for Santa Cruz (mid-1993 prices were $9 one way/$17 round trip) and Monterey ($13.40/$27), stopping at San Francisco Airport en route. From Monterey on the coast, buses veer inland to Salinas, another major hub. Five buses traveling from San Francisco to Los Angeles pass through San Luis Obispo ($25/$50) on the coast at mid-journey and, thereafter, follow Highway 1 to Santa Barbara ($43.75/ $83.15).

From Los Angeles, Greyhound schedules ten buses daily on its San Francisco route; they stop at Santa Barbara ($10.50/$21) and San Luis Obispo ($21/$42) before heading inland.

Call Greyhound's San Francisco depot (415/558-6789) or Los Angeles station (213/620-1200) for exact departure and arrival times.

Peerless Stages travels between San Jose Airport and Santa Cruz four times daily ($7/$13.30). Call Santa Cruz Peerless (408/423-1800) for exact departure and arrival times.

BY PLANE

Listed below are the state's major international airports and the regional fields that have connecting express flights to the primary hubs, as well as the airlines that serve them. You might also call your local Federal Aviation Administration flight service station for information about your destination's weather.

San Francisco International Airport: 415/876-7809; all major airlines fly into SFO.

Oakland International Airport: 510/577-4000; all major airlines.

San Jose International Airport: 408/277-4759; all major airlines.

Monterey Peninsula Airport: 408/648-7000; American Eagle, Skywest-Delta, United, United Express, USAir Express.

San Luis Obispo County Airport: 805/781-5205; American Eagle, Mesa, Skywest-Delta, United Express.

Santa Barbara Municipal Airport: 805/967-7111; includes Skywest, United, United Express, USAir Express.

Los Angeles International Airport: 310/646-5252; all major airlines

BY RAIL

Amtrak's (800/USA-RAIL) Oakland to Los Angeles *Coast Starlight* makes a daily run up and down the California coast with stops in Salinas, San Luis Obispo, and Santa Barbara's lovely mission-style station. For the ultimate in armchair travel, the train can't be beat. Fares from Santa Barbara to San Francisco begin at a cost-effective $60 (one-way). The scenery travelers can enjoy from the Starlight's windows, however, is priceless: crashing surf, smooth beaches, wetlands, and sloughs, as well as rugged mountain peaks and canyons, glide by while you relax.

The track hugs the edge of the land most of the way between Monterey and Santa Barbara counties, offering glimpses of hard-to-get-to pristine coastal stretches. Between Monterey and Santa Barbara, the train threads its way through artichoke fields and lagoons and provides eye-popping vistas of Morro Rock and its neighboring volcanic peaks as it starts down the San Luis Obispo side of Cuesta Pass. Travelers stopping in the city of San Luis Obispo can connect at the station by bus for tours of Hearst Castle. Continuing south, the train follows the inside curve of the voluptuous sand dunes stretching between Pismo Beach and Santa Barbara.

Soquel Creek empties into the Monterey Bay at the lively beach community of Capitola.

Shmuel Thaler

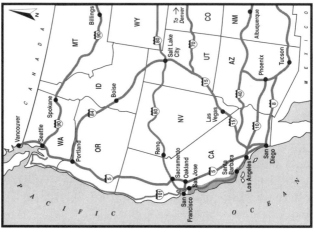

CENTRAL COAST ACCESS

Miles and approximate driving times from the following cities to Santa Cruz:

City	Miles	Hours
Albuquerque	1090	22:00
Bakersfield	290	6:15
Denver	1380	28:00
Eureka	360	7:15
Fresno	210	4:15
Las Vegas	580	12:00
Los Angeles	385	8:00
Phoenix	770	15:15
Portland	750	14:15
Reno	315	6:30
Sacramento	175	3:45
Salt Lake City	835	16:45
San Diego	500	10:15
San Francisco	80	1:45
San Jose	35	0:45
San Mateo	70	1:30
Seattle	915	17:30

Miles and approximate driving times to Santa Barbara:

City	Miles	Hours
Albuquerque	910	17:30
Bakersfield	155	3:00
Denver	1160	22:30
Eureka	650	13:15
Fresno	250	5:00
Las Vegas	390	7:30
Los Angeles	95	2:00
Phoenix	480	9:15
Portland	1040	20:15
Reno	600	12:30
Sacramento	505	10:00
Salt Lake City	820	16:00
San Diego	120	2:15
San Francisco	370	7:45
San Jose	320	7:00
San Mateo	360	7:45
Seattle	1200	23:45

CENTRAL COAST TOWN ACCESS

Following are approximate driving distances from the region's four main cities to selected towns and cities of interest. Travel time may vary depending on weather, road conditions, and the traveler's pace (the speed limit is 55 mph). The listings are the vehicular equivalent of a no pause, straight as an arrow forced march. We encourage everyone to slow down and enjoy the scenery.

From Santa Cruz

City	Miles	Hours
Half Moon Bay	57	1:00
Santa Cruz		
Moss Landing	23	:28
Monterey/Carmel	46	:56
Big Sur	75	1:30
San Simeon	140	2:48
Morro Bay	168	3:22
San Luis Obispo	181	3:37
Santa Ynez Valley	243	4:52
Santa Barbara	286	5:43

From Monterey

City	Miles	Hours
Half Moon Bay	101	2:04
Santa Cruz	46	:55
Moss Landing	23	:28
Big Sur	29	:35
San Simeon	94	1:53
Morro Bay	122	2:26
San Luis Obispo	135	2:42
Santa Ynez Valley	197	3:56
Santa Barbara	242	4:50

From San Luis Obispo

City	Miles	Hours
Half Moon Bay	239	4:47
Santa Cruz	182	3:38
Moss Landing	159	3:11
Monterey/Carmel	136	2:43
Big Sur	107	2:08
San Simeon	41	:49
Morro Bay	13	:16
Santa Ynez Valley	62	1:14
Santa Barbara	106	2:87

From Santa Barbara

City	Miles	Hours
Half Moon Bay	345	6:54
Santa Cruz	288	5:46
Moss Landing	265	5:18
Monterey/Carmel	242	4:50
Big Sur	213	4:16
San Simeon	147	2:56
Morro Bay	119	2:23
San Luis Obispo	105	2:15
Santa Ynez Valley	38	:40

The charming mission and college town of San Luis Obispo is a gateway to many recreational destinations.

San Luis Obispo Chamber of Commerce

GETTING AROUND THE CENTRAL COAST

BY CAR

Highway 1 is the majestic lifeline caressing the Central Coast and connecting all points surveyed in this book. Stretching the length of California, it links the major cities of San Diego, Los Angeles, and San Francisco, and feeds into the freeways of the interior via myriad scenic mountain back roads.

However tortuous the turns, steep the cliffs, or slow the traffic during summer weekends, Highway 1 is, to most who have driven it, the most beautiful road in the world (certainly in California, at least). Often it's a snug fit just to find room enough for two cars to pass each other safely in narrow corridors blasted by dynamite through solid rock. This isn't the route for those in a hurry.

Running from the Canadian border to Los Angeles, and generally just west of Highway 1, Highway 101 offers its own scenic stretches, as well as opportunities for food and lodging along the way. Highway 101 fuses with 1 for the short jaunt between San Luis Obispo and Pismo State Beach, and again for a longer coastal stretch between Goleta and Oxnard, just south of Santa Barbara.

For information on driving to various Central Coast points, see "Getting To The Central Coast" above, and consult the "Central Coast Access" section for distances and driving times.

BY RENTAL CAR

Although car culture originated elsewhere, it hit its stride in California. The Central Coast offers plenty of wheels-to-rent options. Here are listings of the top reliable agencies in the region:

Agency Rent-A-Car	800/321-1972
Alamo Rent-A-Car	800/327-9633
Avis Rent-A-Car	800/831-2847
Budget Rent-A-Car	800/527-0700
Dollar Rent-A-Car	800/800-4000
Enterprise Rent-A-Car	800/325-8007
Hertz Rent-A-Car	800/654-3131
National Car Rental	800/227-7368
Sears Rent-A-Car	800/527-0700
Thrifty Car Rental	800/367-2277
USA Rent-A-Car	800/872-2277

BY BUS AND RAIL

See those sections in "Getting To The Central Coast" above.

BY LIMOUSINE

For the ultimate in leisurely, customized sightseeing, limousines are the way to go. While you look out the windows and sip something cool, someone else drives you to breathtaking locations in style and comfort. Whether you hire a car and driver to simply search out that perfect beach or sign on for a tour of all the top local sights, limousines provide privacy and freedom. Plus, they know the territory. Following is a selection of limo services; call for rates, times, specialties.

Santa Cruz Coast

Club Limo 408/464-2600; PO Box 1775, Aptos.
Michael's Limousine 408/338-7451; 17900 China Grade Rd., Boulder Creek.

Cannery Row, with its destination hotels and fine restaurants, hugs the Monterey coast.

Monterey Coast

At Your Service 408/625-5363; PO Box 323, Pebble Beach.
Bungays Celebrity Limousine 408/624-1407; PO Box 3635, Carmel.

San Luis Obispo Coast

Carousel Limousine 805/545-8381; PO Box 6733, Los Osos.
Daystar Limousine 800/488-3993; PO Box 1401, Arroyo Grande.

Santa Barbara Coast

Pacific Coast Limousine 805/683-0722; 5227 San Simeon Dr., Santa Barbara.
Professional Limousine 805/963-5800; 636 Santa Barbara St., Santa Barbara.

Santa Barbara Trolley Company

An excellent way to appreciate the architectural beauty of Santa Barbara and grasp the lay of the land is to take a 19-stop, 90-minute roundabout that begins and ends at Stearns Wharf and includes a journey through downtown. All-day fares are available and the service operates daily year-round. For more information, call 805/965-0353, or write to PO Box 22316, Santa Barbara.

Santa Barbara, Stearns Wharf, and the magnificent beaches of the Gold Coast.

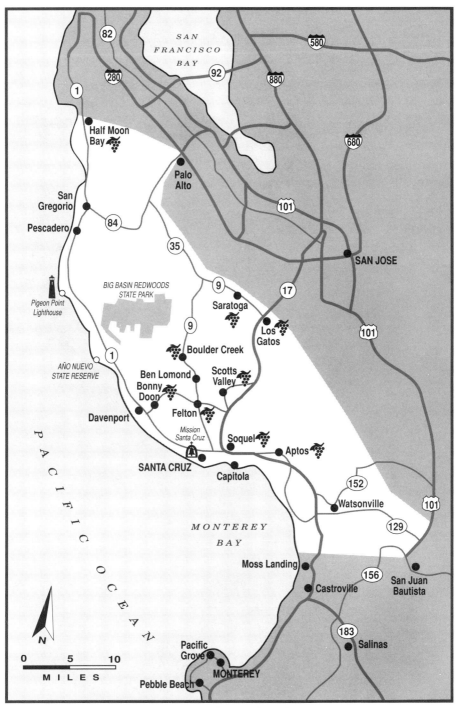

82

SAN FRANCISCO BAY

580

280

92

880

1

680

Half Moon Bay

Palo Alto

San Gregorio

101

Pescadero

84

SAN JOSE

35

101

BIG BASIN REDWOODS STATE PARK

9

Pigeon Point Lighthouse

Saratoga

9

17

Los Gatos

101

Boulder Creek

AÑO NUEVO STATE RESERVE

1

Scotts Valley

Ben Lomond

Bonny Doon

Felton

Davenport

Mission Santa Cruz

Soquel

Aptos

SANTA CRUZ

Capitola

152

Watsonville

101

MONTEREY BAY

129

Moss Landing

156

Castroville

San Juan Bautista

N

183

Salinas

Pacific Grove

0   5   10

MONTEREY

MILES

Pebble Beach

PACIFIC OCEAN

SANTA CRUZ COAST

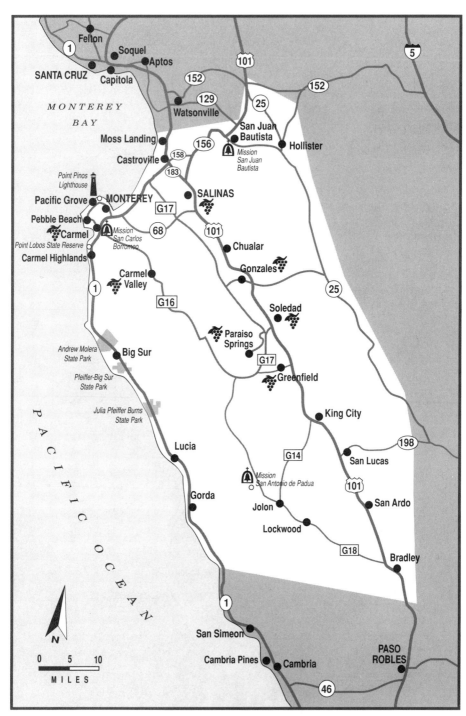

MONTEREY COAST

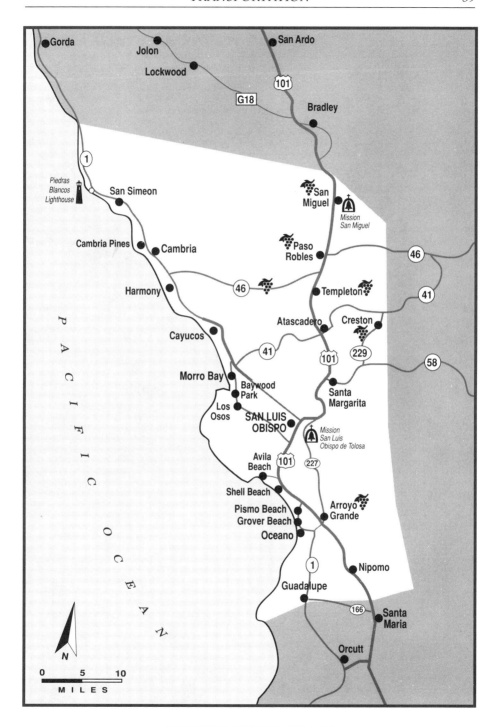

SAN LUIS OBISPO COAST

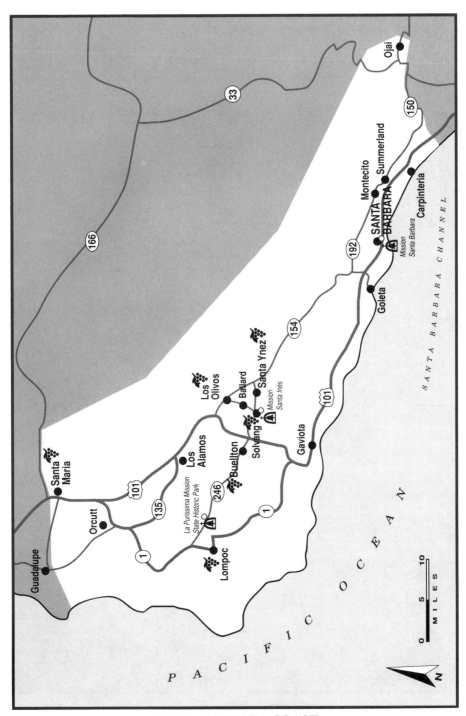

SANTA BARBARA COAST

CHAPTER THREE

Coastal Comforts

LODGING

Brimming with many resort accommodations designed to soothe the spirit and cater to every conceivable whim, the Central Coast offers the full range of overnight lodging, from full-service luxury hotels to charming bed and breakfast bungalows. Along the sparsely populated stretches of the Carmel and Big Sur coast, contemporary lodges showcase architecture featuring regional materials and appointed with the finest of handmade coastal crafts. In Santa Cruz, Pacific Grove, San

Grant Huntington

The Green Gables in Pacific Grove features turn-of-the-century atmosphere a stroll from the crashing surf.

Luis Obispo, and Santa Barbara, vintage homes have been transformed into inviting bed and breakfast lodgings. Given the spectacular Central Coast setting, many of these rooms offer the coveted ocean view.

CENTRAL COAST LODGING NOTES

Most — but not all — accommodations offer breakfast as part of the package; a "B" after the price range in these listings indicates that breakfast is included. Remember that rates and other specifics are subject to change; we recommend calling ahead. Lodgings are listed alphabetically under their town, which also are given alphabetically within each of the four Central Coast regions.

RATES

Inexpensive	Up to $75
Moderate	$75 to $150
Expensive	$150 to $225
Very Expensive	$225 or more

CREDIT CARDS

AE — American Express
CB — Carte Blanche
D — Discover Card
DC — Diner's Club
MC — MasterCard
V — Visa

SANTA CRUZ COAST

No visit to this seaside playground would be complete without a stay near the beach, where accommodations present panoramic views of the blue Pacific and the sensation of waves ushering you into the soundest night's sleep. Also not to be missed are the B&Bs along the shore and in the redwood forests that offer an eclectic blend of architectural styles. Here is a selection of quintessential Santa Cruz overnights.

Aptos/Rio Del Mar

APPLE LANE INN
Innkeepers: Diana & Doug
　Groom.
408/475-6868.
6265 Soquel Dr., Aptos.
Price: Inexpensive to Moderate; B.
Credit Cards: D, MC, V.
Children: Allowed with
　limits.
Smoking: Outside only.
Handicap Access: No.

At the end of a country lane between the villages of Soquel and Aptos and a few minutes from the ocean, this graciously restored Victorian farmhouse offers warm hospitality in the form of five cozy rooms — three with private baths — decorated with period antiques, fabrics, and lighting fixtures. The mood is pure country charm, and the peace and quiet of the surrounding hills belies this inn's location central to the area's top beaches and sights. Afternoon sherry is served in the lovely sitting room, with a player piano and adjoining library; sometimes guests take their drinks out to the pretty white gazebo with views of the surrounding orchards and vineyards. Afternoon tea is taken in the charming second floor sitting room. Breakfast is a hearty affair, featuring eggs from the inn's resident chickens, homemade pastries, and fresh fruits and juices. Games are available in the sitting room and a dart board in the wine cellar.

BAYVIEW HOTEL BED & BREAKFAST INN
Innkeepers: Barry & Sue Hooper.
408/688-8654.
8041 Soquel Dr., Aptos.
Price: Moderate to Expensive; B.
Credit Cards: AE, MC, V.
Children: Allowed with limits.
Smoking: Outside only.
Handicap Access: No.

Built as a lodging in 1878 during the Santa Cruz mountains logging boom, this three-story Victorian has been attractively renovated with lovely antiques and simple period furnishings that blend beautifully with its old-fashioned 10-foot ceilings. The stairway to eight second-floor guest rooms (including one two-room suite), all with private baths, ascends from a cozy guest parlor with a fireplace. A full breakfast is served in the beautifully restored destination restaurant, The Veranda, adjoining the hotel (see *Restaurants*). The Bayview is near a bevy of small antique stores, shops, and restaurants in tiny Aptos Village, just across Highway 1 from fine beaches. The natural splendor of the redwood Forest of Nisene Marks, with miles of hiking and equestrian trails, is just outside the front door.

The 100 year old Mangels House adjoins the Forest of Nisene Marks, just outside Aptos Village.

MANGELS HOUSE
Innkeepers: Jacqueline & Ron Fisher.
408/688-7982.
570 Aptos Creek Rd./PO Box 302, Aptos.
Price: Moderate; B.
Credit Cards: AE, MC, V.
Children: Over 12 only.
Smoking: Common rooms only.
Handicap Access: No.

Brothers-in-law (and sugar kings) Claus Mangels and Claus Spreckles built this Italianate mansion in the 1880s as a summer home for their families. Today, the Victorian ambiance is combined with modern conveniences: the six rooms have private baths and antique appointments (one has its own fireplace). The inn's four acres border the 10,000-acre redwood sanctuary of the Forest of Nisene Marks, ideal for leisurely walks or all-day hikes. Afternoon tea is served in the spacious sitting room — highlighted by a fireplace and grand piano — and sherry in the evening. A bountiful homemade breakfast complete with fresh fruit, an egg specialty, scones, and pastries properly begins the day. Lovely English gardens offer pastoral seclusion, yet the inn is only a few minutes drive to many expansive beaches.

SEASCAPE RESORT
Innkeeper: Jim Maggio.
800/929-7727, 408/688-6800, 408/685-3059 Fax.

An upscale retreat on the bluffs overlooking Monterey Bay, Seascape offers an array of amenities for those who like to play hard before

1 Seascape Resort Dr., Aptos.
Price: Expensive.
Credit Cards: AE, MC, V.
Children: Yes.
Smoking: Outside only.
Handicap Access: Limited.

unwinding in comfort. Beachfront, all-suite accommodations are equipped with gleaming kitchenettes stocked with coffee makers (and coffee), balconies, fireplaces, cable TV, and luxury bathroom amenities. The facility, also catering to conferences, encompasses an excellent restaurant specializing in fresh seafoods and locally grown produce creations. After a day of golfing at the PGA-rated 18-hole Seascape Golf Course just five minute away, you can soak in an outdoor spa, practice your serve on one of nine tennis courts, or cool off in the Olympic-size swimming pool.

Capitola/Soquel

BLUE SPRUCE INN
Innkeepers: Pat & Tom
  O'Brien.
800/559-1137, 408/464-
  1137.
2815 South Main St.,
  Soquel.
Price: Moderate; B.
Credit Cards: AE, MC, V.
Children: Yes.
Smoking: Outside only.
Handicap Access: No.

In a 120-year-old home around the corner from the heart of the historic village of Soquel, this very private inn offers contemporary comfort with the flavor of yesterday. All but one of the inn's six handsomely decorated overnight rooms offer a gas fireplace and two are equipped with whirlpool spas; each room has a private bath, distinctive appointments such as Amish quilts, and examples of the best work of local artists, a special interest of the innkeepers. The inn contains lovely garden and patio areas, where a redwood hot tub promises relaxation and a sound night's sleep. Every evening, wine and snacks are served in front of the parlor fireplace. Within walking distance are many of the area's best boutiques and ethnic restaurants. After donning a soft robe and enjoying a nightcap provided in the room at bedtime, guests rise to hearty breakfasts in the gardens or sitting rooms that begin with freshly squeezed juice, hot muffins, and breads and continue with serious food like blueberry pancakes and sourdough waffles with strawberries.

INN AT DEPOT HILL
Innkeepers: Suzie Lankes
  & Dan Floyd.
408/462-3376, 408/462-
  3697 Fax.
250 Monterey Ave./PO
  Box 1934, Capitola.
Price: Expensive; B.
Children: No.
Smoking: Outside only.
Credit Cards: AE, MC, V.
Handicap Access: Yes.

Crowning a knoll within a few minutes' walk of the sparkling beach and downtown Capitola Village, this stalwart 1901 railway station has been lavishly transformed. In keeping with the architectural features of this former depot, the elegant decor showcases an Orient Express-style theme. Each room bears the name of a glamorous destination and offers appropriately sophisticated appointments. All eight suites boast wood-burning fireplaces, TV, and private baths. The rooms are shamelessly sybaritic; the swank Paris Suite has a black and white marble bathroom with a spacious two-person shower and

French doors leading to the outdoor garden. The sky-blue Delft Room offers a sumptuous featherbed draped in linen and lace, plus a sitting room and Jacuzzi tub for two in its private garden. The Railroad Baron's Room — with deep red velvet upholstery, damask wall treatments, and a dramatic domed ceiling — recreates the feel of a Pullman coach and provides its own enormous soaking tub under a skylight. In sunny weather, breakfast is taken in an outdoor brick patio where sheltering shrubbery walls and musical fountain create the illusion of being in a Mediterranean villa. At the end of the day, a selection of fine wines and hors d'oeuvres is laid out on a marble sideboard in the beautiful public rooms, which are filled with antique furniture, a vintage baby grand piano, and a wall of bookshelves running to the top of the 16-foot ceilings. A luscious dessert is served each evening with coffee. Rooms come with telephones, Fax/modems, bathrobes, and hair dryers. Off-street parking — always scarce in this bustling beach town — is included in the price of the room.

Davenport

NEW DAVENPORT BED & BREAKFAST INN
Innkeeper: Doreen Devorah.
408/425-1818.
31 Davenport Ave. (Box J).
Price: Inexpensive to Moderate; B.
Credit Cards: MC, V.
Children: Allowed with limits.
Smoking: Outside only.
Handicap Access: Yes.

At the heart of this picturesque village, a former whaling port just north of Santa Cruz, is the Davenport Cash Store, not only a tile-floored, high-ceilinged restaurant, plus a fine international and local arts emporium, and also a B&B. The 12 rooms with private baths occupy two locations, one a charming turn-of-the-century bathhouse accented with antiques, the other offering bracing ocean vistas on the floor above the Cash Store. The upstairs rooms have been gorgeously decorated with ethnic treasures gathered from the global travels of artist/owners Bruce and Marcia McDougal, and the wraparound porch provides prime viewing of the migrating gray whales just offshore during winter months. Champagne greets guests upon check-in and a bountiful continental breakfast features delectable pastries from the Cash Store's bakery. The downstairs restaurant has long been a mecca for locals and exudes casual California ambiance (see review in *Restaurants*). Atmospheric cove beaches beckon just across Highway 1.

Half Moon Bay

MILL ROSE INN
Innkeepers: Eve & Terry Baldwin.
800/829-1794, 415/726-9794, 415/726-3031 Fax.
615 Mill St.
Price: Expensive to Very Expensive; B.

Sheer indulgence in a garden setting, this wonderful retreat features four rooms and two suites with TV/VCR, well-stocked refrigerators, and amenities including a coffee maker, fruit basket, liqueurs, and hair dryer. Five of the rooms boast fireplaces and all are decorated with Victorian and Arts and Crafts antiques, as well as down

Stan Cacitti

Half Moon Bay's popular Mill Rose Inn is graced by abundant gardens and secluded patios.

Credit Cards: AE, D, MC, V.
Children: Over 12 only.
Smoking: Outside only.
Handicap Access: Limited.

comforters and brass beds. All rooms have private entrances, and the front garden pays colorful tribute to the horticultural expertise of the innkeepers, who have filled this blooming sanctuary with roses, poppies, irises, delphiniums, and lilies. A back garden showcases yet more flowers, an inviting brick patio, and a gazebo with a whirlpool spa. A champagne breakfast can be brought to your room; multi-course morning offerings also include hot chocolate, fresh fruit drinks, soufflés, and hot dishes. Wine and light appetizers are provided at sundown. The historic village of Half Moon Bay offers fine dining and shopping, plus splendid coastal scenery and beaches a short drive away.

OLD THYME INN
Innkeepers: George & Marcia Dempsey.
415/726-1616.
779 Main St.
Price: Moderate; B.
Credit Cards: MC, V.
Children: Allowed with limits.
Smoking: Outside only.
Handicap Access: No.

The innkeepers at this restored 1890 Queen Anne Victorian offer Old World hospitality and a sweet-scented garden; its 80 varieties of herbs perfume the teas and freshly made dishes at the inn's full breakfast. All six rooms are decorated in turn-of-the-century style and offer private baths. Two rooms have fireplaces and three have whirlpool tubs big enough for two. One detached suite ($165 weekdays, $220 weekends) has its own private garden

Old Thyme Inn offers Victorian comfort perfumed by a lush herb garden.

Stan Cacitti

entrance and is equipped for a romantic stay with fireplace, oversized whirlpool tub, TV/VCR and plush four-poster bed. Evening wine and sherry are all the more relaxing in front of the main room's blazing fireplace. The innkeepers are happy to provide sightseeing tips and restaurant recommendations.

ZABALLA HOUSE
Innkeepers: Simon Low-
  ings & Kerry Pender-
  gast.
415/726-9123.
324 Main St.
Price: Inexpensive to
  Expensive; B.
Credit Cards: AE, D, MC,
  V.
Children: Yes.
Smoking: Outside only.
Handicap Access: No.

Reportedly Half Moon Bay's oldest structure, this cheerful inn with nine guest rooms was built by Estanislao Zaballa in the mid-1800s. Appointed with antiques and boasting 10-foot ceilings, the rooms have private bathrooms, some with old-fashioned claw-foot soaking tubs and others with whirlpool tubs for two. Comforts extend to pre-dinner sherry and wine in the parlor, and breakfast is bountifully family-style, including hot breads and muffins, fresh juices, fruit, and cereals, all taken in the friendly kitchen. The inn is surrounded by graceful gardens; ample shopping and dining await along the tiny, straight-from-a-Western-movie Main Street of this seaside village.

San Gregorio

**RANCHO SAN GREGO-
  RIO**
Innkeepers: Bud & Lee
  Raynor.
415/747-0810, 415/747-
  0184 Fax.
5086 La Honda Rd. (Rte. 1,
  Box 54).
Price: Moderate; B.
Credit Cards: AE, D, MC,
  V.

A secluded California Mission-style coastal re-treat, the inn is set on 15 acres of rolling ranch land affording fine views of the surrounding red-wood forests and lush farmlands just a few miles from San Gregorio Beach. The graceful home is adorned with terra cotta tile floors and an antique-laden courtyard. Each of five guest rooms is distinc-tively decorated and has its own bathroom accom-modations and private porch. Three rooms provide the charm of wood-burning stoves. In addition to old-fashioned country games like badminton,

Children: Yes.
Smoking: Outside only.
Handicap Access: No.

horseshoes, and croquet — as well as a creek-side picnic area — the rancho offers a full country breakfast highlighted by home-baked breads, muffins, and fresh fruit specialties. This is a charming hideaway offering easy access to the dramatic cliffs, beaches, and coastal mountain scenery between Half Moon Bay and Santa Cruz.

Santa Cruz

**BABBLING BROOK BED
& BREAKFAST INN**
Innkeeper: Helen King.
800/866-1131, 408/427-
2437, 408/427-2457 Fax.
1025 Laurel St.
Price: Moderate; B.
Credit Cards: AE, CB, D,
MC, V.
Children: Allowed with
limits.
Smoking: Outside only.
Handicap Access: Yes.

A romantic getaway in a central location between residential and downtown Santa Cruz, the Babbling Brook is charm itself. Innkeeper Helen King has made each of 12 rooms a secluded oasis. The guest rooms are clustered around a central, multi-level cedar building; its stone foundations date from the late 18th century when the property was a gristmill. The soft sounds of the creek flowing through the property's lovely gardens can be heard from each room, and the Honeymoon Suite's private deck overlooks a waterfall. All rooms have private baths, phones, and TVs, and are decorated in a French country theme; many offer decks and fireplaces. An elegant full breakfast is served in the charming living room, and in the sitting room a blazing fireplace is the centerpiece of afternoon wine tastings. The gardens and white gazebo are a favorite wedding site.

CASABLANCA INN
Innkeepers: Glyn & Ray
Luttrell.
408/423-1570, 408/423-
0235 Fax.
101 Main St.
Price: Moderate to Expensive.
Credit Cards: AE, DC, MC,
V.
Children: Yes.
Smoking: Yes.
Handicap Access: Limited.

This red-tile-roofed former seaside retreat of a San Francisco judge (circa 1920) has long been a distinctive landmark. Just across the street from the popular main Santa Cruz beach and the colorful Boardwalk and Cocoanut Grove Ballroom, the Casablanca offers bountiful ocean views and the soothing sounds of the waves. Over the years, innkeepers Glyn and Ray Luttrell have combed antiques emporia for the attractive, unpretentious furnishings of each distinctive room. Some rooms retain the original bathroom tilework and fixtures, and spacious Room 22 sports a fireplace, four-poster bed, and private terrace overlooking the seacoast sites. Essentially a small hotel ringed with a satellite of attractive motel units, the multi-level, Mediterranean-style main building hangs on the hillside just above its own Casablanca Restaurant (see *Restaurants*).

The view from Casablanca Hotel overlooks Santa Cruz' main beach, pier, and nearby Boardwalk.

Buz Bezore

CHAMINADE AT SANTA CRUZ
Innkeeper: Tom O'Shea.
1 Chaminade Lane.
800/283-6569, 408/475-5600, 408/476-4942 Fax.
Price: Moderate.
Credit Cards: AE, D, DC, MC, V.
Children: Yes.
Smoking: Yes.
Handicap Access: Yes.

A contemporary conference center with state-of-the-art lodgings surrounds a lovely pink neo-Deco warren of meeting rooms, terraces, and dining rooms high on a eucalyptus-scented hill overlooking the Santa Cruz Yacht Harbor and Monterey Bay. Handsome rooms with all the amenities have private patios opening on to a surrounding forest of towering oaks. The 80-acre grounds offer hiking trails through the redwoods, outdoor Jacuzzis, tennis courts, and swimming pool; a fine restaurant and plush lounge are just a stroll down landscaped paths. The fully equipped fitness center — aerobics room, basketball court, weight room, sauna, and enormous whirlpool spa — is this retreat's secret weapon. A few minutes from beaches and charming coastal villages, Chaminade feels like it's a million miles away from the madding crowd.

CHATEAU VICTORIAN BED & BREAKFAST INN
Innkeepers: Alice-June & Franz Benjamin.
408/458-9458.
118 First St.
Price: Moderate; B.
Credit Cards: AE, MC, V.
Children: No.
Smoking: Outside only.
Handicap Access: No.

A true "painted lady" only a block from the main beach and famous seaside amusement park, this late Victorian is adorned with dazzling berry hues. The hospitable innkeepers have lovingly decorated the seven rooms with fine antique armoires and lush upholstery; each has its own private bath, queen-size bed with luxurious linens, and fireplace. The inn, on a hillside affording an ocean view, cleverly conceals a secluded patio garden and several decks where sunsets are enjoyed over wine and cheese. The location is ideal for the salt-air action of the nearby Boardwalk, with its historic Giant Dipper roller coaster, and the inviting municipal wharf. Breakfast involves an expanded continental menu of fine coffees and teas, fruit, croissants, and pastries. Many restaurants and shops are within short walking distance.

CLIFF CREST BED & BREAKFAST INN
Innkeepers: Bruce & Sharon Taylor.
408/427-2609.
407 Cliff St.
Price: Moderate; B.
Credit Cards: AE, MC, V.
Children: No.
Smoking: Not in building.
Handicap Access: No.

The beautiful interiors of this lovely Queen Anne Victorian — a historic landmark home built by California's Lieutenant Governor William Jeter in 1890 — immediately cast a spell on visitors. Period details such as Oriental rugs and antique furniture blend with the small mansion's stained and beveled glass and intricate built-in woodwork. Only one block from the main beach, the inn's five rooms each offer a private bath, fireplace, and unique decoration. The charming Pineapple Room is named for its queen-size four-poster bed; the bed posts feature an artfully carved pineapple design. The spacious Empire Room offers turn-of-the-century ambiance with a 12-foot ceiling, king-size canopy bed, beveled glass armoire, and a view of the garden through lace-covered windows. The lush estate gardens were created by John McLaren, the man who designed San Francisco's Golden Gate Park. At sunset, regional wines, cheeses, and appetizers are offered in the antique-filled parlor. Coffee is served in the evening at the main fireplace. Breakfast in the garden solarium includes multiple courses of fresh juices, fruits, and just-baked pastries, plus crêpes, quiche, French toast, and pancakes.

The Cliff Crest sits in Victorian splendor atop Beach Hill in Santa Cruz.

Buz Bezore

The Darling House on West Cliff Drive in Santa Cruz was designed by celebrated architect William Weeks.

Buz Bezore

DARLING HOUSE
Innkeepers: Darrell & Karen Darling.
800/458-1958, 408/458-1958.
314 West Cliff Dr.
Price: Moderate to Expensive; B.
Credit Cards: AE, D, MC, V.
Children: Yes.
Smoking: Cottage only.
Handicap Access: Limited.

The beveled-glass windows and red-tiled roofs of this distinguished Mission Revival mansion overlook a spectacular view of the Santa Cruz coast, municipal wharf, and Monterey Bay beyond. Built as a private home in 1910 by California architect William Weeks, this gorgeous home — lavished with hardwood interiors, Tiffany lamps, and a tile-decorated fireplace — is at the foot of Santa Cruz' scenic West Cliff Drive. Each of its eight rooms (two with private baths) has period antiques. Hearty continental breakfasts are served each morning in the ornate dining and sitting rooms; sherry is offered in late afternoons. The expansive ocean-view verandah is the top spot to take in the sights of sailboats and surfers. Each overnight room is appealing, but especially noteworthy is the large second floor chamber overlooking the ocean, with its own fireplace and telescope for viewing the marine life of the Monterey Bay. One of the shared bathrooms sports an enormous claw-foot "bordello" tub, great for extended soaking for two. A small cottage in the mansion's back gardens sleeps four and an outdoor hot tub spa offers a pampering soak after a day on the beach.

SEA & SAND INN
Innkeeper: Lisa Morley.
408/427-3400.
201 West Cliff Dr.
Price: Moderate to Expensive; B.
Credit Cards: AE, D, DC, MC, V.
Children: Yes.
Smoking: Yes.
Handicap Access: Limited.

Twenty cozy rooms and suites, some with hot tubs and kitchenettes, all prettily decorated with Pacific-blue comforters and upholstery, are tucked into what looks like a long, white cottage on a bluff overlooking the white sandy beach just north of the Santa Cruz Boardwalk. A tiny lawn dotted with white chaise longues fronts the private ocean-view expanse; every room boasts stunning coastal vistas. A favorite getaway for locals and their guests, the inn provides a fine continental breakfast and is a terrific location for strolling West Cliff Drive, watching the world-class surfing action at Lighthouse Point, and for beach and shopping access.

MONTEREY COAST

Monterey and its coastal neighborhoods have been hosting guests since the Spanish first settled here at the end of the 18th century. The number of high quality overnight possibilities testifies to this area's charisma as a destination for visitors from all over the world. The conference trade thrives in this spectacular waterfront setting; contemporary hotel giants offer rooms with a view and all the amenities. Aficionados of the well-turned Victorian B&B consider Pacific Grove a treasure trove. Carmel's abundance of irresistible overnight inns is as legendary as its haunting shoreline. And world-class resorts dot the coastal hills along Big Sur.

Big Sur

POST RANCH INN
Innkeeper: Larry Callahan.
800/527-2200, 408/667-2200, 408/667-2824 Fax.
Hwy. 1/PO Box 219.
Price: Very Expensive; B.
Credit Cards: AE, MC, V.
Children: Yes.
Smoking: Outside only.
Handicap Access: Limited.

Almost 100 acres bordering the spectacular Big Sur coast support this environmentally correct sanctuary offering breathtaking vistas, nature walks, world-class hiking, and innovative California cuisine. One of the area's newest resorts, it's an "eco-inn" — 30 guest rooms blend unobtrusively with the gorgeous, redwood-studded terrain, and recycling bins are part of the scenery. Poised high above the Pacific, guest facilities — some literally in the trees, others with grass-growing roofs — all offer fine views and lush comfort. Bathroom toiletries are vegetable-based and non-animal tested. In addition to the fine restaurant, the resort boasts a lap pool, spa, and bracing hiking trails.

VENTANA
Innkeeper: Robert Bussinger.
800/628-6500 CA, 408/667-2331, 408/624-4812, 408/667-2419 Fax.
Hwy. 1, 28 mi. S. of Carmel.
Price: Expensive to Very Expensive; B.
Credit Cards: AE, CB, D, DC, MC, V.
Children: Allowed with limits.
Smoking: Yes.
Handicap Access: Yes.

This collection of weathered cedar lodges clinging to the ancient oak groves overlooking the wild Big Sur coastline forms a dramatic retreat. Spreading across a summit ridge 1000 feet above the coast, the Ventana complex — including a landmark restaurant (see *Restaurants*), two swimming pools, a general store, and fabulous tiled sunken spas — is one of the ultimate Central Coast resorts. The guest rooms (many with raised fireplaces and hot tubs sunk into private decks) are lavishly decorated with natural wood and tilework, including huge shower, bathing, and dressing rooms areas.

Relaxing at Big Sur's Ventana can be as simple as taking a hot tub on a private deck adjoining your guest room.

Still, the feeling is distinctly rustic, harmonizing effortlessly with the mountain terrain that brings grazing deer to your door and ravens soaring through the nearby sheltering forests. Each room, suite, and secluded cottage has a TV/VCR and refrigerator. The suite of central spas offers hot swirling water deep enough to swim in and private enough for honeymooners. Breakfast, taken before the main lodge's roaring stone fireplace, involves fresh juices, fruit, home-baked coffee cakes and breads, and pots of excellent coffee. Walk through the woods or ride a golf cart shuttle to the trend-setting restaurant, from whose enormous decks sunset takes on new meaning.

Carmel

HIGHLANDS INN
Innkeeper: David Fink.
800/682-4811 CA,
 408/624-3801, 408/626-
 1574 Fax.
Hwy. 1/PO Box 1700.
Price: Very Expensive.
Credit Cards: AE, D, DC,
 MC, V.
Children: Yes.
Smoking: Yes.
Handicap Access: Yes.

A California landmark since 1916, this world-class resort perched in the Carmel Highlands overlooking the spectacular coastline of Point Lobos features natural wood and stone elegance. In 1984, a $40 million renovation transformed accommodations into cozy, contemporary retreats with fireplaces and fully equipped kitchens. The rooms are equipped with huge beds, fireplaces — stacks of firewood are strategically located all over the property — TV, spacious dressing area, plush terry robes, well-stocked refrigerators, coffee makers with a variety of coffees, and amazing king-size whirlpool tubs built for two. Lavish landscaping — with native shrubs like the elegant California wild lilac — hugs the network of walkways leading down to the magnificent stone lodge, headquarters for a bistro overlooking the swimming pool, cocktail lounge, and the sparkling Pacific's Edge dining room with breathtaking views of the swirling surf and tide pools below (see *Restaurants).* Across the street are the natural wonders of Point Lobos State Park — viewable from your balcony through the binoculars helpfully provided in each room. The room service menu, a miniature of the restaurant's, is outstanding.

LA PLAYA HOTEL
Innkeeper: Tom Glidden.
800/582-8900 CA,
    408/624-6476, 408/624-
    7966 Fax.
Camino Real at 8th
    Ave./PO Box 900.
Price: Moderate to Very
    Expensive.
Credit Cards: AE, CB, DC,
    MC, V.
Children: Yes.
Smoking: Yes.
Handicap Access: Yes.

Built in 1902 and a member of Historic Hotels of America, this dream of a Mediterranean villa is a few steps away from Carmel's white sand beaches. La Playa's 73 rooms, two suites, and five storybook cottages combine ocean views with terraced gardens and a jewel of a swimming pool. Award-winning cuisine is served in the hotel's elegant Terrace Grill (see *Restaurants*) and many of the plushly decorated rooms come with fireplaces and inviting patios. Decor is Old World elegant throughout and this charming village's shops, boutiques, and galleries are a short stroll away.

**MISSION RANCH
    RESORT**
Innkeeper: John Purcell.
800/538-8221, 408/624-
    6436, 408/626-4163 Fax.
26270 Dolores Ave.
Price: Moderate to Expen-
    sive; B.
Credit Cards: AE, MC, V.
Children: Allowed with
    limits.
Smoking: No.
Handicap Access: Limited.

The lush ranchlands of this historic acreage near the Carmel Mission offer terrific views of peaceful meadows and sheep, and of the fog creeping in from the beaches of Monterey Bay. This farmhouse B&B was recently upgraded by new owner Clint Eastwood — yes, that Clint Eastwood — and combines country ambiance with contemporary comfort, especially attractive to guests who like to unwind yet stay close to sights, shopping, and the dining attractions of Carmel and Monterey. Overnights come with continental breakfast, tennis courts are nearby, and the hiking is excellent. The property offers fine dining at its California cuisine restaurant, which includes a cozy '30s bar and sandstone fireplace.

**QUAIL LODGE RESORT
    AND GOLF CLUB**
Innkeeper: Csaba Ajan.
800/538-9516, 408/624-
    1581, 408/624-3726 Fax.
8205 Valley Greens Dr.
Price: Expensive to Very
    Expensive.
Credit Cards: AE, CB, DC,
    MC, V.
Children: Yes.
Smoking: Yes.
Handicap Access: Yes.

The word "luxury" takes on a new meaning at this Mobil 5-Star resort, with plush overnight accommodations, a destination golf course, tennis courts, swimming pools, hot tubs, fine continental cuisine, trout fishing ponds, and hiking trails that stretch 850 acres deep into the Carmel hills. It is run like a Swiss watch on a California timetable. One hundred rooms and 14 suites pamper guests in designer trappings with exquisitely tailored furnishings, generous use of mirrors, fireplaces, plants, and private decks with wooden hot tubs and tiled fireplaces. Lodgings run the gamut from lakeside lodges with balconies and terraces to cottages with wet bars, and villas straight from *Architectural Digest*. Every amenity you can think of is already in place, and a short walk through extraor-

Carmel's Quail Lodge offers world class attention in a ranchland setting.

dinary plantings that blend in with the spectacular scenery leads to award-winning cuisine at The Covey (see *Restaurants*).

SANDPIPER INN
Innkeepers: Graeme and Irene MacKenzie.
800/633-6433 CA, 408/624-6433, 408/624-5964 Fax.
2408 Bay View Ave.
Price: Moderate to Expensive; B.
Credit Cards: MC, V.
Children: Allowed with limits.
Smoking: Outside only.
Handicap Access: Yes.

Fifty yards from Carmel Beach, this 1920s prairie-style residence is distinguished by spacious rooms, open-beam ceilings, wood-burning fireplaces, and horizontal lines. The antique-decorated, art-filled inn is suffused with Old World warmth, generating the feeling of staying overnight at a gracious private home. Peace and quiet reigns (though there is one in-room TV). Sherry is served in the fireside lounge each evening and morning brings a fresh continental breakfast. The inn's lovely garden is filled with rhododendrons, camellias, and azaleas. Two-night minimum on weekends.

STONEHOUSE INN
Innkeeper: Nicki Westbrook.
408/624-4569, 408/624-4602 Fax.
8th below Monte Verde/PO Box 2517.
Price: Moderate; B.
Credit Cards: AE, MC, V.
Children: Allowed with limits.
Smoking: Outdoors only.
Handicap Access: No.

Retaining the bohemian "artist's colony" flavor that attracted guests like Jack London and Sinclair Lewis, this historic house (built in 1906) oozes charm in its stonework exterior, fetching gardens, old-fashioned glass-front porch, and white wicker furniture set off by colorful cushions and vibrant hand-woven rugs. Each of six overnight rooms — three with private baths — is uniquely decorated, some with four-poster beds and sloping ceilings. Most rooms present dramatic ocean views; the inn is within easy walking distance of the beach, shopping, and restaurants. A breakfast of juices, coffee, fresh fruit and home-made muffins (plus quiche on the weekends) is provided. The extraordinary living room stone fireplace is kept blazing and afternoon port and cookies may be enjoyed in gardens, the cozy interior, or inviting porch area. Two-night minimum on weekends.

TICKLE PINK INN
Innkeeper: Mark Watson.
800/635-4774, 408/624-1244, 408/626-9516 Fax.
155 Highland Dr., Carmel Highlands.
Price: Moderate to Very Expensive; B.
Credit Cards: AE, MC, V.
Children: Allowed with limits.
Smoking: Yes.
Handicap Access: Partial.

Despite the cute name, this getaway has been popular with savvy travelers since the 1950s, when the secluded hotel was established on the site of Senator Edward Tickle's private retreat. Sharing a main driveway off Highway 1 with the Highlands Inn, the facility's 35 rooms and suites line the Carmel Highlands cliffs overlooking the ocean and an exquisite hidden cove beach, and boasts ample amenities. Rooms are outfitted with bright floral comforters, tiled bathrooms, and private balconies overlooking deluxe views. Coffee makers, TVs, terrycloth robes, and morning newspapers come with each room, and some suites feature wood-burning fireplaces and spa tubs. A stand-alone cottage from the original Tickle estate can accommodate two families. A substantial continental breakfast and evening wine and cheese on the terrace lounge are included.

Carmel Valley

ROBLES DEL RIO LODGE
Innkeepers: Adreena & Glen Gurries.
800/833-0843, 408/659-3705, 408/659-5157 Fax.
200 Punta del Monte.
Price: Moderate to Very Expensive; B.
Credit Cards: MC, V.
Children: Yes.
Smoking: Outside only.
Handicap Access: Yes.

Deep in the heart of the Old Spanish ranch country of Carmel Valley, this 1920s lodge — the oldest resort operating in this gorgeous setting — has hosted myriad celebrities, including *Masterpiece Theatre* legend Alistair Cooke. The rustic board-and-batten ambiance today enjoys a Laura Ashley designer flourish. Thirty-one rooms (including six in the main lodge), and cottages with fireplaces and kitchens, are strewn across nine beautiful acres. A hearty continental breakfast is served in the lodge's main dining room; the house restaurant, The Ridge, offers expert California cuisine based on the freshest seafood and produce from the Monterey Bay area. Amenities include a swimming pool, tiled hot tub with Jacuzzi, sauna, and tennis courts. Nearby is world-class golfing and horseback riding, with Carmel and beaches only a 10-minute drive away.

STONEPINE ESTATE RESORT
Innkeeper: Daniel Barduzzi.

Imagine a French country chateau with an Italian red-tile roof set on a 330-acre estate and equestrian center in the heart of verdant Carmel Valley.

408/659-2245, 408/659-5160 Fax.
150 East Carmel Valley Rd.
Price: Very Expensive; B.
Credit Cards: AE, MC, V.
Children: Allowed with limits.
Smoking: Yes.
Handicap Access: Yes.

You now have a rough idea of the comfortable and tasteful oasis that is Stonepine, named for a stately glen of 60-year-old Italian pines. Designed in the 1930s for the wealthy California Crocker banking family, this pink Mediterranean villa *cum* chateau has won the highest award for small hotels from the elite *Relais & Chateaux*. The tone is set by the Rolls Royce Phantom that scoops up guests arriving at the Monterey Airport. The main drawing room is ablaze with European antiques and elegant furnishings. Rooms and suites are sumptuously decorated in natural textiles; all suites have private balconies or gardens, whirlpool baths, designer toiletries, and TVs, plus some have fireplaces. Stonepine offers myriad leisure time activities, from world-class horseback riding and swimming to celebrity-gazing at the splendid dining room.

Hot Springs

One of the most famous continuations of Carmel Valley Road swings 20 miles inland from the coast to **Tassajara Hot Springs**. For those (preferably with four-wheel drive vehicles) who can handle the sheer cliffs, hairpin turns, and rocky conditions, the reward is sweet release in rock tubs hollowed millennia ago by Native Americans who revered these waters. The earliest mineral springs in the West known to outsiders, the sulphur baths steam away in an idyllic oak grove setting shared with the **Tassajara Zen Center**, which offers simple and delicious vegetarian meals. Guests who don't mind the center's rather Spartan conditions can soak and meditate to their hearts' content. For full accommodations — $100 per weekend double room, including private bath and three meals a day — write in advance to the Zen Center (300 Page St., San Francisco, CA 94102; 415/863-3136). In addition to providing a laid-back cutting edge to the West Coast's human potential movement, the sybaritic sanctuary of **Esalen Institute** (Big Sur, 408/667-3005), made famous in the consciousness-raising '60s, also houses legendary stone tubs once used by Native Americans. Today's meditating pleasure-seeker can listen to the inner child in hot mineral water bliss while taking in one of the most stunning seascape views on the planet. The quickest way to an overnight here is to sign up for a workshop, though lodgings are much sought-after. On the site of a former stagecoach and railroad depot, rustic **Sycamore Mineral Springs Resort** (1215 Avila Beach Dr., Avila Beach, 800/234-5831, 805/595-7302), with its own California cuisine restaurant and swimming pool, ascends a hillside of oak groves with scores of very private outdoor hot tubs. Even overnight rooms have decks with tubs, where the soaking in pepper- and sulphur-scented 110° mineral waters is excellent. Catering to families is **Avila Hot Springs Spa** (250 Avila Beach Dr., 805/595-2359), highlighted by a steaming full-sized swimming pool fed by mineral-rich hot springs.

The Monterey Plaza commands a spectacular marine vantage point near Cannery Row.

Monterey

MONTEREY PLAZA
Innkeeper: Daniel Kelly.
800/631-1339 USA,
   800/334-3999 CA,
   408/646-1700, 408/646-
   5843 Fax.
400 Cannery Row.
Price: Moderate to Very
   Expensive.
Credit Cards: AE, CB, DC,
   MC, V.
Children: Yes.
Smoking: Yes.
Handicap Access: Yes.

Draped on pilings that extend out over the tide pools and kelp beds of Monterey Bay, this contemporary Mediterranean resort hotel enjoys a prime location just a stroll away from Cannery Row and the Monterey Bay Aquarium. Sheer elegance from its over-the-water piazza to its splendid Chinese carpeting and Biedermeier reproduction furnishings, Monterey Plaza specializes in rooms with a coveted view. You can enjoy the spectacle of sea otters and seals frolicking just outside your balcony, sip afternoon tea amidst the Pacific Rim antiques and gleaming brass appointments of the plush main lobby, or take a tub in your marble bathroom before dinner in the hotel's magnificent Delfino Restaurant, showcase for contemporary Italian cuisine.

SPINDRIFT INN
Innkeeper: Helen Callahan.
800/841-1879 USA,
   800/225-2901 CA,
   408/646-8900, 408/646-
   5342 Fax.
652 Cannery Row.
Price: Moderate to Expensive; B.
Credit Cards: AE, CB, D,
   DC, MC, V.

A tastefully rebuilt vintage hotel provides superb location right on the beach at Cannery Row, only a block away from the Monterey Bay Aquarium. Each of 41 guest rooms is romantically decorated with plush canopy feather beds, imported carpeting, window seats with terrific waterfront views, and fireplaces; plus TV, refrigerators, and marble and brass bathrooms with phones and hair dryers. In-room saunas are available and a fresh continental breakfast is delivered to rooms

Children: Yes.
Smoking: Yes.
Handicap Access: Yes.

Pacific Grove

CENTRELLA HOTEL
Innkeeper: Canan Bari-
man.
800/233-3372, 408/372-
3372, 408/372-2036 Fax.
612 Central Ave.
Price: Moderate to Expen-
sive; B.
Credit Cards: AE, MC, V.
Children: Allowed with
limits.
Smoking: Outside only.
Handicap Access: Yes.

GATEHOUSE INN
Innkeeper: Suzi Russo.
800/753-1881, 408/649-
8436, 408/648-8044 Fax.
225 Central Ave.
Price: Moderate to Expen-
sive; B.
Credit Cards: AE, MC, V.
Children: Yes.
Smoking: Outside only.
Handicap Access: Limited.

along with the morning paper. A rooftop garden patio is the perfect place for a sunset glass of wine.

Built in 1889 as a private boarding house, this award-winning Victorian restoration has earned a place on the National Register of Historic Places. Twenty-four of 26 high-ceilinged, comfortably decorated rooms — including suites and cottages — have private bath and telephone. A full buffet breakfast awaits in the dining room each morning, and the evening wine, sherry, and appetizer spread involves substantial fare ranging from pâté and cheeses to marinated artichoke hearts and vegetable platters. The Centrella is aptly named, being within walking distance of Monterey's Cannery Row and world-famous aquarium.

Local lore has it that John Steinbeck regularly discussed historical trivia with the original owner of this Italianate 1884 residence. And this magnificently decorated inn still recalls its Victorian heyday. Much of the original decor — including lincrusta walls — has been enhanced with silk-screened period reproduction wallpaper, wicker furnishings, and opulent themes: one chamber feels like a sultan's tent with a mother-of-pearl inlaid headboard, Persian carpet, and camel saddle chair. Each of eight double rooms has a private bath (yes, even claw-foot tubs) and four rooms boast fireplaces. A fine full breakfast is served in the morning, as are afternoon wine and hors d'oeuvres. The location, very near the ocean, invites strolling and access to Monterey's

Guestrooms at Pacific Grove's Gatehouse are sunny and comfortable.

top sights. This is one of six destination B&Bs in the quality Four Sisters Inns enterprise.

GOSBY HOUSE INN
Innkeeper: Jillian Brewer.
800/527-8828, 408/375-1287, 408/655-9621 Fax.
643 Lighthouse Ave.
Price: Moderate; B.
Credit Cards: AE, MC, V.
Children: Yes.
Smoking: Outside only.
Handicap Access: Limited.

The distinctive front door turret and pointed cupola announce this gabled inn as a showpiece Queen Anne Victorian, circa 1887. Filled with distinctive antiques and charming whimsy from the last century, this beautiful facility was originally built as a boarding house and today offers lodgings in 22 rooms of varying sizes, most with private baths. Two rooms have kitchens, and fireplaces in 12 rooms provide coziness to match the antiques, period reproductions, and plump bed linens. It's like spending the night in the last century, but with phones by your carved wood bedside. Breakfast is substantial and unpretentious, with guests helping themselves to huge breakfast rolls, muffins, scones and hot egg dishes, and then moving out to the garden. The parlor, straight out of a Ivory-Merchant film, is the location for afternoon sherry and hors d'oeuvres. Bicycles are available to help maximize enjoyment of the nearby Pacific coastline and Cannery Row. A three-night reservation at this outpost of the Four Sisters empire provides a free fourth night.

GREEN GABLES INN
Innkeeper: Shirley Butts.
408/375-2095.
104 Fifth St.
Price: Moderate to Expensive; B.
Credit Cards: AE, MC, V.
Children: Yes.
Smoking: Outside only.
Handicap Access: Yes.

One of oceanfront Pacific Grove's landmarks, this multi-gabled Queen Anne mansion was built in 1888 by a southern California businessman for his paramour. The intricate results of the original owner's passion for bay windows, gingerbread, and stained-glass have been turned into a gracious inn, one of the prestigious Four Sisters Inns. Of the charmingly Victorian-style 10 rooms and one suite, some boast ocean-view rooms with fireplaces and six provide private baths. Morning brings the day's newspapers with coffee and continental breakfast to your room, or you can partake of a full, family-style breakfast buffet with fresh egg dishes, fruit, scones, pastries, and pancakes served in the parlor. In the afternoon, wine and appetizers are served by helpful staff members, who will also provide bicycles for touring the dramatic coastline.

SEVEN GABLES INN
Innkeepers: Susan, Ed, John, & Nora Flatley.
408/372-4341.
555 Ocean View Blvd.
Price: Moderate to Expensive; B.

A Victorian confection of multi-gabled gingerbread, the grand mansion's exterior is more than matched by an inviting interior of museum-quality antiques, ornate rugs, and gilded light fixtures. Fourteen elegant guest rooms, including several in adjoining cottages, have private baths and a

Credit Cards: MC, V.
Children: Age 12 and over.
Smoking: Outside only.
Handicap Access: Limited.

stunning coastal view. The second-floor Bellevue Room offers an especially sunny exposure and bay view from cozy window seats. The inn's period theme extends to guest room appointments like antique sideboards, stained glass windows, plush couches, huge armoires, and velvet-upholstered chairs. English high tea is served in the stately dining room each afternoon and a full breakfast greets guest in the morning. Innkeeper Susan Flatley grew up in the showy mansion and can spin great yarns about the area's history, as well as offer suggestions on Monterey's many historic attractions.

Pebble Beach

INN & LINKS AT SPAN-ISH BAY
Innkeeper: John Chadwell.
800/654-9300, 408/647-7500, 408/647-7443 Fax.
2700 17 Mile Dr.
Price: Very Expensive.
Credit Cards: AE, DC, MC, V.
Children: Yes.
Smoking: Yes.
Handicap Access: Yes.

On fabled 17 Mile Drive at the edge of the brooding pines of Del Monte Forest and only a few hundred yards from the Pacific shore, this 236-acre Mediterranean-style enclave is embraced by some of the finest championship golf terrain on the planet. Over 270 luxurious rooms and suites — each boasting four-poster beds, marble baths, fireplaces, and cable TV, and most with balconies, patios, and stupendous ocean views — make this a matchless resort in perhaps the most spectacular setting on the Central Coast. Guests are treated to preferred tee times at such world-class links as Pebble Beach Golf Links, Spyglass Hill Golf Course, and the Tom Watson, Robert Trent Jones, Jr., and Frank Tatum–designed Links at Spanish Bay. If golf isn't your bag, there's tennis, swimming, spa-going, or simply soaking up magnificent views from any of four restaurants and lounges. Complete indulgence here tends to make every guest feel like one of the rich and famous — and many are.

THE LODGE AT PEBBLE BEACH
Innkeeper: Gary Davis.
800/654-9300, 408/624-3811, 408/624-6357 Fax.
17 Mile Drive.
Price: Very Expensive.
Credit Cards: AE, DC, MC, V.
Children: Yes.
Smoking: Yes.
Handicap Access: Yes.

Since 1919, this elegant retreat has catered to international celebrities, sports legends, and those who crave the ultimate in pampering lodgings. The view through the lobby salon's windows is straight out of the Golden Age of Hollywood, overlooking the emerald expanse of the golf course's 18th hole and on to the white Pacific surf swirling along the craggy shoreline. In addition to golf, there are luxury tennis, swimming, horseback riding, and fitness facilities. The 155 spacious guest rooms continue the luxurious theme, with views of the ocean, fairways, or gardens. In addition to fine restaurants, the Lodge boasts a dark wood Tap Room sanctuary lined with a fascinating collection of golf memorabilia.

SAN LUIS OBISPO COAST

Where the emphasis is on beach-oriented action, well-appointed and conveniently located motels are the dominant form of lodging. Visitors will also encounter a healthy selection of cozy B&Bs, some ensconced in creatively renovated 19th-century hotels, offering romance, seaside gardens, and rooms with a view. Here are the essential stops that make this area such a great escape.

Cambria

BEACH HOUSE BED & BREAKFAST INN
Innkeepers: Joan Apathy, Penny Hitch, Kernn MacKinnon.
800/549-6789, 805/927-3136.
6360 Moonstone Beach Dr.
Price: Moderate; B.
Credit Cards: MC, V.
Children: Two people per room limits.
Smoking: Not in rooms.
Handicap Access: No.

Looking like the quintessential Central Coast private beachhouse, this comfortable wood and glass oceanfront home consists of seven rooms of varying sizes, all with private bath and cable TV. Two rooms come with fireplaces and one lofty second-floor room provides a king-size bed and private deck that opens onto the stunning seascape vistas of gorgeous Moonstone Beach. Refreshments, including wines and cheeses, are offered at sunset and morning is the best time to explore the grassy bluffs networked with inviting walking trails that overlook the tide pools and surf just outside the front door. The full breakfast offers fresh juice, cereals, delicious pastries, and entrées. The sunsets are beautiful, and Hearst Castle is 15 minutes up Highway 1.

BLUE WHALE INN
Innkeeper: Fred Ushijimi.
805/927-4647.
6736 Moonstone Beach Dr.
Price: Moderate to Expensive.
Credit Cards: MC, V.
Children: Allowed with limits.
Smoking: Not in rooms.
Handicap Access: No.

Each of this fine B&B's six spacious rooms soothes guests with soft pastel upholstery, plump comforters, canopy swags, comfortable couches, charming contemporary wallpaper, vaulted ceilings, and airy skylighting. A long dressing room area counter is lavishly appointed with beautifully packaged amenities, and there's a refrigerator, fireplace, separate bathroom — with a view of the rolling hills behind the shoreline — and cable TV tucked away in a colorful armoire. Guests also enjoy taking in the sunset and complimentary wine on their decks, or gazing through the telescope in the main lounge at whales and waterfowl cruising the coast. You can hear the soothing waves all night long. An inviting gift shop stocked with fine local crafts and beachy souvenirs is just off the picture window-lined dining room, where full breakfasts involve terrific coffee, fresh juices and fruits, cereals, and yogurt, as well as utter decadence like gingerbread pancakes with lemony syrup fresh from the adjoining kitchen. Regulars — and there are many who return to their favorite rooms each year — like to take a bracing walk along the hiking trails lacing the bluffs over spectacular Moonstone Beach, right across the lane from the inn.

CASTLE INN BY THE SEA
Innkeepers: Diane & Ed Maher.
805/927-8605, 805/927-3179 Fax.
6620 Moonstone Beach Dr.
Price: Inexpensive to Moderate; B.
Credit Cards: AE, D, MC, V.
Children: Yes.
Smoking: Yes.
Handicap Access: Yes.

Sprawling attractively in the pines and cypresses of the windswept bluffs overlooking Moonstone Beach, this AAA favorite caters equally to honeymooners and families attracted to the inviting setting within a short drive of Hearst Castle. Besides 31 overnight rooms, the motel offers a heated pool and Jacuzzi, plus in-room amenities like cable TV/VCR, direct dial phones, and mini-refrigerators. A trail to the beach begins at the facility's front door and a delicious continental breakfast appears at your guest room door in the morning. One-stop shopping for comfort without fussiness and the ease of beachfront location.

FOGCATCHER INN
Innkeepers: Dirk & Lauren Winter.
805/927-1400, 805/927-4016 Fax.
6400 Moonstone Beach Dr.
Price: Moderate; B.
Credit Cards: AE, D, DC, MC, V.
Children: Allowed with limits.
Smoking: Yes.
Handicap Access: Yes.

Conjuring scenes from a Brontë novel, this contemporary neo-English inn with multi-paned windows, thatched roof, and subtle half-timbering offers accommodations a few steps from the surf and tide pools of Moonstone Beach. Set on bluffs crisscrossed with hiking trails, the inn offers such luxuries as a heated pool and hot tub, as well as 60 guest rooms with refrigerator, fireplace, microwave, coffee maker, TV/VCR, and honor bar. There's even a bridal suite — this is honeymoon country. In the main gathering room, a breakfast of fine muffins and pastries, coffee, cereals, fresh fruit, and juices precedes a day of beachcombing, antiquing in Cambria village, or touring the eye-popping sights of San Simeon.

J. PATRICK HOUSE
Innkeeper: Molly Lynch.
805/927-3812.
2990 Burton Dr.
Price: Moderate; B.
Credit Cards: MC, V.
Children: Yes.
Smoking: No
Handicap Access: Limited.

This cozy two-story log house set in the pines overlooking Cambria's east village fronts an old-fashioned arbor leading to eight guest rooms, seven with a wood-burning fireplace and all with private bath. The early American decor of the main house is echoed in the attractive rooms, adorned with floral wallpaper and wicker furniture. Afternoon wine and cheese is offered at the sitting room fireplace and the sunny dining room serves up a full breakfast highlighted by freshly ground coffee, fruits, juices, muffins, and sumptuous cinnamon rolls. Personalized service and friendly atmosphere are added bonuses.

OLALLIEBERRY INN
Innkeepers: Carol Ann & Peter Irsfeld.
805/927-3222, 805/927-0202 Fax.
2476 Main St.
Price: Moderate; B.
Credit Cards: MC, V.
Children: Not appropriate.
Smoking: Not in rooms.
Handicap Access: Yes.

A romantic, period-decorated 1873 Greek Revival home provides six inviting rooms, two with fireplace and each with private bath, updated for contemporary convenience at no sacrifice of yesteryear ambiance. A casual, wicker-appointed main parlor is the setting for evening wine tastings with appetizers, and more than one libation has been enjoyed at the wooded glade and creek bordered by the inn's back lawn. Each guest room is uniquely decorated, with Victorian antiques accentuating the graceful high ceilings. A full breakfast greets guests in the morning and the turn-of-the-century cottages, shops, and galleries of downtown Cambria are a pleasant stroll away.

Morro Bay

INN AT MORRO BAY
Innkeeper: Larry Shupnick.
800/321-9566, 805/772-5651, 805/772-4779 Fax.
19 Country Club Rd.
Price: Inexpensive to Very Expensive.
Credit Cards: AE, CB, D, DC, MC, V.
Children: Yes.
Smoking: Yes.
Handicap Access: Limited

Overlooking the glittering expanse of Morro Bay and its dramatic Morro Rock (and just 30 minutes drive from Hearst Castle), this full-service facility offers inviting accommodations. Swim in the expansive pool, sip local wines in contemporary ambiance of the public rooms-with-a-view, or enjoy breakfast in your own brass bed. Rooms, many with fireplace, offer full amenities, and the inn's restaurant serves up fine seafood and California cuisine featuring the area's renowned fresh produce. Beaches and a bounty of rare waterfowl are right outside your window.

Pismo Beach

SANDCASTLE INN
Innkeeper: Valerie Smith.
800/822-6606, 805/773-2422, 805/773-0771 Fax.
100 Stimson Ave.
Price: Moderate to Expensive; B.
Credit Cards: AE, CB, DC, MC, V.
Children: Yes.

Attractions of this contemporary Mediterranean seaside retreat include plump couches and chairs, huge beds with soothing floral prints, and the ocean panorama viewed from patios, decks, and picture windows. Fifty-nine overnight rooms, including suites with fireplaces, offer complete comfort and views of the picturesque fishing pier and oceanfront. Each room has its own TV/VCR, refrigerator, and coffee maker. The continental breakfast is ideal just after

Smoking: Yes.
Handicap Access: Yes.

SEAVENTURE HOTEL
Innkeeper: Mike Schofield.
800/237-7804 USA,
   800/662-5545 CA,
   805/773-4994, 805/773-
   4693 Fax.
100 Ocean View Ave.
Price: Moderate to Expen-
   sive; B.
Credit Cards: AE, D, DC,
   MC, V.
Children: Yes.
Smoking: Yes.
Handicap Access: Limited.

San Luis Obispo

APPLE FARM INN
Innkeepers: Bob & Kath-
   leen Davis.
800/255-2040 CA,
   805/544-2040, 805/541-
   5497 Fax.
2015 Monterey St.
Price: Moderate to Expen-
   sive.

you've exited the swirling Jacuzzi on the glass-enclosed deck.

Fifty comfortable rooms — 20 with spas and wet bars, some with private decks, all with cable TV and thoughtful toiletries — serve as headquarters for exploring the endless seashore recreational opportunities of this popular coastal resort. Right on the beach, the full-service destination motel boasts its own rooftop restaurant, cocktail lounge, and heated swimming pool for those foggy morning laps. A substantial continental breakfast is included and, yes, the setting is shamelessly romantic.

Even an overworked word like "charming" finds new currency in reference to this Victorian inn, which is a veritable country village of cozy overnight rooms in and around an old millhouse and farm residence. Four-poster beds, flowered wallpaper, ruffled linens, overstuffed couches, and deep tubs add romance to contemporary amenities like the heated swimming pool and Jacuzzi. Each room

Apple Farm Inn in San Luis Obispo is next to an old millhouse and working farm.

Credit Cards: AE, D, MC, V.
Children: Yes.
Smoking: Yes.
Handicap Access: Yes.

boasts its own fireplace and morning brings coffee or tea to your door (the inn's fine restaurant serves a full range of culinary classics; see *Restaurants*). There are splendid views of the surrounding hills and the huge waterwheel turns hypnotically on its 19th century foundations.

GARDEN STREET INN
Innkeepers: Dan & Kathy Smith.
805/545-9802.
1212 Garden St.
Price: Moderate to Expensive; B.
Credit Cards: AE, MC, V.
Children: Over 16 only.
Smoking: Not in rooms.
Handicap Access: Yes.

The high ceilings, grand staircase, and jewel-like stained glass trimmings of this Italianate 1887 Stick Victorian have been lovingly restored to the atmosphere of the heyday of this frontier town. Tastefully decorated with antiques and artistic family memorabilia, the inn offers nine rooms and four suites, each with private bath. Romantics will love the five rooms with fireplaces and whirlpool tubs, as well as the evening wine and cheese selection. There's a well-stocked library, and a homemade full breakfast is served amidst the original stained-glass splendor of the house's Morning Room.

MADONNA INN
Innkeeper: Alex Madonna.
800/543-9666, 805/543-3000, 805/543-1800 Fax.
100 Madonna Rd.
Price: Moderate to Expensive.
Credit Cards: MC, V.
Children: Yes.
Smoking: Yes.
Handicap Access: Limited.

There's simply nothing like the Madonna Inn, an only-in-California tribute to fantasy and excess in stonework and shocking pink, where each room is decorated like a B-movie set. No one ever forgets an overnight in the cave-like Flintstones Suite with its rock waterfall shower, not to mention the men's room with its own waterfall urinal. A no-holds-barred "motel," this epic of red velvet and chandelier overkill (matched by an architectural hodgepodge of an exterior) is wonderful fun. The bar looks like an old-fashioned carousel and the amazing restaurant (yes, you have seen it in many Hollywood movies) serves up serious homemade fare and gargantuan barbecued steaks. There are oodles of souvenir, gift, clothing, and coffee shops. Expect to be amazed by the eccentric decor of any one of the 110 rooms and suites. You may not be planning a second honeymoon — all rooms do have cable TV — but you'll end up having one anyway given the fantasy sensory bombardment.

Megan's Friends Bed & Breakfast Reservation Service

A list of San Luis Obispo County bed & breakfast accommodations in real peoples' homes is available by writing or phoning this placement service (1776 Royal Way, San Luis Obispo; 805/544-4406).

SANTA BARBARA COAST

Luxurious resort retreats favored by magnates and movie people, and elegantly cozy inns of Victorian, Craftsman, and Spanish-style architecture — the following accommodations should be on the discerning Santa Barbara visitor's short list.

Montecito/Summerland

INN ON SUMMER HILL
Innkeeper: Verlinda
  Richardson.
800/845-5566, 805/969-
  9998.
2520 Lillie Ave., Summerland.
Price: Expensive to Very
  Expensive; B.
Credit Cards: AE, MC, V.
Children: Allowed with
  limits.
Smoking: Outside only.
Handicap Access: Limited.

Sixteen inviting rooms comprise this peaceful retreat just south of Santa Barbara in elegant Summerland. Rooms offer expansive ocean views, private balcony, fireplace, cable TV, and canopy beds with floral print swags that match wallpaper and upholstery themes. In the morning, an elaborate full breakfast sets guests up for a day of wandering the stunning local beaches or sightseeing in historic Santa Barbara. Afternoon hors d'oeuvres and wine and evening dessert are served in a soothingly romantic setting.

MONTECITO INN
Innkeeper: Linda Span.
800/843-2017; 805/969-
  7854, 805/969-0623 Fax.
1295 Coast Village Rd.,
  Montecito.
Price: Moderate to Very
  Expensive; B.
Credit Cards: AE, CB, D,
  DC, MC, V.

Rumors abound as to the illicit romps and rendezvouses negotiated for decades at this inn, which inspired *There's a Small Hotel*. But it is clear that even if Charlie Chaplin and Fatty Arbuckle didn't build this elegant bungalow of Spanish tiles and fountains in 1928, they certainly spent time entertaining guests there. The 48 guest rooms and five suites are decorated in French country style and the amenities — besides small-hotel ambiance

The Montecito Inn's French country-style ambiance has long catered to visiting Hollywood celebrities.

Children: Yes.
Smoking: Yes.
Handicap Access: No.

— include cable TV in rooms, a spa/fitness center, a pool, and bicycles on which to explore the swanky surroundings of exclusive Montecito. You'll need the exercise after sampling the menu at the Montecito Cafe: Santa Barbara resident Julia Child is enamored of the fresh seafood and innovative gastronomy here (see *Restaurants*). Two-night minimum on weekends.

SAN YSIDRO RANCH
Innkeeper: Janis Clapoff.
800/368-6788, 805/969-5046, 805/565-1995 Fax.
900 San Ysidro Lane, Montecito.
Price: Expensive to Very Expensive.
Credit Cards: AE, MC, V.
Children: Yes.
Smoking: Yes.
Handicap Access: Yes.

Once a working ranch attached to the Mission Santa Barbara, the gorgeous 550-acre spread has been upgraded to the plush comfort standards of a European inn. The pedigree of the rooms, suites, and cottages — all offering cable TV, fireplace, private deck, wet bar, refrigerator, and whirlpool tub — adds to the atmosphere. Owned by Ronald Colman in the 1930s, the luxury facility has hosted the world's great and glamorous. Here Jack and Jackie Kennedy honeymooned, Vivian Leigh and Laurence Olivier were married, and Somerset Maugham unwound. The country-style room decor is cozy and piney. Guests can play, swim, ride, tennis, and schmooze to their hearts' content and embark for the beach just a few minutes' drive away.

Santa Barbara

BLUE QUAIL INN & COTTAGES
Innkeeper: Julia Marek.
800/676-1622 USA,
800/549-1622 CA,
805/687-2300.
1908 Bath St.
Price: Inexpensive to Expensive; B.
Credit Cards: AE, D, DC, MC, V.
Children: Allowed with limits
Smoking: Allowed with limits.
Handicap Access: No.

A brace of antique-filled bungalows offers relaxing country charm free of fussiness. A place to unwind completely, yet within quick reach of downtown and beaches, Blue Quail offers five double rooms with bath and four suites (two of which share a bath and one with fireplace), each uniquely decorated in a soothing blend of French elegance, white wicker comfort, and early Americana. In the tiny main house, a living room is the setting for afternoon hors d'oeuvres and wine; evening sweets and hot cider can be enjoyed in the lush gardens. Full breakfast is taken near the fragrant country kitchen or in warm weather (which means almost always) on the brick patio. Picnic lunches are available for the beach and there's a solo TV in the main building.

CHESHIRE CAT INN
Innkeeper: Christine Dunstan.

Two adjacent Victorian beauties form the heart of this very British monument to the textiles

805/569-1610, 805/682-1876 Fax.
36 West Valerio St.
Price: Moderate to Very Expensive; B.
Credit Cards: MC, V.
Children: Allowed with limits.
Smoking: Outside only.
Handicap Access: No.

designed by Laura Ashley, whose floral and striped wallpapers and linens adorn every inch of this charming B&B. Innkeeper Christine Dunstan also owns an inn in Scotland and has lovingly recreated an Old World feel here from the turreted exterior to the smashingly decorated six double rooms and six suites. Four rooms have their own fireplaces and whirlpool tubs, two offer TV, some have balconies and kitchenettes. All are beautiful. The gazebo features a soothing spa and there are myriad garden areas. A consummate continental breakfast, served on Wedgwood china at white tables and chairs on the outdoor brick patio, includes croissants, homemade preserves, cereals, and juices. Liqueurs and chocolate greet guests as they check in and the designer restaurants and shops of State Street are only a few blocks away. A two-night minimum is required on weekends.

EL ENCANTO HOTEL & GARDEN VILLAS
Innkeeper: Thomas Narozonick.
800/346-7039 CA, 805/687-5000, 805/687-3903 Fax.
1900 Lasuen Rd.
Price: Moderate to Very Expensive.
Credit Cards: AE, CB, DC, MC, V.
Children: Allowed with limits.
Smoking: Yes.
Handicap Access: Limited.

A colony of Mediterranean villas set in a lush jungle of landscaping crowned by a breathtaking view of the indigo ocean below, El Encanto is considered one of the top small resorts in the West. Red-tile roofs, forests of eucalyptus and banana palms, and a warren of very secluded patios surround the resort's 30-plus rooms, 45 suites and villas, many with fireplaces and private decks. From the terrace of the inn's popular restaurant — reservations are a must — you can also feast on a world-class vista as you enjoy outstanding new American cuisine. Exuding old Santa Barbara romance, this retreat is highly fashionable with jetsetters, rock stars, visiting dignitaries, and romantics. Lots of atmosphere for the price, plus a swimming pool (of course) and tennis courts. Two-night minimum on weekends.

FOUR SEASONS BILTMORE HOTEL
Innkeeper: Chris Hart.
800/332-3442, 805/969-2261, 805/969-5715 Fax.
1260 Channel Dr.
Price: Very Expensive.
Credit Cards: AE, CB, D, DC, MC, V.
Children: Yes.
Smoking: Yes.
Handicap Access: Yes.

Oceanfront location, 21 acres of tropical grounds, sumptuous Mediterranean decor, and graceful architecture create an elegant facility considered the premiere resort in a town of world-class lodgings. The beautiful estate, opened as a lodging in 1927, has been handsomely updated to maximize both its celebrity heritage and deluxe amenities. Spanish balconies look over a labyrinth of splendid gardens and every window in the palatial main building frames incomparable views of the Pacific. Many of the rooms and cottages have private patios overlooking expanses of green and the gorgeous Santa Lucia Mountains. Fireplaces abound, as do ceiling fans, tastefully ensconced TV/VCR centers, room safes, mini-bars, and gleaming white-tiled bathing areas appointed with luxury amenities, hairdryers, and robes. Cool tile-lined walkways lead to the sunny terrace dining, where consummate breakfasts include an authentic Japanese repast and world-class eggs Benedict. The rich and famous congregate on the outdoor terrace at lunch and cocktail hour, or on soft leather-upholstered banquettes in a private lounge for exquisite finger foods that accompany pourings of fine local wines. Savvy guests start the day across the palm-lined front drive at a circa 1930 swimming club where laps in the almost-Olympic size pool appear to take you out into the ocean beyond. A gym, sauna, Jacuzzi, lighted tennis courts, a putting green, and croquet courts await your pleasure.

OLD YACHT CLUB INN
Innkeepers: Nancy Donaldson, Sandy Hunt, Lu Caruso.
800/676-1676, 805/962-1277, 805/962-3989 Fax.
431 Corona del Mar Dr.
Price: Moderate; B.
Credit Cards: AE, CB, D, DC, MC, V.
Children: Allowed with limits.
Smoking: Outside only.
Handicap Access: Limited.

A 1912 California Craftsman bungalow and its 1925 neighbor were reincarnated in 1980 as the Santa Barbara area's first B&B. Each of nine guest rooms — five in the main house, four next door — offers a phone and private bath. TV is available and a suite sports a whirlpool tub. Some rooms have balconies and others patios where evening wine can be enjoyed. Sherry can also be taken amidst the antiques and oriental carpets surrounding the fireplace in the former yacht club's main parlor. A wonderful full breakfast includes homemade breads, juices, fruit, and omelets. Spectacular candlelight dinners are offered on Saturdays for guests. The inn provides bicycles, beach towels, and chairs to enhance a day at the beach only a half block away. Two night minimum on weekends.

PARSONAGE BED & BREAKFAST
Innkeepers: Dick & Audrey Harmon, Holli & Terry Harmon.
800/775-0352, 805/962-9336.
1600 Olive St.
Price: Moderate to Expensive; B.
Credit Cards: AE, D, MC, V.
Children: Allowed with limits.
Smoking: Outside only.
Handicap Access: No.

This beautifully restored Queen Anne Victorian, formerly a minister's home, presents period charm and highly romantic seclusion. A collection of French and American antiques fill the first-floor living rooms, and the five spacious rooms (all with private bath) and elegant Honeymoon Suite offer fine views of ocean and mountains. Homemade cookies fresh from the kitchen, often accompanied by espresso, greet relaxing guests, and in the evenings wine is available on the sprawling verandah. Ample breakfasts of homemade muffins and breads, omelets, fresh juices, and serious coffee are served each morning. The inn is close to shops, fine restaurants, and historic sights, and the Harmon family of innkeepers special-ize in warm personal attention.

Built in 1874, Santa Bar-bara's Simpson House fea-tures authentic Victorian atmosphere.

SIMPSON HOUSE INN
Innkeeper: Gillean Wilson.
800/676-1280, 805/963-7067, 805/564-4811 Fax.
121 East Arrellaga St.
Price: Moderate to Very Expensive; B.
Credit Cards: MC, V.
Children: Allowed with limits.
Smoking: On one veran-dah only.
Handicap Access: Yes.

Large guest rooms (six in the main house, four suites in the adjoining barn) lend this unusual Eastlake Victorian built in 1874 an authentically elegant atmosphere. Some rooms open onto a pri-vate deck overlooking an acre of stately trees and gardens; all afford the luxury of down comforters and graceful antique touches. Afternoon tea and wine are taken in front of the sitting room fireplace, or while ensconced in one of the wicker settees on the wraparound verandah. A bountiful buffet breakfast features hot specialties like French toast and fresh-from-the-oven muffins. Beach chairs and towels may be taken for a day in the sun, and the historic downtown is right around the corner.

UPHAM VICTORIAN HOTEL & GARDEN COTTAGES
Innkeeper: Jan Martin Winn.
800/727-0876, 805/962-0058, 805/963-2825 Fax.
1404 De la Vina St.
Price: Moderate to Very Expensive; B.
Credit Cards: AE, D, DC, MC, V.
Children: Yes.

A few blocks from downtown theaters, restau-rants, and shopping, this Victorian Italianate lodging, built as a hotel in 1871, is peacefully sur-rounded by a carriage house and cottages that offer old-fashioned relaxation and genuinely comfort-able accommodations. The five garden cottages have miniature front porches and private lawns, and some come with fireplaces and whirlpool tubs. All of the 40 rooms and suites offer cable TV (neatly hidden in armoires) and phones, handsome four-poster beds, and antique-appointed bath-

Smoking: Yes.
Handicap Access: Limited.

rooms. Wine and cheese are served in the afternoon in a homey parlor filled with recent menus from the area's top restaurants, and in the morning guests can help themselves to a substantial buffet breakfast or start the day with coffee in the garden gazebo. The inn also provides its own highly acclaimed dining at its verandah restaurant. Manager Jan Martin Winn and staff are exceptionally helpful — you might even get to peek upstairs at the outstanding view through cupola windows — and historic old Santa Barbara is a two-minute stroll away.

VILLA ROSA INN
Innkeeper: Annie Puetz.
805/966-0851, 805/962-
    7159 Fax.
15 Chapala St.
Price: Moderate to Expensive; B.
Credit Cards: AE, MC, V.
Children: Over 14 only.
Smoking: Outside only.
Handicap Access: Limited.

Echoing the splendid Spanish heritage of this sun-drenched resort town, Villa Rosa is accented with wrought-iron balconies, tiled courtyards, beamed ceilings, and vibrant Mediterranean plantings. Sophisticated and low-key, the 18 overnight rooms — four with fireplaces — are decorated in Southwestern tones and provide luxurious amenities like terrycloth robes and fresh roses. A pool, spa, and courtyard offer quiet settings for the complimentary afternoon wine and cheese or evening port and sherry. A continental breakfast is served each morning, and the location of this comfortable lodging affords easy walking to the gorgeous main beaches and fine restaurants.

Santa Ynez Valley

ALISAL GUEST RANCH
Innkeeper: David Lautensack.

Part guest ranch, part golf resort, all Western hospitality, this legendary facility opened its 10,000 acres of working ranch to guests in 1946.

The swimming pool, tennis courts, and golf courses of the Santa Ynez Valley's Alisal Guest Ranch exist to pamper.

805/688-6411, 805/688-2510 Fax.
1054 Alisal Rd., Solvang.
Price: Very Expensive; B, Dinner.
Credit Cards: AE, MC, V.
Children: Yes.
Smoking: Yes.
Handicap Access: Yes.

Some visitors never leave the sprawling swimming pool, tennis courts, or two golf courses with their own PGA pro on staff. Others fish for catfish, bluegill, and large-mouth bass, or sail on the ranch's lakes. But most come to forget the cares of civilization and take to the miles of equestrian trails winding through magnificent hills and sycamore groves. Leaving at dawn, wranglers lead guests into the beautiful country where a campfire breakfast of ham and pancakes awaits. But it's not all rustic. After cocktails at the Oak Room Lounge, guests can enjoy California cuisine in the Old West ambiance of the dining room. Overnight rooms all boast wood-burning stoves and cozy decor. A two-night minimum is required and, during midweek and most weekends, all golf, tennis, and horseback riding is free as part of the package deal. This is a very special getaway for those who like to "rough it" in style.

BALLARD INN
Innkeeper: Kelly Robinson.
800/638-2466, 805/688-7770, 805/688-9560 Fax.
2436 Baseline Ave., Ballard.
Price: Expensive; B.
Credit Cards: AE, MC, V.
Children: Allowed with limits.
Smoking: Outside only.
Handicap Access: Yes.

Fronted by one of tiny Ballard's two or three streets, this contemporary inn could be from the late 19th century, with its wraparound verandah, polished wood dining room, and antique-filled guest rooms. Each room holds its own special charm, built around Old West themes and featuring fine craftwork, brass and wicker beds, magnificent comforters, quilts, and upholsteries, plus Victorian armoires and commodes transformed into sinks. Seven of the 15 rooms have wood-burning fireplaces and each has a full private bath. The parlor lays out an afternoon appetizer display that can include smoked trout, cheeses, pickled asparagus, and crackers to accompany the excellent vintages of Santa Ynez wineries. In the morning, the inn's friendly staff serves up a full breakfast of pancakes or poached eggs and thick slabs of outstanding country bacon, and there's a continental buffet on the carved sideboard. The inn recently earned its fourth AAA star. Staff members are highly knowledgeable about the local micro-wineries and will guide you to memorable tastings; a tour of this captivating wine country is ideal via the Ballard's complimentary mountain bikes. A two-night minimum is required on weekends.

LOS OLIVOS GRAND HOTEL
Innkeeper: Mike Healey.
800/446-2455, 805/688-7788, 805/688-1942 Fax.
2860 Grand Ave./PO Box 526, Los Olivos.

In the gem-like western village of Los Olivos, this luxury hideaway combines turn-of-the-century atmosphere with 20th-century comforts. A terrific base for exploring the scenic wineries of the Santa Ynez Valley, the elegant hotel has 21 spacious overnight rooms, public rooms, an award-winning

Price: Expensive to Very Expensive; B.
Credit Cards: AE, D, MC, V.
Children: Yes.
Smoking: Yes.
Handicap Access: Yes.

restaurant, swimming pool, and Jacuzzi. Each room has been tastefully decorated in period style with armoires, brass beds, floral comforters, and antique chandeliers. Every room also offers a fireplace, remote control TV, wet bar, refrigerator, and welcoming bottle of locally made wine. Continental breakfast is served in-room each morning, after which guests can simply relax poolside or stroll the hotel's arbors and gardens. Bicycles are available for touring tiny Los Olivos, with its art galleries and wine tasting rooms.

CHAPTER FOUR
Preserve and Promote
CULTURE

The cultural tone of California's Central Coast was set long ago by its spectacular natural beauty and welcoming climate, beckoning to and nurturing the creativity of writers, mavericks, and artistic freethinkers for over 200 years. The same coastal splendor that inspired the pens of Robert Louis Stevenson, Robinson Jeffers, John Steinbeck, Jack Kerouac, and Henry Miller now hosts the music masters of the world at

Shmuel Thaler

The early mission days of Central California still linger in the serene walkways of Mission Carmel.

the annual Monterey Jazz Festival and Cabrillo Music Festival. In a part of the country where filmmaking is literally part of the scenery, the cinematic *nouvelle vague* plays nightly at handsomely restored Deco movie palaces. Contemporary artisans push the edges of handmade forms within the shadow of Franciscan mission. Here the historic co-exists comfortably with culture's latest wave.

ARCHITECTURE

The thick adobe walls, sunny courtyards, and Moorish arches of the Spanish missions created by Franciscan padres in the late 18th century have influenced architectural thinking ever since, and still dominate the psychic landscape of the region. Many missions have been restored over the centuries as centerpieces in Central Coast communities, most notably in Santa Barbara, San Luis Obispo, and Carmel.

After the missions were secularized following Mexican independence from Spain, their stylistic influence spilled over into adobe ranch houses and town homes, which today still exist in handsome profusion, especially in the heart of Old Monterey and Santa Barbara. When Mexico lost its claim to California, and American entrepreneurs enthusiastically moved in, they made themselves at home with clapboard houses, New England-style churches, and white picket fences.

With prosperity came ornate displays of Victorian decoration and a profusion of Eastlake streetscapes. To proclaim their arrival as full-blown townships, mercantile districts and industrious downtowns soon turned to building in the Italianate style. The main streets of San Luis Obispo boast whole blocks of beautifully maintained 19th-century stores, banks, workshops, and warehouses.

In the carefully groomed residential streets surrounding downtown Santa Cruz, rows of pastel-hued cottages and mansions preserve the aura of the 19th-century boom in this seaside mecca. City fathers filled Walnut St. with the curved archways, steep gables, and ornate turrets marking the high point of Stick, Gothic Revival, and Queen Anne fashion, all of which flourish today surrounded by historic landscaping and vintage trees. Wealthy land and cattle barons filled the town's Beach Hill district with majestic Victorian mansions; the Oceanview Avenue district overlooking the city is lined with ornate Queen Anne beauties.

Similarly, Santa Barbara's Brinkerhoff Avenue and De La Vina St. nurture that city's early Yankee era in graceful Victorians framing the Spanish heart of downtown. In Pacific Grove, founded in the 19th century as a seaside retreat, distinctive mansions still enjoy vigorous life, many as fine inns.

As the 20th century dawned, the fashion for Art Deco, Moderne, and Mission Revival flourished along the Central Coast, followed by a distinctly California spin on the growing Arts and Crafts movement. To the delight of the area's new generation of moviegoers, Santa Barbara's Arlington Theater rose with its Moorish arches, enormous ceiling beams, and tiled entry filled with fountains. Now a performing arts venue, the lavishly decorated theatrical

One of many restored — and continually maintained — Victorian residences updates the past on San Luis Obispo's Buchon Street.

palace — along with its newly refurbished counterpart, the Lobero Theater — continues to keep faith with the 1920s.

The architect William Weeks was just hitting his stride in the '20s, creating memorable schools, libraries, courthouses, hotels, and public buildings throughout the state. The colorful tiles, Spanish Mission revival polychromed ceilings, and curved roof line of Santa Cruz' Palomar Hotel carry on his legacy. A half mile away, on West Cliff Drive overlooking the Santa Cruz Boardwalk, one of Weeks' rare private homes still boasts its arched terrace, red-tile rooflines, and copper flashing details as the exquisite Darling House bed and breakfast inn.

The most vivid example of the Central Coast revival of its early Spanish architectural roots is downtown Santa Barbara: after destruction by earthquake in 1925, it rebuilt itself from the ground up in a single, harmonious theme. Resplendent with sensuous curved archways, adobe walls, copious plantings, and red-tiled roofs, this breathtaking downtown district allowed no compromise in its architectural design. Down to the last balcony and palm tree, it is the quintessential Central Coast variation on the area's Mediterranean theme.

The Spanish influence also joined the baroque, with two notable examples built a century and a half apart. One is the Royal Presidio Chapel in Monterey. A Spanish colonial gem, the ornate stone façade of the chapel was created in 1794 by master designers from Mexico City. With its bell tower and original 18th-century statues and stations of the cross, this living legacy of the original Spanish capital in the New World recalls the founding spirit of the Central Coast.

The other example, one hundred miles down the coast, is Hearst Castle, where the fantasies of William Randolph Hearst were given form in a fabulous Spanish baroque castle that still astonishes visitors to this incomparable setting between the Santa Lucia Mountains and the ocean.

CINEMA

R aised in proximity to Hollywood's filmmaking capital and frequently recognizing their home towns and coastal settings in many contemporary movies, Central Coastans are savvy silver screen consumers. Alfred Hitchcock and Clint Eastwood — who reigned as elected mayor of Carmel for a time — chose coastal landscapes to play key roles in many of their films. Even before the presence of major university campuses provided zealous audiences for films of every stripe, the region boasted its share of palaces from the Golden Era of movies. The 1930s Moderne Del Mar in Santa Cruz, the Fremont in San Luis Obispo, and the Granada in Santa Barbara — with tiled façades, old-fashioned marquees, and free-standing ticket booths — continue to lure cinema buffs to the latest offerings of celluloid magic. The Central Coast is also enamored of its small art and foreign film houses — like the Nickelodeon in Santa Cruz and the Dream Theater in Monterey — which host film festivals and retrospectives.

Santa Cruz Coast

Capitola Theatre (408/475-3518; 120 Monterey Ave., Capitola) A labor of love by local film buff Audrey Jacobs, who has owned and operated this user-friendly, low-price second-run house for four decades. Great popcorn, beachfront location.

41st Avenue Playhouse (408/476-8841; 1475 41st Ave., Capitola) Mid-county four-plex with Dolby SR sound system, comfortable rocking chair seating, and bright, young staff.

Nickelodeon (408/426-7500; 210 Lincoln St., Santa Cruz) This intimate four-screen complex specializes in the best current art films from the U.S. and abroad. A favorite with area culturati and the university crowd; freshly made popcorn with real butter and fresh fruit juices.

Rio Theatre (408/423-2000; 1205 Soquel Avenue, Santa Cruz) A large, vintage movie palace with plush seats, tiled restrooms, and an upstairs "crying room" for very young filmgoers. Usually screens mainstream blockbusters.

Sash Mill Cinema (408/427-1711; 303 Potrero, Santa Cruz) Mini-festivals, retrospectives, and off-the-wall cult films are the specialty of this appealing film house with its own terrific breakfast and lunch cafe.

Pacific Rim Film Festival

(408/475-2050; 2-1130 East Cliff Dr., Santa Cruz) Free screenings of rarely seen contemporary films from directors representing many countries of the Pacific Rim and Asia come to Santa Cruz each spring thanks to Hawaii's East-West Center, the University of California, Santa Cruz and the enthusiastic endorsement of the town. Guest appearances by directors, after-film discussions, and great wrap parties make this event a hotbed of culturally diverse entertainment.

Monterey Coast

Carmel Village Theater (408/625-1200; Dolores & 7th, Carmel) A single screen throwback to simpler times, this charmer features some art films and a cute, tiny balcony.

Dream Theater (408/372-1331; 301 Prescott Ave., Monterey) Decorated like the Victorian parlor of your favorite aunt, this local institution offers the tops in contemporary art films (viewed from close-to-the-floor recliner seats) and boasts real, hot-buttered popcorn.

Golden Bough (408/372-4555; Monte Verde & 8th, Carmel) Quaint neighborhood theater books first-run fare.

San Luis Obispo's Edward's Fremont Cinema showcases first-run contemporary cinema in a 1930s Deco movie palace setting.

Jay Swanson

Lighthouse Cinema (408/372-7300; 525 Lighthouse Ave, Pacific Grove) First-run screenings in an intimate, neighborhood movieland ambiance are the specialty of this main street theater.

State Cinemas (408/372-4555; 417 Alvarado St., Monterey) Lamentably, this 1928 beauty was cleaved into a tri-plex and shows only Hollywood's latest.

San Luis Obispo Coast

Edward's Fremont (805/541-2141; 1025 Monterey, San Luis Obispo) Another beauty from a bygone era carved up to fit modern small screen needs. Thirties Deco outside, first-run four-plex inside.

Palm Theatre (805/541-5161; 817 Palm, San Luis Obispo) A longtime favorite with the college crowd and local buffs, this thinking person's movie palace specializes in first-run art films.

Santa Barbara Coast

Riviera Theatre (805/965-3886; 2044 Alameda Padre Serra, Santa Barbara) Closest thing to an art film house the city has. Latest foreign flicks and new print film classics are the mainstays.

Metro (805/963-9503; 618 State St., Santa Barbara) Downtown four-plex books blockbusters and event films.

Cinema Twin (805/963-9503; 6050 Hollister Ave., Goleta) One screen shows a mainstream Hollywood biggie, while the other's double bill features a foreign sleeper and prestige independent.

DANCE

Most of the finest dance groups regularly tour the Central Coast's performing arts venues. Santa Cruz is the home base of the nationally acclaimed *Tandy Beal & Company* (408/429-1324), an innovative touring

Mark Wagner

Dancer/choreographer Tandy Beal leads her Central Coast-based modern dance company on international tours.

ensemble that performs its engaging blend of soaring contemporary choreography and witty multi-media work several times each year in Santa Cruz and Monterey (as well as major big city venues). The annual *University of California, Santa Cruz Performing Arts* (408/459-2159) calendar offers the work of innovative dance faculty choreographers and the campus *Arts & Lectures Series* (408/459-2826) books top multi-cultural troupes from around the world to dance on the university's Performing Arts Theatre stage. *Performance Carmel* (408/624-3996) offers world-class dance as part of its annual schedule of international artists and the light-footed *Civic Ballet of San Luis Obispo* (805/544-4363) mounts a yearly performance season. The *University of California, Santa Barbara Arts & Lectures* series (805/893-3535), the school's *Drama & Dance Department* (805/893-3535) and the *Lobero Theatre* (800/883-PLAY, 805/963-0761) all offer a year-round schedule of fine regional, national, and international dance offerings.

GARDENS

The balmy Mediterranean climate of the Central Coast nurtures an exhaustive range of native and cultivated flora, many of which are on view in the form of creatively landscaped formal gardens. However "formal," all bear the unmistakably casual signature of this region's year-round al fresco lifestyle.

Santa Cruz Coast

Antonelli Brothers Begonia Gardens (408/475-5222; 2545 Capitola Rd., Capitola) World headquarters for production of begonia seed, this colorful sprawl of nurseries and plantings is a treat. Also on view and for purchase are azaleas, camellias, rhododendrons, and fuchsias. Open 9–6 daily.

University of California, Santa Cruz Arboretum (408/427-2998; off Empire Grade Rd., Santa Cruz) Experimental and showpiece gardens, both emphasizing indigenous plants, are on display along the arboretum's many trails. Amidst the groves of various eucalyptus trees, the collections of plants from Australia and South Africa are considered among the best in world. Open 9–5 daily.

University of California, Santa Cruz Farm and Garden Project (408/459-4140; off Coolidge Dr., Santa Cruz) A working farm/agroecology project nestled at the foot of the hilltop campus, this 25-acre meadow filled with vegetable and flower beds, orchards, and row crops was founded by French-intensive master gardener Alan Chadwick, whose students have continued organic experiments in these fertile fields. An opportunity to observe a hotbed of ecologically correct Central Coast growing techniques. Open daily dawn to dusk for self-guided tours; docent tours noon Thurs., 2pm Sun.

Monterey Coast

Carmel Valley Begonia Gardens (408/624-7231; 9220 Carmel Valley Rd., Carmel) This lavish nursery specializes in flowering plants, Mediterranean perennials, and, of course, richly hued begonias. The extensive growing beds and nursery may be toured. Open 8:30–5 daily.

La Playa Hotel Gardens (408/624-6476; 8th & El Camino Real, Carmel) The gardens of this graceful Mediterranean-style hotel are lavishly maintained with formal plantings of Icelandic poppies, tulips, primroses, and hyacinths, as well as year-round perennial plantings.

San Luis Obispo Coast

Hearst Castle Gardens (800-444-7275; San Simeon) To surround his 130-room hilltop castle, media baron William Randolph Hearst envisioned gardens on an opulent scale. A 20-person crew headed by Nigel Keep hauled acres of soil up the hillside to create a series of terraces that were then planted with over 100,000 trees, thousands of rose bushes, and acres of Hearst's favorite flower, the camellia. More than a half million flowers were propagated in the castle's greenhouses to stock the fabulous grounds, which include a mile-long pergola. Tour IV of the many Hearst Castle guided visits is largely devoted to the gardens. Open 8:30–3 daily.

Mission Plaza (805/543-6850; Chorro & Monterey Sts., San Luis Obispo) At the site of the Mission San Luis Obispo, founded in 1772, visitors may enjoy the sunny cloistered garden where early Franciscan fathers meditated. In front, a terraced plaza offers soul-soothing landscaping and plantings winding down to and along the banks of peaceful San Luis Creek. Open dawn–dusk daily.

Santa Barbara Coast

Abbey Gardens (805/684-5112; 4620 Carpinteria Ave., Carpinteria) An astonishing array of 2000 varieties of cacti and succulents. Nursery, gift shop open 9–5 Tues.–Sun.

Alice Keck Park Memorial Gardens (805/564-5433; Arrellaga, Garden, Micheltorena, & Santa Barbara Sts., Santa Barbara) Soothing and sybaritic flowers, trees, massed plantings, streams, and a pond. Open dawn–dusk daily.

Moreton Bay Fig Tree (intersection of Chapala St. & Hwy. 1010, Santa Barbara) A much-loved local landmark, this giant fig was brought from its Australian home of Moreton Bay and planted in 1874. It was transplanted to its present location in 1877. The largest tree of its kind in the country, its 160-foot crown provides 21,000 square feet of shade.

Santa Barbara Botanic Gardens (805/682-4726; 1212 Mission Canyon Rd., Santa Barbara) A 65-acre Mission Creek garden of native cacti, shrubs, trees, and wildflowers with three miles of nature trails. Open 9–sunset daily; guided tours 2pm daily; Thurs., Sat., Sun. 10:30am.

Stewart Orchids (805/684-5448; 3376 Foothill Rd., Carpinteria) The Santa Barbara area is an international center for the cultivation of orchids and this huge nursery, which houses over 80,000 square feet of greenhouse space, grows and sells myriad exotic varieties. Open 8–4 Mon.–Fri.; 10–4 Sat.

International Orchid Show

Twice a year, Santa Barbara is inundated with growers and collectors of rare and unusual orchids for sumptuous displays of some of the finest cymbidia on the planet. The Santa Barbara International Orchid Show (805/967-6331) fills the Earl Warren Showgrounds each March with patio, garden, and pool displays of orchid varieties. The International Orchid Fair (805/967-1284) draws growers and vendors from around the world every July.

HISTORIC PLACES

Those who settled the Central Coast over the past two centuries left their mark in seaside attractions and ambitious architectural compounds that still bear witness to the dreams, energy, and civic vision of their builders. Representing all the periods of human habitation here — Native American, Spanish, Mexican, and American — many of the most notable and atmospheric of these historic places allow rare access to other eras. Thanks to our temporal proximity to those earliest immigrant days, many of these landmarks continue to enjoy a vital contemporary life, often forming the centerpiece of their modern communities.

Santa Cruz Coast

**EVERGREEN HISTORI-
CAL CEMETERY**
408/425-7278.
Evergreen & Coral Sts.,
Santa Cruz.

One of the oldest Protestant cemeteries in the state, this verdant hillside became a final resting place for area settlers, from judges to courtesans, in 1850. Beneath the weathered and tottering

Open: Dawn–dusk daily;
  docent-led tours by
  appt. only.
Admission: Free; tours 50¢
  child, $1 adult.

headstones, lie Civil War veterans, Freemasons, and civic fathers (and mothers). An entire section devoted to graves of Chinese immigrants commemorates those who came to build the region's railroads, bridges, and roads.

The New England-style James Johnston House has stood watch over the Half Moon Bay coastline since the middle of the 19th century.

Stan Cacitti

**JAMES JOHNSTON
  HOUSE** AND
**WILLIAM JOHNSTON
  HOUSE**
No telephone.
Higgins Purissima Rd.,
  Half Moon Bay.
Open: Dawn–dusk daily.
Admission: Donations.

The only remaining example of the New England saltbox style dwelling on the northern Central Coast, the two-story, white clapboard house built in 1853 by one of the original '49ers, Ohio-born James Johnston, remains one of this area's most important and earliest structures. Built in the 1860s, the neighboring home of William Johnston still shows off its wooden peg construction and original shutters and corner boards. The lovely country road itself curves for almost 10 miles by old Santa Cruz Mountains farmhouses, pastures, and meadows before rejoining Hwy. 1.

**SANTA CRUZ MUNICI-
  PAL WHARF**
408/429-3628.
Beach & Washington Sts.,
  Santa Cruz.
Open: 5am–2am daily.
Admission: Free.

The incessant bellowing of the resident colony of harbor seals who lounge among the wharf's huge pilings welcomes visitors to this shop and restaurant-lined fishing pier. Offering wraparound views of the surfing action at Steamers Lane and the turn-of-the-century Boardwalk casino and arcade, the wharf buzzes with open-air fish markets, gift and sporting boutiques, and bay excursion craft for hire. Constructed in 1914, this fishing and pleasure pier extends out into Monterey Bay near where four earlier versions were built, the first one in 1853 to fill sailing ships with the produce of the fertile Santa Cruz Mountains countryside. Today the casual pace begins at dawn for local fisherfolk and continues with de rigueur sunset cocktails for locals and visitors alike.

Shmuel Thaler

An authentically restored 19th-century cattle ranch and dairy are open to the public at Wilder Ranch State Park, just north of Santa Cruz.

WILDER RANCH STATE PARK
408/426-0505.
1401 Coast Rd. off Hwy. l, Santa Cruz.
Open: 8–dusk daily; docent-led tours 10–4 Weds.–Sun., with reservations; general ranch tour Sat., Sun. 1pm.
Admission: $6/vehicle parking fee.

Stretching over 5000 acres of the most sumptuous and varied terrain on the Central Coast, this former dairy ranch turned cattle ranch turned state park sprawls from its seaside tide pools and plover sanctuary all way up to redwood groves crowning a 2000-foot mountain top. Along the way, the spread encompasses magnificent meadows, ponds, springs, and wildlife habitats, including blue heron rookeries, and fox and coyote dens.

At the foot of the property is the beautifully maintained Victorian compound of the Wilder dairy ranch. All the buildings — including the long barn that housed the state's first cream separator, antique stable, workshop with original water-driven machinery, bunkhouse, and the owners' large, period-furnished Victorian manor house — are open to the public. Nearby are the remains of the original adobe, where Russian José Bolcoff married Spanish land grant heiress Maria Castro back when the ranch was part of the 10,000-acre Rancho Refugio.

The full exhilaration of this land is best enjoyed with sturdy shoes, a day pack filled with food and water, and a camera and binoculars for the ranch's many hiking, biking, and equestrian trails. It's a trip back into the solitude and open grandeur of the Old West.

Monterey Coast
CASA SOBERANES
408/649-7118.
Del Monte & Pacific Sts., Monterey.
Open: Tours 10, 11, 12 exc. Tues., Thurs.

Built during the 1840s by Custom House Warden Don José Rafael Estrada and later sold to Don Feliciano Soberanes, this lovely tile-roofed colonial adobe was Europeanized with a Mediterranean-style balcony. The interior, including what

Admission: $2 adults,
$1.50 youth, $1 children.
2-day pass.

has long been considered the prettiest adobe salon in Monterey, is decorated with period New England furniture and Mexican folk art.

COLTON HALL & OLD JAIL
408-646-5640.
522 Pacific St., Monterey.
Open: 10–5 daily (winter 4pm).
Admission: Free.

Designed as a town hall by Yankee *Alcade* (mayor) Walter Colton in 1847-49, this important historic landmark of local stone housed the first Constitutional Convention of the State of California during the autumn of 1849. Over the years, it served as a school, county seat, municipal court, and police headquarters, and was handsomely restored for the Centennial of 1949. The tables and benches of the upstairs assembly hall are arranged as they were when the 48 delegates from around the new state gathered to design the emerging government. The original designs for the grizzly bear, which still adorns the state flag, are displayed here. At the next-door jail, desperadoes ruminating on their few final hours on earth carved their names into the walls.

COOPER-MOLERA ADOBE
408/649-7109.
508 Munras Ave. Monterey.
Open: Tours 10, 11, 12 daily exc. Mon.; 2-day pass.
Admission: $2 adults, $1.50 youth, $1 children.

One of the largest extant adobes in the state, this structure was built in 1826 by English sea captain John Rogers Cooper, who converted to Catholicism and became a Mexican citizen in order to marry the renowned Californio beauty Encarnacion Vallejo, sister of General Mariano Vallejo. A successful businessman, Cooper added to the original single-story adobe as his fortune from hides, tallow, and sea otter pelts grew. Tours place the visitor dramatically in touch with affluent life in the early colonial period.

CUSTOM HOUSE
408/649-7188.
1 Custom House Plaza, Monterey.
Open: 10–5 daily.
Admission: Free.

The oldest public building in California, this 1814 adobe and tile structure flew the flags of Spain, Mexico, and the U.S. during its tenure as the most important port of entry into Alta California. At this site, custom taxes were levied on all trading ships during Spanish rule to help finance government expenses for the entire region. Fandangos were danced here to celebrate the arrival of foreign trading vessels, many laden with finery like Chinese silks. Under the direction of wealthy Yankee Thomas Larkin, the facility was enlarged and renovated in 1841. Later, in 1846, Commander Sloat proclaimed the takeover of California by the United States by raising the stars and stripes over what was perceived then as a symbol of foreign domination. Today, this State Historical Monument is packed with reminders of Monterey's former shipping glory, including harpoons, vintage portraits, and brocade garments worn by the wealthy Californios.

LARKIN HOUSE
408/649-7188.
510 Calle Principal, Monterey.
Open: Tours 2, 3, 4 daily exc. Tues.
Admission: $2 adults, $1.50 youth, $1 children; 2-day pass.

In creating what was to be the first two-story adobe in the Spanish capital in 1835, leading merchant Thomas O. Larkin invented the graceful Monterey style of Mexican adobe architecture. The encircling second-story verandah and low-hipped roofs that characterize this house were Larkin's own design and represent a fusion of the Spanish-style adobe with New England innovations, like the extensive use of glass in windows and a symmetrical floor plan. Today, the house is beautifully restored and decorated with period antiques, including many of Larkin's own furniture and belongings.

OLD WHALING STATION
408/375-5356.
391 Decatur St. at Heritage Harbor, Monterey.
Open: 10–2 Fri.; gardens dawn–dusk daily.
Admission: Free.

When adventurous Scotsman David White built this adobe residence in 1847, the walkway leading up to the house was paved with whale vertebrae. This calcified evidence of the sheer numbers of whales being dispatched from this busy Monterey Bay location was apt, since, upon White's departure, the house was taken over by the Old Monterey Whaling Company as headquarters for the lucrative, and messy, processing of whale oil. The station shares its gardens with what is thought to be the first brick building constructed in California.

STEVENSON HOUSE
408/649-2905.
530 Houston St., Monterey.
Open: Tours 2, 3, 4 daily exc. Mon.
Admission: $2 adults, $1.50 youth, $1 children; 2-day pass.

A highlight of Old Monterey's many attractions is this two-story adobe built in the late 1830s as a private residence with upstairs rooms rented out to boarders. One of the most famous guests of what was called The French Hotel in the 1870s was Robert Louis Stevenson. In his late 20s, and not yet the celebrated author he would become, Stevenson took rooms here to be near his paramour, Fanny Van de Grift Osbourne. Stevenson enjoyed his Monterey idyll for four months, during which he wrote an account of 1870s Monterey in *The Old Pacific Capital*, later drawing on the rugged coastal scenery for *Treasure Island*. The house is furnished with Stevenson's books, furniture, and memorabilia, including several portraits of the author. His bed and writing desk are still in place in the Robert Louis Stevenson Room of this beautifully restored monument.

MONTEREY PRESIDIO
408/647-5119.
Pacific St., north of Scott
St., Monterey.
Open: 24 hours daily.
Admission: Free.

Founded on June 3, 1770, when Gaspar de Portolá claimed Monterey for the King of Spain, the second military fort in Alta California first took shape as a structure of huts and crude barricades. The presidio was moved in 1800 to its present site overlooking the majestic port immortalized by Richard Henry Dana in *Two Years Before the Mast*. First the Mexican government (1822), then the Americans (1846) erected blockhouses and gun sites, spots now shown with plaques. The Sloat Monument commemorates the first raising of the American flag over Monterey by U.S. naval commodore John Drake Sloat. Today, this oldest military reservation in the United States is one of the largest Army posts in the country and site of the Defense Language Institute (408/647-5000). Historic markers dot the reservation, indicating Indian ceremonial rocks and the first landfalls of Sebastian Vizcaino (1602) and Father Junipero Serra (1770). The view overlooking Monterey Bay is daunting.

TOR HOUSE
408/624-1813.
26304 Ocean View Ave.,
  Carmel.
Open: Fri., Sat. by reservation; call or write Robinson Jeffers Tor House Foundation, PO Box 2713.
Admission: $5. No children under 12.

As ruggedly romantic as the poet's words, this charismatic stone house and tower was built by Robinson Jeffers, who first came to Carmel with his wife, Una, in 1914. With its commanding view of the rocky coastline and stone Hawk Tower, which the poet built for his wife, the house creates a haunting Gothic image in its quiet residential setting. The stalwart rock walls were raised with Jeffers' own hands and contain stones gathered from the four corners of the globe, including one from the Great Wall of China, some from England, lava from Hawaii, even a porthole from the ship that took Napoleon to exile on Elba. Lovely gardens may be toured, as well as the burnished redwood interior filled with antique Oriental rugs.

San Luis Obispo Coast

AH LOUIS STORE
805/543-4332.
800 Palm St., San Luis Obispo.
Open: 10–5 Mon.–Sat.
Admission: Free.

This brickwork monument to its 1874 builder — an enterprising Cantonese immigrant named Ah Louis — still stands on the corner of the former Chinese district of downtown San Luis Obispo, dispensing an eclectic inventory of Asian goods along with architectural ambiance. The store was just a small corner of the enterprising Ah Louis' empire. Coming to California to find gold in the 1850s, he

A monument to its 1874 builder — an enterprising Cantonese immigrant who became a wealthy businessman — the Ah Louis Store still stands on the corner of the former Chinese district of downtown San Luis Obispo.

Jay Swanson

also helped create county roads, established the area's first brick works, and ran a seed business and half a dozen farms.

HEARST CASTLE
Hwy. 1, San Simeon.
Open: 8–4 daily.
Admission: $14 adults, $7 children ages 6–12; tickets must be reserved by calling MISTIX (800/444-4445); tours daily, starting at 8:20am, exc. major holidays.

The site of America's only genuine castle by the sea, overlooking the Pacific Ocean north of Cambria, was the setting of family camping trips when future media magnate and political starmaker William Randolph Hearst was a boy. In 1919, Hearst hatched his grandiose scheme of transforming a magical spot on his father's quarter-of-a-million acre ranchland into a showpiece of architecture and international artwork. Hearst dismantled entire medieval chapels, Renaissance villas, and Greco-Roman temples, hauling back priceless artifacts to decorate the interior of the 100-room Casa Grande — a Spanish Baroque theme park designed by San Francisco architect Julia Morgan — and a spate of palatial guest houses for his celebrity friends.

Splendid Greco-Roman pools are among the fabulous treasures of San Simeon's Hearst Castle.

Shmuel Thaler

Byzantine tilework now gleams from the lofty towers and spectacular indoor swimming pool. A library Hearst built for his personal study contains over 5000 volumes of one of the world's finest rare book collections and one of the greatest caches of Greek vases. Surrounding this part sublime, part outrageous monument to consumption was once the world's largest private zoo, and zebras, Barbary sheep, Himalayan goats, and deer still remain to delight contemporary visitors.

During the '20s, '30s and '40s, the world's rich and famous visited Hearst Castle for opulent weekends of fancy dress partying. Guests included Winston Churchill, Charlie Chaplin, Gary Cooper, Ben Hecht, Groucho Marx, Douglas Fairbanks, Joan Crawford, Charles and Ann Morrow Lindbergh, Louella Parsons, Cary Grant, and, of course, Hearst mistress Marian Davies, whose relationship with the eccentric millionaire was immortalized in Orson Welles' *Citizen Kane*.

The castle may be visited only on guided tours. Given the sheer scale of the monument, it takes four tours to encompass all the sites. Tour I is designed for first-time visitors and includes the astonishing gardens, one of the Mediterranean guest houses, the ground floor of the main house, and outdoor Roman pool. Tour II moves through the upper floors of the main house, including Hearst's private suites, libraries, guest room, kitchen, and both pools. Tour III sweeps through the 36 bedrooms of the guest wing, as well as pools and gardens. Tour IV, offered only in the summer, wanders along the grounds, gardens, wine cellar, and ground floor of the largest guest house. All tours involve climbing many stairs; for arrangements for visitors in wheelchairs, call 805/927-2020. It's helpful, before calling for any reservations, to know when you plan to visit, how many people in your party, and what areas of the castle you want to see.

Santa Barbara Coast

COURTHOUSE
805/962-6464.
1100 Anacapa St., Santa
 Barbara.
Open: 8–5 weekdays, 9–5
 Sat., Sun., holidays;
 guided tours 2 Mon.–Sat.,
 10:30 Weds., Fri.
Admission: Free.

This 1929 Spanish revival masterpiece with Moorish outlines shimmers with lavish Tunisian tilework, a soaring clocktower, and curvaceous windows and doorways, all frosted with red-tile roofing. Palatial in impact, the stunning structure is adorned with painted ceilings, massive wrought iron chandeliers, monumental murals in the second floor chambers, and stunning sunken gardens. The ascent of the 70-foot tower affords visitors a stunning 360-degree view of the city below and ocean beyond.

**CHUMASH PAINTED
 CAVE STATE PARK**
805/968-1711.
Off Hwy. 154 on Painted
 Cave Rd., Santa Barbara.
Open: 8–dusk daily.
Admission: Free.

An ancient cave surrounded by rugged mountain terrain once attracted Chumash Indian artists, who, many hundreds of years ago, filled the cave walls with brightly colored pictographs believed to be of religious significance. A rare glimpse into the Native American past of this region.

Start at the dolphin statue for a Stearns Wharf tour.

Kim Reierson

STEARNS WHARF
805 /564-5518.
Foot of State St., Santa Barbara.
Open: Dawn–2am daily.
Admission: Free.

Built in 1872 by John Peck Stearns, this high profile landmark provides magnificent views of the surrounding city, mountains, and coastline, as well as numerous seafood stands, restaurants, wine tasting rooms, and souvenir stands. Once purchased by Hollywood legend Jimmy Cagney, this is the oldest operating wharf on the West Coast. Public parking is available on the wharf, but the short walk out to the end — starting at downtown's dolphin statue landmark — is the best way to soak up maximum panoramas.

HISTORIC WALKING TOURS

Neighborhood clusters of original and restored buildings still mark the earliest Spanish and American settlements along the Central Coast. There is no better way to appreciate the living past than by walking these areas armed with maps issued by local tourism offices or historical societies . . . and with a pair of comfortable shoes.

Half Moon Bay/Pescadero

A self-guided tour brochure of 19th-century dwellings built by fishing and ranching settlers is available from the local Chamber of Commerce (415/726-5202; 225 520 Kelly Ave., Half Moon Bay). Highlights include *Spanishtown* landmarks of the 19th-century Spanish and Portuguese settlement, the Half Moon Bay community *Methodist Church* (built in 1872), 1853 *Johnston House* — one of the finest examples extant of the New England saltbox style — and the 1820 *Pilarcitos Catholic Cemetery.*

Santa Cruz Mission Plaza

In addition to a historic mission adobe, the plaza surrounding the *Santa Cruz Mission State Historic Park* (408/425-5849; 144 School St. at Adobe St.) was the first area populated by the earliest influx of American settlers. Built in 1822 to house Native Americans who worked at Mission Santa Cruz, the adobe house here is the only authentically restored Indian residence in the California Mission chain. The seven rooms show how occupants lived; open 10–4 Thurs.–Sun., tours throughout weekend; $2 adults, $1 children under 12/seniors. To see impressive early homes, walk by Santa Cruz' oldest house, the 1850 *Francisco Alzina* home (107 Sylvar St.), an intricate Stick villa (207 Mission St.,) built in 1883, and a splendid Gothic home with classical railings and gable (127 Green St.) built in 1867.

Monterey Path of History

In the heart of Old Monterey, clustered near Fisherman's Wharf, a score of fine 19th-century casas, adobes, and public buildings are landmarks of this city's rich historic past. A walking tour around this **Path of History** provides an encounter with the abundant Spanish, Californio, and early American period. Administered by the **Monterey State Historic Park** (408/649-7118; 525 Polk St., Monterey), a two-day $5 admission pass ($3 youth, $2 kids) gains access to over twenty sites. Maps and guided tour details are available at *Pacific House, Colton Hall,* and the *Cooper-Molera Adobe.*

Pacific Grove Victorian House Tour

Founded in the late 1870s as a Methodist summer retreat, Pacific Grove quickly blossomed with Victorian mansions — many now open to the public as bed and breakfast establishments — ornate Gothic, turreted Queen Anne, and even a few English castle styles dominate. Some of the loveliest of these are along Ocean View Boulevard and Lighthouse Ave., including the *Green Gables Guest House,* the *Gosby House Inn, Hart Mansion,* the *Trimmer Home,* and *Sea Star.* Each year, usually in October, a *Victorian House Tour* (408/373-3304) gives visitors access to some of these architectural beauties.

San Luis Obispo Heritage Walk

The seven-square-block heart of downtown San Luis Obispo offers a walking tour through the eclectic architectural and historic past of the mission town. A Visitors' Guide from the Chamber of Commerce for $3.16 (805/781-2777; 1039 Chorro St.) will get you started. In addition to the *Ah Louis Store* and the splendid *Mission San Luis Obispo de Tolosa,* stop at the *Dallidet Adobe* (1185 Pacific St.), built in the 1850s by Frenchman Pierce Hyppolite Dallidet, one of the area's pioneer viticulturists. Among the Victorian mansions of the area, must-visits include the 1875 *Jack House* (546 Marsh St.) and the grand

The 1893 Andrews Bank Building is one of the sights of a self-guided Heritage Walk of downtown San Luis Obispo.

Jay Swanson

1895 *Erickson Home* (687 Islay St.). The ornate brick and terra façade of the circa 1893 *Andrews Bank Building* (Osos & Monterey Sts.) is a prime example of turn-of-the-century mercantile prosperity, and several fine adobes are windows on the town's Mexican era, most notably the *Murray Adobe* (747 Monterey St.) and *Sauer-Adams Adobe* (964 Chorro St.), built in 1830.

Santa Barbara Red-Tile Walking Tour

A map of this 12-block walking tour is available from the Visitor's Center at Cabrillo Boulevard and Santa Barbara St. Winding through the heart of downtown and encompassing the old Spanish foundations and adobes of Santa Barbara, this tour — best begun at the stately *Courthouse* (corner of Anacapa & Santa Barbara Sts.) — affords intimate appreciation of the efforts of philanthropic matriarch Pearl Chase. After a destructive 1925 earthquake leveled the previous hodgepodge of civic building styles, Chase single-mindedly engineered her vision of a unified Spanish/Mediterranean architecture and a harmonious, red-tiled rebuilding of the downtown. Of special interest: the *Casa de la Guerra Adobe* (15 E. De la Guerra St.), built in 1827 as the home of the Spanish-born Comandante of the Presidio and remodeled in a stunning wrap of 1920s Andalusian architecture as the El Paseo shopping arcade; the *Lugo Adobe* (114 E. De La Guerra St.), remodeled in 1922 to house studios for artists; the L-shaped *Casa Covarrubias* (75 Santa Barbara St.); the *Rochin Adobe* (820 Santa Barbara St.), constructed in 1855 of adobe bricks salvaged from the Presidio; *El Presidio* (123 E. Canon Perdido St.), site of the Spanish fort founded in 1782, and including parts of the original barracks — *El Cuartal* — across the street and the reconstructed Presidio *Chapel* with restored 18th-century decorations. *The Santa Barbara Trolley,* a free downtown shuttle, conveniently cruises State St. the length of the Red Tile district and back down to Stearns Wharf every 15 minutes. *Heritage Tours of Santa Barbara* (805/962-8578; 519 Fig Ave.) offers guided walking tours — complete with maps and restaurant tips — departing from City Hall at de la Guerra Plaza 10–11:30am Mon.–Sat.; 1–2:30 Sun.

KID STUFF

Children and their young at heart parents have myriad opportunities for major fun on the Central Coast. The diverting stops mentioned here mostly require a full day's commitment to be fully enjoyed. So slow down, and have a little play time.

Santa Cruz Coast

Mystery Spot (408/423-8897;1953 Branciforte Dr., Santa Cruz) A wacky local landmark where trees grow at weird angles and buildings defy the laws of physics. People seem to change size and balls roll uphill. Is it due to the mysterious force of some buried meteor, or is it simply an optical illusion? Whatever it is, this wooded 150-foot plot offers lots of brain-tickling fun.

Santa Cruz Beach Boardwalk (408/423-5590; 400 Beach St., Santa Cruz) More than 20 exciting rides, including an old-fashioned wooden roller coaster, the Giant Dipper. Rides at either end of the Boardwalk — including a mellow Ferris wheel, bumper cars, "underground" train excursions, and a colorful, vintage carousel — will please the very young. Wilder rides, including the state-of-the-art, stomach-churning Typhoon, will test the endurance of teenagers and impress even the most jaded thrill-seeker. Neptune's Kingdom is an indoor, pirate-theme amusement center with a video arcade, historical displays, snack bars, and a two-story miniature golf course.

Monterey Coast

Dennis the Menace Playground (408/646-3866; at the Camino El Estero Park, Monterey) Designed by cartoonist Hank Ketcham, who created that little cartoon and movie rascal, Dennis the Menace. This is a fun spot for romping on slides, futuristic jungle gyms, and a steam locomotive, or just soaking up the peaceful beauty of El Estero Lake.

Monterey Bay Aquarium (See description in "Museums" below.)

Dennis the Menace Playground in Monterey, a popular family recreation spot, was designed by cartoonist Hank Ketcham.

Shmuel Thaler

San Luis Obispo Coast

Bubblegum Alley (733-737 Higuera St., San Luis Obispo) Sometime in the early 1960s, some bubblegum chewer left his or her calling card on the side of this narrow brick corridor. And a tradition was born, the result of which is a veritable wall of pastel-hued chewing gum deposits, many fashioned into imaginative pop art, all properly gooey.

San Luis Obispo Children's Museum (805/544-5437; 1010 Nipomo St., San Luis Obispo) Lots of fun, educational, and please-touch exhibits: slip down a dinosaur slide, explore the engines of a fire station, design homes, serve lunch at a diner, play with computers, and watch each other on closed-circuit TV monitors. Check out the beehive and ant farm — they aren't hands-on, but maybe that's just as well.

Santa Barbara Coast

Santa Barbara Zoological Gardens (805/962-5339; 500 Niños Drive, Santa Barbara) The small scale of this exceptionally attractive zoo makes it perfect for children. Over 700 lions, elephants, lemurs, monkeys, giraffes, flamingos, and their exotic friends live in open, natural habitat settings and young ones will especially enjoy the farmyard petting area, playground, and miniature train ride.

Santa Barbara Museum of Natural History (805/682-4711; 2559 Puesta del Sol Road, Santa Barbara) At the entrance of this popular attraction, a 72-foot blue whale skeleton sits to the invariable delight of youngsters. The museum's 14 exhibit halls offer plenty of sights, sounds, and hands-on displays, including a wave machine, seismograph, and displays devoted to insects, birds, mammals, geology, Native American cultures, and marine life. Weekend planetarium shows astonish both adults and children (over ten). The hilltop setting, just two blocks from the Mission Santa Barbara, makes this an ideal start for an all-day excursion. $5 adults; $3 children 2–12.

LIGHTHOUSES

Necessity and technology were joined in these brilliant beacons clinging to the rockiest edges of the Central California coast during the 19th century, warning with their illuminated message of jagged perils lurking in the fog. Armed with the high candle power of the French Fresnel lens, which ingeniously used over 1000 pieces of cut glass to magnify its light, the slender lighthouses and their stalwart attendants kept faith with mariners until the coming of automation and the computer. Always a romantic sight, a few of these towers continue to shed light along the Central Coast. The *Point Pinos Lighthouse* (Asilomar Ave. off Ocean View Blvd., in Pacific Grove) was built in 1855, the oldest continuously operating lighthouse on the West Coast. Open on weekends for self-guided tours between 1–4, it is furnished with Victorian

The 1872 Pigeon Light-house, the second tallest lighthouse on the California coast, is home to a youth hostel.

Shmuel Thaler

antiques and helpful explanations of its automated workings. The *Pigeon Point Lighthouse*, just south of Half Moon Bay, was built in 1872 on a murderous outcropping of rocks and contains a Fresnel lens first used on Cape Hatteras during the Civil War. It still pierces the pea-soup fog clinging to the North Central Coast and now functions as both a Coast Guard outpost and hostel run by American Youth Hostels. *Piedras Blancos Lighthouse* (Hwy. 1, 5 miles north of San Simeon) is on white guano-encrusted rocks named by Portuguese explorer Juan Rodriquez Cabrillo in 1542. A lookout was built here in 1864 during the heyday of the whaling era and, in 1875, the first brick and steel lighthouse was completed. The glass prisms of its French Fresnel lens were illuminated by a vapor lamp that consumed up to five tons of kerosene annually. Visible for up to 25 miles, the original lamp was automated in 1949 and today sheds its light out to sea every 15 seconds (closed to public tour).

MISSIONS

Between 1769 and 1823, Junipero Serra and his successor, Fermin Francisco Lasuén, established 21 missions, spaced at roughly the length of a day's ride along the California coast. Selection of each site was based on proximity to fresh water, land for grazing and growing, and a population of prospective native converts. Like their adjacent military presidios, mission complexes were organized around a central quadrangle. Constructed of the abundant adobe provided by native clay soils, they were further protected from the elements by a plaster coating of lime.

As the missions prospered and grew, long open-air galleries of graceful arches connected padres' living quarters and offices with the main chapel.

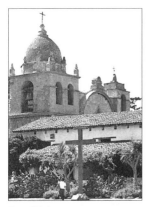

Mission Carmel was erected in 1771 as headquarters of California's ambitious Franciscan crusade.

Shmuel Thaler

Deeply shaded cloisters and three-foot-thick walls — some elaborately decorated with stenciling and murals created with native dyes and pigments — kept mission interiors cool during the hottest summers. Beyond the mission walls were stables and corrals, mills, orchards, vineyards and lime kilns.

Trained by imported stone masons and wood carvers, many of the missions' Christianized flock — called neophytes — became competent artisans whose handiwork still adorns original altars and pulpits.

At San Luis Obispo in 1776, the mission was destroyed by fire, thanks to a flaming arrow shot by a non-pacified native into the original thatched tule roof. Since that time, the red tiles associated with Spanish California became the missions' roofing of choice. After Mexico achieved its independence from Spain, the missions were secularized in 1834, and their vast holdings of land and cattle auctioned or granted to leading immigrant citizens. Over the years the missions have been creatively restored and are among the top attractions of the Central Coast region.

Santa Cruz Coast

MISSION LA EXALTA-CION DE LA SANTA CRUZ
408/426-5686.
126 High St. at Emmet St., Santa Cruz.
Open: Daily 2–5.
Admission: Free.

Founded in 1791, this was the twelfth California mission. With a large native population, fertile grazing lands, and proximity to ocean trade, this setting promised to be one of the richest in the Franciscan empire. But all turned sour when the civilian Pueblo of Branciforte sprang up across the river, populated by a rough crew of former convicts, pirates, and opportunists, who lured the Ohlone converts away with the temptations of drink and gambling. After falling into disrepair during the early 19th century, the original mission was leveled by an earthquake in 1857. Today, the mission site is occupied by a Catholic church built in 1889. Across the street, a one-third scale replica of the mission and its domed tower houses a chapel and the mission's original paintings and statues.

Monterey Coast

MISSION CARMEL (SAN CARLOS BORROMEO DEL RIO CARMELO)
408/624-3600.
3080 Rio Rd. & Hwy. 1, Carmel.
Open: 9:30–4:30 Mon.–Sat., 10:30–4:30 Sun.
(June–Aug. till 7:30pm).
Admission: Donations.

Though founded by Father Junipero Serra in 1771, the second mission in the wide-ranging Franciscan enterprise was moved to its present location and completed with sandstone blocks quarried from the Santa Lucia Mountains by Serra's successor Lasuén in 1797. In its prime, it furnished the former Spanish capital of Monterey with the bounty from its orchards, fields, and stables and was the official headquarters of the Franciscan missionary effort in Alta California. Buried within this mission he loved so well, Father Serra is now entombed in a splendid bronze sarcophagus near the sanctuary, where he awaits the canonization for which his faithful are currently petitioning. Two other great California Franciscans — Lasuén and expedition diarist Crespi — are buried here as well. The handsome mission interior boasts a vaulted, ribbed ceiling, baroque altar, and hand-carved doorway lintels. The oval domed tower recalls Spanish architecture's debt to the conquering Moors, as does the sanctuary's star window. The adjoining museum displays the silver religious ware Serra brought from Mexico and California's first library, as well as a restored kitchen and cell in which Serra lived and corresponded with his far-flung brethren. Planted with vintage olive and pepper trees, the garden and cemetery contain the graves of over 3000 Native Americans, plus members of Monterey's pioneer families.

MISSION SAN JUAN BAUTISTA
408/623-2127.
2nd & Mariposa Sts., San Juan Bautista.
Open: 9:30–4:30 daily.
Admission: $1.

Founded in 1797, Mission San Juan Bautista basilica — 10 miles inland from Monterey — is the largest in the California mission family. The 40-foot polychromed chapel walls were originally painted in 1818 by Bostonian Thomas Doak, a deserter from the ship *Albatross*; the lofty beams of the chapel interior are crowned by an ornate baroque altar. Today, the mission's large plaza skirts the entire 184-foot length of the graceful arched portico; its thick walls keep interior rooms cool in the blazing heat of summer. Olive and cypress trees encircle the small Indian burial ground behind the mission, where the view takes in a dramatic panorama of the San Andreas Fault zigzagging through Hollister in the distance. The mission's adjoining bell tower — now closed to the public — figured prominently in the climactic conclusion of Alfred Hitchcock's *Vertigo*.

Each summer the adventurous Cabrillo Music Festival fills the plaza and the acoustically perfect mission interior with the sounds of the living present. The innovative Hispanic performance troupe El Teatro Camposino also makes its home base here.

San Luis Obispo Coast

MISSION SAN LUIS OBISPO DE TOLOSA
805/543-6850.
Monterey & Chorro Sts., San Luis Obispo.
Open: 9–5 daily.
Admission: Donations.

The fifth in the series of missions personally founded by busy Franciscan Padre Serra and named for Saint Louis, bishop of Toulouse, this settlement was one of the wealthiest of the missions. A large population of Native American converts helped tend the extensive holdings of cattle, sheep, horses, and fertile land on the banks of San Luis Obispo Creek. An extensive restoration, which uncovered hand-hewn beams, began in the 1930s. Still a thriving parish church, the mission is graced by a bell tower and cool cloister gardens. A fine museum provides glimpses of early mission life and daily work habits of the resident fathers and neophytes.

Santa Barbara Coast

LA PURISSIMA MISSION STATE HISTORIC PARK
805/733-3713.
2295 Purissima Rd., Lompoc.
Open: Daily 10–5, exc. major holidays.
Admission: $5 per vehicle.

Founded in 1787 as the eleventh of California's Franciscan missions, La Purissima was once a huge ranch and farming complex situated near a thriving Chumash Indian village called Alsacupi. After a devastating earthquake in 1812 shook the adobe walls to ruins, the mission was moved, reconstructed, and eventually fell back into decay. While original walls remain, an extraordinary restoration was begun nearby that today is a living museum, the only recreation of an entire mission structure — its corrals, workshops, storerooms, padre's apartments, and aqueduct system. So seamless is the restoration that visitors to the 900-acre grounds can essentially sample mission life on tours of the gardens, tannery, reservoir, soap factory, residences, workrooms, and main church.

MISSION SANTA BARBARA
805/682-4713.
Laguna St., Santa Barbara.
Open: 9–5 daily.
Admission: $2 adults; free under 16.

Founded in 1786, this self-proclaimed "Queen of the Missions" commands an astonishing view of the city and waterfront of Santa Barbara from its hilltop location. Its twin bell towers are crowned with Moorish domes, lending its stately exterior proportions considerably more charm than its rather stolid interior. Self-guided tours of the adjoining museum rooms give visitors a glimpse of daily monastery life, including authentically furnished sleeping and working rooms. Outside is a fine garden and a cemetery for founding fathers, both sacred and secular, as well as more than 4000 native converts.

MISSION SANTA INÉS
805/688-4815.
1760 Mission Drive,
  Solvang.
Open: 9–7 daily.
Admission: $2.

Founded in 1804, the original simply rendered mission chapel was replaced after a mighty 1812 earthquake with a brick and adobe structure complete with tile roof and floors. After the inevitable decline that afflicted missions after secularization, the building was restored in the 20th century and is now famed for its extensive gardens, lovely bell tower campanile, Indian-crafted frescoes, and hand-carved door. This mission boasts a fascinating museum showcasing rare artifacts from the Franciscan colonization.

MUSEUMS

One of the highlights of any trip is a visit to the destination's primary museum for a journey back in time to make the acquaintance of previous inhabitants and eras. The Central Coast boasts a wide range of specialty museums and many fine state-of-the-art general interest repositories of history, culture, and environmental lore. Most are open free to the public or request only nominal donations.

Santa Cruz Coast

**LIGHTHOUSE SURFING
  MUSEUM**
408/429-3429.
West Cliff Dr. near Felton
  Ave., Santa Cruz.
Open: Noon–4 Wed.–Mon.
  (weekends till 5).
Admission: Free.

Billing itself as the only surfing museum in the world, this eclectic collection of vintage longboards, videos, photographs, and memorabilia — including the first wetsuit — tracks the history of surfing in Santa Cruz. The tiny collection is housed inside the Mark Abbott Memorial Lighthouse poised overlooking the world-class surf action of Steamer Lane and features a sweeping view of the Santa Cruz beach and Boardwalk. On this spot, in the late 1800s, Hawaiian princes first brought the ancient Polynesian sport to the New World.

**MCPHERSON CENTER
  FOR ART AND HIS-
  TORY**
408/454-0697.
705 Front St. at Cooper St.,
  Santa Cruz.
Open: 11–4 Tues.–Sun.,
  11–8 Thurs.
Admission: $3 adults, $2
  students/seniors; free
  first Thurs.

This joint cultural venture of the Art Museum of Santa Cruz County and the Santa Cruz County Historical Trust offers revolving exhibitions highlighting regional history and contemporary artists. A permanent installation on the second floor of the main building — packed with heirloom clothing, tools, trunks, telegraphs — accesses the entire history of human habitation in the area, from Ohlone Indian days through the frontier logging boom to

Shmuel Thaler

A cornerstone of downtown Santa Cruz culture, the McPherson Center for Art and History offers a diversity of exhibitions.

the Boardwalk fantasy world. The museum presents talks, tours, and films on art and history, and features a rental gallery of work by area artists.

OCTAGON MUSEUM
408/454-0697.
705 Front St., Santa Cruz.
Open: 11–4 Tues.–Sun.,
   11–8 Thurs.
Admission: Free.

The Victorian fad for octagonal buildings, for their space efficiency and presumed health-giving properties, produced this charming 1882 brick structure with pedimented portico. Designed as the county's Hall of Records, the local architectural treasure is now an exhibition annex of the McPherson Center for Art and History and offers revolving exhibitions of regional historic interest, as well as showcases for the works of selected California artists.

SANTA CRUZ CITY MUSEUM OF NATURAL HISTORY
408/429-3773.
1305 E. Cliff Dr. at
   Seabright Ave., Santa
   Cruz.
Open: 10–5 Tues.–Sat.,
   noon–5 Sun.
Admission: Donations.

In a graceful seaside mansion across the street from Castle Beach, the museum details the natural and cultural history of the northern Central Coast area. Ohlone Indian artifacts share space with illustrated specimens of local flora and fauna and fossil remains. Docent-led museum tours, field trips, classes, and workshops are available, as well as year-round classes for youngsters on natural history topics. Not to be missed are April's wildflower show and January's Fungus Faire.

Monterey Coast

MARITIME MUSEUM OF MONTEREY
408/373-2469.
5 Custom House Plaza,
   Monterey.
Open: 10–5 Tues.–Sun.
Admission: $5 adults, $3
   youth 13–17, $2 under
   13, free under 5.

Housed in the 18,000-square foot Stanton Center on the historic waterfront, this brainchild of the Monterey History and Art Association fills two levels and seven exhibition areas with history from the Ohlone Indian peoples and Spanish explorers to dramatic displays of Monterey's fishing and sailing heyday. Maritime history artifacts,

Monterey Bay Aquarium

(408/648-4888; 886 Cannery Row at Foam St.) Built on the edge of the enormous Monterey Bay National Marine Sanctuary — whose underwater valley dwarfs the Grand Canyon — the aquarium is state-of-the-art in every respect. Home to more than 6500 marine creatures, it houses living exhibits illustrating the Monterey Bay's many underwater habitats. Velvety leopard sharks cruise along with schools of silvery sardines in the aquarium's vast three-story kelp forests, towering up to the sunlight filtering through 300,000-gallon exhibition tanks. Children tend to fall in love with the Touch Tide Pool, where they can run their hands along the living surfaces of star fish, anemones and sleek bat rays. Playful sea otters soar acrobatically through the waters of their special area, a gorgeous recreation of the bay floor that opens out onto the sunny rocks above. The arrangement allows viewers to watch the sea otters cavorting deep under water as well as up on the surface. Special exhibits show off the frontiers of marine science, creatively wedded with arresting interpretive display design. The tastefully stocked Gift Store is itself worth leisurely exploration. Central Coast visitors shouldn't even consider passing it up: the aquarium truly lives up to its international reputation. Open daily from 10–6, from 9:30 during the summer; advance tickets ($10.50 adults, $7.75 students/seniors, $4.75 ages 3–12 & disabled) can be ordered by calling 800/756-3737.

Visitors from the world over enjoy the awe-inspiring marine displays at the Monterey Bay Aquarium.

Shmuel Thaler

from a five-ton Fresnel lighthouse lens to Portuguese navigation logs and charts, are on view in this exciting new museum.

PACIFIC GROVE MUSEUM OF NATURAL HISTORY
408/648-3116.

The front lawn offers a life-sized gray whale sculpture and the interior is filled with displays of Californiana, from minerals and seashells to hundreds of taxidermy specimens of indigenous

165 Forest Ave., Pacific Grove.
Open: 10–5 Tues.–Sun.
Admission: Free.

wildlife. The popular migrating monarch butterflies boast their own exhibit and colorful video; rare local flora bloom in the small native plant garden just outside. A small gift store offers tempting posters, books, T-shirts, and other educational souvenirs.

WHALER'S CABIN MUSEUM, POINT LOBOS
408/624-4909.
Hwy. 1, south of Carmel.
Open: 12–4 daily; reserve open 9–5 winter, 9–7 summer.
Admission: $6 per vehicle.

Attracted to the huge pods of California gray whale that migrated between Arctic waters and Baja California spawning grounds, whalers began plying Pacific waters in the very early 1800s. By the mid 1840s, the Central Coast had profitable whaling stations at Moss Landing, Davenport, and San Simeon. A circa 1851 cabin, built by Chinese fishing families overlooking Point Lobos' Whaler's Cove, has been carefully preserved as a museum, and recalls the whaling heyday with photographs, harpoons, sailing implements, and other memorabilia of the Portuguese whalers who frequented the cove in the 1860s. This tiny weathered cabin, whose floor joists are supported by six whale vertebrae, overlooks an idyllic cove on the West Coast and is one of the oldest buildings of Chinese origin remaining in Monterey Bay area.

San Luis Obispo Coast

MORRO BAY MUSEUM OF NATURAL HISTORY
805/772-2694.
State Park Rd. at White's Point, Morro Bay.
Open: 10–5 daily.
Admission: $1 adults, 50¢ children 6–17.

Commanding a stunning panoramic view of the bay, estuary, and stately Morro Rock, the museum offers informative dioramas and interpretive displays of local flora, fauna, geology, and history of the Native Americans who once called this area home. A trail leads from the museum, past Indian sites to the top of White's Point.

SAN LUIS OBISPO HISTORICAL MUSEUM
805/543-0638.
696 Monterey St., San Luis Obispo.
Open: 10–4 Weds.Sun.
Admission: Free.

In a graceful Richardsonian Romanesque mansion made of local granite and sandstone by prolific California architect William Weeks, the museum's exhibits present a colorful overview of the history of the county, from Chumash days through the mission and rancho periods to the present day. A complete Victorian parlor invites a glimpse into 19th-century frontier days; many displays are designed for youngsters to enjoy hands-on.

Santa Barbara Coast

**EL PRESIDIO STATE
HISTORIC PARK**
805/966-9719.
123 East Canon Perdido
St., Santa Barbara.
Open: 10:30–4:30 daily.
Admission: Donations.

The restoration of this Spanish military outpost, founded in 1782, has uncovered many of the original foundations. The Presidio chapel reconstruction contains 18th-century decorations. In the padre's quarters are authentically reproduced furniture and architecture. Next door, El Cuartel — the guard's house — is the oldest building in Santa Barbara and dates from the Presidio's founding. Slide shows and scale models provide a fascinating glimpse of life in Old Spanish California. Buildings are subject to closure for on-going restoration work.

**HANS CHRISTIAN
ANDERSEN MUSEUM**
805/688-2052.
1680 Mission Dr., Solvang.
Open: 9:30–6 Sun.–Thurs.,
till 8 Fri., Sat.
Admission: Free.

Lovingly devoted to the author of beloved children's fairy tales, this small museum is filled with exhibits recounting Anderson's life and boasts original letters, photographs, and Andersen artwork and book illustrations.

**SANTA BARBARA HIS-
TORICAL MUSEUM**
805/966-1601
136 East De La Guerra St.,
Santa Barbara.
Open: 10–5 Tues.–Sat.,
noon–5 Sun.
Admission: Donations.

A lovely adobe complex houses treasures from Santa Barbara's Chumash, Spanish, Mexican, and American eras. Casa de Covarrubias (1817) at 715 Santa Barbara St. was the site of the last Mexican Assembly meeting in July 1846. It adjoins the Historic Adobe (built 1836) that once served as headquarters for Colonel John C. Fremont after the city's American takeover in 1846.

**SANTA BARBARA
MUSEUM OF ART**
805/963-4364.
1130 State St., Santa Barbara.
Open: 11–5 Tues.–Sat. (till
9 Thurs.), noon–5 Sun.
Admission: $3 adults,
$2.50 seniors, $1.50 children 6–16; free Thurs. &
first Sun. of month.

An outstanding regional museum with important holdings of American art — O'Keefe, Eakins, Sargent, and Hopper — and 19th-century Impressionist works by Monet, Pisarro, and Chagall. The far-reaching collection was culled from the past four millennia — everything from early Greek and Roman sculpture to modern expressionist and photographic works. Also on display are bronzes and antiques. Guided tours available.

**SANTA BARBARA
MUSEUM OF NAT-
URAL HISTORY**
805/682-4711.
2559 Puesta del Sol Rd.,
Santa Barbara.

A nationally renowned museum specializing in the natural history of California and North America's West Coast. Exhibits highlight the geology, flora, and fauna of the area. Displays interpret the prehistory of the Channel Islands and Pacific

Open: 9–5 Mon.–Sat.; 10–5 Sun. & most holidays; closed major holidays. Admission: $5 adults, $3 children 3–12.

Coast Native Americans. The resident Gladwin Planetarium holds regular star shows and features displays of meteorites.

SANTA YNEZ VALLEY HISTORIC SOCIETY MUSEUM
805/688-7889.
3596 Sagunto St., Santa Ynez.
Open: 1–4 Fri.–Sun.
Admission: Free.

One room of this tiny, fascinating museum is devoted to Native Americans, focusing especially on Chumash culture and artifacts. Other displays bring to life 19th-century Santa Ynez Valley days. Next door, a carriage house shows off a varied collection of stagecoaches, wagons, carriages, and buggies that once transported human beings, their mail, and their belongings up and down the Central Coast.

SEA CENTER
805/963-1067.
211 Stearns Wharf, Santa Barbara.
Open: 10–5 daily, Tues.–Sun. noon–4pm outside touch tank.
Admission: $2 adults, $1.50 seniors, $1 children 3–18.

On the oldest operating wharf in California, Santa Barbara Channel marine life is on exhibit in exciting live displays and interpretive data at a computer learning center. Many aquarium and touch tanks for an up close and personal view of intriguing sea life.

MUSIC

As enamored of classical revivals as of innovative new music festivals, the Central Coast boasts its share of well-attended symphony concert, chamber music presentations, and jazz venues, all of topnotch caliber and many, like the Cabrillo Music Festival and Monterey Jazz Festivals, uniquely Central Coast in style and attitude.

Santa Cruz Coast

Cabrillo Music Festival (408/662-2701; tickets 408/429-3444; Santa Cruz Civic Auditorium, Santa Cruz) For over a quarter of a century, this internationally acclaimed two-week summer festival of new and avant garde music has been a Central Coast cultural fixture. Guest artists have included John Cage, Philip Collins, Lou Harrison, Philip Glass, and Keith Jarrett, showcasing world premieres and masterworks of the modern repertoire. The season's emotional highlight is the closing day of performances in and around Mission San Juan Bautista.

Mission San Juan Bautista annually hosts concerts of the Cabrillo Music Festival within its beautifully preserved sanctuary.

Shmuel Thaler

Santa Cruz Baroque Festival (408/336-5731; First Congregational Church, Santa Cruz) Top baroque interpreters and virtuosos of harpsichord, fortepiano, and vocal repertoire from around the San Francisco and Monterey Bay areas perform in this stellar series of early masters concerts. Bach, Vivaldi, Mozart, Scarlatti, and friends are brilliantly represented by solo and chamber specialists during its winter-spring season.

Santa Cruz County Symphony (408/462-0553; Santa Cruz Civic Auditorium, Santa Cruz) A dynamic series of classical and contemporary orchestral masterworks performed by resident symphony and guest virtuosos in the acoustically renovated Art Deco civic landmark during a fall-spring season.

Monterey Coast

Camerata Singers (408/484-1217; Carmel Mission Basilica, Mission San Antonio) The soaring, seamless voices of this world-class vocal ensemble are shown off to full advantage each winter in the atmospheric acoustics of Old California's mission settings.

Maestro Larry Granger brings a modern touch to the acclaimed Santa Cruz County Symphony.

Paul Schraub

Carmel Bach Festival (408/624-2046; Sunset Cultural Center, Carmel Mission Basilica, Carmel) The best of Bach, and plenty of his Baroque colleagues, pours forth in this splendid, celebrated three-week (July-August) annual love affair with great music that draws devotees from around the Central Coast. Passionate performances, concerts, recitals, lectures, opera, symposia, receptions, and a children's concert fill the bill, all top quality and enthusiastically attended.

Carmel Music Society (408/625-9938; Sunset Cultural Center, Carmel) After seven decades, this musical institution is still going strong during its fall-spring season, offering distinctive solo recitals for voice — by reigning divas like Frederica von Stade — piano, flute, and violin. The society also stages annual vocal and instrumental competitions and international touring ensembles.

Chamber Music Society (408/625-2212; Sunset Cultural Center, Carmel) Long the performance venue of choice for generations of Carmel culturati, the society regularly hosts visitors like the Los Angeles Piano Quartet and the Arden Piano Trio, as well California's leading string quartet ensembles, as part of this exciting six-concert series each winter and spring.

Monterey Bay Blues Festival (408/394-2652; Monterey Fairgrounds) Rapidly establishing a red-hot reputation, this sizzling music fest brings blues greats together two days every June for performances and jamming. New discoveries share the stage with heavyweights like B.B. King, the Neville Brothers, and Etta James.

Monterey County Symphony (408/624-8511; Sunset Cultural Center, Carmel) Internationally acclaimed guest artists join the resident professional symphony orchestra for an annual October-May series of concerts from the classical and modern repertoires.

Monterey Jazz Festival (408/373-3366; Monterey Fairgrounds) The oldest jazz festival in the U.S. features living legends and youthful contenders. Three days of September jazz sessions on multiple stages, an intimate "night club" hot spot, and outdoor performance arena make the granddaddy of West Coast music fests a world-famous, perennial "with it" winner. This legendary jazz venue has featured Dizzie Gillespie, Ray Charles, Tito Puente, Joe Williams, Ella Fitzgerald, Wynton Marsalis. All proceeds are for the education of budding Monterey County jazz musicians.

San Luis Obispo Coast

California State Old Time Fiddlers Association (805/773-4382, 800/443-7778; Moose Lodge, 180 Main St., Pismo Beach) Music the way they used to make it sets toes tappin' the first and third Sunday of each month.

San Luis Obispo County Symphony (805/543-3533; 1160 Marsh St., Suite 204, San Luis Obispo) This resident orchestra enlists the talents of top area soloists and guest virtuosos in presenting its fall-spring season of classic repertoire symphonies and concertos throughout the area.

Santa Barbara Coast

Alameda Park Band Concerts (Anacapa & Micheltorena, Santa Barbara) Every Sunday afternoon from 3–4 at this old-fashioned park bandstand, generous local singers and musicians perform for the absolutely free enjoyment of all.

Santa Barbara Chamber Orchestra (805/564-8887; Lobero Theatre, Santa Barbara) Six concerts during a fall-spring season offer chamber classics with featured solo virtuosi.

Santa Barbara Choral Society (805/965-7905; First Presbyterian Church, Santa Barbara) Four decades strong and still giving voice to the great masterpieces of the choral repertoire, this vigorous company chooses its winter-spring season's offerings from Broadway to Baroque.

Santa Barbara Civic Light Opera (800/549-0899; Lobero Theatre, Santa Barbara) Light opera and musical comedy gems — from Gilbert and Sullivan to Rodgers and Hammerstein — come to life in four beautifully mounted productions in a fall-spring season.

Santa Barbara Symphony (805/965-6596; Arlington Theatre, Santa Barbara) The lavish interior of this Spanish revival playhouse resounds with the talents of world-renowned guest artists like violinist Itzhak Perlman who join this fine resident symphonic orchestra in a fall-spring season of classical concerts, followed by a summer concert series.

NIGHTLIFE

A handsome oak interior and plenty of live rock make Emi's an after-hours dance mecca in Santa Cruz.

Shmuel Thaler

Nightlife on the Central Coast can involve just about anything for all tastes. Western dancing is popping up all over, as is that hot new opportunity to make a fool of yourself called karaoke. Small clubs specialize in intimate jazz to sip with cocktails and there's plenty of diehard rock 'n' roll venues for serious let-it-all-hang-out dancing. And good old down and dirty blues is enjoying a renaissance at the region's roadhouses and smoky bars.

Santa Cruz Coast

Santa Cruz: *Callahan's Pub* (408/427-3119; 507 Water St.) Blues, blues, nuthin' but blues seven nights a week. *Catalyst* (408/423-1336; 1011 Pacific Ave.) One of the coast's top venues, the friendly, courting-serious dance hall offers billiards room, three bars, great sound and light system, and a massive dance floor. Every form of rock and world fusion music is booked, primarily top bands of the San Francisco Bay Area and local lights. Periodic sit down shows feature top jazz acts and traveling troubadours. The Friday afternoon Happy Hour is a local tradition, attracting writers, artists, and talkers to the long, curving downstairs bar. Full bar and music nightly. *Crow's Nest* (408/476-4560; 218 East Cliff Dr., Yacht Harbor) A little DJ dancing, some rock and soul on weekends, and comedy on Sunday. Great views, great boy-girl rituals, lively ambiance — the quintessential Santa Cruz club. *Emi's Upstairs Bar* (408/423-7502; 1001 Cedar St.) Funk, soul, rock and blues every night except Sunday. Hottest place in town for quality music, dancing, drinks, and food. *Kuumbwa Jazz Center* (408/427-2227; 320-2 Cedar St.) Premier jazz club between San Francisco and Los Angeles. Co-director Tim Jackson heads the Monterey Jazz Festival. This is the place to catch top headliners for a reasonable price. Big time stars love to play this room and for the club's appreciative, knowledgeable audiences. Other promoters take over the room on off-nights and import quirky talents from the fields of progressive country, Euro-folk, and women's music. *Moe's Alley* (408/479-1854; 1535 Commercial Way) Blues club with full bar. Taking the stage are locals, San Francisco Bay Area hotshots, and touring headliners passing through town en route to the big cities. Plugged in every night of the week. Women admitted free on Tuesdays. *Seabright Brewery* (408/426-2739; 519 Seabright Ave.) Great afternoon rock and beer Fridays starting at 5:30. Get your fun in early.

Bach Dancing & Dynamite Society

(415/726-4143; PO Box 302, El Granada) Jazz nut and beach bum (self-anointed) Peter Douglas has run this homey music emporium on Miramar Beach for over 25 years. $10 gets you great music (often from touring headliners or up-and-coming young Turks between gigs in San Francisco and Los Angeles) and incomparable ocean views. For a few dollars more, you can partake of a buffet. Attention: bring your own wine. Mailer of coming attractions available upon request. Open Sunday from 4:30–9.

Monterey Coast

Monterey: *Brasstree Lounge* (408/649-4511; atop the Doubletree Hotel) Prime dancing and schmoozing at this popular venue for serious rock and pop music; it all goes down smoothly with the very special drinks whipped up by ace bartender Eric Robb. *Club (The)* (408/646-9244; Alvarado & Del Monte) Progressive dance music, DJ spins, and live rock fill two entire floors with dancing. *Doc Ricketts' Lab* (408/649-4241; 95 Prescott Ave.) Area's top spot for live music, specializing in rock 'n' roll and blues in an intimate setting. *Planet Gemini* (408/373-1449; 625 Cannery Row, Third Floor) Rock, country, salsa, and comedy seven nights a week. Long on dancing (especially line dancing), short on laughs.

Pacific Grove: *Portofino Cafe* (408/373-7379; 620 Lighthouse Ave.) Folk, ethnic, and contemporary acoustic musical stylings in a bohemian coffee house setting. *Tinnery at the Beach* (408/646-1040; 631 Ocean View Blvd.) A late night bar menu keeps company with romantic live music.

San Luis Obispo Coast

Cambria: *Old Camozzi's Saloon* (805/927-8941; 2262 Main St.) Live music, local color and plenty of watering hole ambiance housed within an authentic 19th century saloon.

Pismo Beach: *Harry's* (805/773-1010; Cypress & Pomeroy) Dancing to one of the area's top country and country rock bands every single night.

San Luis Obispo: *Loco Ranchero* (805/545-9015; 1772 Calle Joaquin) Regular line-up of best local and out-of-town bands pump irresistible dance music into this popular club with a sensational view of the entire town. *Rose and Crown* (805/541-1911; 1000 Higuera St.) Live bands play a bit of jazz and rock weekends at this English-style pub that offers traditional darts as well as not-so-traditional dancing. *Tortilla Flats* (805/544-7575; 1051 Nipomo St.) Mad, passionate dancing to creative DJ music every night of the week.

Santa Barbara Coast

Goleta: *Alex's Cantina* (805/683-2577; 5918 Hollister Ave.) A favorite with UCSB students, this place pumps with DJ dance tunes nightly.

Montecito: *The Grill* (805/565-3272; 1279 Coast Village Rd.) A longtime hot spot with nightly jazz, rhythm 'n' blues, and contemporary acoustic guitar.

Santa Barbara: *Beach Shack* (805/966-1634; 500 Anacapa St.) The town's biggest dance floor shakes non-stop with live rock action and playful, summertime ambiance. *Bluebird Cafe* (805/966-7778; 1221 State St.) Live alternative music in a chi-chi dining atmosphere. *Joseppi's* (805/962-5516; 434 State St.) The area's oldest club features live jazz and sizzling rhythm 'n' blues every night in a smoke-free setting. *Fess Parker's Red Lion Resort* (805/564-4333; 630 E. Cabrillo Blvd.) Use the high caliber lounge and jazz acts playing nightly at the Barra Los Arcos Lounge as an excuse to check out this sprawling lodging across from the main beach. *Zack's at the Beach* (805/963-0744; 1111 E.

Cabrillo Blvd.) Gorgeous ocean views, American regional cuisine, tasteful live soft rock and jazz. *Zelo* (805/966-5792; 630 State St.) Progressive rock, techno, DJ dancing, plus tasty food and drinks have made this place one of Santa Barbara's feet-down favorites.

THEATER

The Wild West had a soft spot in its cantankerous collective hide for touring Shakespearean acting troupes, and that affection continues into the present on the stage-friendly Central Coast. Most local performance groups feature classically trained actors with a few rogues and renegades who have escaped from Hollywood thrown into the mix for good measure.

Santa Cruz Coast

Actors' Theatre (408/425-7529; 1001 Center St., Santa Cruz) Dramatic and musical performances, plus a series of readings of new plays, are offered by this lively, local year-round production company in a handsome and intimate small theater venue.

Shakespeare Santa Cruz (408/459-2121; Performing Arts Complex, University of California, Santa Cruz) A vivacious professional theater company of top American and British actors hosts innovative and critically acclaimed productions of Shakespeare and related contemporary dramatic works. The four-play summer festival holds forth in repertory performances on the large Performing Arts Theater stage, as well as the outdoor redwood glen.

Fresh takes on theatrical classics are the specialty of the innovative summer Shakespeare Santa Cruz festival.

Ann Parker

Monterey Coast

Carmel Shakespeare Festival (408/649-0340, tickets 408/655-3200; Outdoor Forest Theater, Santa Rita & Mountainview Sts., Carmel) For six weeks beginning in September, two productions of Shakespearean classics run in repertory in the oldest outdoor amphitheater in the West, built in 1910 by Carmel's bohemian founders.

Monterey Bay Theatrefest (408/649-0340; Fisherman's Wharf, Monterey) Free outdoor theater during July and August fills Monterey's waterfront with lively thespian action from the sublime to the delightfully comic.

Sunset Cultural Center (408/624-3996; 8th & San Carlos Sts., Carmel) The cultural heart and longtime gathering spot for intensely arts-minded local citizenry, the center houses a wide array of events all year round, including the Carmel Bach Festival, the Monterey County Symphony and Performance Carmel.

San Luis Obispo Coast

Cal Poly Theatre (805/541-5369; San Luis Obispo) Pacific Repertory Opera performances are among the many theater offerings presented on the stage of the California State Polytechnic University campus, throughout the fall-spring academic year.

Santa Barbara Coast

Circle Bar B (805/965-9652; Goleta) A long-standing dinner theater showcase to delight the appetites of those who enjoy melodrama with their main entrées.

Lobero Theatre/Pasadena Playhouse (800/883-PLAY; 33 East Canon Perdido, Santa Barbara) Award-winning contemporary stage entertainment from a new production group.

Solvang Theater Under the Stars (800/549-PCPA; Solvang Festival Theater, Second St., Solvang) Nightly, except Monday, all summer long, the outdoor

Civic pride and a passion for Spanish revival architecture have made Santa Barbara's Lobero Theatre a year-round venue for award-winning contemporary stage entertainment.

Kim Reierson

theater rings with myriad theatrical treasures ranging from heavy-weight classics and Shakespearean gems to contemporary and comic capers performed by the repertory company of the Pacific Conservatory of the Performing Arts.

SEASONAL EVENTS

Flamenco entertainment is popular at Santa Barbara's Old Spanish Days Fiesta in August.

Kim Reierson

From the Avocado Festival to the Zoo-B-Que, there's a celebration for everyone and everything on the Central Coast, year-round.

January

Fungus Fair 408/429-3773; Santa Cruz
Heritage Day Festival 415/726-2418; Half Moon Bay
Living History Day 408/623-4881; Monterey
Mozart's Birthday Party 805/543-4580; San Luis Obispo

Each January, Santa Cruz area mycologists gather to trade notes, sample wild mushrooms, and sport costumes at the Fungus Fair.

Shmuel Thaler

February

Boardwalk's Clam Chowder Cook-Off 408/429-3477; Santa Cruz
Carnival Monterey 408/373-3250; Monterey
Gourmet Gala 408/373-8482; Monterey
Highlands Inn Masters of Food & Wine 408/624-3801; Carmel
Hot Air Affair 408/649-6544; Monterey
Mumbo Gumbo Mardi Gras 805/634-1414; San Luis Obispo
Storytelling Festival 805/688-6144; Solvang

March

Colton Hall Birthday Party 408/375-9944; Old Monterey
International Film Festival 805/963-0023; Santa Barbara
Taste of Solvang 805/688-6144; Solvang
Wine Festival 800/525-3378; Monterey

April

Carnival Santa Cruz 408/427-2227; Santa Cruz
Hans Christian Andersen Fairy Tales Festival 805/688-3317; Solvang
Petal and Palettes Art and Flower Show 805/927-3624; Cambria
Presidio Days 805/966-9719; Santa Barbara
Spring Wildflower Show 408/429-3773; Santa Cruz
Vintner's Festival 805/688-0881; Solvang
Wildflower Show 408/648-3116; Pacific Grove

May

Antique Fly-In & Airshow 408/373-3366; Watsonville
Artists Studio Tour 408/373-1685; Monterey
Chamarita Festival 415/726-2729; Half Moon Bay
Cinco de Mayo Celebration 408/429-3504; Santa Cruz
Cinco de Mayo Festival 805/965-8581; Santa Barbara
Cinco de Mayo Festivities 805/541-8000; San Luis Obispo
Italian Street Painting Festival 805/569-3873; Santa Barbara
La Fiesta de San Luis Obispo 805/543-1710; San Luis Obispo
Los Rancheros Visadores 805/688-3317; Solvang
Pacific Rim Film Festival 408/475-2050; Santa Cruz
Spring Fair 408/462-0494; Santa Cruz
Squid Festival 408/649-6547; Monterey
Wine and Food Festival 805/967-4618; Goleta

June

Afternoon of Epicurean Delight 805/543-1323; San Luis Obispo
Chili Cook-Off 805/927-3163; Cambria
Harbor Festival & Boat Show 408/462-2338; Santa Cruz
Japanese Cultural Fair 408/475-2115; Santa Cruz
Sand Sculpture and Sandcastle Contest 805/966-6110; Santa Barbara
Scandinavian Midsummer Festival 805/688-6144; Solvang

Summer Art Festival 408/659-5099; Carmel
Summer Solstice Celebration 805/965-3396; Santa Barbara
Vintners' Festival 408/458-5030; Santa Cruz

July

Art in the Park and Fireworks 805/772-4467; Morro Bay
Big Little Backyard Fourth of July Party 408/646-3866; Old Monterey
Estival Festival 408/429-8433; Santa Cruz
Fireworks off the Pier 805/995-1200; Cayucos
Fourth of July Beach Fireworks 805/773-4382; Pismo Beach
Fourth of July Celebration 408/429-3477; Santa Cruz
Fourth of July Parade 805/543-1323; San Luis Obispo
Fourth of July Parade and Fireworks 805/927-3624; Cambria
Greek Festival 805/966-9222; Santa Barbara
Japanese Friendship Festival 805/543-1323; San Luis Obispo
KUSP Cajun Chomp 'n' Stomp 408/476-2800; Aptos
Mission Arts & Crafts Fair 805/682-4713; Santa Barbara
National Horse Show 805/687-0766; Santa Barbara
Old-Fashioned Fourth of July 415/728-3313; Half Moon Bay
Portuguese Celebration 805/995-1200; Cayucos
Renaissance Faire 805/543-1323; San Luis Obispo
Rib Cook-Off 805/541-8000; San Luis Obispo
Stow House Fourth of July 805/967-4618; Goleta
World's Shortest Fourth of July Parade 408/688-2428; Aptos
World's Worst Poetry Contest 805/773-4382; Pismo Beach

August

Calamari Festival 408/427-3554; Santa Cruz
Festival of the Bears 805/528-4884; Los Osos
Mission Santa Inés Fiesta 805/688-4815; Solvang

Santa Cruz' India Joze Restaurant hosts an August-long month of eclectic international dining — the Calamari Festival — entirely devoted to the culinary joys of squid.

Paul Schraub

Museum of Natural History Wine Festival 805/682-4711; Santa Barbara
Old Spanish Days Fiesta 805/962-8101; Santa Barbara
Scottish Festival & Highland Games 408/394-1129; Monterey

September

Art and Wine Festival 408/688-7377; Capitola
Artichoke Festival 408/633-2465; Monterey
Central Coast Wine Festival 805/543-1323; San Luis Obispo
Chili Cook-Off & Horseshoe Tournament 408/429-3477; Santa Cruz
Concours d'Elegance 805/564-7888; Santa Barbara
Danish Days 805/688-3317; Solvang
Fiesta de San Carlos Borromeo 408/624-1271; Carmel
Greek Festival 408/424-4434; Monterey
Harbor Festival 408/462-2338; Santa Cruz
National Begonia Festival 408/475-6522; Capitola
Oktoberfest 805/966-9222; Santa Barbara
Old Monterey Santa Rosalia Festival 408/626-2050; Old Monterey
Outdoor Dance Festival 805/962-6945; Santa Barbara
Pacific Country Picnic 408/476-6116; Swanton
Sons of Norway 805/773-4382; Pismo Beach

October

Art Association Home Tour 805/927-8190; Cambria
Arts & Crafts Festival 408/438-6038; Aptos
Avocado Festival 805/684-0038; Carpinteria
Butterfly Parade 408/646-6520; Pacific Grove
Celebration of Harvest 805/688-6144; Solvang
Clam Festival 805/773-4382; Pismo Beach
Harbor Festival 805/772-1155; Morro Bay
Italian Heritage Festival 408/423-5590; Santa Cruz
Jewish Food Festival 408/624-2015; Carmel
Mission Parade and Fiesta 408/429-3663; Santa Cruz
Oktoberfest 408/372-5863; Monterey
Oktoberfest 805/528-4884; Los Osos
Open Studio Tour 408/688-5399; Santa Cruz
Pumpkin and Art Festival 415/726-9652; Half Moon Bay
Hallcrest Vineyards Harvest Fair 408/335-4441; Felton
Sand Castle and Sculpting Contest 805/966-9222; Santa Barbara
Slugfest 408/429-8433; Santa Cruz
Valley Days Lemon Festival 805/967-4618; Goleta
Zoo-B-Que 805/962-5339; Santa Barbara

November

Christmas Street Fair 805/772-4467; Morro Bay
Harvest Celebration 805/541-5868; San Luis Obispo

Holiday Arts and Crafts Fair 408/646-3866; Monterey
Robert Louis Stevenson's Un-Birthday 408/649-7118; Monterey

December

Candlelight Tour 408/623-2425; San Juan Bautista
Children's Holiday Parade 408/429-8433; Santa Cruz
Christmas at the Castle 805/927-2093; San Simeon
Christmas Festival 805/927-3624; Cambria
Christmas in the Adobes 408/649-7111; Monterey
Christmas in the Plaza 805/543-1323; San Luis Obispo
La Posada and Piñata Party 408/646-3866; Old Monterey
Lighted Boat Parade 408/867-5297; Santa Cruz
Lighted Boat Parade 805/772-4467; Morro Bay
Parade of Lights 805/564-5519; Santa Barbara
Una Pastorella 805/966-9719; Santa Barbara
Victorian Christmas 805/964-4407; Goleta

CHAPTER FIVE

Matters of Taste

RESTAURANTS & FOOD PURVEYORS

With its year-round harvests and the influence of Pacific Rim neighbors, California cuisine has a vivacious reputation the world over. Food historians like to trace the origins of this bold, light culinary style to the Central Coast. After all, it was at Ventana in Big Sur that California food artist Jeremiah Tower roasted his first red bell pepper and launched the evolving trend toward mesquite grilling. With an emphasis on fresh produce — organically grown

Kim Reierson

Acacia in Montecito offers a creative approach to traditional American cuisine.

whenever possible — and Pacific seafood, Central Coast restaurants serve their share of uncompromising and innovative California cuisine, where sauces are thickened by reduction (rather than flour and butter) and vegetables are given as much respect as entrée presentations. Locally made goat cheeses, free-range poultry, seasonal game, roasted peppers, and garden-fresh herbs highlight the culinary trend now accepted at dining capitals the world over. Also showcased here are popular contemporary Italian menus, authentic Mexican recipes, and Asian influences, so much so that wild mushrooms, black beans, lemon grass, ginger, and cilantro have become standards of the repertoire. The single most pervasive influence on the dining styles of this coastal region is the mild Mediterranean climate that enables fresh-grown produce to reach the tables of the Central Coast all year long. Diners here are happily spoiled, and just as happy to share the wealth.

PRICE GUIDE

The price ranges below include the cost of a single dinner including appetizer, entrée, dessert, and coffee. Not included is the price of wine, beer, or spirits.

Inexpensive	Up to $10
Moderate	$10 to $25
Expensive	$25 to $40
Very Expensive	$40 or more

CREDIT CARDS

AE — American Express
CB — Carte Blanche
D — Discover Card
DC — Diner's Club
MC — MasterCard
V — Visa

Selected food purveyors — bakeries, coffee houses, farmers' markets, ice cream shops, and micro-breweries — are highlighted throughout this chapter.

SANTA CRUZ COAST

The educated palates of university residents and world-traveled artists have long demanded and consumed an astonishing variety of exotic cuisine in what otherwise appears to be a rustic resort community. Dining is as much an attraction as the fabled beaches and redwoods, so don't travel far without sampling the food at these inimitably Santa Cruz area restaurants.

Capitola/Soquel

GAYLE'S BAKERY AND ROSTICCERIA
408/462-1127.
504 Bay Ave., Capitola.
Open: Daily.
Price: Moderate.
Cuisine: Bakery, Deli.
Serving: B, L, D.
Credit Cards: Cash, checks only.
Handicap Access: Yes.

One-stop shopping for gourmet take-out and dine-in excellence. The Italian/California deli, fueled by oak ovens and rotisserie, turns out roasted meats, pasta salads, and focaccia sandwiches. The bakery, highlighted by an array of superior breads developed by author/breadmaker Joe Ortiz — the *franchese* is a knockout — offers beautiful cakes, berry tarts, and croissants from the imagination of Gayle Ortiz. The recent addition of an espresso bar and outdoor patio seating pack in devoted fans who come from miles around to indulge in continental breakfasts and then take home multi-course meals, complete with a fine selection of wines. This place is extremely popular, but no one seems to mind taking a number and ogling the gorgeous showcases while waiting.

*Ranjeet Lal, chef and owner
of Ranjeet's in Soquel, offers
a world cuisine menu.*

Suzette Lucich

RANJEET'S
408/475-6407.
3051 Porter St., Soquel.
Open: Daily.
Price: Moderate.
Cuisine: Continental.
Serving: D.
Reservations: No.
Credit Cards: AE, MC, V.
Handicap Access: Yes.

Just off the main street of this historic village, Ranjeet's is an oasis of culinary integrity, custom cooking, and top value. A creatively spiced world cuisine menu stresses the Pacific Rim as well as freshly prepared seafoods, steaks, and chicken dishes, all infused with provocative herb and spicing choices. Bountiful portions and the casual atmosphere of this converted Victorian home have made Ranjeet's extremely popular with savvy diners who crave restaurant experiences yet keep an eye on the bottom line.

SEAFOOD MAMA
408/476-5976.
820 Bay Ave., Capitola.
Open: Daily.
Price: Moderate.
Cuisine: Seafood
Serving: D.
Reservations: For 6 or
  more.
Credit Cards: AE, MC, V.
Handicap Access: Yes.

Lots of clean woodwork, an oyster bar, an aromatic mesquite grill, and a menu devoted to a dazzling array of fresh seafood has earned Seafood Mama a place in the hearts of discerning catch-of-the-day aficionados. Healthfully prepared, seafoods range from calamari, halibut, and salmon to scallops, bass, mahi mahi, roughy, and New Zealand green-lipped mussels. All entrées are attractively presented with zesty salads and fresh vegetables. The wine list features the Central Coast.

SHADOWBROOK
408/475-1511.
1750 Wharf Rd., Capitola.

Proof that even long-standing restaurant legends do earn their reputations, the Shadowbrook is not only de rigueur for out-of-town visitors and

Capitola's multi-level Shadowbrook Restaurant hosts residents and visitors in rustically elegant dining rooms.

Open: Daily.
Price: Moderate to Expensive.
Cuisine: California.
Serving: D; Sun. Br.
Reservations: Recommended.
Handicap Access: Yes.
Credit Cards: AE, D, DC, MC, V.

special occasions, it's on the cognoscenti's short list of consistently fine dining experiences. Under the skill of owner Ted Burke and chef Tom Grego, this rustically elegant sprawl of multi-level stone and wood-beamed dining rooms turns out expert California cuisine served by an unerring wait staff. From the full bar upstairs, guests wander down past the central stone fireplace to a favorite private booth or round oak table overlooking Soquel Creek below. Fresh seafoods are a specialty, but many swear by the prime rib served with horseradish-laced sour cream. Sunday brunches on the patio feature inventive seafood Benedict, a grilled chicken on penne pasta, and a marvelous Italian-style roast beef sandwich piled with sweet red peppers and Fontina cheese. Ride the charming funicular down from street level to the restaurant below, and then stroll back through waterfalls and gardens.

Davenport

NEW DAVENPORT CASH STORE
408/426-4122.
Hwy. 1 & Davenport Ave.
Open: Daily.
Price: Moderate.
Cuisine: New American.
Serving: B, L, D.
Reservations: No.
Credit Cards: MC, V.
Handicap Access: Yes.

Lofty, heavy-beamed ceilings and brick walls lined with museum-quality Mexican and South American crafts lend a rustic charm to this local landmark that exudes quintessential California funk. Encircled by a fine B&B, the restaurant adjoins a spectacular import and arts store. Breakfasts here attract visitors from up and down the coast. The first on its block to provide freshly ground French roast before coffee houses became cliché, the Cash Store also makes its own substantial cinnamon rolls, muffins, and pies. Chef Henry Lehr's dinners are straightforward and wonderful, featuring creative pastas and seafoods, a fine char-

Davenport Cash Store's Henry Lehr combines the freshest ingredients from north Central Coast fields and waters in fine California cuisine.

George Sakkestad

broiled New York steak, and fat tostadas loaded with fresh chicken, luscious beans, guacamole, and sour cream. Soups and salads are gorgeous and generous. Views from the windows capture cliffs, waves, and migrating whales. Excellent listing of Santa Cruz Mountains wines, made only miles from the restaurant.

Half Moon Bay

PASTA MOON
415/726-5125.
315 Main St.
Open: Daily.
Price: Moderate.
Cuisine:
  California/Mediter-
  ranean.
Serving: L, D.
Reservations: Recom-
  mended.
Credit Cards: AE, MC, V.
Handicap Access: Yes.

Innovative and made-before-your-very-eyes pasta dishes are the signature of this new, very smart café-style eatery at the end of Half Moon Bay's tiny, atmospheric Main Street. Service is accommodating and knowledgeable and the tiny tables are close enough together to allow plenty of menu comparisons with fellow diners, trattoria-style. Creative salads here involve intriguing herb blends and baby lettuces; even the Caesar salad is first-rate. But the homemade sauces, sausages, and pastas that make up the main creations are truly stunning. An entrée cioppino, as good as it looks and packed with shellfish, could feed three hungry adults. A selective wine list — long on bright, young Italians and vintage Californians — complements the sassy cuisine, and the art-lined ambiance is vibrant. Terrific value for the money.

SAN BENITO HOUSE
415/726-3425.
356 Main St.
Open: Thurs.–Sun.
Price: Moderate.
Cuisine: Contemporary.

The country inn setting of this inviting California cuisine restaurant provides an instant sense of comfort and ease. Executive chef Carol Mickelsen trained with French culinary masters and combines her gourmet gifts with her co-chef, son

San Benito House offers memorable meals in its popular restaurant on Half Moon Bay's historic Main Street.

Stan Cacitti

Serving: D; Sun. Br.
Reservations: Recommended.
Credit Cards: MC, V.
Handicap Access: Yes.

Greg Regan; they use the very freshest in seasonal produce for a changing menu of prix fixe dinners. Especially desirable are the mesquite-grilled fresh fish items, as well as wonderful roast leg of lamb. The fabulous Sunday brunch provides luxury fuel for a day wandering the spectacular coast range countryside embracing this tiny seaside town.

Pescadero

DUARTE'S TAVERN
415/879-0464.
202 Stage Rd.
Open: Daily.
Price: Inexpensive.
Cuisine: Classic Central Coast.
Serving: B, L, D.
Reservations: Recommended for weekend dinner.
Credit Cards: AE, MC, V.
Handicap Access: Yes.

Long a local legend, this dark wood roadhouse, with a bar straight out of a Hollywood Western, is enormously popular with locals who can't get enough of this flavorful cuisine. An abalone sandwich is outstanding; intensely flavored soups include their famous artichoke concoction. If you eat at the counter, you can watch cooks preparing your order of simple luxuries like fresh crab sandwiches, flavor-running steaks, and some of the finest omelets in the land. Among the major listing of fresh berry pies, the locally grown olallieberry — a variety of blackberry — version is unforgettable. A regional treasure.

Rio Del Mar/Aptos

CAFÉ SPARROW
408/688-6238.
8042 Soquel Dr., Aptos.
Open: Daily.
Price: Moderate to Expensive.
Cuisine: Continental.

Updated continental classics find a home in this small, pretty café. Very popular with residents of the village and beach communities surrounding Aptos, Café Sparrow turns sandwiches and salads into memorable experiences. Dinner entrées are an eclectic assortment of continental variations, and

Serving: B (Sat. only), L, D;
Sun. Br.
Reservations: Recom-
mended for dinner.
Credit Cards: MC, V.
Handicap Access: Yes.

include an excellent peppered Angus filet mignon in sauce Diane, rich New Zealand venison in a brandied cherry demi-glacé, and bistro-fare-like grilled chicken and fresh breaded oysters with a lemon caper creme. Attractive desserts and an award-winning wine list.

Chez Renee in Aptos regu-
larly wins awards for chef
Jack Chyle and his
partner/wife Renee.

Shmuel Thaler

CHEZ RENEE
408/688-5566.
9051 Soquel Dr., Aptos.
Open: Tues.–Sat.
Price: Moderate to Expen-
sive.
Cuisine: Continental.
Serving: L (except Sat.), D.
Reservations: Recom-
mended.
Credit Cards: MC, V.
Handicap Access: Yes.

Superbly run by California Culinary Academy-trained owners Jack and Renee Chyle, Chez Renee has been showered with awards in its ten-year career. Considered by many to be among the very top dining spots of the Monterey Bay area, the intimate ambiance is personally orchestrated by the vivacious Renee, who also creates some of the exquisite desserts. The soft peach-toned dining room has a stone fireplace, lit in cool months for a roman-tic atmosphere. The award-winning wine list is espe-cially strong in French and California vintages (including many from the Santa Cruz Mountains), but the food is the whole brilliant point. Jack Chyle is a sorcerer with duck, which he finesses with fresh, seasonal fruit and berry sauces, and splashes with an imaginative palette of wines or liqueurs. The house smoked salmon is an exquis-ite opener, as are Pacific Northwest oysters on the half shell and ripe figs with prosciutto. Pastas, veal, and seafoods are all amazing, and beef-eaters swear by the filet mignon served with a port wine sauce, crumbled Stilton cheese, and a walnut garnish. The freshly made desserts — especially warm soufflés and the ethereal cheesecake — are the stuff of lifelong memories. A serious selection of single malt Scotches and premium vodkas is available at the tiny adjoining bar.

Dan Coyro

Manuel Santana and his partner/wife Alice preside at Manuel's, Aptos' bravura home of Mexican dining.

MANUEL'S
408/688-4848.
261 Center St., Aptos.
Open: Daily.
Price: Inexpensive.
Cuisine: Mexican.
Serving: L, D.
Reservations: Recom-
  mended.
Handicap Access: Yes.
Credit Cards: MC, V.

Talented artist Manuel Santana would be a local legend even if he and his wife Alicia hadn't founded this Mexican restaurant overlooking Sea-cliff State Beach. But they did, and for more than 25 years diners have given thanks over bottles of ice cold Corona, tangy margaritas, and plates of rich refried beans. Always crowded with convivial regulars who all seem to have grown up with each other, Manuel's feels like a culinary fiesta, with artwork on the dark wood walls and south-of-the-border tilework. Menu highlights include the soothing chiles rellenos, fruity enchiladas tropicales, and snapper smothered in chili and sour creme sauce. The guacamole and hot sauce are addictive, as are house salads topped with guacamole, tomato slices, garbanzo beans, and a very vinegary vinaigrette. Full bar.

PALAPAS
408/662-9000.
21 Seascape Village, Aptos.
Open: Daily.
Price: Moderate.
Cuisine: Mexican, Seafood.
Serving: L, D.
Reservations: Recom-
  mended weekends.
Credit Cards: AE, MC, V.
Handicap Access: Yes.

The feel of a contemporary hacienda with a view of the Pacific has been created in this sky-lighted dining room in an upscale resort community. With enormous booths, lots of tilework, and boldly colored textile decorating, the beautiful dining room serves skilled and imaginative Mexican seafood specialties. The entire Pacific Rim, from Mexico to Asia, inspires the culinary concepts of chef Ron Romo, who has filled the menu with dazzling fresh seafoods sided with salsas and tropical produce. Not to be missed are the charbroiled camarones (prawns) marinated in fresh orange juice, lime butter, and garlic in a toasted chili sauce. Also wonderful are succulent grilled chicken tostadas topped with world-class guacamole and house-made tomatillo sauce. The fresh fish entrées are sumptuous — the sashimi is perfection — and the menu also includes interesting vegetarian selections, like enchiladas filled with marinated tofu, guacamole, or creamy cheese. The full bar pours a terrific selection of aged tequilas and the whole place feels like a quick trip to the Mexican Riviera.

VERANDA
408/685-1881.
8041 Soquel Dr., Aptos.
Open: Daily.
Price: Moderate to Expensive.
Cuisine: Regional American.
Serving: L (Mon.–Fri.), D; Sun. Br.
Reservations: Recommended weekends.
Credit Cards: AE, D, MC, V.
Handicap Access: Yes.

Tucked into several high-ceilinged rooms and one converted, window-lined verandah, this bastion of New American cuisine offers contemporary, fresh dishes in a romantic turn-of-the-century setting. Recipes here are influenced by many regional American styles; the menu offers welcome alternatives to California cuisine. Intricate and beautifully presented pâtés and wonderful crab and salmon cakes served with exceptional tartar sauce are among the appetizers. Fine soups, including an earthy Kentucky burgoo, are house specialties. Vegetables are brilliantly executed and fresh salmon creations often approach epic proportions. The chef has a gift for desserts and the house crème brûlée is exceptional, as is the bread pudding with bourbon custard sauce. Adjoins the Bayview Inn (see *Lodging*).

Santa Cruz

RISTORANTE AVANTI
408/427-0135.
1711 Mission St.
Open: Daily.
Price: Moderate.
Cuisine: Italian.
Serving: L, D.
Reservations: A good idea.
Credit Cards: AE, MC, V.
Handicap Access: Yes.

A small trattoria popular with the nearby University of California at Santa Cruz, Avanti makes patrons feel at home with its warm service and unfussy ambiance. Many lunch patrons like to dine at the long wine bar counter, where a good selection of Italian and locally made vintages come by the glass. Excellent bruschettas, roasted garlic with crostini, grilled eggplant, and roast peppers get diners warmed up for generous entrées like the garlicky linguine with clam sauce, sensuous lasagna, sprightly flavored three-cheese ravioli, and fresh fish specials. Don't miss the chicken with creamy polenta at lunch time — a fantasy dish seemingly from the hands of an Italian grandmother. Prices are reasonable and the camaraderie irresistible.

BLACK'S BEACH CAFÉ
408/475-2233.
15th Ave. & East Cliff Dr.
Open: Daily.
Price: Moderate.

Opened recently in a quiet beach neighborhood by California Culinary Academy-trained chef/owner Robert Morris, this light, airy dining room forms a contemporary canvas for exciting

Cuisine: New American.
Serving: B (weekends only), L, D.
Reservations: For 6 or more.
Credit Cards: AE, MC, V.
Handicap Access: Yes.

and fresh food ideas. The emphasis is on seasonally fresh ingredients with a nod toward the Pacific Rim. So you'll find ahi tuna available in a variety of recipes, from a grilled filet served over organic baby greens with Asian vinaigrette to a sandwich with crimson tuna topped by cilantro ginger sauce, Napa cabbage, and sprouts. Very beachfront bistro, the café specializes in huge, healthy sandwiches and salads — such as a Chinese chicken salad topped with plum sauce vinaigrette with organic local greens and crisp green apples — and there are hot entrée specials with pasta, chicken, and vegetarian ingredients each evening.

CAFÉ BITTERSWEET
408/423-9999.
2332 Mission St.
Open: Tues.–Sun.
Price: Moderate.
Cuisine: Continental.
Serving: D.
Reservations: Recommended.
Credit Cards: MC, V.
Handicap Access: Yes.

A new kid on the block, this inviting bistro proved an instant success fueled by the skill of chef Thomas Vinolus and partner Elizabeth Clark. Banquette and booth seating provide cozy people-watching, but the amazingly low-priced menu of utterly fresh, expertly prepared California bistro fare is the top draw. Starters include succulent grilled shrimp or salmon over wilted baby greens with sides of perfect garlic and sage-spiced white beans. Main courses include classic rib-eye steaks grilled with a shallot Merlot sauce, bountiful lamb pot pie, and gorgeous roasted chicken — all served with exceptional vegetables, highlighted by the house signature scalloped potatoes. The chef, trained in intricate pastries, finesses a lemon raspberry napoleon of crisp filo pastry layered with creamy lemon custard and tart raspberry coulis. The crème brûlée is outstanding.

CASABLANCA
408/426-9063.
101 Main St.
Open: Daily.
Price: Expensive.
Cuisine: Continental.
Serving: D; Sun. Br.
Reservations: Advised.
Credit Cards: AE, DC, MC, V.
Handicap Access: Limited.

R omantic is the word for this fine dining room set in a 1920s Mediterranean estate-turned-inn perched on the hillside over the main Santa Cruz beach and wharf. Gleaming brass and candlelight enhance the dining room; enormous picture windows frame a captivating view of the water, all the prettier at night. Chef Randy Chowning has creative fun with contemporary California cuisine, enhanced by an award-winning list of over 400 wines. Superior fresh seafoods, filet mignon, rack of lamb, and grilled duck are standards here. An appetizer of roasted ancho chili pepper stuffed with cheese and served with a red bell pepper sauce is wonderful, as is the cold smoked salmon with dill aïoli. The house salad of baby butterhead lettuce and Dijon vinaigrette is a standout and all the fresh seafood ideas work brilliantly, especially a linguini

*Casablanca Restaurant, over-
looking the Santa Cruz main
beach and wharf, serves
renowned Sunday brunches
and dinners.*

Buz Bezore

with prawns, sea scallops, and clams in lemon thyme and fresh tomato cream.
Elegant desserts feature seasonal berries and creamy pastries. The Sunday
brunch is, for reasons of beachfront view and superlative egg specialties
served with lots of champagne, justly popular.

CHINA SZECHWAN
408/423-1178.
221 Cathcart St.
Open: Tues.–Sun.
Price: Inexpensive.
Cuisine: Szechuan.
Serving: L, D.
Reservations: No.
Credit Cards: MC, V.
Handicap Access: Yes.

As regular as clockwork, most downtown Santa Cruz workers end up here in their favorite red booth each week. The multi-generational family of master chef Yuen still smartly run the entire establishment. The menu is classic, flavorful Szechuan, with creative spicy seafood and vegetable dishes, consummate pot stickers and barbecued spare ribs, and the finest hot and sour soup outside of the Middle Kingdom. Especially bold is the outstanding broccoli and garlic sauce, with freshly picked greens (this *is* broccoli country), slender strips of lean pork, and copious quantities of garlic. The bean curd Szechuan-style comes with a fiery meat sauce. In fact, anything you order "Szechuan style" arrives redolent of chilies and garlic, but brilliantly balanced. Prices are rock bottom for the exceptional quality and fast service.

CROW'S NEST
408/476-4560.
2218 East Cliff Dr.
Open: Daily.
Price: Moderate.
Cuisine: Seafood.
Serving: L, D.
Reservations: Recom-
  mended.

Especially on Wednesday evenings, when there's plenty of boat racing action on the Monterey Bay, the Crow's Nest and its incomparable Yacht Harbor location never fail to deliver a classic beachfront experience. Many devotees of this handsome, split-level establishment right on the beach make tracks upstairs to the extremely popular bar, a gath-

The Crow's Nest is a required dining adventure for visitors to the scenic Yacht Harbor in Santa Cruz.

Suzette Lucich

Credit Cards: AE, D, DC, MC, V.
Handicap Access: Yes.

ering place for singles, with live music on weekends. There's also an oyster bar in the upper level and some outdoor seating. Downstairs and out on the glass-enwrapped decks, a menu of seafood standards is served along with the area's most comprehensive and inviting salad bar. Fresh grilled fish here is fine — especially the teriyaki salmon — as are the fat sirloin steak sandwiches at lunch and aged filet mignon at night.

EL PALOMAR
408/425-7575.
1336 Pacific Ave.
Open: Daily.
Price: Inexpensive to Moderate.
Cuisine: Mexican.
Serving: L, D; Sun. Br.
Reservations: Accepted only weekdays.
Credit Cards: AE, D, MC, V.
Handicap Access: Yes.

A wildly popular dining room that has it all — inventive and invitingly priced Mexican cuisine, world-class margaritas, and the charismatic setting of a historic 1930s Spanish Revival hotel whose lofty, heavy-beamed, polychromed ceilings encompass the non-stop action. Fine cocktails are served under the airy skylighting of the adjoining lounge. The warm housemade corn tortillas are the real thing and wrap perfectly around tender cooked pork and shredded chicken in outstanding lunch tacos. For $5 you can fill up on crisp puffy *sopes* filled with chicken, vegetables, shredded cabbage, and sour cream, or work through something grander in the form of fresh garlic grilled prawns bathed in cilantro-laced, fiery hot guajillo chili sauce. Late brunches of refried beans topped with a fried egg are without peer and the house *pozole* — a rich pork and fresh hominy laced soup topped with lime, cabbage, and cilantro — will cure the worst cold (or hangover). Housed in the tallest building in downtown Santa Cruz, El Palomar is hard to miss and impossible to beat.

Proprietress Suki Kang has turned Emi's beautiful oak wood dining rooms into a showcase for authentic Korean cuisine.

Shmuel Thaler

EMI'S KOREAN RESTAURANT & BAR
408/423-7502.
1003 Cedar St.
Open: Daily.
Price: Inexpensive to Moderate.
Cuisine: Korean.
Serving: L (exc. weekends), D.
Reservations: Recommended weekends.
Credit Cards: MC, V.
Handicap Access: Yes.

Occupying the spacious oak and stained glass second floor of a turn-of-the-century hotel building, this dining room appointed with deep blue linens and Asian artwork showcases the richly seasoned authentic cuisine of Korea. Tiny dishes of fiery condiments like pickled garlic stem, pressed fish cake, silken bean sprouts, and fiery kim chee arrive with complex entrées like stews of lean pork, tofu, and scallops in a soy-laced sauce, served in a simmering cast iron pot. Carnivores regularly succumb to the addictive sizzling platters of highly seasoned lean barbecue rib-eye or chewy short ribs. The spicy seafood and vegetable-laden Special Noodle Soup will cure whatever ails you. Appetizers include mung bean pancakes filled with assorted vegetables and prawns in bite-sized wedges along with a wonderful sweet-sour dipping sauce. Lunch specials of grilled glazed chicken come with fruit garnishes, beautiful salads of carrot "roses," and a tangle of fresh cabbage. After hours the place is transformed by live bands into one of the top blues clubs in town.

INDIA JOZE
408/427-3554.
1001 Center St.
Open: Daily.
Price: Moderate to Expensive.
Cuisine: Pacific Rim/Middle Eastern.
Serving: L, D; Sun. Br
Reservations: Recommended for dinner.

No visit to Santa Cruz is complete without a stop at this destination for gourmet globe-trotters and power brokers of the Monterey Bay area. Launched in the '70s by the culinary genius of chef/guru Joseph Schultz, the spacious, art-lined dining rooms and outdoor patios of this landmark have hosted visitors from all over the world. Headquarters for the annual Calamari Festival, Joze specializes in world fusion cooking featuring innovative interpretations of Indonesian, Middle Eastern,

India Joze Restaurant is a longtime Santa Cruz hotspot for freshly prepared variations on exotic world cuisines.

Don Fukuda

Credit Cards: D, MC, V.
Handicap Access: Yes.

and Mediterranean classics. Fresh seafoods and exquisite produce receive inspired saucings and seasonings, and pungent condiments arrive at your table to add firepower and further spice to servings of basmati rice, salads of neon-hued pickled vegetables, and grilled filets of salmon topped with tamarind and basil glaze. Not to be missed are pergedels — corn fritters served with a peanut/coconut milk dipping sauce — and glorious exotica like dragon chicken, slathered in a fresh mint and cilantro glaze with black Asian mushrooms. The house-made desserts alone merit more than one visit. The wine list is extensive and long on local vintages. Terrific people-watching comes compliments of the house.

MOBO SUSHI
408/425-1700.
105 South River St.
Open: Tues.–Sun.
Price: Moderate.
Cuisine: Japanese/Sushi.
Serving: L (except Sun.), D.
Reservations: No.
Credit Cards: MC, V.
Handicap Access: Yes.

A vibrant scene, intriguing taped musical selections, and imaginative, sparkling fresh sushi creations make this a hit. The very young, skilled staff here keeps the orders flowing and all the classic tekkamakis, nigiris, and anari sushis are prepared, as well as variations that could only have been created on the Central Coast by head honcho Scott Maddox. For example, the Rock & Roll is filled with freshwater eel and avocado; Sushi Rage involves avocado, garlic, and macadamia nuts as well as buttery hamachi tuna and sticky rice. The Presto Roll is a local favorite, packed with fresh basil and crimson ahi tuna. Adventure dining at its best — nothing too precious and everything fresh, fresh, fresh.

O'MEI RESTAURANT
408/425-8458.
2316 Mission St.
Open: Daily.
Price: Moderate.
Cuisine: Contemporary
Asian.
Serving: L (except week-
ends), D.
Reservations: Recom-
mended.
Credit Cards: AE, MC, V.
Handicap Access: Yes.

The Pacific Rim culinary genius of Roger Grigsby has made these sleek, serene dining rooms one of the area's most popular and consistently excellent restaurants. Trips to the Far East recharge Grigsby's inventive menu, translated through contemporary California emphasis on light, fresh presentation. Tiny dishes of intriguing appetizers are brought to each table, and diners can choose from baby pickled corn cobs, chili-infused carrots, or vinegary straw mushrooms — whatever moves the kitchen that evening. The seasonally transmuting menu is always tantalizing; appetizer standouts include the sumptuous red oil dumplings and fabulous slender green beans tossed with fermented shrimp. Vegetables like the yu xiang eggplant, vibrant with the perfume of Szechuan peppercorns, or asparagus in garlicky black bean sauce, are meals unto themselves. More complex, but equally accessible, are special creations such as pan-fried noodles with smoked bacon, tiny clams, and yellow zucchini or a stir-fry of chicken, sweet potatoes, and black dates infused by an earthy sauce of rice wine and molasses. Desserts are equally inventive and the wines-by-the-glass include the finest from area micro-wineries. A favorite with visiting celebrities, politicos, artists, and University of California folks.

Marc Westburg, chef of the Pearl Alley Bistro & Wine Bar, offers exquisite contemporary fare influenced by international seasonings and fresh produce.

Shmuel Thaler

**PEARL ALLEY BISTRO &
WINE BAR**
408/429-8070.
110 Pearl Alley (upstairs
bet. Pacific Ave. & Cedar
St.).
Open: Daily.

Before culinary *wunderkind* Marc Westburg opened this accessibly chi-chi bistro on the site of a longtime favorite winebar, he had cooked all over the world, including a stint as Trader Vic's personal chef. The multicultural flavor, texture, and seasoning ideas from his extensive experience

Price: Moderate to Expensive.
Cuisine: Contemporary Continental.
Serving: D.
Reservations: Recommended.
Credit Cards: AE, MC, V.
Handicap Access: No.

power some of the most innovative dishes on the Central Coast. The small dining room — the hardwood floors accentuate the convivial hubbub — offers a constantly changing menu, big on small dishes. The Pacific Rim influence appears in the exquisite fresh kim chee salmon served with house-made pickled cabbage and toasted nori, and the spicy sambar lamb curry; more European are signature dishes like a vegetable flan — the beautiful bands of beet, carrot, spinach, and potato mousse resemble an edible rainbow — a caramelized onion tart, and sweetbreads in fig cream sauce. Pastas are accented with whatever the chef found in the day's marketplace; look for risottos with unusual ingredients like burdock root. Special menus feature the cuisine of different parts of the globe for a week each month, so adventuresome gourmands can eat everything from kangaroo to antelope when their timing is right. The long wood bar attracts solo diners as well as connoisseurs of Pearl Alley's lengthy listing of outstanding Central Coast and French vintages, most available by the glass.

REAL THAI KITCHEN
408/427-2559.
1632 Seabright Ave.
Open: Daily.
Price: Inexpensive.
Cuisine: Thai.
Serving: L, D.
Reservations: Recommended weekend dinner.
Credit Cards: AE, MC, V.
Handicap Access: Yes.

Fans of the brilliant flavor complexities of Thai cuisine have made this small, colorfully decorated restaurant their second home. Using fresh local produce and seafoods as a primary base, chef Prasit Saranyaphiphat expertly applies the traditional seasonings of chilies, garlic, basil, lemon grass, and lime to a wide range of authentic dishes. The creamy pad Thai stir-fried rice noodles beautifully support a flotilla of shrimp, chicken, egg, tofu, and ground peanuts. Southern Thai curries — layered with sweet basil, fiery chilies, and coconut milk — are unforgettable, especially those with roasted duck or fresh seafoods. Many come simply for sensuous appetizers like the spicy shrimp soup filled with mushrooms, lemon grass, and coconut milk, or the chicken larb (minced poultry, toasted rice powder, lime, chilies, basil, cilantro, and shredded lettuce). Don't miss the barbecued pork ribs. Hostess/partner Ellen Saranyaphiphat is a gem.

SEA CLOUD RESTAURANT & SOCIAL CLUB
408/458-9393.
Municipal Wharf 4913.
Price: Moderate to Expensive.
Cuisine: California.

The contemporary nautical theme at the Sea Cloud is enhanced by glorious burnished woodwork, and the friendly bar serves superior cocktails and fine local wines. Afternoon drinks here are a religion, offering clear views of the waves and surfing action at Lighthouse Point. From one of the main dining rooms, the panoramic

Manager Peter Loustalet, owner Lou Caviglia, and chef Steve Elb collaborate on the casual sophistication of the Sea Cloud Restaurant & Social Club on the Santa Cruz Wharf.

Shmuel Thaler

Serving: L (exc. weekends), D.
Reservations: Recommended.
Credit Cards: AE, MC, V.
Handicap Access: Yes.

view is filled by the main beach, colorful Boardwalk attractions, and Santa Cruz Mountains beyond. Masterminded by chef Steve Elb, the menu offers fresh seafoods with touches of Southwestern and Pacific Rim inspiration. Tiny muyagi oysters on the half shell and excellent clam chowder start things off, followed by an innovative shellfish pasta creation or a sumptuous filet mignon. The warm confit of duck salad is an intensely flavored pleasure of baby lettuces, rich tender duck, and fresh local goat cheese bathed in a warm balsamic vinaigrette. Elb is a master of fresh produce and visually arresting garnishes. The heart of romaine salad with gorgonzola and balsamic vinaigrette is splendid, as are the freshly made desserts, especially the hazelnut mousse. Service is flawless and views of marine life, ubiquitous gulls and pelicans, seals and the occasional dolphin and whale add to the waterfront ambiance.

SUKEROKU
408/426-6660.
1701 Mission St.
Open: Tues.–Sun.
Price: Moderate.
Cuisine: Japanese.
Serving: L (Tues.–Fri.), D.
Reservations: No.
Credit Cards: MC, V.
Handicap Access: No.

Since the late '70s, this tiny Japanese restaurant and even tinier sushi bar have satisfied the cravings for soy, sake, and sushi on the part of neighbors and university regulars in this Westside Santa Cruz community. Blonde wood tables and the occasional travel poster make up the spare decor, but the real star here is the wonderful food. Exceptional bowls of fat udon noodles filled with shiitakes, prawns, and vegetables are available at dinner, while lunches offer consummate teriyaki

Isao and Tishiko Hamashi have made Sukeroku in Santa Cruz a haven for Japanese food lovers.

Shmuel Thaler

salmon and pork, or feather-light tempura. The sushi is first-rate, served up with friendly flair — and the occasional outburst of song — by legendary chef/owner Isao Hamashi. A local treasure.

MONTEREY COAST

It's no surprise that in this stretch of the Central Coast, seafood is king, especially the silken flesh of the Monterey spot prawn, farm-raised abalone, and wild Monterey Bay king salmon. Italian cuisine, a legacy from the pioneering fishing families, is another great specialty. Educated palates won't want to miss the epicurean treasures offered up by the following fine Monterey area restaurants.

Big Sur

NEPENTHE
408/667-2345.
Hwy. 1, 30 mi. S. of
   Carmel.
Open: Daily.
Price: Moderate.
Cuisine: Tapas, Regional
   American.
Serving: L, D; Br. (every
   day).
Reservations: Not neces-
   sary.
Credit Cards: AE, MC, V.
Handicap Access: Yes.

A legendary bohemian pit stop since 1949, Nepenthe always has been a gathering spot for literary lights seeking escape from the urban jungle. Henry Miller was a regular and Orson Welles purchased a cabin on the property for his bride, Rita Hayworth. A central fireplace and rustic woodwork add to the charm of this terraced establishment hugging the rocky coastline. The new Kiva Restaurant serves a daily brunch and offers a tapas menu until dusk on its outdoor deck. The view from the terrace affords an unsurpassed glimpse of the wild beauty of this magic spot. Sooner or later everyone makes the pilgrimage here, sometimes for an evening cocktail — the Bloody Marys have few rivals — sometimes for the fine salads and exceptional burgers, but always for the view and the unique moody Central Coast atmosphere. The charming Phoenix Shop arts and crafts emporium adjoins the restaurant. Don't forget your camera.

**VENTANA RESTAU-
RANT**
408/667-2331.
Hwy. 1, 28 mi. S. of
  Carmel.
Open: Daily.
Price: Expensive.
Cuisine:
  California/Mediter-
  ranean.
Serving: L, D.
Reservations: Required for
  dinner.
Credit Cards: AE, D, DC,
  MC, V.
Handicap Access: Yes.

Here in the heart of Big Sur is the ultimate retreat, and perhaps the most beautiful setting for an inn (see *Lodging*) and restaurant in the world. Perched a thousand feet above the Pacific Ocean, framed by the lush Santa Lucia mountain range, Ventana seems hoisted on top of the world. On a clear day, the panoramic view alone is worth the visit and, not surprisingly, Ventana is a favorite respite for locals and travelers alike. The restaurant interior, like that of the inn's overnight rooms, is rustic yet very polished and sophisticated. Both the lunch and dinner menus are distinctive, but unified in their California-Mediterranean themes, reflecting the Central Coast "Riviera" setting. Appetizers include warm zucchini, goat cheese, and tomato tart with Big Sur greens. Entrées, like grilled salmon with artichoke and potatoes, and the tower of grilled summer vegetables with roasted red pepper sauce, are complemented by an award-winning wine list with an emphasis on the vintages of California, especially the Central Coast. The staff is amiable and exceptionally competent. The restaurant has an in-house bakery and offers an extensive array of desserts, breads, cakes, and pastries. The tab is rich — but so is the experience.

Carmel

CAFÉ STRAVAGANZA
408/625-3733.
241 Crossroads Center,
  Hwy. 1 & Rio Rd.
Open: Daily.
Price: Inexpensive to Mod-
  erate.
Cuisine: Regional Mediter-
  ranean.
Serving: L, D.
Reservations: Recom-
  mended for dinner.
Credit Cards: AE, MC, V.
Handicap Access: Yes.

Popular Carmel restaurateur Fuad Bahou has infused this colorful and friendly café with true Mediterranean warmth and the voluptuous flavors of Greece, Italy, and the Middle East. The walls are vibrant with bold artworks and charming Mediterranean crafts in bright colors. The riot of visual decor is echoed in the menu that urges diners to sample the lush roasted eggplant *baba ghannouge* with fresh vegetables for dipping, fat grilled sausages with Dijon yogurt, and pizzas topped with almost anything. Nightly specials of fresh seafoods and pastas are bountiful; irresistible grilled prawns come with feta cheese, drizzled with lime and mint vinaigrette. Many swear by the gloriously messy paella and everything from the grill exudes flamboyant flavoring. Locally made wines by the glass are available and the homemade desserts are prepared with love. The casual yet festive atmosphere is maintained by regulars who all love to table hop. The cuisine is sophisticated and down-home, and newcomers will immediately feel welcome.

Bakeries

The Central Coast taste for superior breads and pastries has prompted a delicious groundswell of exceptional bakeries. Most serve excellent coffees and provide table seating and are fashionable meeting spots for movers, shakers, and artsy types. *Alfaro's Café & Bakery* (408/426-9240; 920 Pacific Ave., Santa Cruz) bakes up splendid breakfast pastries and earthy individual pizzas in addition to fabulous sourdough and seed breads. *The Buttery* (408/458-3020; 702 Soquel Ave., Santa Cruz) bakes great breads, but the sumptuously frosted cakes and elegant cookies are even better (don't miss the zucchini muffins and pecan sandies). *Emily's Good Things to Eat* (408/429-9866; 1129 Mission St., Santa Cruz) offers the aromatic attractions of pumpkin muffins and round fragrant sourdough bread. *Kelly's French Pastry* (408/423-9059; 1547 Pacific Ave, Santa Cruz & 408/662-2911; 7486 Soquel Dr., Aptos) creates authentic French breads, cakes, and pastries, killer pear tarts, and *pain d'almond*. *Fifi's Café & French Bakery* (1188 Forest Ave., Pacific Grove; 408/372-5325) is the crème de la crème of Monterey area bakeries, famed for napoleons, cheesecakes, petit fours, and berry delights, to take away or consume with espresso on the premises. The name says it all at *Old West Cinnamon Rolls* (861 Dolliver St., Pismo Beach; 805/773-1428), an exhibition bakery that whips up monster cinnamon rolls, old-fashioned donuts, cookies, breads, and rolls. *SLO Baked* (763A Foothill Blvd., San Luis Obispo; 805/541-1438) is a perennial favorite with plump scones, crisp croissants, pies, cookies, amazing bran muffins, and fancy, beautiful cakes. *Astrid's Café* (2030 Cliff Dr., Santa Barbara; 805/965-0180) serves authentic croissants, gemlike fruit tarts, picture-pretty pastries, and superb French breads from a master baker. *Pierre Lafond* (833 State St., Santa Barbara; 805/966-2276 — also three other locations in the area) creates mouth-watering designer muffins, elegant European-style pastries, biscottis, and outrageously seductive cookies to scarf down immediately or take home for later.

Baker-turned-entrepreneuse, Kelly Sanchez parlayed her knack for superb French breads and pastries into Kelly's French Pastry, in Aptos and in downtown Santa Cruz.

Paul Schraub

CASANOVA
408/625-0501.
5th Ave. bet. Mission &
   San Carlos Sts.
Open: Daily.
Price: Moderate to Expen-
   sive.
Cuisine: Country French
   and Italian.
Serving: B, L, D; Sun. Br.
Reservations: Recom-
   mended for dinner.
Credit Cards: MC, V.
Handicap Access: Yes.

Consistently voted "Carmel's Most Romantic Restaurant," this appealing family-run restaurant is a bastion of fine continental classics matched by an award-winning wine cellar excavated under the charming residence-turned-restaurant. The atmosphere of an Italian hideaway is enhanced by a menu offering superbly light gnocchi verde, excellent melanzane, and a fine version of braised veal provençal with mushrooms, peppers, tomatoes, and white wine. Dinner here can include grilled rack of lamb or salmon with mushroom duxelles, as well as creamy pasta entrées with fresh local shellfish or earthy cheeses. Main courses come with antipasto and a choice of appetizers. Dessert tarts of seasonal fruits and berries can tempt even the strongest resolve, and there's a fine selection of vintage ports to extend the sensation of delicious indulgence. Brunches at Casanova are equally tempting, ranging from eggs Florentine to smoked salmon salad or lobster tail in saffron broth with angel hair pasta. Even if the fog is in, the al fresco dining is romantic, warmed, if need be, by convenient space heaters.

CRÈME CARMEL
408/624-0444.
8th Ave. & San Carlos St.
Open: Daily.
Price: Expensive.
Cuisine: French/Califor-
   nia.
Serving: D.
Reservations: Recom-
   mended.
Credit Cards: AE, CB, D,
   DC, MC, V.
Handicap Access: Yes.

Tucked at the back of a courtyard, behind an eye-wear store and an appliance repair shop, this is one of Carmel's best known secrets. The dining room is small and intimate, with white-clothed tables close together, and is complemented by soft music and subdued lighting. The friendly waitstaff, well-versed sommelier, and the seasonal French/California menu add a casual accent to the atmosphere. Starters include Pacific oysters on the half shell with mignonette sauce, smoked salmon and potato pancakes with crème fraîche, and Sonoma foie gras with caramelized onion and caviar with port sauce. Entrées include Pacific salmon with chervil broth and fennel ratatouille, and sliced breast of duck served with green peppercorn-Madeira sauce. The menu draws widely on locally grown products. Desserts are rich without heaviness and the wine list is exceptional for such a small restaurant. The entire mood is unpretentious, making for a relaxing dining experience popular among locals.

**GIULIANO'S RIS-
   TORANTE**
408/625-5231.
Mission St. & 5th Ave.
Open: Daily.

The low-key intimacy and casual elegance of this small, sophisticated dining room have earned the devotion of a savvy clientele since its 1981 opening by Susan and Robert Negri and their family.

Price: Expensive.
Cuisine: Northern Italian.
Serving: L (Tues.–Sat.), D.
Reservations: Recom-
mended for dinner.
Credit Cards: AE, MC, V.
Handicap Access: Yes.

The rose-toned decor, punctuated with sculptural flower displays, is delightfully easy on the eyes. The specialties here are poems to the fashionable cuisine of northern Italy, including buttery carpaccio appetizers and sweet, tender roasted peppers Piémontaise. The veal piccata and homemade pastas are all impeccably executed and expertly served.

KATY'S COTTAGE
408/625-6260.
Lincoln St. bet. Ocean &
7th Aves.
Open: Daily.
Price: Inexpensive.
Cuisine: Country Ameri-
can.
Serving: B, L (except Sun.).
Reservations: Recom-
mended.
Credit Cards: Cash, checks
only.
Handicap Access: Yes.

Bountiful homecooked breakfasts until closing time are some of the welcoming features that have made this tiny charmer such an underground favorite with Carmelites. Run with care and expertise by Katy Curry, the pretty pink and green dining room with antique touches and a fireplace specializes in breakfasts of old-fashioned luxuries like panettone French toast, serious oatmeal, and addictive miniature pancakes. Lovely lunches can involve artichoke soup and chicken salad, and the famous eggs Benedict may be made with lox, chicken, or fresh vegetables in lieu of the traditional Canadian bacon.

PACIFIC'S EDGE
408/624-3801.
Highlands Inn, 4 mi. S. of
Carmel on Hwy. 1.
Open: Daily.
Price: Expensive.
Cuisine: New
American/California,
emphasis on Central
Coast.
Serving: L, D; Sun. Br.

The Highlands Inn — a prestigious, architectural award-winning property — offers beautiful views of the spectacular Carmel coastline, the refined luxury of a world-class historic hotel, *and* this superior restaurant. The menu — orchestrated by young superstar chef Brian Whitmer — features seasonal California cuisine showcasing abundant regional foods. Highlights include an appetizer of Monterey Bay smoked king salmon and Carmel Val-

Chef Brian Whitmer of Pacific's Edge supervises the meticulous preparation of his renowned cuisine.

Reservations: Recom-
mended.
Credit Cards: AE, CB, D,
DC, MC, V.
Handicap Access: Yes.

ley greens with sweet corn fritters and roasted pepper relish; a stunning filet of beef with homemade,
oversized black pepper ravioli; and a strudel of baby
artichokes, goat cheese, sun-dried tomatoes and
sautéed mushrooms. The seasonal menu is augmented by a nightly prix fixe "Sunset Dinner
Menu," usually consisting of three courses and dessert with selected wines by
the glass. And there are no shortage of vintage possibilities here: the wine cellar
is spectacular, featuring an inventory of 28,000 bottles. Each winter the
acclaimed international "Masters of Food & Wine" marathon of dinners and
tastings fills the inn and restaurant with celebrity chefs, vintners, and gourmands.

RIO GRILL
408/625-5436.
Hwy. 1 at Rio Rd.
Open: Daily.
Price: Moderate.
Cuisine: American South-
west/California.
Serving: L, D; Sun. Br.
Reservations: Recom-
mended.
Credit Cards: AE, MC, V.
Handicap Access: Yes.

This is *the* place for beautiful people — at the
bar, behind the bar, waitressing, waitering, and
on the walls (literally — the walls in the bar display
full-color cartoons of celebrities and friends). And
everybody is having a good time. Maybe that's
why the Rio Grill is constantly winning the "Best
Place to Meet People" accolade. The restaurant
wins on other points too: for excellent, warm service; innovative, delicious food; and an atmosphere
and menu that successfully mixes the exotic (fresh
swordfish with Jack Daniels-infused sun-dried
tomato pesto) with the casual (one of the best egg-
plant sandwiches around). Book a table here in advance or expect a long wait
at the door. The hyper-attractive dining rooms emulate the open-air Santa Fe
look — stylish artwork, live cacti, and butcher-paper tablecloths plus crayons.
So be playful. The menu is famous for its place on the cutting edge of New
American cuisine. The daily blackboard list of specials sports fresh pastas, fish,
and shellfish with a global culinary theme. The wine list offers over 200 selections of top-flight, mostly California wines, and the desserts are decadent.

SANS SOUCI
408/624-6220.
Lincoln St. bet. 5th & 6th
Aves.
Open: Daily.
Price: Expensive.
Cuisine: French.
Serving: D.
Reservations: Recom-
mended
Credit Cards: AE, MC, V.
Handicap Access: Yes.

Tucked inside one of Carmel's numerous courtyards is one of the long-standing dining treasures of the Monterey Peninsula, the Sans Souci.
The name, French for "without a care," says it all.
The atmosphere is elegant and the tuxedoed waiters knowledgeable. Despite appearances, the tone
here is casual and unpretentious. The owner, John
Jay Williams, is on hand virtually every night to
assure his patrons' satisfaction. Chef Jean Hubert,
while French-trained, instills his dishes with a subtle California accent. Exotic starters include Russian

Beluga caviar with garnishes and toast points; the prized wild California abalone; and tortellini filled with greens and Sardo cheese in a carrot-walnut oil coulis. Entrées feature skate wings lightly sautéed in brown butter, and boneless, free-range chicken robed in aromatic green herbs. The delightfully evolving wine list features rare vintages of French and California red wines. Homemade desserts are light yet very satisfying. And you can walk off dinner by strolling Carmel by starlight.

SILVER JONES
408/624-5200.
3690 The Barnyard, Hwy. 1
  & Carmel Valley Rd.
Open: Daily.
Price: Moderate.
Cuisine:
  American/Mediter-
  ranean/Vegetarian.
Serving: L (except Sun.), D;
  Sun. Br.
Reservations: Recom-
  mended.
Credit Cards: AE, MC, V.
Handicap Access: Yes.

At the mouth of Carmel Valley, Silver Jones is a consistent winner of accolades and a famous local hangout, as much for the humor of the proprietor and staff as for the fine food and wine. The open air dining room, with its cozy fireplace, wood floors, wall rugs, and wood tables, exudes a hospitable blend of Mediterranean and American Southwest ambiance. The menu changes daily and blends Italian, California, and vegetarian influences; the result is great food and fun. The staff's charm carries over to the crowd, which can get a bit loud at night. Appetizers include numerous gourmet pizzas made in the house brick oven; grilled spinach polenta with eggplant caponata; wild rice salad with walnut, feta, mushrooms, and roasted vegetables; and Castroville artichokes with basil dressing. Entrées include local sand dabs poached in Chardonnay, garlic, and butter. There are exciting pasta and seafood dishes, and classic American fare, like meatloaf and mashed potatoes. Specials usually include "heart-smart" options, among them some very creative salads. The wine list is eclectic and desserts are delicious — try the bread pudding with Jack Daniels sauce.

TERRACE GRILL
408/624-4010.
La Playa Hotel, Camino
  Real & 8th Ave.
Open: Daily.
Price: Moderate.
Cuisine:
  Mediterranean/Ameri-
  can Southwest.
Serving: B, L, D; Sun, Br.
Reservations: Recom-
  mended for dinner.
Credit Cards: AE, MC, V.
Handicap Access: Limited.

A heated, awning-covered outdoor dining area with surrounding gardens gives the Terrace Grill a casual, relaxed Mediterranean ambiance perfectly complemented by the menu. In the evening, the outdoor gas lights and candle-lit tables create a romantic mood — accentuated by the peaceful, neighborhood location. The cuisine is a highly successful combination of Mediterranean, Middle-Eastern, California, and American Southwest. Prices are very reasonable for the quality and quantity offered. The menu changes regularly to accommodate in-season foods, like local Monterey Bay king salmon. Some lunch stand-outs include crab gazpacho, herb-roasted shrimp, and a zesty

Continental dining in the coastal valley elegance of Quail Lodge has made The Covey a favorite site for celebrity guests.

grilled chicken quesadilla. Dinner fare includes prime rib, swordfish, pastas, Moroccan prawns with couscous, and seared duck with sesame, orange, and ginger. Desserts, while homemade, don't always live up to their billing and the wine list is a bit short, but adequate.

Carmel Valley

THE COVEY
408/624-1582.
Quail Lodge Resort, 8205
    Valley Greens Dr.
Open: Daily.
Price: Expensive.
Cuisine: European/Cali-
    fornia.
Serving: D.
Reservations: Required.
Credit Cards: AE, CB, DC,
    MC, V.
Handicap Access: Yes.

With countless awards for food, service, and wine, and overlooking a gorgeous setting, this restaurant gives new meaning to the words "romantic," "fabulous," and "expensive." Those who don't mind being treated like royalty can join celebrity residents of this exclusive area (If you're discreet, you'll spy Doris Day — a Carmel Valley resident who dines here weekly) at sumptuously set tables, where brilliant creations featuring updated classics are all heightened by fresh herbs grown in the restaurant's own gardens. Outstanding duck, lamb, and veal dishes are not to be missed, the shrimp and scallop quenelle is feath-erlight, and the desserts are extravagantly satisfying. This elegant place caters to a very worldly set, and diners not dressed for the occasion will tend to feel out of place. But for a true taste of the luxurious, it's that very special spot.

WILL'S FARGO
408/659-2774.
12 mi. from Hwy. 1, in
    center of Carmel Valley
    Village.
Open: Daily.
Price: Moderate to Expen-
    sive.
Cuisine: American/Conti-
    nental.

A steak house perhaps without peer on the Central Coast, Will's Fargo has been serving up bountiful portions of superbly prepared beef entrées since 1959. Patrons select their main course in the butcher shop, a mini-recreation of what you might have found in a Midwest town during the 1950s. Steaks are cut to order and served with a house-made relish tray, soup or salad, hot cheese

Coffee Houses

Like all artistically fertile places on the globe, the Central Coast cultivates its café society in coffee houses so numerous they're practically underfoot. *Caffe Pergolesi* (418 Cedar St., Santa Cruz; 408/426-1775) attracts young and avant garde students and artists who congregate to swill industrial strength coffee and wait to be discovered. *Georgiana's* (1520 Pacific Ave., Santa Cruz; 408/427-9900) is a new caffeine-infused meeting spot housed in the front of Bookshop Santa Cruz and wildly popular with outdoor café types. *Jahva House* (120 Union St., Santa Cruz; 408/459-9876), a '60s-style neo-hippie hangout, features weathered couches, big leafy plants and terrific caffe latte. *Mr. Toots* (221 Esplanade, Capitola; 408/475-3679) offers an ocean view and upper room, dark-wood ambiance that has attracted a long-standing following. *Pacific Grove Coffee Roasting Company* (510 Lighthouse Ave., Pacific Grove; 408/655-5633), a popular java joint, specializes in house roasted cappuccinos, dark French roasts, and special blends. *The Coffee Merchant* (1065 Higuera, San Luis Obispo; 805/543-6701) deals in biscottis and muffins along with fine espresso and fresh roasts served in a bohemian atmosphere. *Side Street Café* (2375 Alamo Pintado, Los Olivos; 805/688-8455) provides a laid-back forum for lovers of movies, live music, and fine coffee and tea, especially in the lovely back garden shaded by rose arbors and magnificent locust trees. *Earthling Bookshop Inc.* (698 Higuera, San Luis Obispo; 805/543-7951; also 1137 State St., Santa Barbara; 805/965-0926) provides soothing bookshop atmosphere, as well as a selection of splendid coffees, desserts, and literary events.

The Central Coast cultivates a café society in an explosion of coffee houses, many with sidewalk tables like those at Santa Barbara's Earthling Bookshop.

Kim Reierson

Serving: D.
Reservations: Recommended.
Credit Cards: AE, DC, MC, V.
Handicap Access: No.

bread, stuffed baked potato, and fresh vegetable. The warm, turn-of-the-century dining room is studded with Western relics and artifacts. The filet mignon, New York cut steak, double-thick lamb chops, and prime rib-eye are stand-outs. Chicken and seafood are also offered. The wine list is quite good and predictably heavy on reds. The service is snappy, knowledgeable, and friendly — many of the staff members are veteran employees. For just a quick bite, consider the lounge menu featuring pasta, Caesar salad, and a superb French dip sandwich au jus. Desserts include many standards: cheesecake, strawberry shortcake, homemade apple pie, and a delicately rich walnut pie. There's an excellent selection of after-dinner drinks at the bar and a friendly mix of patrons.

Monterey

BINDEL'S
408/373-3737.
500 Hartnell St.
Open: Daily.
Price: Moderate to Expensive.
Cuisine: California.
Serving: D; Sun Br.
Reservations: Recommended.
Credit Cards: AE, CB, D, DC, MC, V.
Handicap Access: Yes.

Even the architecture of this 1840 landmark two-story adobe — refurbished as a gracious dining house — offers a taste of Old Monterey. Elegantly decorated with valanced draperies, tapestried chairs, and romantic chandeliers, Bindel's serves up stylish, unpretentious California cuisine showcasing the outstanding harvests of the fertile Salinas Valley and the Monterey Bay. In addition to house favorites like Monterey Jack cheese bread and artichoke cream soup, appetizer highlights include soft snapper tacos with black beans and avocado salsa, and crab cakes with lime and caper butter. Appealing entrées like roast Petaluma duck with bing cherry-Merlot sauce and wild rice, or steamed Pacific salmon with dill Chardonnay sauce, provide a dining tour of California's finest flavors. Besides a full bar, a fine wine list features top Monterey area wines.

CAFÉ FINA
408/372-5200.
47 Fisherman's Wharf #1.
Open: Daily.
Price: Moderate to Expensive.
Cuisine: Contemporary Italian.
Serving: L, D.
Reservations: Recommended.
Credit Cards: AE, CB, D, DC, MC, V.
Handicap Access: Yes.

Energetic Italian spirit fills this waterfront trattoria equipped with its own wood-burning pizza oven imported from the Old Country. Café Fina offers lighthearted atmosphere with zesty mesquite-grilled seafoods and chicken or beef specialties. The fine pizzas come with inventive toppings and fragrant fresh herbs; the handmade pastas and raviolis reflect the warmth of proprietors Dominic and Naida Mercurio, whose family portraits line the walls of this charming café. Don't miss the smoked salmon pizzettes with tomatoes and mozzarella and a goat cheese and black olive ravioli in cream sauce. Full bar, very cozy, terrific flavors, and lots of fun.

DUCK CLUB
408/646-1706.
Monterey Plaza Hotel, 400 Cannery Row.
Open: Daily.
Price: Moderate to Expensive.

Dangling out over the aquamarine Monterey Bay, this fine restaurant offers elegant atmosphere and breathtaking vistas of the ocean. While jackets are required, the management seems happy to supply them to casually dressed guests. A long copper counter frames the exhibition kitchen and

Cuisine: International/Cal-
ifornia.
Serving: B, L, D.
Reservations: Recom-
mended for dinner.
Credit Cards: AE, CB, DC,
MC, V.
Handicap Access: Yes.

Italian wood-burning ovens of the lovely dining room, where generously spaced tables provide plenty of romantic privacy. In addition to a full bar, there's a substantial listing of top California and Italian wines — all the better to accompany appetizers of grilled vegetables with Mediterranean vinaigrette, or grilled prawns wrapped with pancetta in sun-dried tomato beurre blanc. Also exceptional are pasta entrées and the game, beef, and fresh seafood dishes, and the pastry cart is straight from Italian heaven. The renowned brunch buffet is lavishly laid out on an al fresco terrace that juts out over the water.

FRESH CREAM
408/375-9798.
100-C Heritage Harbor, 99
Pacific St.
Open: Daily.
Price: Expensive.
Cuisine: French/Califor-
nia.
Serving: L (Fri. only), D.
Reservations: Recom-
mended.
Credit Cards: AE, CB, D,
DC, MC, V.
Handicap Access: Yes.

When you want everything to be "just so" and you're willing to pay for it, you will not be disappointed at Fresh Cream, which has built its reputation on perfection. Guests ascend a spiral staircase leading to a full-service bar and dining rooms with beautiful views of Fisherman's Wharf and Monterey Bay. Stylish Impressionist artworks create an intimate setting for the enjoyment of chef Tim Nugent's truly inspired cuisine, a deft blend of French and California influences. The menu changes daily and includes a half dozen appetizers, such as a fresh salmon torte with capers, herbed crumbs, and red pepper butter; a three-fowl and peppercorns sausage wrapped in puff pastry on compote of fresh apple; and ravioli of lobster with shrimp butter, topped with black and gold caviar. Entrées include luxurious veal dishes and an impeccable Holland Dover sole grilled in browned butter and lemon and boned at the table. A focused wine list, stellar service, and outstanding desserts add to the joy of dining at this very polished, romantic restaurant.

MONTEREY JOE'S
408/655-3355.
2149 N. Fremont St.
Open: Daily.
Price: Moderate.
Cuisine: Italian country-
style.
Serving: L (exc. week-
ends), D.
Reservations: Recom-
mended.
Credit Cards: AE, D, MC,
V.
Handicap Access: Yes.

A favorite with knowledgeable local gourmets, this California grill crossed with Italian bistro creates mouth-watering temptations from the vivacious exhibition kitchen. The award-winning interior of this contemporary adobe is reminiscent of the vintage Italian eateries in San Francisco. Everything is served with flair — from classic antipasto dishes like carpaccio, prosciutto with melon, or bold pastas, to a bounty of fresh seafood, veal, rabbit, pork, and beef specialties. The pizzas from the wood-burning oven are little classics. And the Italian-style desserts — especially the ultra-creamy tiramisu — are as delicious as they are beautiful. A fine listing of locally made vintages joins the large selection of Italian wines. A power lunch and dinner destination.

TARPY'S ROADHOUSE
408/647-1444.
Hwy. 68 & Canyon Del
    Rey Rd.
Open: Daily.
Price: Inexpensive to Moderate.
Cuisine: Regional American.
Serving: L (except Sun.), D;
    Sun. Br.
Reservations: Recommended.
Credit Cards: AE, D, MC, V.
Handicap Access: Yes.

A relatively new star in the Monterey Peninsula dining heavens, Tarpy's was created by the restaurateurs of the famed Rio Grill and is housed in a weathered turn-of-the-century roadhouse just off Highway 1. A tangle of trees and landscaping embraces the popular patio dining area, a setting for lunches of serious sandwiches like pork loin with chili barbecue mayonnaise or grilled chicken breast with roasted shallot and mushroom aioli. Inside the old stone house, American country favorites like house-aged beef with garlic mashed potatoes, venison rib chop with green peppercorn sauce, and pecan barbecue duck are offered along with a superb listing of California wines. Old-fashioned desserts like fresh peach crisp à la mode and tapioca with fresh berries continue the contemporary spin on a country comfort food theme.

Pacific Grove

CENTRAL 159
408/372-2235.
529 Central Ave. (bet.
    Lighthouse & Central).
Open: Mon.–Sat.
Price: Moderate to Expensive.
Cuisine: New
    American/California.
Serving: L, D.
Reservations: Not necessary.
Credit Cards: AE, DC, MC,
    V.
Handicap Access: Yes.

A favorite with local winemakers and restaurateurs on their days off, this inviting and casual contemporary dining room bears the New American cuisine signature of chef David Beckwith, whose emphasis is on seasonings and regional styles of the Americas. The intimate, California grill mood is enhanced by seating inside at bistro-like banquette tables or outside on the cozy patio. In addition to intriguingly presented fresh seafood and grill items, the kitchen turns out provocative selections based entirely on the harvests from fine Monterey Bay area farmers' gardens.

EL COCODRILO
408/655-3311.
701 Lighthouse Ave.
Open: Wed.–Mon.
Price: Moderate.
Cuisine: Coastal Central
    American/Caribbean.
Serving: D.

A menu of authentic Central American and Caribbean dishes, a lively, festive decor (intriguing artifacts and photographs from the collection of proprietress Marie Perruca-Ramirez), and clever presentations have made El Cocodrilo ("the crocodile" in Spanish), a favorite of locals seeking the exotic. This casual and hospitable restaurant consistently

---

Farmers' Markets

The weekly tradition of cruising the freshest locally grown produce, displayed in colorful booths by the growers themselves, has become a fixture of Central Coast life. It's a chance to meet the growers and select their freshly harvested, certified organic fruits, nuts, vegetables, and honey; plus eggs, cheeses, flowers, and just-caught seafood, all in an open-air market setting. *Downtown Farmers' Market of Santa Cruz* (Pacific between Cathcart & Lincoln, Santa Cruz; 408/429-8433; Weds. 3–7) bounces with friendly, festive, folksy atmosphere with live music, and street entertainment. *UCSC Farm & Garden Project* (University of California at Santa Cruz, Bay Ave. & Empire Grade Rd., Santa Cruz; 408/459-4140; Tues. & Fri. noon–5) sells produce and flowers from UCSC experimental agroecology fields, remarkable for their diversity, freshness, and downright unusualness. *Aptos Certified Farmers' Market* (6500 Soquel Dr., Cabrillo College lower parking lot, Aptos; 408/423-7308; Sat. 8–noon) is considered the granddaddy of area open-air organic produce emporia, with everything from brown eggs to purple potatoes. *Old Monterey Farmer's Market* (Alvarado, between Pearl and Del Monte, Monterey; 408/655-8070; Tues. 4–7) features scores of grower's displays, plus live music and finger food booths. *Monterey Certified Farmer's Market* (Fremont St. off Aguajito Rd., Monterey Peninsula College, Monterey; 916/654-0824; Thurs 2:30-6:30) draws purveyors from the boutique organic produce fields of Carmel. *San Luis Obispo Certified Farmers' Market* (Higuera & Chorro Sts., San Luis Obispo; 805/544-9570; Thurs. 6:30–9 at night) fills this block of downtown SLO with one of the most spectacular street markets on the Central Coast, featuring street musicians and jugglers, oakwood barbecues stocked with grilling meats and, of course, the legendary fresh produce, flowers, nuts, honey, eggs and herbs of this hothouse growing area. Everybody in town shows up. *Cambria Certified Farmers' Market* (Cambria Dr. & Main St., Cambria off Hwy. 1; 805/927-4715; Fri 2:30–5:30) presents the best looking and tasting produce the coast can generate. The *Santa Barbara Farmers' Market* (corner of Cota & Santa Barbara Sts., downtown Santa Barbara; 805/962-5354; Sat. 8:30–noon) is the region's largest certified farmers' market with 120 growers, all year round. *Santa Barbara Farmers' Market II* (500 block of State St., Santa Barbara; Tues. 4–7:30) unveils the freshest from 60 area farms, orchards, dairies, and seafood suppliers.

Reservations: Recommended.
Credit Cards: D, MC, V.
Handicap Access: Yes.

delivers bountiful portions of nutritious, good-tasting food (nothing is too spicy) that is far-removed from what most consider home cooking. And it's that new experience — dishes such as the bayou brochette of prawns, chicken, farm-raised alligator, tomatoes, onions, and peppers marinated in raspberry/tamarind vinaigrette — that brings people back for more. Other highlights include the Jamaican curry crab cakes with roasted cashew nuts, and the *pupusa*, Salvadoran-style handmade tortillas stuffed with cheese and chicken. A nightly Happy Hour stands out for the delectable appetizers and daily wine-by-the-glass specials. Service is attentive, the wine list more than adequate, and the desserts sinfully rich.

Every Thursday evening a block of downtown San Luis Obispo overflows with fresh produce, flowers, street musicians, and oakwood barbecues, all part of the acclaimed Certified Farmers' Market.

Jay Swanson

Pebble Beach

BAY CLUB
408/647-7433.
Inn at Spanish Bay, 2700 17
  Mile Dr.
Open: Daily.
Price: Moderate to Expen-
  sive.
Cuisine: Northern Italian.
Serving: D.
Reservations: Recom-
  mended.
Credit Cards: AE, CB, D,
  DC, MC, V.
Handicap Access: Yes.

Intimate and romantic, this charming club within the plush resort and golf complex on 17 Mile Drive specializes in contemporary Northern Italian cuisine. The wine list has taken the *Wine Spectator* Grand Award for the past several years. Everything, as you'd expect in such a setting, is beautifully presented. Light yet intense risottos tinged with regional flavors of artichoke and crab are irresistible. House pastas such as rigatoni with lobster are excellent; or try the antipasto of poached veal loin with caper and tuna sauce. From luxurious beef to brilliant seafoods, the dining here is as lovely as the surroundings.

CLUB XIX
408/625-8519.
The Lodge at Pebble
  Beach, 17 Mile Dr.
Open: Daily.
Price: Expensive.
Cuisine: Contemporary
  continental.
Serving: L, D.
Reservations: Recom-
  mended for dinner.
Credit Cards: AE, DC, MC,
  V.
Handicap Access: Yes.

Unabashedly posh, Club XIX takes its name from the age-old tease about what comes after the 18th hole of golf. In fact, one of the world's fabled sites — the 18th fairway of the Pebble Beach Golf Links — fills the view from the intimate dining room, whose sensitive cuisine is created by Lisa Magadini, a Culinary Institute of America graduate. Exceptional dinners, heightened by award-winning wine selections and luxury liqueurs from the full bar, are the rule here. From duck and crab appetizers to entrées of grilled salmon and medallions of veal, every dining move is flawless and enhanced by fine china and crystal. Outdoor patio dining also maximizes the stunning view.

SAN LUIS OBISPO COAST

In addition to sparkling fresh seafood plucked each day from teeming Pacific waters, this area features a long-standing tradition of Western-style dining, headlining aromatic oak pit grills, steaks slathered in barbecue sauce, even buffalo burgers. The exceptional produce from surrounding small farms is legendary, even in a state graced with a year-round growing season. The following San Luis Obispo eateries provide some of the top gastronomic occasions to experience the best this stretch of the coast has to offer.

Avila Beach

OLD CUSTOM HOUSE
805/595-7555.
324 Front St.
Open: Daily.
Price: Moderate.
Cuisine: Seafood.
Serving: B, L, D.
Reservations: No.
Credit Cards: AE, D, MC, V.
Handicap Access: Yes.

In 1927, when San Luis Obispo Bay was an official U.S. Port of Entry, this charming structure was built to house the business of customs. Today it serves as an atmospheric waterfront restaurant specializing in the bountiful fresh seafoods harvested along the Central Coast. The outdoor patio dining is popular, with views of gardens and fish ponds (and warding off marine fog with strategically placed heaters). An oak pit barbecue turns out beef and pork classics and the casual breakfasts offer eggs done every way imaginable. A popular local hangout.

Cambria

BRAMBLES
805/927-4716.
4005 Burton Dr.
Open: Daily.
Price: Moderate to Expensive.
Cuisine: Continental.
Serving: D; Sun. Br.
Reservations: Recommended.
Credit Cards: AE, CB, D, DC, MC, V.
Handicap Access: Yes.

Long one of the village of Cambria's top dinner houses, Brambles occupies an English-style home built in 1874. Numerous additions over the years have turned the building into charming dining rooms surrounded by a thicket of garden. While prime rib of beef with Yorkshire pudding is a house signature dish, the salmon broiled over the oakwood pit is exceptional, as are all the fresh, continental seafood dishes. Steaks come sizzling from the oakwood pit, and a selection of attractive chicken and pasta specialties rounds out the menu. Greek and Caesar salads are created from the fresh bounty of local market gardens. Sampling regional wines difficult to find outside the area is made effortless by the restaurant's extensive wine list, winner of a *Wine Spectator* Award for Excellence.

IAN'S
805/927-8649.
2150 Center St.

A sleek, contemporary dining room with upholstered banquettes, sophisticated wall sconces, and bold original artwork, Ian's creates some of the

Ice Cream Shops

The universal favorite dessert is showcased in myriad Central Coast creameries. *Donatello's Gelato* (113 Walnut Ave., Santa Cruz; 408/425-8908) specializes in fine-textured Italian-style ice cream in a rainbow of fresh and decadent flavors. *Marianne's* (1020 Ocean, Santa Cruz; 408/458-1447), for decades a landmark for creaminess like vanilla bean milkshakes, serves sugar cones filled with California 17, a killer version of Rocky Road. *Polar Bear Ice Cream* (1224 Soquel Ave., Santa Cruz; 408/425-5188) has fine espressos and delectable ice creams, including good berries and a superior pumpkin flavor. *TCBY Yogurt* (188 Country Club Gate, Pacific Grove; 408/649-8229), home of extraordinarily rich-tasting frozen yogurt, makes indulgence practically a health regimen. *Cocogelato* (Ocean between Mission & San Carlos, Carmel; 408/625-3122) serves sinfully delicious frozen yogurts and luscious Italian ice creams in a charming café. *Pieces of Heaven* (3686 The Barnyard, Carmel; 408/625-3368) offers world-famous Ben & Jerry's ice cream flavors like Cherry Garcia. *Debbie's Ice Cream Factory* (1023 Monterey, San Luis Obispo; 805/541-5520) invites patrons to watch homemade ice cream being created (through an observation window), and then sit down to a legendary mud pie. *SLO Maid Ice Cream Factory* (728 Higuera, San Luis Obispo; 805/541-3117) is an outpost for nationally renowned, award-winning ice cream, sorbet, sherbet, and frozen yogurt, all made, sold, and consumed at this popular spot in downtown SLO. *Great Pacific Ice Cream Co.* (219-A Stearns Wharf, Santa Barbara; 805/962-0108) features zillions of flavors of creamy goodness served right on the wharf so you can feast on an ocean view along with your calories.

SLO Maid Ice Cream Factory is an outpost for extraordinary ice cream made and sold in downtown San Luis Obispo.

Jay Swanson

Open: Daily.
Price: Moderate to Expensive.
Cuisine: California.
Serving: L (Fri. & Sat.), D; Sun. Br.
Reservations: Recommended.
Credit Cards: AE, MC, V.
Handicap Access: Yes.

finest California cuisine in the area. Fresh produce from area farms and gardens collaborate in an array of appetizers, especially beauties like the duck quesadilla studded with pumpkin seeds and golden raisins and topped with salsa fresca, avocados, tomatoes, and cilantro. Also wonderful are warm grilled asparagus on baby greens with goat cheese and toasted pine nuts, and the roast chicken with creamy garlic mashed potatoes. Duck, rabbit, and lamb appear in exciting guises on this menu, as do Central Coast abalone and prawn orchestrations. The service is excellent, the ambiance sophisticated yet casual, and the wine list excels in Central Coast vintages. The entire restaurant, including the bar, is non-smoking.

LINN'S MAIN BIN
805/927-0371.
2277 Main St.
Open: Daily.
Price: Moderate.
Cuisine: Country American.
Serving: B, L, D; Sun. Br.
Reservations: No.
Credit Cards: D, MC, V.
Handicap Access: Yes.

A Cambria original ensconced on picturesque Old West Main Street, Linn's is partly a huge café, like an American country tea room, and partly gourmet gift shop and bakery. The area's largest regional wine list complements a menu of homemade soups, signature pot pies, and imaginative sandwiches, all with fresh produce from Linn's own farms.

MUSTACHE PETE'S
805/927-8589.
4090 Burton Dr.
Open: Daily.
Price: Inexpensive to Moderate.
Cuisine: Italian.
Serving: L, D; Sun. Br.
Reservations: No.
Credit Cards: AE, D, MC, V.
Handicap Access: Yes.

The front of this convivial hangout is a laid-back sports bar, complete with pool table and giant TV. Behind that a spacious Italian eatery takes over. Sooner or later, everybody in town stops by to see friends, unwind over a beer, or feast on two-fisted pizzas topped with everything from pesto to roasted garlic chicken. Fresh seafood is turned into substantial scampi, cioppino, and Alfredo specialties, and there are plenty of Italian chicken classics. The pastas come loaded with fine marinara, cheeses, pesto, and fresh vegetables. Expect lots of local color.

ROBIN'S
805/927-5007.
4095 Burton Dr.
Open: Daily.
Price: Inexpensive to Moderate.
Cuisine: Eclectic ethnic.
Serving: L (except Sun.), D.
Reservations: Recommended summer weekends.
Credit Cards: AE, MC, V.
Handicap Access: Limited.

Tucked into a 1930s Spanish-style house set with antique oak tables and ethnic crafts on the walls, Robin's is a charming, eclectic dining experience. The emphasis here is on natural ingredients — the menu contains a wealth of vegetarian dishes — and ethnic cuisines ranging from the Far East to Latin America. The result is an exciting menu and even more exciting spicings and seasonings. Produce packed with just-picked flavor is mated with curries, toasted nuts, and glorious dressings to create inventive salads. The curried chicken salad sandwich served on a croissant with lettuce, tomatoes, cucumbers, and toasted almonds is divine.

Thai stir-fried beef explodes with the flavor of mint, ginger, garlic, chilies, and peanuts; all the black bean and pasta dishes are also imaginative. The finest

Micro-Breweries

In the 1980s, the repeal of a prohibition against selling and making beers on the same location prompted an explosion of micro-breweries all over the Central Coast, where freshly made and boldly flavored handmade brews are on tap at on-site pubs. These beers bear absolutely no relation to those lite beers advertised on TV. Tours are usually available and, in many cases, glass walls allow a full view of the "exhibition brewing." **Santa Cruz Brewing Company/Front Street Pub** (516 Front St. Santa Cruz; 408/429-8838) offers fine house lager, amber, porter, and seasonal items like barley wine and wheat beer on tap (or by the bottle at area markets) at a lively brewpub that's always packed with thirsty bodies. **Seabright Brewery** (519 Seabright Ave #107, Santa Cruz; 408/426 2739) features outdoor patio seating to enjoy Pelican pale, Seabright Amber, Ace's Ale, and Oatmeal Stout, all made on the sleek contemporary premises and all award-winners. **Monterey Brewing Company** (638 Wave, Monterey; 408/375-3634) is a popular brewpub close to Cannery Row that cooks up huge vats of pale, amber, and dark stout, plus unusual specialty brews like passionfruit and apricot. **SLO Brewing Company** (1119 Garden St., San Luis Obispo; 805/543-1843) offers fine brews like Brickhouse Pale, Garden Alley Amber, and Cole Porter, plus seasonal specialties and a classic pool hall straight out of *The Hustler*. **Brew House Grill** (202 State St., Santa Barbara; 805/963-3090) is a combination working brewery and fun pub with witty coastal specialties like Anacapa Amber and East Beach Blonde.

Gerry and Bernie Turgeon, the father and son entrepreneurs of Santa Cruz Brewing Company/Front Street Pub, were pioneers in the Central Coast micro-brewery boom.

Shmuel Thaler

from small local wineries is available by the glass or by the split — an excellent tasting opportunity. And nobody gets past the lavish counter of fresh desserts, of which French apple pie, tiramisu, and frangipane tart with wine-poached pears are only a few temptations. The patio seating, surrounded by a lush arbor, is especially appealing.

SOW'S EAR CAFÉ
805/927-4865.
2248 Main St.
Open: Daily.
Price: Moderate.
Cuisine: American.
Serving: D.
Reservations: Recom-
   mended.
Credit Cards: MC, V.
Handicap Access: Limited.

Locally grown herbs and vegetables pack vibrant flavor into each dish graciously served and skillfully presented in this fine country café. The entrées run the gamut of country American favorites, all given a uniquely Central Coast spin. Shellfish linguini with Greek olives, fennel, feta cheese, and tomatoes is a justifiably popular item, as are the chicken and dumplings and grill roasted chicken breast with fresh rosemary. An appetizer salad of fresh spinach is topped with sesame crusted chicken, oranges, almonds, and honey-lime dressing. The heartland attitude is continued by desserts like luxurious warm blueberry bread pudding with brandy hard sauce and milk chocolate cheesecake with hazelnut crust. The freshly baked bread is wonderful and the mood is unpretentiously friendly.

Harmony

**OLD HARMONY PASTA
   FACTORY**
805/927-5882.
2 Old Creamery Rd. &
   Hwy. 1.
Open: Daily.
Price: Moderate.
Cuisine: Italian.
Serving: L (sandwiches
   only), D; Sun. Br.
Reservations: Recom-
   mended weekends.
Credit Cards: AE, MC, V.
Handicap Access: Yes.

A stone's throw from the coast, the tiny village of Harmony is devoted to a community of thriving arts studios housed in renovated farm buildings. In what was once the butter cooling room of an old creamery, the Old Harmony Pasta Factory presents imaginative Italian cookery in the mellowest possible setting. Fetchingly decorated with lush plants and encircled by tiny gardens setting off the weathered wood buildings, this skylighted restaurant whips up a dreamy orange cream linguini and tiny pizzas, as well as classics like scampi, pork tenderloin Marsala, chicken Alfredo, and myriad other pastas. The garden patio, with its relaxing view of the splendid coastal foothills, is the place to take meals. Sunday brunches include favorites like eggs Benedict and omelets of garden-fresh produce and herbs.

Morro Bay

BLUE HERON
805/772-5651.
Inn at Morro Bay, 19
   Country Club Dr.
Open: Daily.
Price: Expensive.
Cuisine: California.
Serving: B, L, D; Sun. Br.
Reservations: Recom-
   mended.
Credit Cards: AE, CB, D,
   DC, MC, V.
Handicap Access: Yes.

Within a popular lodge, the Blue Heron showcases fine California cuisine, often with a French accent, and romantic views of the ocean at Morro Bay State Park. The elegant and comfortable dining room excels in sophisticated dinners, where appetizers can include zucchini blossoms stuffed with chicken truffle mousse and balsamic butter or country pâtés and salads of seasonal greens. Local king salmon is poached with fresh sorrel sauce and roast duckling arrives napped with blueberry cream sauce. A grilled halibut served with tomato basil fettucini, lemon-olive oil, and ginger is especially memorable. Classic breakfasts and lunches featuring seafoods and pastas are also served.

DORN'S ORIGINAL BREAKERS CAFÉ
805/772-4415.
801 Market St.
Open: Daily.
Price: Moderate.
Cuisine: Country American.
Serving: B, L, D.
Reservations: Recommended weekends.
Credit Cards: MC, V.
Handicap Access: Yes.

Converted from a vintage World War I real estate office in the early 1940s, and a success since the day it opened, Dorn's specializes in seafood served in an inspirational setting — overlooking the dramatic ancient volcanic plug of Morro Rock and the silvery Morro Bay harbor. Breakfasts are served until 2pm daily, offering a huge choice of pancakes, egg dishes, and French toast creations. Those in the know also come for the classic Boston clam chowder and highly prized Morro Bay abalone. Freshly made pastas are also quite good.

Nipomo

JOCKO'S
805/929-3686.
Corner of Tefft St. & Thomas Rd.
Open: Daily.
Price: Inexpensive to Moderate.
Cuisine: Steak house/Oak pit barbecue.
Serving: B, L, D.
Reservations: Required weekends.
Credit Cards: MC, V.
Handicap Access: Limited.

Seemingly in the middle of a very beautiful nowhere, Jocko's is legendary throughout the Central Coast for carrying high the torch of world-class beef. The interior decor — featuring paper placemats, hanging plants, and cattle brands burned into the woodwork — seems never to have left the '50s (when Jocko's was founded). Even the separate bar, well-worn by regulars, seems from another time. But the steaks are the real McCoy: witness the ranchlands right outside the front door. Massive Spencer steaks — thick, tender, and loaded with the sort of flavor that evokes nostalgia — start at around $7. And that includes serious french fries, homemade tomato salsa, and pots of succulent pinquito beans. Jocko's could convert even the most diehard vegetarian. Okay, so it's a couple miles from the coast. The drive through the rolling hills of the southern Salinas Valley is worth the detour.

San Luis Obispo

APPLE FARM
805/544-6100.
2015 Monterey St.
Open: Daily.
Price: Moderate.
Cuisine: American.
Serving: B, L, D.
Reservations: Recommended.
Credit Cards: AE, D, MC, V.
Handicap Access: Yes.

In a cutely decorated B&B complex with gardens, orchards, and a working water wheel, this welcoming country-style restaurant specializes in generous portions of down-home, fresh-cooked foods with all the trimmings. Fresh grilled fish specials of Louisiana catfish, halibut, and New Zealand orange roughy come, as do all dinners, with homemade soup or salad (or for a few dollars more, a trip to the farm-fresh salad bar), hot cornbread, vegetable, and choice of potatoes. Turkey pot pie, barbecued baby back ribs, even homemade meat loaf will please those look-ing for hearty, old-fashioned comfort foods. Apple desserts are the house sig-nature.

GARDENS OF AVILA
805/595-7365.
1215 Avila Beach Dr.
Open: Tues.–Sun.
Price: Moderate to Expen-
    sive.
Cuisine: California.
Serving: L, (except Sun.),
    D; Sun. Br.
Reservations: Recom-
    mended.
Credit Cards: AE, D, MC,
    V.
Handicap Access: Yes.

From the windows and terraces of this contem-porary restaurant in a popular inn, diners can feast on the view of oak groves and secluded min-eral water tubs dotting the hillside. Another feast awaits inside, showcasing local produce and wines, seafoods, and grilled meats. Appetizers like Mediterranean crab cakes served with ricotta penne or a Jamaican jerk vegetable quesadilla show off the kitchen's passion for multicultural flavor-ings. Roasted tri-tip and grilled chicken sand-wiches are on the lunch menu; dinner offers tiger prawns, duck confit calzone, and blackened snap-per with fried soft-shell crayfish. The smoke-free ambiance is relaxed, and the atmospheric harbors of Avila Beach are just down the road.

LINNAEAS CAFÉ
805/541-5888.
1110 Garden St.
Open: Daily.
Price: Inexpensive.
Cuisine: Eclectic vegetar-
    ian.
Serving: B, L (except Sun.).
Reservations: No.
Credit Cards: Cash only.
Handicap Access: Yes.

A true splash of local color is this funky, bohemian outpost of '60s Central Coast crossed with multiple ethnic cuisines. Charmingly primitive decor includes lots of artwork (both whimsical and serious offerings by local artists), a wooden order counter, tiny round tables for seat-ing, and a back garden patio for all-day reading over cups of the fine house café au lait. The menu is all over the map, but strikes gold, for example, in the soft Armenian crackerbread sandwiches filled with all manner of fresh goodies and cream cheese.
Homemade soups and salads are healthful and bountiful. A breakfast of Swedish rice pudding with steamed milk is a simple luxury. Big fat freshly made pies, tortes, breads, and carrot cakes complete the illusion of being in a friendly home kitchen. Music in the evenings serves up folk, light jazz, and classical as eclectic as the menu. Open until midnight.

RHYTHM CAFÉ
805/541-4048.
1040 Broad St.
Open: Daily.
Cuisine: California fusion.
Serving: B, L, D; Sun. Br.
Price: Inexpensive to Mod-
    erate.

Overlooking the landscaped terracing and native plantings along the sleepy San Luis Creek — where Father Junipero Serra established the area's wealthiest mission in the late 18th cen-tury — this attractive little bistro affords a peaceful view of ducks and waterfowl. An exciting menu concentrates on fresh produce and California atti-

Reservations: No.
Credit Cards: Cash, checks only.
Handicap Access: Yes.

tudes, with dashes of Asian, Mediterranean and East Indian stylings. Grilled oysters on the half shell are presented with mignonette and fiery wasabe soy sauce, and a Greek salad comes with grilled lamb on skewers. Entrées include baked whole trout with polenta, sautéed leeks, and pancetta; and seared fresh sea scallops with orange-ginger butter and crispy udon noodles. A nice place for light meals of soup, salad, and freshly made sourdough before crossing the creek and taking in the historic mission sights.

Shell Beach

F. MCLINTOCK'S SALOON & DINING HOUSE
805/773-1892.
750 Mattie Rd.
Open: Daily.
Price: Moderate to Expensive.
Cuisine: Steak, Seafood.
Serving: L, D; Sun. Br.
Reservations: Not accepted for dinner Fri. & Sat.
Credit Cards: D, MC, V.
Handicap Access: Yes.

A rip-roaring saloon and dining room aggressively adorned with hunting trophies and cattle ranch implements, McClintock's is a very busy place, filled with fun-loving regulars serious about their 30-ounce T-bones, buffalo burgers, or oak-barbecued ribs. For those who consider beef something that belongs in a pasture, this place also offers a huge menu of other goodies, like pan-fried rainbow trout, and chicken and seafood specialties. The bar is the sort of thing you'd expect to see John Wayne hanging around, and every night the action heats up with live country and western music. A major brunch of cowboy-sized proportions, with steak 'n' eggs, or biscuits and gravy, is served Sundays.

SANTA BARBARA COAST

Santa Barbara restaurants, while representing the full range of fine dining possibilities, can be at their best offering the flavors of the Central Coast's original settlers: Italian, Japanese, and Mexican (along with seafood restaurants). Settings range from the cozy to the opulent. Any of the following eateries provide fine introductions to Santa Barbara dining excellence.

Carpinteria

PACIFIC GRILL
805/684-7670.
3765 Santa Claus Lane.
Open: Daily.
Price: Inexpensive.
Cuisine: American burger.
Serving: B, L, D.

From the freeway, it looks like little more than a shack with a huge "Burgers" sign over the door (and, anyway, your attention is immediately caught by the startling sight down the road of a gigantic Santa Claus emerging from a rooftop chimney). This is Santa Claus Land, just south of Carpinteria, and you can pass it in the blink of an

Reservations: No.
Credit Cards: MC, V.
Handicap Access: Yes.

eye. But if you exit on Santa Claus Lane, you'll find a pristine, appealing spot serving the kind of hamburgers that make Americans wax nostalgic: delicious big burgers with high grade meat, wonderful buns, and all the pickles you want. This hot spot also does vegetarian garden burgers, as well as chicken, calamari, and even buffalo burgers. The folks here make a nice seafood salad with luscious greens and an excellent chili. California wines, beer, and fresh squeezed lemonade are served as accompaniments. Eat indoors or out on the patio overlooking a grassy tree-shaded oasis, a few hundred yards from a sea wall of boulders and the picture perfect beach beyond.

Santa Barbara

BRIGITTE'S
805/966-9676, 805/965-
6012 Fax.
1325 State St.
Open: Daily.
Price: Moderate to Expensive.
Cuisine: California.
Serving: L (except Sun.), D.
Reservations: No.
Credit Cards: MC, V.
Handicap Access: Yes.

Brigitte's is a favorite spot for Santa Barbarians who appreciate wonderful California cuisine at reasonable prices. A lively bistro-type restaurant, Brigitte's smoothly juggles style with casualness. The dining room uses plenty of white linen, but takes no reservations. The menu is brief, with a select handful of tantalizing salads, appetizers, pizzas, and pastas mixed with savory entrées from the grill. Classic dishes include watercress and arugula salad with fried brie, apples, and almonds; lamb sausage pizza with roasted garlic, wild mushrooms, and mozzarella; and tomato linguine with chicken, chilies, ginger, pine nuts, cilantro, and olive oil. The excellent list of local wines served at the wine bar features many reasonably priced offerings. Desserts are wonderful. (The adjoining deli and bakery serves coffee, baked goods, sandwiches, etc. from 7:30–6.)

**BROPHY BROTHERS
RESTAURANT &
CLAM BAR**
805/966-4418.
119 Harbor Way.
Open: Daily.
Price: Moderate.
Cuisine: Seafood.
Serving: L, D.
Reservations: No.
Credit Cards: AE, MC, V.
Handicap Access: No.

There's lots of waterfront hustle and bustle to take in from your table overlooking Santa Barbara's busy working harbor: fisherfolk mending nets, huge pelicans begging for scraps, and divers returning from morning abalone and sea urchin foraging. Brophy's best seats line the narrow wraparound verandah where you catch a fine view of the water. Popular with both visitors and local professionals, Brophy's can get very boisterous and very busy — so don't be in a hurry. Though it looks and feels like a rickety old wharf fish house, this place serves terrific, huge platters of a dozen fresh seafoods. Grilled local yellowtail arrives glazed with lime and oyster cream sauce and the grilled king salmon with fresh tarragon is superb. Naturally, myriad variations on oysters, clams, crab, and mussels are tops. The house cole slaw is a classic, as are the sturdy french fries and enormous seafood sandwiches. There's a substantial listing of wines made in the Santa Ynez Valley, and this place "will blacken anything."

CITRONELLE
805/963-0111.
901 Cabrillo Blvd.
Open: Daily.
Price: Expensive.
Cuisine: Contemporary
 California.
Serving: B, L, D.
Reservations: Recom-
 mended.
Credit Cards: AE, CB, D,
 DC, MC, V.
Handicap Access: Yes.

If you eat at Citronelle before dark, you can treat yourself to one of the most beautiful views in Santa Barbara. The restaurant is upstairs in a hotel, the Santa Barbara Inn, across the street from the wide, lovely vista of East Beach and the Santa Barbara harbor. Citronelle is the first offshoot of the famous Los Angeles eatery Citrus, owned by chef Michel Richard, and the menus are quite similar. Because it is so well known in Los Angeles, the restaurant is often peppered with visitors from there, not all of whom bring their best manners. The food can be spectacular — to look at as well as to taste. Richard is known for his delightful food trickery: tuna disguised as pepper steak, fried potatoes made to look like a bird's nest, delicious crunchy shrimp that resemble porcupines, and delicate noodles that turn out to be fashioned from turnips. Sauces are exceedingly tasty and light, derived from essences of vegetables, mushrooms, and fruits. The desserts alone are worth a visit, and no wonder: Richard first achieved culinary fame as a pastry chef.

At Citronelle, Santa Barbara's first cousin to the famed L.A. eatery Citrus, chef Michel Richard creates culinary masterpieces.

Kim Reierson

COLD SPRING TAVERN
805/967-0066.
5995 Stagecoach Rd. (off San Marcos Pass).
Open: Daily.
Price: Moderate.
Cuisine: Classic California.
Serving: B (weekends only), L, D.
Reservations: Recommended.
Credit Cards: AE, MC, V.
Handicap Access: Yes.

Heading over the pass from Santa Barbara towards the Santa Ynez Valley, about 14 miles from town you'll find the Cold Spring Tavern. It's been a way station for travelers for more than a century. These days, you're just as likely to see half a dozen motorcycles as you are a couple of Mercedeses parked under the great old elm and sycamore trees surrounding this historic shingled tavern. To step inside is to step back in time: huge stone fireplaces and kerosene lamps cast a glow on a veritable museum of memorabilia. The tavern is known for the quality of its steak and for its game dishes. Pepper steak, rabbit, and venison dishes are classic standards. Cold Spring chicken is a boneless breast of chicken with tavern bread stuffing, raisins, almonds, and a mushroom sherry sauce. Pasta and seafood dishes are generally found on the nightly specials. They're proud of their trio of chilies: the delicious Cold Spring chili, black bean chili with wild game, and a fine chili verde. (The spring water, known as "Hobo Soda," is delicious.)

DOWNEY'S
805/966-5006.
1305 State St.
Open: Tues.–Sun.
Price: Expensive.
Cuisine: California/Continental.
Serving: L (exc. weekends), D.
Reservations: Recommended.
Credit Cards: AE, MC, V.
Handicap Access: Yes.

Downey's has consistently been known as one of the finest restaurants in North America. John Downey, who trained as a chef in his native England, was one of the first to introduce nouvelle cuisine to Southern California in the late '70s and he has continued to be on the forefront of creativity and excellence in food. His restaurant, in a small State Street store front, is simple, spare, and pristine. Here you will find waiters reciting with reverence the brief, constantly evolving menu. Included might be dishes like venison sausage with fresh blackberries and spinach; Ojai squab with mulberries, thyme, and braised spring greens; or chayote squash with shallots and sherry. Be warned: midway through your meal, you will find yourself plotting how to return as soon as possible.

LA SUPER-RICA TAQUERIA
805/963-4940.
622 North Milpas.
Open: Daily.
Price: Inexpensive.
Cuisine: Mexican tacos al carbon.
Serving: L, D.

The inspiration came from the taquerias found on street corners in Mexico City serving *tacos al carbon*. There is no sign to mark the location here, although there is usually a line spilling out onto the sidewalk. Construction workers and celebrities mingle in patient, happy anticipation of the meal to come. You order at a window and find a table out in the canvas-covered patio. One bite and you'll

Reservations: No way.
Credit Cards: Cash only.
Handicap Access: Yes.

understand why this has been called "the best Mexican food in America." Small, thick corn tortillas, made before your eyes, are the backbone of the menu. Have them with utterly simple grilled steak or chicken, or try more elaborate versions with green peppers, chilies, onions, and cheese along with the meat. Three kinds of salsa include a fresh tomato salsa that's practically a salad. Look for specials on the blackboard, like *sopes* — little cups of crispy tortillas filled with chicken, melted cheese, avocado, and radish slices.

MOUSSE ODILE
805/962-5393.
18 East Cota St.
Open: Mon.–Sat.
Price: Moderate.
Cuisine: French home
  cooking.
Serving: B, L, D.
Reservations: Dinner only.
Credit Cards: AE, D, DC,
  MC, V.
Handicap Access: Yes.

One of the oldest and best French restaurants in Santa Barbara, Mousse Odile specializes in *cuisine bourgeoise* — classic French home cooking. If only we'd all had home cooking like this. The casual, comfortable restaurant has two spacious, light rooms with high ceilings, cheerful posters, and lots of big funky plants. The small back patio with high brick walls and a shady loquat tree could be anywhere in Paris. The restaurant is popular among the locals who return again and again for the good coffee, marvelous French bread, and some classic dishes available only here. At breakfast, French omelets are authentically tasty. Try the wonderful carrot soup and delicious celery Victor — a dish of cooked celery with capers, anchovies, and a cool fermiére sauce — during lunch visits. In the evening, the North African couscous with succulent lamb and vegetables is a palate-pleaser. Filet mignon and duck are excellent. There's a full bar, a fine wine list, and a selection of light dinners. The salad dressing is so good, the restaurant sells it to customers by the bottle.

Mousse Odile is a warm and casual rendezvous spot in Santa Barbara offering legendary breakfasts and appealing French country cooking.

Kim Reierson

OYSTERS
805/962-9888.
9 West Victoria St.
Open: Daily.
Price: Moderate.
Cuisine: California.
Serving: L (except Sun.), D.
Reservations: Recom-
    mended weekends.
Credit Cards: AE, D, MC,
    V.
Handicap Access: Yes.

Specializing in a small selection of exquisitely prepared fresh fish in lovely sauces, Oysters is a pearl of a restaurant. Simply decorated, with green carpeting and snowy linens, the slightly formal feeling of elegance is due to the style of service. The restaurant consists of one simple room and a pleasant patio, screened from the sidewalk by lush trees. From a tiny wine bar you can watch owner/chef Jerry Wilson concocting one of his ingenious, improvised sauces like tomato, basil, and lime salsa. Oysters offers a tiny but appealing selection of salads, pasta, and chicken, as well as meat dishes such as the pumpernickel crusted leg of lamb with artichoke cream. And, of course, oysters — served as shooters, or fried, grilled, and on the half shell — are the big draw. Oyster stew is smartly prepared with spinach and glazed shallots. With good reason, the restaurant has been described as "one of the 10 best bistros in California."

PALACE CAFÉ
805/966-3133.
8 East Cota St.
Open: Daily.
Price: Expensive.
Cuisine: Cajun, Creole,
    Caribbean.
Serving: D.
Reservations: For 5:30–6
    only on Fri., for 5:30
    only on Sat.
Credit Cards: AE, MC, V.
Handicap Access: Yes.

Local diners like the Palace because it has the feel of a big city hot spot. Out-of-towners like it because they've been clever enough to find the most happening place in town. This mostly Cajun, somewhat Creole, and slightly Caribbean restaurant specializes in a kind of wilder-than-life dinner experience that has proven to be a very successful formula for the owner/entrepreneurs. They employ a bunch of fresh, young waiters and waitresses who use a vigorous, upbeat, team approach to taking care of their customers. The food is rich, well-seasoned, generously proportioned, very fresh, and exotic. Southern bayou crawfish, flown in from Louisiana, appear in dishes like fried Cajun crayfish popcorn or crawfish étouffée. You'll also find classics such as Louisiana gumbo, oysters Rockerfeller, and blackened redfish. The ovens turn out four kinds of delicious muffins that are whisked to the table throughout the meal. You'll be stuffed but you'll still have to try the Louisiana bread pudding soufflé with whiskey cream sauce and the Florida key lime pie, both done to perfection. A sax soloist performs for those waiting in line on Saturday.

PIRANHA
805/965-2980.
714 State St.
Open: Tues.–Sun.
Price: Moderate to Expen-
    sive.

Santa Barbara has its share of excellent Japanese restaurants, but Piranha is one of the finest and most interesting. It's also a stunningly designed restaurant. Heather and Koji Numura met each other in a Japanese language class at University of

Cuisine: Japanese/California.
Serving: L (except Sun.), D.
Reservations: Recommended.
Credit Cards: AE, MC, V.
Handicap Access: Yes.

California, Santa Barbara, and their menu is as bicultural as their marriage. In addition to excellent sushi, they offer a selection of robata — wonderful Japanese-style grilled meats and vegetables. You'll also find eclectic salads like warm scallop and Asian pear salad or the house salad — a tasty mixture of cucumber, spicy sprouts, gobo, asparagus, broccoli, crab, and shrimp with a zesty dressing that blends Southwestern and Japanese flavors. Other choices at this delectable restaurant include angel hair pasta with exotic mushrooms, fresh mussels with saffron cream sauce, and a potato onion cheese pie.

STEAMERS
805/966-0260.
214 State St.
Open: Daily.
Price: Moderate.
Cuisine: Seafood.
Serving: L, D.
Reservations: Recommended for dinner Fri., Sat.
Credit Cards: AE, MC, V.
Handicap Access: Yes.

One of the hottest scenes on vivacious State Street, Steamers is more than just a pretty face. One of the area's top fresh seafood houses, it caters to a lively clientele attracted as much to the open-air patio dining as to the appealing interior brick walls and golden oak booths. From the exhibition kitchen come sizzling appetizers like Anchor Steam beer-battered scallops, Hawaiian ahi with pineapple-ginger salsa, the eponymous steamed clams, and some of the tastiest Buffalo-style chicken wings west of the Great Lakes. Daily specials offer half a dozen fresh seafood choices — mahi mahi, orange roughy, white sea bass, local mussels, king salmon, whatever's fresh. You can also find fine pastas, cioppino, and a great Caesar salad. Local Central Coast vintages are showcased by the glass and the house wine list — which won a 1992 *Wine Spectator* Award of Excellence — keeps pace with the cuisine. In addition to seafoods, Steamer's offers mesquite broiled steaks and contemporary chicken entrées as well, and the beer listing runs to over 50 domestic, imported, and handmade brews from California's fine young micro-breweries. The casual ambiance makes each patron feel instantly among friends.

21 VICTORIA
805/962-5222.
21 West Victoria St.
Open: Tues.–Sun.
Price: Moderate to Expensive.
Cuisine: Mediterranean/Pacific Rim.
Serving: D.
Reservations: Recommended weekends.

In a setting of California Victorian charm, chef Michael French (young, classically trained, and attractive, like everyone else working here) works magic in the open kitchen. He describes his artfully simple menu as "Mediterrasian" — combining flavors of the Riviera (notably France and Italy) with those of the Pacific Rim. You might find an exquisite appetizer like salmon pot stickers served with a duo of curry and ginger beet sauces. Or gnocchi in a sherry/shiitake mushroom reduction. Another must-taste is sesame scallops linguini with vegeta-

Credit Cards: AE, MC, V.
Handicap Access: Yes.

bles and coconut curry sauce. Roast quail appetizer is napped with a reduction of wild mushrooms. A simple grilled vegetable salad with basmati rice and braised greens is as memorable as a nine course dinner. Creamy desserts, like a fresh raspberry napoleon with house puff pastry and a billion calories, are bold and memorable. Live jazz Weds.–Sun. after 9:30pm.

WINE CASK
805/966-9463.
813 Anacapa St.
Open: Daily.
Price: Moderate to Expensive.
Cuisine: Bistro.
Serving: L (exc. weekends), D.
Reservations: Recommended weekends.
Credit Cards: AE, MC, V.
Handicap Access: Yes.

It began modestly as a wine shop that served soups and appetizers at the tasting bar. Ambition, hard work, and good taste have transformed the Wine Cask into a truly elegant restaurant. In the heart of the historic El Paseo, the restaurant has a lovely patio and fountain outdoors, and a stunning dining room with gorgeous hand-painted wooden beams and a huge ornate stone fireplace. It combines the best of Santa Barbara's architectural heritage with bistro-style contemporary cuisine. Dishes like roast Muscovy duck with orange-cumin sauce and ginger-scallion fried rice, or blackened spicy chicken roll with spinach, avocado, sour cream, and cilantro tomato relish are examples of the deft, sophisticated blending of cultural flavors. Smoked salmon is a classic here. Desserts like warm caramelized pear orange sabayon are magic, and the wine selection is marvelous. The adjacent wine store stocks more than 2000 selected wines and offers wine tastings.

Santa Ynez Valley

BALLARD STORE
805/688-5319.
2449 Baseline, Ballard.
Open: Weds.–Sun.
Price: Moderate to Expensive.
Cuisine:
    American/French.
Serving: D; Sun. Br.
Reservations: Recommended weekends.
Credit Cards: MC, V.
Handicap Access: Yes.

A conspicuous landmark in this minuscule hamlet, the Ballard Store is a 1930s grocery filled with rural ambiance and the sweet smells of fresh bread. The restaurant is something of a religious shrine to locals who treat out-of-town guests visiting the Santa Ynez viticultural region to its heavenly fare. The eclectic menu offers an early bistro supper featuring sturdy presentations of freshness from local farms and gardens, a prix fixe dinner menu, and à la carte selections. Among seafood options, the cioppino has won many converts, and the duck and beef entrées are presented with a delicious French accent. The champagne Sunday brunch is bountiful and wildly popular. No visit to the wine country is complete without a visit to this rustic gourmet outpost.

MATTEI'S TAVERN
805/688-4820.
Hwy. 154, Los Olivos.
Price: Moderate to Expensive.
Cuisine: Regional American.
Open: Daily.
Serving: L, D.
Reservations: Recommended.
Credit Cards: MC, V.
Handicap Access: Yes.

This gracious roadhouse built in 1886 was a stagecoach overnight stop linking Santa Barbara with outposts north, and is still steeped in vintage Western ambiance. The long front verandah is draped with wisteria; the huge bar, fireplace, and fir floors are originals; and the wicker sunroom and brick patio provide atmospheric dining surrounded by lovely gardens and a magnificent bower of heirloom yellow roses. Still a lure for locals and visitors alike (who come for the tavern action as much as the fine regional dining), Mattei's has seen its share of film world celebrities, especially during its days as an overnight hideaway. Mickey Rooney and Ava Gardner were married here, and John Barrymore rented one of the estate cottages each summer during his heyday. Today, fine al fresco lunches are a top draw, especially given the prospect of a sumptuous charbroiled burger with world-class french fries, or that top-drawer homemade chicken pot pie you always imagined must exist somewhere. Contemporary salads, fresh seafoods, and appropriately Western-style steaks complete the bill of fare. The hot apple crisp with vanilla ice cream is the stuff diets are destroyed for. Set in the middle of Santa Ynez Valley wine country, Mattei's boasts a fine listing of locally made vintages and the service is warm and attentive.

Montecito

ACACIA
805/969-8600.
1212 Coast Village Rd.
Open: Daily.
Price: Moderate to Expensive
Cuisine: Regional American.
Serving: B weekends, L, D.
Reservations: Recommended weekends.
Credit Cards: AE, MC, V.
Handicap Access: Yes.

A stylish, comfortable restaurant on Montecito's Coast Village Road, Acacia has all the earmarks of an eatery on the cutting edge of food trends. What is nouvelle here is the urge to serve traditional American fare with surprising twists. You can order a world-class rendition of matzo ball soup (and the hot bagels come with crème fraîche), or a weekend breakfast plate of scrambled eggs on a bed of lightly grilled pasta and baby spinach leaves. Acacia does wonderful things with onions, from the stewed, marinated onions that substitute for butter on the table to the delectable fried lemon pepper rings. Expect a generous, excellent hamburger and an epicurean roasted chicken that comes with succulent vegetables. Lamb T-bone with garlic mashed potatoes provides serious comfort. Desserts like chocolate covered Boston cream pie are sweet extravaganzas of pure Americana.

FOUR SEASONS BILTMORE
805/969-2261.

Built by the ocean as a luxurious resort hotel in 1927, the Four Seasons Biltmore continues to strive for and even surpass the fine standards of its

1260 Channel Dr.
Open: Daily.
Price: Expensive.
Cuisine: Contemporary
  multicultural.
Serving: B, L, D; Sun. Br.
Reservations: Recom-
  mended.
Credit Cards: AE, DC, MC,
  V.
Handicap Access: Yes.

glorious, patrician past. You won't find a staff more eager to please, anywhere. The lavish dining rooms look out over the sparkling Pacific, while the food holds its own against a magnificent backdrop of Mediterranean-Spanish colonial grandeur. Despite the fact that the hotel routinely serves hundreds upon hundreds of meals each day, the food is imaginative, tasteful, and impeccably fresh. Under the guidance of chef Carrie Nahabedian, the finest ingredients are procured from across the continent for menus that change seasonally and accommodate a wide range of tastes. In addition to food magazine cover breakfasts, ranging from designer hearty to healthfully correct, you can find terrific lunch salads like curly endive with goat cheese croutons, garlic, and smoked bacon, or enjoy a sumptuous Channel Island swordfish sandwich with ratatouille mayonnaise. Feast on tangy linguini with rock shrimp, lemon zest, and chervil for dinner. Save room for fantasy desserts.

MONTECITO CAFÉ
805/969-3392.
1295 Coast Village Rd.
Open: Daily.
Price: Moderate.
Cuisine: California.
Serving: L, D.
Reservations: Limited
  number accepted.
Credit Cards: AE, MC, V.
Handicap Access: Yes.

It's often difficult to get into the Montecito Café without a reservation, for it has struck just the right orchestration of glamorous decor, excellent food, and reasonable prices. Residents of exclusive Montecito love to go out and look good; they also appreciate good value for their money and this is where they get a chance to do both, even if it means eating in a spot that can be terribly busy and somewhat noisy. Located in the Montecito Inn, which dates from the '20s (see *Lodging*), it is close to both the beach and the freeway. One of the two dining rooms of the restaurant has a wall of plate glass, a three-tiered fountain, and a lush garden. The goat cheese pancake with smoked salmon, sour cream, and golden caviar appetizer brings people back again and again. So does a marvelous dish of grilled chicken with a creamy sauce of tomato, red onions, and Anaheim chilies.

PANE E VINO
805/969-9274.
1482 East Valley Rd.
Open: Daily.
Price: Moderate to Expen-
  sive.
Cuisine: Northern Italian.
Serving: L (except Sun.),
  D.
Reservations: Recom-
  mended for dinner.

The craze for Italian food has spawned a number of excellent, successful Italian restaurants in this area, but Pane e Vino was the first to bring its truly authentic Northern Italian food here. It continues to be the finest purveyor of one of the tastiest cuisines in the world. It's supposed to be a simple trattoria, adorned with appetizing displays of cheeses and salamis and shelves of Chianti and olive oil. But its wealthy, loyal Montecito clientele

Credit Cards: No.
Handicap Access: Yes.

give it an exclusive tone. More than half the diners sit out on a heated patio overlooking a parking lot that isn't particularly scenic. And because it is so small, when it's busy, it feels crowded. But the crowd inevitably includes movie stars. And the food is great. The much copied cappellini with fresh tomatoes and basil comes with more garlic and intense flavor here than anywhere. Fish is always superb, herbed roasted chicken is delicious, and the risotto special is highly recommended, especially when it comes with mushrooms. Service is *molto Italiano* — that is, charming and sometimes infuriating.

**THE STONEHOUSE AT
  SAN YSIDRO RANCH**
805/969-5046.
900 San Ysidro Lane.
Open: Daily.
Price: Expensive.
Cuisine: Regional Ameri-
  can.
Serving: B (exc. Sun.), L
  (exc. Sun.), D; Sun. Br.
Reservations: Recom-
  mended exc. for break-
  fast.
Credit Cards: AE, MC, V.
Handicap Access: Yes.

Nestled against the bucolic foothills of Montecito, the luxurious, charming San Ysidro Ranch is known as a hideaway for the rich and famous. The sandstone restaurant was once a lemon packing plant, and its historic character remains intact despite extensive remodeling and an apparently unlimited decorating budget. The "regional American cooking" of chef Gerard Thompson inspires a menu that reads like a travel diary of Americana, from Pennsylvania Dutch braised lamb shank with cornmeal mush to cedar planked salmon prepared in a style used by Native Americans. The menu changes constantly to take advantage of seasonal ingredients. The restaurant also caters very tastefully to health and weight conscious patrons. There's a lovely deck for dining and a cozy, lavish bar downstairs where you can also order a meal.

CHAPTER SIX

Grape Expectations
WINERIES

Wines of California . . . inimitable fragrance and soft fire . . . and the wine of bottled poetry.

— Robert Louis Stevenson

Well over three-quarters of the wine made in the United States is produced in California and, of that, the most well-known hails from Napa and Sonoma. But, increasingly, some of the most intriguing California wines are being generated from small wineries along the Central Coast. Thanks to the compactness of these facilities — most are so small their wines rarely leave their areas — winemakers here are famed for their abilities to grow grapes and create wines by hand.

Roland & Karen Muschenetz

Richard Sanford shows off the award-winning grapes at his Sanford Vineyard in the southern section of the Central Coast.

Grape-growing micro-climates weave throughout the region's mountains and sunny coastal slopes, each unique collaboration of soil, climate, and varietal creating intriguing variations in the final products. Thanks to mild temperatures, fog-cooled evenings, and a long, dry growing season, Central Coast wines are celebrated for intensity of flavor, length of life, and elegance of structure.

With the need for sacramental wines used in celebrating the Catholic Mass, wine production arrived in California with the Franciscan missionaries in the late 18th century. After experiments with native grapes proved unacceptable, European vinifera vines were imported for cultivation. By the 1850s, under the

Prominent Varietals

Certain European vinifera grape varieties have been found to prosper famously when catalyzed by Central Coast soils and climate. Producing the most celebrated regional wines are the **Chardonnay** and **Cabernet Sauvignon** grape. **Chardonnay** is the great white wine of French Burgundy, which produces a dry, buttery, apple-like wine whose depth and fruit are heightened by oak aging. **Cabernet Sauvignon**, which produces the celebrated red wine of Bordeaux, is full-bodied, fragrant, often with tones of cherries and bell pepper, and is the top red varietal produced in California.

Zinfandel is a vigorous red grape — one of the earliest planted in California — that produces a bold wine with berry-like aroma. **Pinot Noir**, the Burgundian red wine grape, is finding its way to some fine wines of dry and elegant structure. The spicy Alsatian **Gewurztraminer** wine is another popular California white varietal, as is the fruity, faintly grassy **Sauvignon Blanc**, long used to create the white wines of Bordeaux and the Loire. Rhône varietals — **Syrah** and **Petite Sirah** — are on the ascendance in the Central Coast, their velvety and complex wines gaining increasing attention.

influence of European viticultural entrepreneurs, California winemaking had expanded up and down the state and was a thriving industry during the last half of the 19th century. New World winemaking survived a phylloxera infestation in the 1880s, and the loss of vast cellarings in the infamous earthquake of 1906, only to be dealt a near fatal blow by Prohibition. California winemaking rebuilt and reinvented itself following the Repeal Act of 1933.

Essential Wine Tasting Protocol

There is nothing pretentious about wine tasting on the Central Coast, an activity enthusiastically pursued by weekend visitors to the area's many small tasting rooms. Tasting room staff are happy to guide the novice through winemaking techniques and tips for maximizing appreciation. Like all collaborations of nature and art, wine should be enjoyed by all the senses.

Before tasting, pause to notice the color and clarity of the wine. Hold the glass up to the light to admire its full luster and — ideally — clarity. Rotate the wine gently in the glass and then smell deeply, noticing the bouquet that often will be reminiscent of a wide range of fruits, flowers, and earthiness. Now you're ready to take a small sip. Trilling it against the roof of the mouth — this may take practice — hels to achieve its maximum palate contact. Here's where the wine shows off its range of sweetness, tartness, body, and, when swallowed, its finish.

Clearing the palate with water or bread is crucial for sampling successive wines. And those strategically placed buckets are there for a reason. Spitting out excess wine will insure that both you and your palate stay intact during multiple tastings. If you plan to make an afternoon of it, it's a wise idea to designate a driver who sips nothing stronger than juice or mineral water during a series of winery visits.

Recognizing that the Central Coast region boasted growing conditions similar to those of the great European viticultural centers of the Rhine, Bordeaux, and Burgundy, University of California, Davis experts began rediscovering prime vineyard planting areas along the eastern slopes of the coast ranges, in the Santa Cruz, Monterey, and San Luis Obispo areas, and in the Santa Ynez Valley behind Santa Barbara. The most recent renaissance of wine-growing interest in the state came with a trend in the 1960s away from mega-agriculture. In a resulting boom of micro-wineries in the 1970s, the Central Coast of California came into its own, claiming the attention both of the region's population and international aficionados.

Santa Cruz Mountains Wine Country

When Mission Santa Cruz was founded, the missionaries planted river benchlands below the church with the sweet Spanish grape required for wines used in the Catholic Mass. Commercial winemaking in the area began in 1863 with the first plantings of grapes by brothers George and John Jarvis in the Vine Hill district near the 2000-foot summit of the Santa Cruz Mountains. By 1870, over 300 acres of the mountains had been dedicated to wine grapes, and there were over a dozen winemakers in business in the Santa Cruz County by 1875.

By the late 1880s, three respected vintners — Santa Cruz Mountain Wine Company, Mare Vista, and the Ben Lomond Wine Company — were sending wines to competitions around the country and the world. However, natural disasters, depression, world war and, finally, Prohibition effectively uprooted the young industry.

Then, intent on the rural splendor of the redwoods and seaside, expatriates from urban areas and Silicon Valley decided that doing their own thing would include winemaking. The region has long attracted mavericks, from 1940s forefathers Chaffee Hall and Martin Ray — early believers in the power of the modern premium wine industry — to "Rhône Ranger" Randall Grahm in the mid-'80s. Since the 1970s, Santa Cruz Mountains wines have gained in finesse and renown, fueled by a boom of over two dozen almost exclusively family-run micro-wineries that capture the unique *terroir* of the stony mountain soil and the dry fog-cooled growing season. Latter-day pioneers like David Bruce, Ken Burnap, Dexter Ahlgren, and Robert Roudon were joined in the '80s by a host of new entrepreneurs. Exceptional Chardonnays, Gewurztraminers, Rieslings, and Cabernets are already emerging from this young *appellation*, showing the regional style of elegance and long-lived structure.

BARGETTO WINERY
Winemaker: Paul Wolford.
408/475-2258, 408/475-2664 Fax.
3535 North Main St.,
   Soquel.

The Santa Cruz Mountains' oldest winery has a spacious brick tasting room on Main Street packed with history from pre-Prohibition days when the enterprising Bargetto brothers kept frontier restaurants well-stocked with sturdy red wine

The tasting room at Bargetto Winery hosts guests from all over the world.

Covello & Covello

Tours: 11, 2 Mon.–Fri.
Tastings: 10–5 daily.

based on Italian traditions. Today, a third generation is in charge of the large facility. Visitors can
picnic at an outdoor courtyard overlooking Soquel
Creek. Producing over 30,000 cases annually, Bar-
getto is the largest winery in the area, enjoying a renaissance of excellence on
the elegant structures of its Chardonnay and Cabernet Sauvignon. Don't leave
without sampling the winery's distinctive mead and fruit wines, including the
luscious olallieberry, raspberry, and apricot, distributed under the Chaucer's
label. Another tasting and sales room is on Monterey's Cannery Row.

**BONNY DOON VINE-
YARD**
Winemaker: Randall
Grahm.

The unmistakable sense of adventure of world-
acclaimed winemaker Randall Grahm are
everywhere apparent at this rustic, mountain top
winery with state-of-the-art equipment. The vine-

The Rhône Ranger of Bonny Doon Vineyards, maverick winemaker Randall Grahm, helped put Santa Cruz area wines on the map.

Jock McDonald

408/425-3625, 425-3856 Fax.
10 Pine Flat Rd./PO Box 8376, Santa Cruz.
Tours: By appointment only.
Tastings: Noon–5 Fri.–Mon., noon–5 daily exc. Tues. in summer.

yards here are planted with Grenache, Mouverdre, Syrah, Marsanne, and Roussane, an indication of Grahm's early interest in the Rhône region of France. Innovation here yields velvety dessert wines, award-wining Chardonnays, and Italian varietal white wines, as well as the occasional eau de vie and distilled brandy. Darling of the international media, Grahm — dubbed "America's most avant garde winemaker" by *Connoisseur Magazine* — produces vintage after astonishing vintage of distinctive wines, highlighted by clever labels that play on Old World classics.

DEVLIN WINE CELLARS
Winemaker: Chuck Devlin.
408/476-7288, 479-9043 Fax.
3801 Park Ave./PO Box 728, Soquel.
Tours: No.
Tastings: Noon–5 weekends.

A 30-acre winery at the end of an idyllic country road, Devlin is run by Chuck and Cheryl Devlin and their young son Thomas, whose artwork has graced labels of vintages past. Critically acclaimed for a succession of fine Chardonnays, Merlots, and Cabernets, the winery excels in its emphasis upon premium wines, all affordably priced. The estate overlooks redwood forests and the Monterey Bay, and is a favorite spot for picnics and private parties.

Chuck and Cheryl Devlin of Devlin Wine Cellars are part of the youthful infusion of Santa Cruz area winemaking talent.

HALLCREST VINEYARDS
Winemaker: John Schumacher.
408/335-4441, 800/491-9463 CA, 408/335-4450 Fax.

B egun in the 1940s by post-Prohibition winemaking pioneer Chaffee Hall, the winery created legendary Cabernet Sauvignon and Riesling from its estate grapes, many of which survive today. University of California, Davis–trained winemaker John Schumacher carries on the tradition of exquisite White Rieslings produced from

379 Felton Empire Rd., Felton.
Tours: By appointment only.
Tastings: 11–5:30 daily.

those fabled estate grapes. Full-bodied Zinfandels and crisp, buttery Chardonnays also are specialties of this small, handmade wine facility. Recently, the winery has begun bottling a line of certified organic, sulfite-free wines under the Organic Wine Works label. The sunny vineyards overlook the ancient redwoods of Henry Cowell State Park. The wooden cottage tasting room, picnic lawns, and cellars form the background for a superb day of wine tasting and Hallcrest's star-studded outdoor musical concert series, which regularly brings some of the top names in jazz, blues, and acoustic genres to the terraced lawns.

OBESTER WINERY
Winemakers: Paul & Sandy Obester.
415/726-9463, 415/726-7074 Fax.
12341 San Mateo Rd. (Hwy. 92), Half Moon Bay.
Tours: No.
Tastings: 10-5 daily.

From this small, ranch-style winery at the foot of the mountains in the seaside town of Half Moon Bay come exceptional varietals. The handsome tasting room has long been a fixture on any day trip to this charming village, where delightfully floral Gewurztraminers, toasty Chardonnays, and elegantly structured Sauvignon Blancs star. Most of the label's product can be sampled at the tasting room, which also offers specialty food items.

ROUDON-SMITH VINEYARDS
Winemaker: Bob Roudon.
408/438-1244, 408/438-5123 Fax.
2364 Bean Creek Rd., Scotts Valley.
Tours: By appointment only.
Tastings: 11-4 Sat., by appointment Sun.

Wines designed to be partnered with fine food are the specialties of this award-winning house, best exemplified by a full-bodied Zinfandel, elegantly structured Estate Chardonnay, and Santa Cruz Mountain Pinot Noir. Keeping production down to around 10,000 cases a year, Texan-born Roudon likes to "stand back and let the grapes do the work," a technique that has produced vintages

The winemaking quartet of Jim and June Smith and Bob and Annamaria Roudon have made Roudon-Smith wines outstanding.

packed with true varietal characteristics. A visit to the winery takes visitors through some memorable Santa Cruz Mountains scenery.

SOQUEL VINEYARD
Winemakers: Peter Bargetto, Paul Bargetto, Jon Morgan.
408/462-9045.
7880 Glen Haven Rd., Soquel.
Tours: By appointment only.
Tastings: 10:30–3:30 Sat., by appointment other days.

The focus here is on small quantities of handmade wines showcasing the intensely flavored grapes of the region. Still in its infancy, this vibrant young enterprise has already attracted much attention in regional and national competitions — the Cabernets and Chardonnays are justly acclaimed, but the Pinot Noir is especially appealing.

UC Davis-trained winemakers Steve and Pam Storrs specialize in a line of Chardonnays created exclusively with Santa Cruz appellation grapes.

Paul Schraub

STORRS WINERY
Winemakers: Stephen & Pamela Storrs.
408/458-5030, 408/458-0464 Fax.
Old Sash Mill #35, 303 Potrero St., Santa Cruz.
Tours: By appointment only.

The emphasis here is on a series of Chardonnays created from exclusively Santa Cruz Mountain grapes. And, given the widely diverse topography of selected vineyards, the results are as distinct as they are distinctive. The small tasting room regularly attracts inquiring wine buffs and the winemakers are always available to explain, discuss, and compare notes. In the winery, housed behind the sleek tasting area, all the sorcery of winemaking — from blending to cellaring — is on view at a glance. Don't miss the complex, toasty Chardonnay from Gaspar Vineyard, the crisp Vanamanutagi Vineyards Chardonnay, and the supple Merlots.

Other Santa Cruz Mountains Wineries

Ahlgren Vineyard (408/338-6071; 20320 Hwy. 9, Boulder Creek) With grapes from the Santa Cruz *appellation*, Dexter Ahlgren turns out some of the most renowned Cabernet Sauvignons and Semillons in California. Sixteen consecutive vintages of Ahlgren Chardonnay from Monterey's Ventana Vineyard have taken countless awards for their rich, clean bouquet and flavors. The handmade approach and the low volume of production makes these wines coveted by serious collectors. Tours and tastings Sat. noon–4.

Aptos Vineyard (408/688-3856; 7278 Mesa Dr., Aptos) Extremely small bottlings of Pinot Noir, grown on winemaking county Judge John Marlo's small estate, are evocative of the fabled vintages of Burgundy. Regularly honored at California's top competitions, these Pinots are so rare they seldom find their way any further than the cellars of local admirers. Worth looking for when you're in the area. No tours or tastings.

Cinnabar Vineyards (408/741-5858, 408/741-5860 Fax; 23000 Congress Springs Rd., Saratoga) On the eastern slopes of the Santa Cruz Mountains overlooking the Santa Clara Valley, winemaker Tom Mudd's very small facility specializes in limited production of estate-bottled Cabernet Sauvignon and Chardonnay. The wines are aged in French oak in three underground, naturally cooled caves at this beautiful 24-acre vineyard and winery. Arrange visits in advance; tastings on one Saturday open house a month.

Crescini Wines (408/462-1466; PO Box 216, Soquel) Premium Cabernet Franc, Cabernet Sauvignon and Petite Sirah are the specialty of this tiny, family-operated winery located in the redwoods of the Soquel Valley. Headed by winemaker Richard Crescini, it produces under 1000 cases annually. No tours, but tastings are available by appointment only.

Equinox (408/338-2646; 290 Igo Way, Boulder Creek) Barry Jackson produces a Methode Champagne Sparkling Wine that is both rounded and austerely dry. No tours; tastings at select public functions.

McHenry Vineyard (916/756-3202; in Bonny Doon, mailing address is 330 Eleventh St., Davis, 95616) From a small, redwood-encircled winery in the Bonny Doon mountain top area, UC Davis anthropologist/winemaker Henry McHenry turns out lustrous Pinot Noirs from estate grapes planted on 4 acres 5 miles from the ocean. No tastings; November tours for mailing list recipients.

Nicasio Vineyards (408/423-1073; 483 Nicasio Way, Soquel) Small quantities of Cabernet Sauvignon, Chardonnay, Riesling, and Zinfandel handmade from carefully selected vineyards come from Dan Wheeler's small facility, one of the first of the new generation of post-Prohibition wineries. Wines are aged naturally in an enormous sandstone cave hollowed out of the nearby hillside. Tours and tastings by appointment only.

Salamandre Cellars (408/685-0321, 408/685-1860 Fax; 108 Don Carlos Dr.,

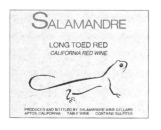

Aptos) Always intriguing, winemaker Wells Shoemaker delights in innovative blends, such as the intensely floral White Riesling and Muscat Canelli called White Dove. Every inch of this minuscule operation is covered by hand, from selective picking of grapes, to crushing, bottling, and lugging of boxes. Salamandre wines may be found in restaurants and wine stores throughout Santa Cruz

County, and the label — with the embossed emblem of the long-toed epony-mous salamander — is a regional keepsake. Tours and tastings by mailing list invitation only.

Santa Cruz Mountains Vineyard proprietor Ken Burnap pio-neered the Central Coast boom in handmade wines.

Dan Coyro

Santa Cruz Mountain Vineyard (408/426-6209; 2300 Jarvis Rd., Santa Cruz) Ken Burnap's winery site, originally planted by John Jarvis in 1863, is one of the oldest vineyard lands in the Santa Cruz Mountain *appellation*, offering southern-exposure hillside terrain and well-drained, rather poor soil that encourages deep roots and intensity of flavor. Vines are hand-tended and hand-harvested, and the labor-intensive production techniques reach fruition in powerful red wines. The Merlots are pure velvet and the Pinot Noirs memo-rable. Tours and tastings by appointment only.

Silver Mountain Vineyard (408/353-2278; PO Box 3636, Santa Cruz) Jerold O'Brien's small win-ery turns out stylish Chardonnay from its estate vineyard at the summit of the Santa Cruz Moun-tains in an area planted by early viticulturists. Other offerings are Cabernet and Zinfandel. Tours and tastings by appointment only.

Trout Gulch Vineyards (408/688-4380; 3875 Trout Gulch Rd., Aptos) Winemaker Bernie Tur-geon specializes in Chardonnay and Pinot Noir. No tours or tastings.

Zayante Vineyards (408/335-7992, 408/335-5770; 420 Old Mount Rd., Felton) Currently expanding vineyards at a historic old hilltop ranch where the winery is housed, winemaker Greg Nolten creates just under 1000 cases annually entirely by hand. The first estate Chardonnay was released in 1992. Available

only at the winery, it is a complex, generously flavored beauty. Also quite special is a spicy Petite Sirah. Tours by appointment only; anniversary celebration on the third weekend in May.

Vintners' Passport Weekend

Four Saturdays a year, the two dozen wineries of the Santa Cruz Mountains collaborate on an "open house" that stretches from the summit of the redwood mountains to hilltops overlooking the ocean in south Santa Cruz County. Many of the tiniest facilities, rarely open to the public, have an opportunity to show off their finest and the weekends allow visitors a chance to meet the winemakers, tour cellars, and sample wines unavailable anywhere else. For dates and locations, contact Mary Liz Cortese at the **Santa Cruz Mountains Winegrowers Association** (408/479-9463; PO Box 3000, Santa Cruz).

Monterey Wine Country

Growers here solved the apparent climactic drawbacks of the dry, breezy valley by planting vines parallel to the prevailing winds, and supply vast quantities of grapes for huge operations like Mirassou, Almaden, Paul Masson, and Wente Brothers.

Given the coolness of this growing area — whose temperatures are the lowest in the Central Coast region thanks to Salinas Valley breezes and the proximity to ocean fogs — Monterey grapes luxuriate in a lengthy ripening process. The leading white grapes — Chardonnay, Sauvignon Blanc and Gewurztraminer — respond especially well to these conditions with pronounced intensity and length of vintage life. Though a relative newcomer to the California winemaking scene, Monterey is earning increasing respect for its grapes and locally produced wines.

CHALONE VINEYARD
Winemaker: Michael
  Michaud.
408/678-1717.
Hwy. 146 & Stonewall
  Canyon Rd., Soledad.
Tours: 11–4 weekends, by
  appointment weekdays.
Tastings: 11–4 weekends,
  by appointment weekdays.

World-famous for its lusty and elegant Chardonnays and Pinot Noirs, Chalone cultivates its 100-plus acres of grapes at a 2000-ft. elevation on the east face of the Coast Range. Founded in 1969 by influential winemaker Richard Graff, Chalone was an early leader in coaxing Burgundian-style wines out of the coastal climate. Today, the winery is part of an empire that includes Edna Valley Vineyard, Carmenet, and Acacia wineries.

Graff's never-ending quest for the great California Pinot Noir continues to be well received, and Chalone's Chardonnays are regarded among the top made in the country.

CHATEAU JULIEN WINERY
Winemaker: William Anderson.
408/624-2600, 408/624-6138 Fax.
8940 Carmel Valley Road, Carmel.
Tours: By appointment only.
Tastings: 8:30–5 weekdays, 11–5 weekends.

This award-winning winery is ten minutes from Carmel on Carmel Valley Road. Tastings of its splendid Chardonnays and Cabernet Sauvignons are available at a glittering French-style country chateau, complete with copper flashing, stained glass, and antique furnishings. Set in the heart of the Old Spanish California ambiance of Carmel Valley, the winery is famous for full-bodied, accessible vintages of complex, spicy Chardonnay and satiny Merlots. The varietals — all made from Monterey County grapes — also include a delightful blend of Semillon and Sauvignon Blanc, called Meritage White. Look for the 1989 Cabernet Sauvignon that took a double gold in the 1993 San Francisco Fair National Wine Competition.

CLONINGER CELLARS
Winemaker: John Estell.
408/758-1686, 408/758-9769 Fax.
1645 River Rd., Gonzales.
Tours: By appointment only.
Tastings: 10:30–6 Thurs.–Mon.

A new, small winery, Cloninger Cellars has already won acclaim for its first release, a 1988 full-bodied, creamy Chardonnay. The first vintage of this splendid partner for fine dining was a very limited 1000-case release. The intention is to increase the vineyard size from its current 10 acres to 200-plus acres, with a production focus on Cabernet Sauvignon and Pinot Noir, in addition to the award-winning Chardonnays.

JEKEL VINEYARDS
Winemaker: Joel Burnstein.
408/674-5522, 408/674-3769 Fax.
40155 Walnut Ave., Greenfield.
Tours: By appointment only.
Tastings: 10–5 daily.

In less than 20 years, an original planting of 140 acres of vineyards east of the Coast Range has resulted in an established winery producing upwards of 80,000 cases of fine wines each year. The superb Chardonnays and Cabernet Sauvignons are local legends. A red barn houses the main facility and the tasting room arbor is draped with wisteria. Jekel bottles Cabernet Franc — long the favored blending grape of Bordeaux-style Cabernet Sauvignons — as a varietal unto itself, with berry- and pepper-laden results. The extensive grounds, tasting and sales rooms are open to wanderers. The tasting room atmosphere is friendly and helpful and the sampling pours are generous; picnicking under the wisteria arbors is a treat.

MONTEREY VINEYARD
Winemaker: Phil Fran-
scioni.
408/675-2316, 408/675-
3019.
800 South Alta St., Gonzales.
Tours: 11–3 on the hour
Thurs.–Sun, noon, 1, 3
Mon.–Wed.
Tastings: 10–5 daily.

Owned by the giant Seagrams Company, this high-profile winery produces sturdy varietals and blends on its 1100 acres in the southern Salinas Valley. This is a large, half-million-case per year operation; the lavishly appointed Spanish-style tasting center boasts an exhibition gallery and park-like grounds, with ponds and geese, and picnic tables on the lawn. The tour provides a close look at high-production winemaking techniques. The specialties of the house, including red and white blends, as well as a range of Chardonnays, Pinot Noirs, and Cabernets, are all astonishingly affordable.

VENTANA VINEYARDS
Winemaker: Rick Boyer.
408/372-7415, 800/237-
8846, 408/655-1855.
2999 Monterey-Salinas
Hwy. 68, Monterey.
Tours: No.
Tastings: Noon–5 daily.

Grapes flourish in this 400-acre vineyard planted in gravely soil on the arid banks of the Arroyo Seco River, one of the single most award-winning vineyard properties in the country. The wines are excellent, notably the engagingly fruity Sauvignon Blanc and peppery Cabernet Sauvignon. The charming stonework tasting headquarters and grounds are elegantly rustic. One of the top growers in California; Ventana grapes invariably find their way to the most prestigious vintages from this *appellation*.

Other Monterey Wineries

Bernardus Winery (408/659-4300, 408/626-9313 Fax; 21810 Parrot Ranch Rd., Carmel Valley) Tucked into the rolling ranchlands of Carmel Valley, this new operation directs its attention to the reds and whites of France's fabled Bordeaux. Winemaker Don Blackburn produces especially notable Cabernet Franc, Cabernet Sauvignon, Merlot, and Sauvignon Blanc vintages from its estate Jamesburg vineyards. Tours and tastings by appointment only.

Durney Vineyard (408/625-5433; Cachagua Rd., Carmel Valley) Over 80 acres of estate vines planted over the past 25 years are fed by underground springs and grown without the use of herbicides or pesticides at this 1200-ft. elevation winery in a beautiful Carmel Valley side pocket of the Santa Lucia Mountains. Winemaker Peter Watson-Graff creates the award-winning wines from the fruit of estate vineyards, over half of which are of planted to the superior Cabernet Sauvignon grape. Durney's excellent varietals are showcased at area restaurants and wine stores. No tours or tastings.

Georis Winery (408/625-6731, 408/625-0409 Fax; PO Box 702, Carmel) Winemaker Walter Georis, who owns Carmel's renowned Casanova Restaurant — justly praised both for its food and wine list — makes nothing but Merlots. But what Merlots they are. All are prize winners and releases average around 500 cases. If you can find a bottle at a Monterey Peninsula restaurant or wine shop, snatch it up. Tours and tastings by appointment only.

Joullian Vineyards (408/659-2800; 20300 Cachagua Rd., Carmel Valley) The Joullian and Sias families, with winemaker Ridge Watson, devote over three-quarters of their vineyard land to the noble varietals of Bordeaux, resulting in an array of complex Cabernets, Merlots, and Sauvignon Blanc vintages. Their vineyards include 655 acres of 1400-ft. elevation benchland in the heart of the Carmel Valley viticultural *appellation*, and 40 acres of rocky Arroyo Seco loam. Tours and tastings by appointment only.

Lockwood Vineyard (408/753-1424, 800/753-1424, 408/753-1238 Fax; PO Box 1997, Salinas) In only a decade, estate-grown grapes from this winery in southern Monterey wine country have turned out bold, gold-medal vintages. Sales are strictly through mail order. Small amounts of proprietary wine are grown on the vast vineyard acreage, wines that regularly sell to other fine wine producers. Lockwood wines, produced on 1650 acres of vineyards, have taken many top awards since the first 1989 vintage. Winemaker Steve Pessagno uses a variety of production techniques, varying the aging conditions of a specific batch of grapes in order to produce several very distinctive wines from a single vintage. Tours by appointment only; no tastings.

Masson Vineyards (408/675-2481; 800 South Alta St., Gonzales) Winemaker Larry Brink heads the project to revitalize the famed Masson name and elevate it to rarer critical climes. Success in that mission appears to be within sight. Blanc de Noir Sparkling Wine, Cabernet Sauvignon, Chardonnay and Merlot are good values and quite tasty. Tours and tastings by appointment only.

Monterey Wine Country Association

To receive a colorful, fact-filled brochure on the Monterey wine area, contact this group — an organization that knows how to disseminate information on its wines (408/375-9400, 408/372-4142 Fax; PO Box 1793, Monterey; Attention Duane K. Harris).

Monterey Peninsula Winery (408/372-4949; 786 Wave St., Monterey) Big reds and full-bodied whites are the specialty of this winery. The facility is south of Monterey, but tastings — along with other fine premium labels from this region — are available in an old Victorian a block from Cannery Row. Winemaker Tom Bates' Zinfandels are loaded with spicy varietal quality and his lush Merlots are award-winning. Barbera and Pinot Noir also are featured. Tastings from noon–5 daily; no tours.

Morgan Winery (408/422-9855, 408/422-9880 Fax; 526 Brunken Ave., Salinas) Morgan Chardonnays consistently win awards for this small winery in the heart of John Steinbeck country. Producing 20,000 cases annually of Sauvignon Blanc, Pinot Noir, Cabernet Sauvignon, and Chardonnay, winemaker Joseph Davis uses time-honored methods of barrel fermentation, contact on lees, and aging in a variety of French oak barrels, with dramatic results. Tours and tastings by appointment only.

San Saba Vineyard (214/821-4044; Central Coast location, Dallas home office) This 68-acre vineyard nestled in the foothills of the Santa Lucia Mountains excels in the production of award-winning Cabernet Sauvignons, and affordably priced Chardonnays and Merlots, thanks to winemaker Barry Jackson. Tours and tastings by appointment only.

Paul Masson Museum and Wine Tasting

This second floor mecca of wine nostalgia is housed in an old cannery building over the blue waters of Monterey Bay. Wines may be purchased by the glass, and there is major array of souvenir gifts and specialty foods. The museum is filled with photos, wine paraphernalia, and memorabilia tracing the history of the long-standing California winery, founded in 1900 by French vintner Paul Masson on the eastern slopes of the Santa Cruz Mountains. A wide range of vintages produced by the huge facility now in the Salinas Valley (closed to the public) is available for sampling and, of course, purchasing (408/646-5446, Cannery Row, Monterey).

San Luis Obispo/Paso Robles Wine Country

The history of winemaking in this warm growing area (which is cooled by both coastal fogs and afternoon Salinas Valley breezes) began at Mission San Miguel Archangel in 1797. The Franciscan missionaries established winemaking as part of the California heritage. In fact, the first grapes at Mission San Luis Obispo were brought by Father Junipero Serra himself.

Eventually, European settlers who stayed after the Gold Rush brought French and Italian varietals to these rich farmlands. One early winery, established by Andrew York in 1882, is still in operation as York Mountain Winery.

Armed with evidence provided by University of California researchers of the potential of the area's climate and soils for grape growing, a wine boom got underway in the 1960s. Today, more than 25 wineries cluster in the hills surrounding Paso Robles and stretch down to the cooler coastal valleys of Edna and Arroyo Grande. Inland, the red wine grapes of the Rhône and Bordeaux produce award-winning vintages, while along the coast, the Burgundian varietals of Chardonnay and Pinot Noir are the specialties.

ARCIERO WINERY
Winemaker: Malcolm Ceibly.
805/239-2562, 805/239-2317 Fax.
5625 E. Hwy. 46, Paso Robles.
Tours: 10–5 weekdays, 10–6 weekends.
Tastings: 10–5 weekdays, 10–6 weekends.

An impressive Mediterranean-style, red-tile-roofed winery and tasting complex is highlighted by a visitor center, lavish landscaping, and beautiful picnic area, the perfect spot to begin a self-guided tour. A destination unto itself, the upscale facility supports fine winemaking, with a memorable selection of Cabs, Chardonnays, and Petite Sirahs. Well-stocked gift store and an exhibit of racing cars, courtesy of brothers Frank and Phil Arciero.

CASTORO CELLARS
Winemaker: Niels Udsen.
805/238-0725, 805/238-2602 Fax.
1480 North Bethel Rd., Templeton.
Tours: By appointment only.
Tastings: 11–5:30 daily.

Lovely views from the vineyards, a prime picnic area, and an antique-filled tasting room are among the pleasures of a visit to these cellars. Gourmet and wine-theme gift items are available, as well as samples of the award-winning Cabernet Sauvignons, considered among the most consistent, well-priced of all California Cabs. Niels Udsen is also among a handful of California winemakers adding delightful experiments in unfermented grape juice to his bottling line. The results so far have yielded an especially refreshing, non-alcoholic Zinfandel elixir that is blissful on a warm day. (Far from a mere gimmick, non-alcoholic grape juices, created with all the care given to premium wines, stand to be highly competitive in a market fond of its bottled waters and designer soft drinks.)

EBERLE WINERY
Winemaker: Gary Eberle.
805/238-9607, 805/237-0344 Fax.
E. Hwy. 46 (3.5 mi. from Paso Robles), Paso Robles.
Tours: By appointment only.
Tastings: 10–5 daily.

Eberle is a prime destination for discovering the regional flavor of the estate's fine Cabernets, Chardonnay, and luscious Muscat Canelli. The winery has a panoramic view of the estate vineyards; the cellar can be viewed from the elegant tasting room adjoining the winery. The patio is a popular picnic site and monthly gourmet winemaker dinners are held (advance reservations required). Gary Eberle was named Central Coast Winemaker of the Year for 1990.

HARMONY CELLARS
Winemaker: Chuck Mulligan.
805/927-1625, 800/432-9239.
3255 Harmony Valley Rd./PO Box 2502, Harmony.
Tours: No.
Tastings: 10–5 daily.

The long-awaited winery facility was completed in mid-1993, allowing visitors to the charming tasting room in tiny, artsy Harmony an even closer look at the creation of fine varietals, as well as some playful blends like a spicy Zinfandel/Gamay Beaujolais called Zinjolais. Harmony Cellars is scenically wedged between the ocean and the rolling foothills of the Santa Lucia Mountains, offering idyllic picnicking conditions.

MAISON DEUTZ WINERY
Winemaker: Christian Roguenant.
805/481-1763, 805/481-6920 Fax.
453 Deutz Dr., Arroyo Grande.
Tours: By appointment only.
Tastings: 11–5 daily exc. Tues.

The winery's unique cellar is set amidst vineyards and rolling hills, and is devoted solely to the production of sparkling wines made by true French *méthode champenoise* techniques. A lofty tasting room with a view of the ocean showcases the crisp Cuvee Brut. Tastings involve plenty of finger foods, cheeses, crackers, fruits, and nuts.

MASTANTUONO WINERY
Winemaker: Pasquale Mastantuono.
805/238-0676, 805/238-9257 Fax.
100 Oak View Rd., Templeton.
Tours: No.
Tastings: 10–5 daily.

The tasting room here — appointed in Italian hunting lodge fashion — presents a dazzling array of interesting varietals, with a focus on dry-farmed grapes used for lusty Zinfandels and rich, rounded Cabernets. The romantic, castle-like winery building overlooks stands of majestic oaks; picnicking in the winery's charming gazebo is often accompanied by live music during warm weather. There is a well-stocked gift store, with deli items.

MERIDIAN VINEYARDS
Winemaker: Chuck Ortman.
805/237-6000, 805/239-5715 Fax.
7000 E. Hwy. 46, Paso Robles.
Tours: By appointment only.
Tastings: 10–6 daily exc. Tues.

Thanks to savvy marketing and a superior, moderately priced product, Meridian has established itself as a leader in the market for Central Coast wines. Meridian's Chardonnay is highly drinkable, both crisp and creamy, and is fast becoming one of the most popular, affordable Chardonnays in the state. The Pinot Noir is supple and rounded, the 1989 Paso Robles Cabernet Sauvignon took a Gold Medal at the 1992 California State Fair, and the Syrah is rewarding.

PESENTI WINERY
Winemaker: Frank Nerelli.
805/434-1030.
2900 Vineyard Dr., Templeton.
Tours: By appointment only.
Tastings: 9–5:30 daily.

The oldest original family-owned winery in the area, Pesenti was established in 1934 on vineyards planted in 1923, and still carries on the tradition of premium red and wine wines, notably a Gray Riesling, Cabernet Sauvignon, and Zinfandel. The wine-lined tasting room boasts a staggering list of varietals for sampling; the sales offer true bargains on everything from modest blends up to national award-winning premiums. Lots of gift items, too.

TWIN HILLS RANCH WINERY
Winemakers: Caroline Scott & Glenn Reid.
805/238-9148.
2025 Nacimiento Lake Dr., Paso Robles.
Tours: By appointment only
Tastings: Noon–4 daily, 11–5 daily in summer.

Gardens with shaded picnic area and a country French, half-timbered tasting room crown this family-owned estate, encircled by almond trees and vineyards. Along with Zinfandel, Cabernet Sauvignon, and Chardonnay, the winery features an acclaimed California Dry Sherry made in the traditional Spanish *solera* method. Extra attractions include a gift shop, banquet facilities, and art exhibition space.

WILD HORSE WINERY & VINEYARD
Winemaker: Ken Volk.

Wild Horse does a fine job of maximizing the regional potential of bold red varietals and crisp, fruity Chardonnays. Its outstanding white

WILD HORSE™

1989
CABERNET SAUVIGNON
PASO ROBLES

PRODUCED AND BOTTLED BY WILD HORSE
TEMPLETON, CALIFORNIA BW 5169 ALC. 13.2% BY VOL.

805/434-2541, 805/434-3516 Fax.
1437 Wild Horse Winery Court, Templeton.
Tours: By appointment only.
Tastings: 11–5 daily.

wines include a spicy Gewurztraminer, as well as Pinot Noir vintages. At its welcoming tasting room, these wines, as well as specialties available only at the winery — Orange Muscat, Cabernet Franc and Malvasia Bianca — are displayed for the enjoyment of visiting tasters.

YORK MOUNTAIN WINERY
Winemaker: Steve Goldman.
805/238-3925.
W. York Mountain Rd., Templeton.
Tours: No.
Tastings: 10–5 daily.

Having remarkably stood the test of time — including Prohibition — this winery is over 100 years old and even boasts its own wine growing designation, the York Mountain Appellation. The venerable winery offers atmospheric antique appointments and a tasting room with a sturdy stone fireplace. The fine tasting here includes not only a wide range of time-honored Central Coast varietals, but complex sherries and ports, as well. Everything made here can be tasted for a nominal fee; the gift area stocks plenty of wine books, wine paraphernalia, and gourmet food items.

Other San Luis Obispo/Paso Robles Wineries

Adelaida Cellars (805/239-8980, 805/239-4671 Fax; 5805 Adelaida Rd., Paso Robles) The winery enjoys a dramatic setting on picturesque ranchlands ranging well above 2300 feet. The views from the tasting room, the site of many memorable wine dinners around the central wood-burning oven, create the perfect setting for tasting winemaker John Munch's spicy Zinfandels and rounded Cabernets. The 1991 Chardonnay took a Gold Medal at the 1993 San Francisco Fair Wine Competition. Tastings daily from 10:30–4:30; tours by appointment only.

Claiborne and Churchill (805/544-4066; 860-E Capitolio Way/PO Box 12742, San Luis Obispo) A small premium winery rapidly ascending in the California winemaking community, C&C is becoming justly famous for dry, spicy Gewurztraminers and elegant Chardonnays. Winemaker Claiborne Thompson also offers bottlings of Muscat Canelli, Pinot Noir, and Riesling. Tours and tastings by appointment only.

Corbett Canyon Vineyards (805/544-5800, 805/544-7205 Fax; 2195 Corbett Canyon Rd., Arroyo Grande) About 8 miles southeast of San Luis Obispo on a hilltop with a stunning view of the Santa Lucia Mountains, this expansive Spanish-style winery blends in with the Old California scenery. The large,

The estate and tasting facility at San Luis Obispo's Corbett Canyon Vineyards Winery welcome visitors.

sunny tasting room offers samples 10–4:30 daily of winemaker John Clark's highly respected estate Cabernet Sauvignon, Chardonnay, Merlot, Pinot Noir, and Sauvignon Blanc. Tours 11, 1, 3 on weekends.

Cottonwood Canyon Vineyard & Winery (805/549-9463, 805/546-8031 Fax; 4330 Santa Fe Rd., San Luis Obispo) Winemaker Roland Shackelford's very new winery specializes in Chardonnay and Pinot Noir made from local grapes. Tours and tastings by appointment only.

Edna Valley Vineyard (805/544-9594; 2585 Biddle Ranch Rd., San Luis Obispo) A member of the internationally renowned Chalone Wine Group, this mid-sized (60,000 cases annually) winery employs classic Burgundian techniques to create delightful Pinot Noir and Chardonnay, made exclusively from grapes grown in the Edna Valley. Tastings 10–4 daily; tours can be arranged for groups larger than 10.

Hope Farms Winery (805/238-6979, 805/238-4063 Fax; 2175 Arbor Rd., Paso Robles) The charming country atmosphere of this small, family-run winery showcases winemaker Steve Rasmussen's classic Central Coast Cabernet Sauvignon and Zinfandel made from estate vineyard grapes. Also try the Chardonnay and Muscat Canelli. Tastings 11–5 daily; no tours.

Jankris Winery (805/434-0319; W. Hwy. 46 at Bethel Rd., Templeton) A Victorian farmhouse headquarters this winery; and its atmospheric setting of vineyards, lawns, and rose garden is a popular site for picnics and weddings. Winemaker Michael Black won a Gold Medal at the 1992 California State Fair with his 1989 Jankris Vineyard, Paso Robles Zinfandel. Also try his Chardonnay, Gamay, Merlot, and Pinot Noir vintages. Tastings 11–5 daily; no tours.

Justin Vineyards & Winery (805/238-6932, 805/238-7382 Fax; 11680 Chimney Rock Rd., Paso Robles) The beautiful Paso Robles countryside forms the

The picnic area at Justin Vineyards & Winery hugs the vineyards.

backdrop for formal English gardens and monthly candlelight guest chef dinners at this creative winery. Sprawling vineyards yield grapes for winemaker Jim Spear's especially rewarding Chardonnay and a Bordeaux-style Meritage created from Cabernet Sauvignon, Cabernet Franc, and Merlot grapes. Other offerings include Nebbiolo and Orange Muscat. Tastings and tours 10–6 daily.

Martin Brothers Winery (805/238-2520, 895/238-6041 Fax; E. Hwy. 46 at Buena Vista, Paso Robles) Italian varietals are the specialty of winemaker Dominic Martin, including Aleatico, Cabernet Etrusco, Chardonnay in Botti, Grappa de Nebbiolo, Nebbiolo Vecchio, Vin Santo, Zinfandel Primitivo, and the new sparkling Moscato Allegro, all sampled on lawns overlooking the vineyards. Seasonal concerts are held in the winery amphitheater in spring and summer. Tastings 11–5 daily; tours by appointment only.

Mission View Estate Vineyard & Winery (805/467-3104, 805/467-3719 Fax; Hwy. 101 at Wellsona Rd., San Miguel) Just east of historic Mission San Miguel, the winery's extensive vineyards generate especially fine Cabernets and Zinfandels. Winemaker Robert Nadeau's Chardonnay, Muscat Canelli, and Sauvignon Blanc also can be tasted in a room accented by Spanish tilework and heavy beamed ceilings. Picnicking on the redwood deck offers a view of the vineyards and the mission beyond. Tastings 10–5 daily; no tours.

Peachy Canyon Winery (805/237-1577; Rte. 1, Box 115C, Paso Robles) One of winemakers Doug Beckett and Toby Shumrick's definitive Zinfandels took a Gold Medal in the prestigious San Francisco Fair 1993 National Wine Competition. The Cabernet Sauvignon also tastes like a winner. No tours; tastings by appointment only.

Saucelito Canyon Vineyard & Winery (805/489-8762, 805/543-2111 Fax; 1600 Saucelito Creek Rd., Arroyo Grande) With acclaim from connoisseurs and restaurateurs throughout the state, winemaker Bill Greenough specializes in Zinfandel made from century-old, dry-farmed vineyards. Tastings noon–5 daily; tours by appointment only.

Talley Vineyards (805/489-0446, 805/489-5201 Fax; 3031 Lopez Dr., Arroyo

Grande) In one of the Edna Valley's newest vineyards, winemaker Steve Rasmussen creates fruity Chardonnays and meaty Pinot Noirs. Picnicking is encouraged on the lawns and gazebo. Tastings 11–5 Thurs.–Sun. (daily in summer) in a two-story adobe dating to the 1860s. No tours.

Tobin James Cellars (805/239-2204; E. Union Rd. at E. Hwy. 46, Paso Robles) Tiny quantities of distinctive Cabernet Sauvignon, Chardonnay, Merlot, Pinot Noir, and Zinfandel are produced at winemaker Tobin James Shumrick's intensive winery. The new facility, on one of the most beautiful country roads in the Central Coast, opened in mid-1993. Tours and tastings 10–5 daily.

International Wine Center

A few steps from the windswept bluffs of Cambria's Moonstone Beach, the center is nestled in the spectacular plantings of Moonstone Gardens. This one-stop international wine shopping spot is staffed by knowledgeable wine raconteurs who will guide you through top regional wines, as well as a spate of world-class and off-beat vintages from the rest of California and the world beyond. Proprietor Calvin Wilkes even stocks a world-class selection of rare teas and boutique beers. Over 200 wines are poured for tasting here each year. All your questions about wine protocol, growing techniques, and tasting etiquette will be answered graciously. Bottle and case prices offer tempting bargains. Open 11–5 daily; a tasting fee of $1 per person is charged (805/927-1697, 800/733-1648; Moonstone Gardens, Hwy. 1, Cambria). Entrepreneur Wilkes also opened a tasting annex in the village of Cambria at 778 Main St., cleverly called 927-WINE (which is also its phone number). Here, a hefty selection of imported cheeses is served along with several breads for daily tastings of international and California wines.

The Crushed Grape Wine Center

Gifts of gourmet foods and wines from the San Luis Obispo area — as well as around the world — are available at this bonanza for bon vivants. The wine bar is the heart of the action, pouring an eclectic assortment of California vintages with the accent on the Central Coast. Bottled wine selection and gourmet gift baskets make delicious souvenirs of the region (805/544-4449; Madonna Rd. at Hwy. 101, San Luis Obispo).

Linn's at the Granary Wine Tasting Room

Local winemakers without their own tasting rooms pool their resources, so to speak, at this central fruit and vegetable stand-cum-meeting place, recently expanded into an elegant wine tasting room, gourmet food store, bakery, and gift shop. A lengthy and ever-changing tasting list allows visitors to sample over 80 award-winning wines of small local family-owned wineries. A $3 tasting fee includes a souvenir wine glass. Each month a "Meet the Winemaker" program brings one of the top alchemists of local winemaking to Linn's for talks and tastings (805/237-4001; 12th & Riverside Ave., Paso Robles).

Santa Barbara/Santa Ynez Valley Wine Country

Increasingly capturing the fancy of California wine aficionados looking for the new and distinctive in Central Coast wines, the lush valleys and canyons of the Santa Ynez Mountains offer a wide range of possibilities. Over 11,000 acres of Santa Barbara County are planted with grapes. Unique to this versatile wine making area is the transverse range of these coastal mountains. Paralleling the sharp inward angle of the West Coast at Santa Barbara County, the mountains run east-west, allowing the inland flow of cooling fog and ocean breezes. The slow ripening of grapes grown under this coastal influence makes for intense development of varietal characteristics.

The inland valleys offer a warmer, drier micro-climate resulting in a range of characteristics emulating conditions in Bordeaux and the Rhône. Since Santa Barbara area wineries aggressively embrace the grapes of France's Rhône district, this is the place to look for especially fine Syrahs, Petite Sirahs, and Viogniers, in addition to exemplary Sauvignon Blancs, Chardonnays, and Pinot Noirs.

As with the other major winemaking districts of the Central Coast, the Franciscan mission fathers planted the first vineyards in Santa Barbara and then in the Santa Ynez Mountains. Soon, a good 6000 gallons of wine a year were being made, thanks to the labors of Chumash Indian converts who crushed the grapes by footwork and fermented the juices in tar-coated cow hides.

Los Olivos Tasting Room and Wine Shop

This is a user-friendly wine tasting depot that provides a one-stop tasting tour of some of the area's finest wineries — wineries too small to provide their own tasting facilities. For $3, you can sample 6 to 8 pours of outstanding area vintages from tiny facilities like Claiborne & Churchill, Ojai, Qupé, and Au Bon Climat. The man behind the bar, Chris Benzinger, will fill your ear with delicious, behind-the-scenes tidbits about styles, awards, winemaking personalities, and tasting tips. This establishment, smack in the middle of the two streets that make up the atmospheric Western village of Los Olivos, is a required stop for all buffs of the unique charms of Santa Ynez Valley winemaking. 11–6 daily (805/688-7406; 2905 Grand Ave./PO Box 640, Los Olivos).

BRANDER VINEYARD
Winemaker: Fred Brander.
805/688-2455.
Hwy. 154 at Robler/PO Box 92, Los Olivos.
Tours: By appointment only.
Tastings: 10–5 daily.

Overlooking the ranchlands of Ronald Reagan and Michael Jackson, this pink faux chateau winery and tasting facility serves up its fine wines with an alluring views of Santa Ynez Valley scenery. You'll be enthralled by the fruity, butterscotchy Chardonnays and crisp, complex Bordeaux-style Sauvignon Blancs. A very special blend of Cabernet Franc, Cabernet Sauvignon, and

Merlot called Tête de Cuvée Bouchet sings of blackberries, cassis, and spice. Stock up here or sign up for the mailing list: local Brander fans tend to buy up each vintage in advance.

BYRON VINEYARD & WINERY
Winemaker: Byron "Ken" Brown.
805/937-7288, 805/937-1246 Fax.
5230 Tepusquet Rd., Santa Maria.
Tours: 10–4 daily.
Tastings: 10–4 daily.

The road to this well-respected, ten-year-old winery is a splendid country lane. The picnic area on the steep slope of Tepusquet Creek is the site of many special wine and food events. The Spanish, barn-like tasting room provides samples of the winery's award-winning products, highlighted by crisp and distinctive white wines. The excellent Byron Chardonnays — covered with glory at major national competitions — invariably find themselves paired with innovative California cuisine in the south Central Coast's best restaurants.

Alison Green of Santa Ynez Valley's landmark Firestone Vineyard is one of California's pioneer women winemakers.

FIRESTONE VINEYARD
Winemaker: Alison Green.
805/688-3940, 805/686-1256 Fax.
5017 Zaca Station Rd./PO Box 244, Los Olivos.
Tours: Every 45 min. 10–4 daily.
Tastings: 10–4 daily.

Overlooking hundreds of acres planted to all the major grape varietals of the Central Coast, this award-winning winery essentially started the recent surge of interest in the Santa Barbara area as a winemaking contender. While the Chardonnays are exceptional, and have been served in far-flung diplomatic settings, the Rieslings made here set the tone, especially the Late Harvest vintages and a new and unprecedented Dry Riesling. There's a pleasingly dry spin on the much-honored Gewurztraminers. The huge, contemporary hacienda winery, well-appointed tasting and gift area, and adjoining picnic patio all overlook a mosaic of vineyards lining Zaca Station Road, one of the prettiest country lanes in California.

The sprawling Mediter-ranean tasting facility of Gainey Vineyard is a social mecca in the Santa Ynez Valley.

GAINEY VINEYARD
Winemaker: Rick Longoria.
805/688-0558, 805/688-5864 Fax.
3950 E. Hwy. 246/PO Box 910, Santa Ynez.
Tours: 11, 1, 3 weekends; every hour 10:30–3:30 weekdays.
Tastings: 10–5 daily.

Over 60 acres of estate vines surround the red-tile-roofed, Spanish-style winery complex announced by a procession of romantic pepper trees. This is as much a community cultural center as it is tasting facility for Gainey's highly respected vintages. The attractive tasting room overlooks the vineyard-laden hills and pours award-winning Sauvignon Blancs and Chardonnays. The Pinot Noir is also highly regarded. Tours here begin at an instructive "Visitor's Vineyard," a demonstration planting that shows off the various cultivation techniques and trellising required by different grapes, and allows visitors to sample the fruit. The popular winery also is the site for a wide range of cooking classes, art shows, concerts, and wine-appreciation workshops.

MOSBY WINERY AT VEGA VINEYARDS
Winemaker: Bill Mosby.
805/688-2415, 805/686-4288 Fax.
Hwy. 101 at Santa Rosa Rd./PO Box 1849, Buellton.
Tours: By appointment only.
Tastings: 10–4 daily.

Tastings, concerts on the lawn, and cooking classes are among the events at this small, family-run winery that emphasizes Italian varietals, as well as top California grape vintages. An old red barn houses the winery and tasting room; a mid-19th century adobe is also on the farm property. The place is definitely rustic, though the wines are anything but. The elegant Chardonnays and Pinot Noirs set the tone, and the potent grappas attract high honors at major competitions.

FESS PARKER WINERY
Winemaker: Eli Parker.
805/688-1545.
6200 Foxen Canyon Rd./PO Box 908, Los Olivos.

Though his son Eli manages the large, attractive winery, headquartered in a gorgeous building of native stone and roofed in copper, the chance to catch a glimpse of the Western movie and TV hero is part of the deal. The setting is classic California

Veteran western star-turned-winemaker Fess Parker and son Eli sample the estate Syrah at Fess Parker Winery in Los Olivos.

Tours: No.
Tastings: 10–4 daily ($2 fee includes logo glass).

RANCHO SISQUOC WIN-ERY
Winemaker: Stephan Bedford.
805/934-4332, 805/937-6601 Fax.
6600 Foxen Canyon Rd., Santa Maria.
Tours: No.
Tastings: 10–4 daily.

rolling ranchland. The winery is equipped for myriad public tastings, concerts, conferences, and food events; 1992 marked the first harvest of grapes grown on the 715-acre ranch.

The pastoral Sisquoc River Valley frames the large ranch accommodating this tiny stone and redwood winery. The entire line of acclaimed wines produced from estate grapes is available exclusively at the tasting room, which

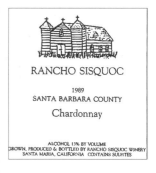

adjoins a shaded lawn, gardens, and delightful picnic area sheltered by huge oaks. Winemaker Stephan Bedford is a knowledgeable host and a gold mine of information about the area's culture and winemaking. The complex Chardonnays and Sauvignon Blancs are outstanding for drinking now and for cellaring.

SANFORD WINERY
Winemaker: Bruno D'Alfonso.
805/688-3300, 805/688-7381 Fax.
7250 Santa Rosa Rd., Buellton.
Tours: No.
Tastings: 11–4 daily.

This small winery is tucked into the foothills of the Santa Lucia Mountains west of Solvang on farmlands accented by weathered buildings — a classic Old West setting. The cozy, rustic tasting room sports a friendly pot-bellied stove; picnic tables sit next to a gentle creek. Sanford wines are respected as some of the finest of this winemaking valley; the lush, toasty Chardonnays and soft, rich Pinot Noirs regularly show up on expert's "best of California" lists.

SANTA YNEZ WINERY
Winemaker: Doug Scott.
805/688-8381, 800/864-3443, 805/688-3764.
343 North Refugio Rd., Santa Ynez.
Tours: On the hour after noon, weekends.
Tastings: 10–5 daily.

On historic ranchlands in the heart of present-day Chumash Indian country, this pioneer winery draws from over 100 acres of vineyards — including those originally planted in the late 1960s — for its premium production of Cabernet Sauvignon, Chardonnay, Sauvignon Blanc, and Gewurztraminer. The small, casually friendly tasting room is set in the midst of vineyards and rolling ranch country. The interesting gift store is lined with awards and trophies; picnics on the redwood deck afford a view of yesteryear in the West. In Santa Barbara, winemaker Doug Scott's Stearns Wharf Vintners (805/966-6624; 217-G Stearns Wharf) offers samples from the winery from 9–6 (till 9 at night, summer).

ZACA MESA WINERY
Winemaker: Dan Gehrs.
805/688-3310, 805/688-8796.
6905 Foxen Canyon Rd./PO Box 899, Los Olivos.
Tours: 10–4 daily.
Tastings: 10–4 daily.

Zaca Mesa wines are some of the best-known and best-received wines made in the area, and the lovely rustic winery has been producing award-winners since 1972, especially delightful Chardonnays, Syrahs, and other Rhône grape varietals. Housed in a wooden barn, the winery is among a bevy of tiny establishments dotting gorgeous Foxen Canyon Road, and a leisurely afternoon picnicking here will have you fantasizing about buying property.

Other Santa Barbara/Santa Ynez Valley Wineries

Au Bon Climat (805/688-8630; PO Box 113, Los Olivos) Especially prized are the Chardonnays and Pinot Noirs created by winemaker Jim Clendenen, well worth pursuing at restaurants and wine shops all over California. This winery showcases the climatic resemblance between this growing area and the fabled Burgundian Côte d'Or, while subtly flaunting the depth of flavor available to grapes nurtured in these long, fog-cooled growing conditions. The Los Olivos Tasting Room and Wine Shop provides samples; no tours.

Babcock Vineyards (805/736-1455, 805/736-3886 Fax; 5175 Hwy. 246, Lompoc) Winemaker Bryan Babcock creates award-winning Rieslings and Gewurztraminers, as well as appealing Chardonnay, Pinot Noir, Sauvignon Blanc and Sangiovese bottlings. Attractive picnic area surrounded by vineyards. Tours and tastings 10:30–4 weekends.

Buttonwood Farm Winery (805/688-3032, 805/688-6168 Fax; 1500 Alamo Pintado Rd. /PO Box 1007, Solvang) It's new, it's small, and the fine Sauvignon Blancs and Merlots made by winemaker Mike Brown are attracting attention. The Cabernet Franc and Cabernet Sauvignon offerings also are smart. Tastings 11–5 Fri.–Sun.; no tours.

Chimère (805/922-9097, 805/922-2462 Fax; 547 W. Betteravia, Suite D, Santa Maria) Gary Mosby was the original winemaker at Edna Valley and left to produce Chardonnay, Gamay, Pinot Blanc, and Pinot Noir at his own independent label in 1988. Tours and tastings by appointment only.

Foxen Vineyard (805/937-4251; Rte. 1, Box 144-A, Foxen Canyon Rd., Santa Maria) Nestling among the vineyards that surround this country road, the small winery boasts the excellent reserve Cabernet Sauvignon, Chardonnay, Chenin Blanc, Merlot, and Pinot Noir of winemakers Richard Doré and Bill Wathen. Tours and tastings noon–4 weekends.

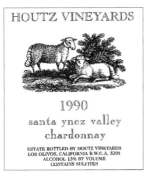

Houtz Vineyard (805/688-8664; 2670 Ontiveros Rd./PO Box 897, Los Olivos) Small and rustic, the winery is housed in a California-style redwood barn in the middle of a fully functional farm filled with all manner of animals. Winemaker David Houtz offers tastings of Cabernet Sauvignon, Chardonnay, and Sauvignon Blanc, as well as picnicking near a small pond, from noon–4 weekends. Tastings; no tours.

J. Kerr Wines (805/688-5337; PO Box 7539, Santa Maria) Sales of the Chardonnay, Pinot Noir, and Syrah vintages produced by this very small winery (winemaker John Kerr II is assistant winemaker at Byron) are conducted through wholesale distribution and at the Los Olivos Tasting Room. No tours.

Kalyra Wines (805/963-0274; PO Box 865, Buellton) Fairly new and very small, the winery produces a few hundred cases each of Chardonnay, Merlot, Port and *natural* German-style Sparkling Wine. Winemaker Michael Brown also experiments with fortified dessert wines. His hand-crafted work can be found at fine wine shops in the Santa Barbara area and at the Los Olivos Tasting Room. No tours or tastings.

Lane Tanner (805/934-0230; Rte. 1, Box 144-A, Santa Maria) Savvy, saucy Lane Tanner is a smart woman winemaker who is on the trail of the perfect Pinot Noir. She just could find it. No tours or tastings.

Respected winemaker Robert Longoria creates stunning Santa Ynez Valley wines under his own label as well as for Gainey Vineyards.

Longoria Wine Cellars (805/688-9804; PO Box 186, Los Olivos) Gainey's winemaker by day, Rick Longoria has been making Pinot Noir on his own since 1982 and now is producing Cabernet Franc and Merlot. Look for a Chardonnay in 1994. No tours; samples at the Los Olivos Tasting Room.

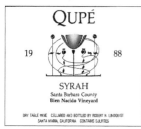

Qupé Wine Cellars (805/688-2477, 805/686-4470 Fax; PO Box 440, Los Olivos) The winery's unusual name is a Chumash Indian word for "poppy," the ubiquitous golden state flower. Enjoying increasing celebrity, the wines are outstanding — notably the black raspberry-scented Syrahs from Santa Barbara's coveted Bien Nacido Vineyard — and are available at fine markets, restaurants, and the Los Olivos Tasting Room. Specializing in Chardonnay and the wines of the Rhône, winemaker Bob Lindquist creates spellbinding vintages of great depth. Most of the tiny output is scooped up by the finest and trendiest Central Coast and Southern California restaurants; buyers should jump at any opportunity to stock their cellars with this rising star. No tours or tastings.

Vita Nova (No phone; PO Box 822, Los Olivos) Two celebrated winemakers, Jim Clendenen from Au Bon Climat and Bob Lindquist from Qupé, have joined forces to whip up some new ideas in Cabernet Franc, Cabernet Sauvignon, Merlot, and Sauvignon Blanc blends, as well as gorgeous Chardonnays. The Los Olivos Tasting Room offers samples. No tours.

Santa Barbara County Vintners' Association

For a map of this area's excellent wineries, the helpful folks at this first-class organization would be glad to send you one if you request it (805/688-0881; PO Box WINE, Los Olivos).

CHAPTER SEVEN
Pump It Up
RECREATION

Obsessed with the sun and drawn to the sea, Central Coast Californians relish reinventing ways to play in the open air. No stretch of scenic road is without its walkers, runners, and cyclists. Rain or shine, beaches bloom with tide pooling and volleyball enthusiasts. Beyond the edge of the land, the ocean simmers with surfers, swimmers and sailors. Parasailers, windsurfers and hang

The sands, dunes, and waves of Zmudowski State Beach, just north of Moss Landing, are ideal for strolling, beachcombing, bird-watching, tide pooling, surfing, and clamming.

gliders tempt the fates in sea and sky. Fishing enthusiasts find reverie and material for tall tales in wave, pond, and stream. Camping along the coast and in its forests and valleys is *de rigueur* for all. Whatever the recreational itch, the Central Coast has the exact pastime to scratch it.

BEACHES

A popular T-shirt here says it all: "Life's a beach." And the Central Coast obliges with beaches of every description — smooth, white, wide, rugged, curved, sheltered, sprawling — for swimmers, surfers, sunbathers, collectors, walkers, lovers. From the intriguing and isolated along the north coast to the warm-water bodysurfing havens of the southern stretches, beaches define the lifestyle of the region.

Santa Cruz Coast

Año Nuevo State Reserve (Hwy. 1 & New Years Creek Rd.) Hiking trails lead along the northern bluffs, dunes, and tide pools of this famous sanctuary. The southern stretch of the reserve is open from December–April to guided walks only by reservation (MISTIX, 1-800/444-7575). Gray whale sightings are

The sheltered sands of Capitola City Beach offer a haven for beach lovers and sandcastle builders of all ages.

Shmuel Thaler

legion during winter months, but the prime attraction remains the elephant seals, who gather here to mate and bear their endearing young. Parking, restrooms, wheelchair-accessible path and viewing platform. Entrance fee.

Capitola City Beach (Esplanade & Monterey St.) Restaurants, shops, galleries, and prime people-watching line the esplanade framing this popular swimming and sunbathing area. A safe play area for children is formed by the curve of Soquel Creek as it meets the sea and nonstop volleyball is a religion. Parking is difficult; take the shuttle at the Hwy. 1 and Park Ave. exit. No entrance fee.

Cowell Beach (West Cliff Dr. & Bay St., Santa Cruz) Stairways lead down to this prime day-use location at the top of Santa Cruz' main beach, featuring volleyball during summer and all-year surfing action at Steamers Lane. Paved walkway leads to restrooms. Wheelchair access to the shore, parking, lifeguard during the crowded summer season. No entrance fee.

El Granada Beach (Half Moon Bay bet. East Breakwater & Mirada Rd.) A seawall makes this sandy stretch particularly sheltered. Come prepared for cool, foggy conditions. Restrooms, parking. No entrance fee.

Hooper Beach (Capitola Wharf, Capitola) Peacefully out of the way from Capitola's main beach action, this secluded stretch is perfect for undisturbed wave watching and picnicking. Parking available but challenging. No entrance fee.

Laguna Creek Beach (Hwy. 1 at Laguna Creek) Another of this stretch of the coast's many hidden, cliff-hewn cove beaches. Undeveloped to the delight of privacy-conscious sun worshippers. No entrance fee.

Lighthouse Field State Beach (West Cliff Dr. & Pelton Ave., Santa Cruz) Just north of Lighthouse Point, this broad stretch of beach offers fine swimming and is accessible by walkways down to the sand. The basic theme here is "endless summer," with plenty of impromptu musical and drumming sessions, frolicking dogs, and kids. Across the street is an undeveloped park of wildflowers and trees with walking and biking paths, and picnic tables. A favored local spot for early morning and sunset walking rituals, cycling, and roller skating, as well as front-row viewing of surfing action just off Lighthouse Point. Parking. No entrance fee.

Lundborgh Beach (N. of Manresa State Beach., La Selva) A very secluded stretch of coast, accessible only by strolling southward from Manresa. Locals call it Trestle Beach. No facilities or parking. No entrance fee.

Manresa State Beach (Hwy. 1 to San Andreas Rd. exit., La Selva) A treasure of this stretch of the coast, Manresa is accessible via stairway and paths from main parking lot and by Sand Dollar Dr. walkway. Restrooms and 63 campsites for tent camping. Stroll and wade with the abundant shorebirds. Swimmers beware: formidable rip currents. For campsite reservations, call MISTIX (1-800/444-7275). Entrance fee.

Moran Lake Beach (2700 East Cliff Dr., Santa Cruz) Moran Lake is a misty lagoon ringed with eucalyptus groves and a nature trail. The wide sandy beach just south of the lagoon offers parking, wheelchair access. No entrance fee.

Natural Bridges State Beach (2531 West Cliff Dr. off Hwy. 1/Mission St., Santa Cruz) At the northern edge of Santa Cruz proper, rugged cliffs and sandstone rock formations sculpted by wind and wave create a romantic setting. (The graceful arches that gave the beach its name have succumbed to the elements.) 50 acres of cypress and eucalyptus groves, where monarch butterflies migrate each year. Weekends from October–February, guided tours of the Butterfly Natural Preserve. Sandy beaches and tide pool areas adjoin picnic sites and much of the property is wheelchair accessible. Restrooms, ample parking. No entrance fee.

New Brighton State Beach (Hwy. 1 Park Ave. exit, 4 mi. S. of Santa Cruz) Pristinely sheltered, these 68 sandy acres are crowned by bluffs of fragrant eucalyptus and offer trails through beachfront forests; beach access by stairway. A good waterfowl viewing area, the long sandy beach offers 115 campsites, showers, bicycle camping sites, wheelchair-accessible restrooms, and fire pits along the beach for al fresco cookery. A splendid view of the Monterey coastline just across the bay. Entrance fee.

Pebble Beach (Hwy. 1 bet. Hill Rd. & Artichoke Rd., 1.5 mi. S. of Pescadero Rd.) Pebbles rolled round and soft by the waves are the specialty here, including varieties of agate. A tiny but inviting a self-guided nature trail leads south to Bean Hollow State Beach. Picnic tables and restrooms. No entrance fee.

Pescadero State Beach (Hwy. 1 at Pescadero Rd.) This mile-long beach offers a diversity of terrain, from soft dunes to tide pools. Just across the Coast Highway from the sights and sounds of the wildlife preserve of Pescadero Marsh with lots of picnic sites and restroom facilities, this is a top all-day setting. Plenty of parking and hiking trails. No entrance fee.

Pomponio State Beach (Hwy. 1, 3 mi. N. of Pescadero Rd.) A luscious stretch of beach, offering prime driftwood-gathering thanks to the confluence of a scenic creek. Many facilities, including picnic tables, cooking grills, ample parking, restrooms. Day-use fee.

Red, White, & Blue Beach (Hwy. 1 at Scaroni Rd., 5.5 mi. N. of Santa Cruz) A red, white, and blue mailbox marks the spot south of Davenport for fans of clothing-optional sunbathing. Long a private beach, this naturists' mecca offers picnic tables but frowns on cameras and dogs. Day-use and camping fee.

Rio Del Mar Beach (S. end of Seacliff State Beach, Seacliff exit off Hwy. 1) An esplanade well-stocked with convenience stores and a fine seafood restaurant and bar fronts this wide expanse of sand with privacy and long stretches of strolling during the week; weekends, the secret is poorly kept. Gentle waves make it attractive for bodysurfing during late summer, early fall. A bike path/walking trail connects with nearby Seacliff State Beach. Restrooms, ample parking. No entrance fee.

San Gregorio Beach (Hwy. 1 & San Gregorio Rd.) At the intersection of an old stagecoach road, this idyllic cove is framed by encircling coastal hills and rolling farmlands. The spot marks one of the campsites of Portola's 1769 Spanish expedition to the San Francisco Bay. Watch out for rip currents. Picnic tables, restrooms. Day-use entrance fee.

Santa Cruz Beach & Boardwalk (829 Beach St. near Front St.) The boardwalk — with its vendors, games, and rides — is the last remaining oceanfront amusement park in California. On a hot day, the adjoining Santa Cruz and Cowell beaches are where the action is — whether it's surfing, sunbathing, swimming, volleyball, or strolling on the pier. Ample pay parking. No entrance fee.

Scott Creek Beach (Hwy. 1 N. of Davenport Landing) A broad expanse of sand for sunbathers and beachcombers. An intertidal reef and tide pools are full of marine life. Restrooms, parking. No entrance fee.

Seabright Beach (East Cliff Dr. & Seabright Ave., Santa Cruz) Known to locals as Castle Beach, this wide, sandy shoreline abuts the wonderful Santa Cruz Museum of Natural History. Good water sport spot. Limited parking. No entrance fee.

Seacliff State Beach (Seacliff exit off Hwy. 1., Rio Del Mar) A natural history center, covered picnic areas, and 26 RV sites along this long, sandy, 85-acre beach stretching below picturesque bluffs. Good swimming areas and fishing is allowed from a pier where the concrete-hulled freighter *Palo Alto* — a user-friendly curiosity left over from World War I — is docked. Showers. Entrance fee.

Sunset State Beach (San Andreas Rd. off Hwy. 1, Watsonville) Diverse flora and fauna, huge sand dunes, and a pine-forested, 90-site tent and RV campground on a long expanse of beach. In a rural area just south of Manresa State Beach, its 7 miles of sandy shoreline are great for beachcombing, picnicking, fishing, clamming. Showers. Entrance fee.

Twin Lakes State Beach (7th Ave. at East Cliff Dr., Santa Cruz) Warm, wide, and sheltered, this inviting expanse of sand curves around the mouth of a lagoon abundantly populated with ducks, geese, and native waterfowl. Popular with lovers, sunbathers, families, and fishing buffs who patrol the nearby harbor jetty. A stretch of powdery white sand, the beach offers windsurfing and volleyball action, plus the eye-appeal of boats weaving in and out of the yacht harbor. Parking on roadway shoulders (dicey during popular summertime), restrooms. No entrance fee.

Waddell Creek Beach (Hwy. 1, 1 mi. S. of San Mateo/Santa Cruz Co. line) The quintessential northern Central Coast beach. At the southwest tip of Big Basin Redwoods State Park, this beautiful setting offers prime beachcombing and romantic walks. Hang gliders soar overhead and the surf beyond is studded with the multicolored sails of windsurfers. Coastal access via plenty of well-marked paths, as well as trails worn over the years by legions of diehard surfers. Use trails through private property with discretion, since some local farmers are not amused by trespassers, however innocent or athletic. But if you feel the need to take your shoes off and gambol in the ebb tide with someone you love — this is the place. Parking, restrooms. No entrance fee.

Monterey Coast

Asilomar State Beach (Pico Ave & Sunset Dr., Pacific Grove) An expanse of world-class tide pools, rocky shoreline, and sandy dunes. Divers frequent the area searching for prized abalone. Neon-hued ice plant colonies hug the edge of the sand. Swimming is unwise due to rocks and hazardous riptides. Adjoins the atmospheric Asilomar Conference Grounds. Restrooms; parking along roadway. No entrance fee.

Carmel City Beach (Ocean Ave., Carmel) Soft white sand extends beyond a border of deep green cypress trees, for picnics, campfires, volleyball, wheelchair-accessible restrooms. Warning: dangerous surf/swimming conditions. Stairways provide beach access to this gorgeous location, predictably crowded on weekends. No entrance fee.

Carmel River State Beach (Scenic Rd. at Carmelo St., Carmel) A favorite with divers and lagoon waterfowl-watchers, this 100-acre sandy beach fronts a teeming marsh, near the site where Spanish explorers first made landfall. The southernmost tip, known as Monastery Beach, is accessible from Hwy. 1. Prime day recreation. Parking, restrooms. No entrance fee.

Fanshell Beach (Signal Hill Rd., at 17 Mile Dr., Pebble Beach) In the heart of scenic 17 Mile Drive, this gorgeous white sand cove offers choice locations for the antics of resident sea otters, and fishing, picnicking, and, for the hardy, swimming. Parking. No entrance fee.

Garrapapa State Park (Hwy. 1, 2 mi. S. of Malpaso Creek, Big Sur) A soaring landscape of steep cliffs, accessible along a panoramic trail, overlooks rich tide pools below and a breathtaking view. Excellent whale- and sea otter-watching. Roadside parking, chemical toilets. No entrance fee.

Jade Cove (Hwy. 1, 12 mi. S. of Lucia) Named for the soft green nephrite jade once found here — and collected by generations past — this rocky cove is today a favorite diving area. Still gorgeous for wandering and sifting through the smooth pebbles to discover some special memento. Reached by a steep trail. No facilities. No entrance fee.

Monterey State Beach (Sand Dunes Dr., Monterey) A lovely stretch of dunes and a bracing view of the entire Monterey Bay highlights this sandy beach. Parking, restrooms. No entrance fee.

Pfeiffer Beach (Hwy. 1, end of Sycamore Canyon Rd., Big Sur) A trail leads from the parking lot through cypress groves to the sandy beach with monumental cliffs and sea caves. Natural rock arches channel the waves into spectacular displays of wild spray and spume. At the beach, Sycamore Creek spills into a hidden lagoon. A gorgeous sanctuary for exploring, though the surf is hazardous and gusty winds require warm clothing for all-day outings. Parking, restrooms. No entrance fee.

Point Lobos State Reserve (W. of Hwy. 1 at Carmel Highlands) Widely considered one of the most spectacular coastal sanctuaries in the country, this 2500-acre preserve shelters ancient cypress groves, rugged cliffs, swirling tide pools, and bottle-green water lapping crystalline cove beaches. Exquisite China Beach offers sheltered swimming. Well-marked trails thread the meadows, bluffs, and shoreline, for stunning views of sea lion and waterfowl habitats. A small museum in a vintage Whaler's Cabin, diving by permit. Ample parking, restrooms. Entrance fee.

Sand Dollar Beach (Hwy. 1, 11 mi. S. of Lucia) Lush fields and cypress groves frame this favorite picnic spot, with trails leading to a half-moon-shaped beach. Hang gliders love this spot. Restrooms, parking. No entrance fee.

Willow Creek Beach (Hwy. 1, 14 mi. S. of Lucia) An excellent picnic spot with views of former coastline now eroded into stately offshore rock formations. Enthusiasts still comb for bits of jade where Willow Creek meets the sea. Parking, restrooms. No entrance fee.

Zmudowski State Beach (Hwy. 1, 1 mi. N. of Moss Landing) A boardwalk leads through the dunes to a prime surfing and clamming beach bordered by verdant farms. Snowy plovers and their wildfowl colleagues nest in the serpentine estuary. A rich marriage of saltwater and freshwater, lined with cattails. Parking, restrooms. No entrance fee.

Tide pools filled with the delicately balanced ecology of tiny marine creatures abound along the rocky stretches of the Central Coast, like this rich expanse near Cayucos in San Luis Obispo County.

Jay Swanson

Tide Pooling Pointers

On rocky stretches of the Central Coast, the outcroppings form pockets that retain water receding after high tide. These tidal pools contain intricately interdependent life zones, miniature aquaria that are home to fabulous seaweeds, periwinkles, mussels, barnacles and, in the lowest intertidal areas, sea stars, sea urchins, hermit crabs, and anemones. The best time for tide pooling is at low tide, when the rocky pockets of life are exposed. And it's best to wear rubber-soled shoes to prevent slipping on the wet rocks. Fascinating to observe up close, these tiny creatures depend on the cycles of the tides and delicate environmental balance for their existence. However tempting, please don't touch or pick up any tide pool residents.

The tide pools of **Pescadero State Beach** and **Año Nuevo State Reserve** in the northern Central Coast well reward those willing to brave often windy conditions to explore these rocky expanses. **Natural Bridges State Park**, just north of Santa Cruz, is famous for its tide pools filled with pink-tentacled anemones, black turban snails, prehistoric-looking mossy chiton, and purple sea urchins. Further south, **17 Mile Drive** and nearby **Asilomar State Beach** showcase tide pools laced with intricate seaweed beds extending into the crashing surf of the rocky coastline. **Point Lobos State Reserve** is another treasure-trove of tide pools hugging soft sand pocket beaches. Further south, guided tide pool exploring is provided by the **Morro Bay State Park Museum of Natural History** (805/772-2694). And the rocky stretches between **San Simeon** and **Piedras Blancas** yield up especially rewarding tide pools. In the Santa Barbara area, **Refugio State Beach** tide pools teem with miniature life and are easily accessible.

San Luis Obispo Coast

Avila State Beach (Front St., bet. Harford Dr. and San Rafael St., Avila Beach) Next to a tiny sailing village, this beach nuzzles the public fishing pier and boasts playground equipment, outdoor showers, restrooms, and a view of San Luis Obispo Bay. Lifeguards spring, summer. Ample parking. No entrance fee.

The public fishing pier at Avila State Beach is the background for games of seaside frisbee at San Luis Obispo Bay.

Jay Swanson

Cayucos State Beach (W. of N. Ocean Dr., Cayucos) A beachfront pier attracts fishing aficionados at this local recreation spot, with barbecue and picnicking facilities. The pier, prettily lit at night, is wheelchair accessible. Restrooms, parking. No entrance fee.

Leffingwell Landing (Hwy. 1 & Moonstone Beach Dr., Cambria) Beautifully maintained hiking trails wander the sagebrush and lupine-filled bluffs and cypress groves above the swirling tide pools and brown sandy beach below. Excellent whale and sea otter watching from benches at vista points. Boat ramp, parking, restrooms, picnic areas. No entrance fee.

Moonstone Beach (Moonstone Dr., Cambria) Prime beachcombing for gnarled driftwood and the occasional moonstone agate along this sheltered stretch adjoining San Simeon State Beach. Tide pools contain an abundance of starfish and anemones. Hiking trails lace the formidable bluffs lining the water's edge. Parking, no facilities. No entrance fee.

Morro Strand State Beach (Studio Dr. bet. 24th St. & Cody Ave., Cayucos [N.]; Hwy. 1 bet. Yerba Buena Ave. & Atascadero Rd., Morro Bay [S.]) The northern stretch of the beach is accessible by numerous stairways and walkways leading from streets intersecting Studio Dr. A paved parking lot at the end of 24th St. offers restrooms, picnic tables. The southern section of the beach offers almost 2 miles of sand and dunes studded with ice plant, a splendid setting for contemplating the volcanic crags of Morro Rock. 100 campsites at the end of Yerba Buena Dr. Restrooms, showers, parking. Fee for camping, none for day-use.

Pismo State Beach (from Wilmar Ave. at Pismo Beach, to Santa Barbara Cty. line) 20 miles of coast are embraced by this beach area, from the sandy beaches with volleyball courts just north of the Pismo Beach Pier, down to the 4000 acres of sweeping Nipomo Dunes, which once starred as the Sinai Desert in Cecil B. DeMille's *Ten Commandments*. Campgrounds, eucalyptus groves, dune buggy playgrounds. and marshlands; parking, restrooms, ample opportunities for seafood restaurant dining. Entrance fees for campgrounds.

Ragged Point Beach (Hwy. 1, 15 mi. N. of San Simeon) Sweeping vistas of Big Sur from the bluff top overlook of this rocky spit of coastline. Near a grassy picnic area with tables, a steep trail leads down to the tiny beach, past a waterfall renewed by winter rains. Restrooms, parking area. No entrance fee.

William R. Hearst Memorial State Beach (Hwy. 1 on San Simeon Rd., San Simeon) One of the many natural playgrounds left to the State of California by the tycoon is this outstanding fishing and swimming area, nestled in the protective beauty of San Simeon Point. A 1000-foot fishing pier, well stocked with fishing equipment and boat rentals, is west of the main parking area. A eucalyptus grove and grassy expanse near the park's entrance offer fine picnicking facilities. Restrooms, parking. Entrance fee.

Santa Barbara Coast

Arroyo Burro Beach Park (2981 Cliff Dr., Santa Barbara) This multi-use county park encompasses coastal bluffs and memorable vistas of the beautiful town and waterfront, and sandy beaches, volleyball courts, picnic area, restaurants, snack concessions. Popular with the horsy set, equestrian trails lead from Cliff Dr. down to the sand. Expect plenty of company summer weekends. Lifeguards in summer, parking, wheelchair-accessible restrooms. No entrance fee.

Carpinteria State Beach (end of Palm Ave., Carpinteria) A broad sandy swath of prime swimming and sunning area bordered by dunes and including a Chumash Indian interpretive display, trailer and tent camping, RV sites. Popular with swimmers, this is considered one of the safest beaches on the Central Coast thanks to a shallow offshore ocean floor sheltering the area from tidal currents. Surfers abound at the south end of the beach, a place locally dubbed "Tarpits." Lifeguards in summer. Uncluttered by commercialism, a true coastal retreat offering ample parking, showers, restrooms, picnic facilities. Day-use and overnight entrance fee.

Beachcombing Tips

All-day beach foraging and wandering can yield countless simple treasures and, at areas where creeks meet the coastline, plentiful driftwood curiosities. Tide pool areas are often surrounded by beautiful rocks and glass fragments, smoothed and rounded by the elements. The trick is to come early in the day, when tiny sand dollars, the odd weathered bottle, and even round, bottle-glass fishing net floats are washed up on the shores. Mornings after storms yield the most interesting sea-tossed objects and driftwood by the ton. Bring a day-pack or canvas bag for collecting and, during foggy mornings and evenings, a warm sweater.

Beachcombers on the wide sand flats of Morro Strand near San Luis Obispo enjoy the year-round balmy climate.

Jay Swanson

East Beach (1100 East Cabrillo Blvd., Santa Barbara) Visible by cruising the palm-lined main drag of Santa Barbara's coastline, East Beach is a dear old friend to natives who line its half-mile-wide length of sand, enjoy grassy barbecue outposts, play in wading pool and children's playground and above all, compete — casually — on wall-to-wall volleyball courts. *The* beach at Santa Barbara, the quintessential beach town. Restrooms, ample parking. No entrance fee.

El Capitan State Beach (Hwy. 101, 12 mi. N. of Goleta) Rugged hiking trails around the nooks and rocky crannies of this 133-acre park lead down to a narrow stretch of sandy beach, famed for world-class surfing conditions. Lifeguards in summer. Ample parking, camping, snacking and restroom facilities. Entrance fees for day-use and overnight camping.

Gaviota State Park Beach (Hwy. 101 at Gaviota Beach Rd., Gaviota) A 2700-acre park encircling splendid wilderness hiking as well as beach activities along 5 miles of shoreline. Campground, picnic areas, boat launch, and a fishing pier. Lifeguards in summer. Parking, wheelchair accessible restrooms. Day and overnight use fee.

Isla Vista Beach (Del Playa Dr., Isla Vista) You don't have to be a student of the university to take the stairways down to this sun-soaked beach, but chances are your fellow sun worshippers will be matriculating if nothing else. Tanning action and tide pools. Parking on-street, no facilities. No entrance fee.

Leadbetter Beach (1000 Shoreline Dr., Santa Barbara) With sparkling white sand, this cove beach just north of Santa Barbara proper has landscaped picnic areas, restrooms, snack bars, and a picturesque view of the busy fishing and yacht harbor. Parking, lifeguard in summer. No entrance fee.

Nude Beach (State St. at end of Mockingbird Lane, Santa Barbara) Popular with locals who find bathing attire restrictive, this powdery strand offers isolation and plenty of convivial company. No facilities. No entrance fee.

Palm Park Beach (500 E. Cabrillo Blvd., Santa Barbara) A perfect postcard of wide white beach lined with palms and brilliant green lawns adjoining the red-tiled downtown and an immaculate blend of picnic facilities, bike path, footpaths for strolling, and people watching. Red-tile-roofed restrooms. Possibly the most elegant beach on the Central Coast. No entrance fee.

Point Sal State Beach (Brown & Point Sal Rds., Guadalupe) Take rugged Point Sal Rd. to the coast, where steep trails wind to the secluded expanse of beach. Romantic or impossibly rustic, depending on your mood and the condition of the poorly maintained road. Harbor seals congregate at the headland of Point Sal. Ample parking, no facilities. No entrance fee.

Refugio State Beach (Hwy. 101 at Refugio Rd., 15 mi. N. of Goleta) Refugio has it all: gorgeous rocky coastline, soft sandy beaches, and tide pools. A bike and hike path leads from the railroad tracks at Hwy. 101 down to the beach, between Refugio and El Capitan State Beach, just to the south. Major campground, snack facilities, restrooms, lifeguards in season. Ample parking. Fees for day and overnight use.

Rincon Beach Park (Hwy. 101 at Bates Rd., Carpinteria) Wooden stairways lead down the steep Rincon Point to the beach, where the smooth sand provides a ringside seat on some of California's hottest surfing action. Parking, restroom facilities. No entrance fee.

West Beach (Cabrillo Blvd., Santa Barbara) Between the harbor and Stearns Wharf, 11 sugar-fine acres of sand offer top sunning and swimming, as well as a boardwalk for walkers, bicyclists, and rollerbladers. Parking, lifeguards. No entrance fee.

BICYCLING

The postcard panoramas and inviting weather of the Central Coast are made for bicycling. Long stretches of scenic roadways attract enthusiasts from all over the West. No town is without its network of clearly marked bike lanes or paths through strings of villages, along meandering country lanes, and into beach and forest parklands. Following are bicycle rental specialists to outfit your cycling sessions.

With palm trees and pathways for bicyclists and roller skaters, Santa Barbara's West Beach is one of the most popular play-grounds on the Central Coast.

Santa Cruz Coast

Bicyclery 415/726-6000; 432 Main St., Half Moon Bay
Dutchman Bicycles 408/476-9555; 3961 Portola Dr. at 41st Ave., Santa Cruz

Monterey Coast

Adventures by the Sea Inc. 408/372-1807; 299 Cannery Row, Monterey
Bay Bike Rentals 408/646-9090; 640 Wave St., Monterey
Bay Bike Rentals 408/625-2453; Lincoln St. bet. 5th and 6th Sts., Carmel
Carmel Bicycle 408/625-2211; 7150 Carmel Valley Rd., Carmel

San Luis Obispo Coast

Central Coast Adventures 805/927-4386; Plaza del Cavalier Suite 5B, San Simeon
Pismo Bike Rental 805/773-0355; 500 Cypress St., Pismo Beach
SLO Spokes Rentals 805/542-9396, 800/653-9391; 1319 Kentwood Dr., San Luis Obispo

Santa Barbara Coast

Beach Rentals 805/963-2524; 8 West Cabrillo Blvd., Santa Barbara
Bicycles Ltd. 805/964-4913; 5707 Calle Real, Goleta

On a clear day the hills of Monterey across the bay are visible to bicyclists enjoying the bluffs above Santa Cruz.

Shmuel Thaler

Cycles Four Rent Inc. 805/966-3804; 101 State St., Santa Barbara
Isla Vista Bicycle Boutique 805/968-3338; 880 Embarcadero Del Mar, Isla Vista

BIRD-WATCHING

Hundreds of species of birds live and nest in or migrate to the Central Coast, one of the richest bird habitats in the U.S. The shallow waters of bays and beach areas attract shorebirds like grebes and sanderlings; the rich waters off the coast swell with shearwater gulls and long-necked cormorants, as well as open-ocean species like the albatross, traveling thousands of miles to feed here. Tidal areas everywhere host sandpipers, delightfully quick and delicate birds continually chasing waves on long pencil-thin legs and digging deep

One of the richest bird habitats in the United States, the shallow waters of bays and beach areas of the Central Coast are home to hundreds of species of waterfowl, such as the snowy egret.

Shmuel Thaler

into the mud for tiny crustacea. Most majestic are the lagoon-loving blue herons — whose wingspans surpass six feet — and plumed white egrets. But nothing matches the sight of a line of pelicans cruising in formation at sunset, diving suddenly straight down into the waves to spear a quick marine dinner.

Santa Cruz Coast

Pescadero Marsh Natural Preserve (Hwy. 1, N. of Pescadero Rd., 15 mi. S. of Half Moon Bay) Over 160 species of birds regularly visit and breed in this gorgeous, undeveloped sanctuary, the largest coastal marshlands between Marin and Elkhorn Slough. In late fall and early spring, the waters teem with loons and grebes, additions to the resident community of egrets, herons, kites, hawks, mallards, and cinnamon teal. Bird watching is allowed along Pescadero Rd. and on marked interpretive trails off Hwy. 1, but tread lightly in this sensitive area.

Scott Creek (Hwy. 1, N. of Davenport) Tule-lined wetlands are encircled by the sandy beach on one side and the canyons and redwood-topped Santa Cruz Mountains on the other. Wood ducks, cinnamon teals, mallards, and coots keep company with grebes, herons, and egrets here, especially beautiful in the early morning when mists rise from the surface of the deep green water.

Twin Lakes State Beach (East Cliff Dr., near 7th Ave., Santa Cruz) Schwan Lagoon, spilling over onto the white sandy beach, originates across the slender roadway as a eucalyptus-ringed wildfowl refuge enjoyed via a wooded path around the park. Here grebes and black-necked stilts glide in company with long-billed curlews and marbled godwits. Loons may be heard in the tall grasses.

Monterey Coast

Andrew Molera State Park (Hwy. 1, N. end of Old Coast Rd., Big Sur) A lively bird sanctuary is at the lagoon where the Big Sur River flows to the ocean. Grebes, wood ducks, geese, scoters, and coots join sea otters enamored of shellfish lodged in huge kelp beds.

Carmel River State Beach (Scenic Rd. at Carmelo St., Carmel) A lovely, protected marsh filled with kingfishers, hawks, pelicans, cormorants, sandpipers, herons, egrets, ducks, and geese. Much to delight novice as well as experienced birdwatchers.

Elkhorn Slough (Hwy. 1 at Moss Landing) An intertidal reserve with 1400 acres of wetland, marsh, and dunes, this is home to hundreds of species of wildlife, including rare California brown pelicans and California clapper rails, plus the occasional peregrine falcon and golden eagle. Thousands of shore birds feed here together in great agitated flocks, especially sandpipers, killdeers, curlews, willets, and sanderlings. Here resident gulls — Western, California, and Heermann's — join mallards and pintail ducks. In the lagoons, observe California murres, grebes, scoters, and coots. Cameras and binoculars are a must. (Elkhorn Slough Foundation, 408/728-5939; 1700 Elkhorn Rd., Watsonville, 95076.)

Point Lobos State Park (Hwy. 1, 3 mi. S. of Carmel) Among the many wonders of this spectacularly beautiful wilderness preserve is an abundance of birdlife (more than 250 species), and rocky outcroppings and islands studded with nesting sites of Brandt's cormorant. Blue herons and white egrets are fond of the marshy meadows.

Salinas River Wildlife Area (Potrero Rd., west of Hwy. 1, Moss Landing) 250 acres of shoreline boast sheltered dunes laced with wildflowers and, just south of the beach, the 500-acre Salinas River National Wildlife Refuge, home to sandpipers, herons, egrets, brown pelicans, and snowy plovers.

San Luis Obispo Coast

Nipomo Dunes Preserve (End of Main St., Guadalupe) Encompassing magnificent dunes, including the largest on the West Coast, this rare habitat shelters myriad bird species, including endangered species such as the California least tern. In autumn, look for cinnamon teals, black brants, ruddy ducks, and mallards.

Montaña de Oro State Park (2 mi. S. of Los Osos via Los Osos Valley/Pecho Rd.) Native and migrating birds find their way to the sheltered coves and windswept bluffs of this sprawling 8400-acre preserve. Albatrosses and pelicans soar above the cliffs, which in summer become the nesting site for the elusive pigeon guillemot and black oyster-catcher. Diverse winged wildlife in a setting of splendid isolation.

Morro Bay State Park (Hwy. 1, Morro Bay) Within this confluence of nutrient-rich mud flats and bay, the 576-foot high volcanic plug Morro Rock is an ecological preserve for the highly endangered peregrine falcon. Nesting falcons are protected here and the rock is closed to entrance. Binoculars are recommended for catching a glimpse of the spectacular raptor. In winter and fall, thousands of other migrating birds can be viewed from the broad beach as they feed on the clams, oysters, and shrimp of the tidal mud. A stopping point on the Pacific Migratory Flyway, the bay and beach attract over 250 species of native and migrating birds. In the bay estuary, a dense stand of eucalyptus trees forms the largest great blue heron rookery between San Francisco and the Mexican border. From January until mid-summer, the enormous birds will build nests, lay eggs, and feed their fledglings in this rookery. Docents at the State Park Museum of Natural History provide guided walks during nesting season (805/772-2694).

Santa Barbara Coast

Andree Clark Bird Refuge (East Cabrillo Blvd. at Hwy. 101, Santa Barbara) Near the glamorous swimming and sunning of East Beach, this 42-acre refuge showcases a sheltered saltwater marsh popular with cormorants, ducks, geese, herons, and egrets. Bike path and grassy area.

Goleta Slough (5990 Sandspit Rd., Goleta) Just beyond the sand dunes fronting Goleta Point, a nutrient-rich wetland caters to stilt-legged egrets, snowy plovers, blue herons, and countless sandpipers.

Monarch Butterfly Migration

Great clouds of brilliant orange and black wings descend upon the Central Coast each winter as monarch butterflies migrate south for the winter. Fond of wintering packed tightly together in astonishing clusters, they enshroud entire groves of eucalyptus as they wait in semi-dormancy for the warmth of spring. Starting in October, monarchs are visible all over the coastline, but several spots are renowned for their annual populations of hundreds of thousands of butterflies. Both Pacific Grove and the Morro Bay area consider themselves "world capitals" of monarch migration. The eucalyptus groves along Pacific Grove's Ocean View Blvd. and along the 1900 block of Lighthouse Avenue are legendary for this autumn influx of lepidoptera, which fly over 3000 miles to these particular trees. The sheltered forests of Montaña de Oro near Morro Bay, and at Natural Bridges State Park, north of Santa Cruz, are also prime viewing spots. Look but don't touch. Docents at Morro Bay State Park Museum of Natural History (805/772-2694) and at Natural Bridges State Park (408/423-4609 or 688-3241) lead "butterfly walks" in fall and winter.

Each winter huge numbers of monarch butterflies migrate south for the winter, blanketing eucalyptus groves throughout the Central Coast, especially in Santa Cruz, Pacific Grove, and Morro Bay.

Shmuel Thaler

Ocean Beach County Park (Highway 246, 10 mi. west of Hwy. 1, Surf) Where the Santa Ynez River forms a lagoon at the edge of the ocean, a 28-acre park provides sanctuary for abundant waterfowl, including rare and endangered species like the California least tern and California brown pelican. Surrounding dunes are a popular nesting site and may be closed to the public during spring and summer.

BOATING

S ince this *is* the Pacific Ocean coastline, dimpled with gentle bays and invigorated by surf, boating of every variation awaits veteran and novice sailors alike. Pioneered by able Chumash Indian navigators, who plied the Central Coast waters in their pitch-coated canoes, boating here will transport you to some of the finest views, fishing, and thrills available. Many feel that a visit to this seaside playground isn't complete without an outing on the Pacific; professionals can provide all the equipment, advice, and safe sailing tips you'll need to sail off into the sunset.

CANOEING AND SEA KAYAKING

Individualists who prefer their boating experiences in splendid isolation will find small, state-of-the-art rental crafts for getting in touch with the blue sea without the distractions of power motors or other people. Remember that basic rules of safety insure maximum enjoyment, and wear appropriate protective gear and life jackets.

Marine kayaking is an increasingly popular Central Coast sport for those who enjoy getting close to the sea.

Shmuel Thaler

Santa Cruz Coast

Adventure Sports Unlimited (408/458-3648; Sash Mill #15, 303 Potrero St., Santa Cruz) Instruction, classes, rentals, sales, tours of Big Sur and Carmel.

Kayak Connection (408/479-1121; Santa Cruz Yacht Harbor, 413 Lake Ave., Santa Cruz) Guided tours, long and short kayak rentals, retail sales.

Monterey Coast

Adventures By the Sea (408/372-1807, 408/372-4103 Fax; 299 Cannery Row, Monterey) Classes, instruction, rentals, sales, and tours by Monterey Bay Aquarium personnel.

Monterey Bay Kayaks (800/649-5357 CA, 408/373-5357, 693 Del Monte Ave., Monterey) One-stop shopping for still-water and marine kayaking; equipment, rentals, classes; tours of Monterey Bay, Carmel Bay, Elkhorn Slough, Big Sur.

San Luis Obispo Coast

Central Coast Adventures (805/927-4386; PO Box 160, San Simeon) Instruction, tours, lessons, sales, rentals.

Good Clean Fun Surf & Sport (805/995-1993; 136 Ocean Front, Cayucos) Instructional tours, lessons, rentals, sales. Private charters, group rates and school outings.

Kayaks of Morro Bay (805/772-1119, evenings & weekends; Morro Bay)

Guided outings and instruction in sea kayaking. No experience needed. Call for reservations, weekends only.

Lost Horizons Sea Kayaking (805/595-7244; First and San Antonio Sts., Avila Beach) Rentals, sales, classes, guided tours.

Morro Bay Outfitter (805/772-1119; 844 Main St., Morro Bay) Kayak and canoe rentals, lessons, tours.

Santa Barbara Coast

Aquatics (805/964-8680; 5370 Hollister Ave., Santa Barbara) Equipment, supplies, rentals, excursions.

Paddle Sports (805/899-4925; 100 State St., Santa Barbara) Lessons, rentals, sales, tours.

CRUISES AND CHARTERS

Some of the finest views of the Central Coast are seen to full advantage from the comfort of a launch piloted by a professional. From catamarans to romantic sloops to sturdy power launches, cruises and charter opportunities abound here.

Private charters and sunset cruises of Monterey Bay are the specialty of Chardonnay Charters, based at the Santa Cruz Small Craft Harbor.

Santa Cruz Coast

Chardonnay Sailing Charters (408/423-1213; PO Box 66966, Scotts Valley) 3-day and sunset cruises, private charters aboard 50-ft. ultra-light racing yacht. Depart from Santa Cruz Small Craft Harbor.

Earth, Sea & Sky Tours (408/688-5544; PO Box 1630, Aptos) Professionally guided tours. Whale-watching, fishing, and diving excursions; sunset, champagne, and dinner cruises.

Pacific Yachting (408/476-2370, 800/374-2626; 333 Lake Ave., Santa Cruz) 2-, 4- or 6-hour cruises.

Monterey Coast

Monterey Sport Fishing Cruises (408/372-2203; 96 Fisherman's Wharf No. 1, Monterey) Specialties include whale-watching, marine mammal, and nature cruises in the Marine Wildlife Sanctuary.

Twin Otters Diving Charters (408/394-4235; Municipal Wharf No. 2, Monterey) Takes up to 20 people for sightseeing and 15 for scuba diving. Will match 2 or 3 interested singles with an already-booked group outing. Cruise wanders the coast as far south as Pt. Lobos to see porpoises, whales, otters, harbor seals, sea lions, and coastal sites.

San Luis Obispo Coast

Central Coast Cruises (805/772-4776; 501 Embarcadero, Morro Bay) Ocean and nature cruises, private parties and weddings, with special event catering.

Morro Bay Sailing Center (805/772-8085; 699 Embarcadero, Morro Bay) Harbor cruises aboard the *African Queen*. The *Clam Taxi* transports clammers to the Morro Bay sand spit.

Tiger's Folly II (805/772-2257, 772-2255; 1205 Embarcadero, Morro Bay) 1-hour cruises of Morro Bay, plus champagne Sunday brunch cruises. Sails daily during the summer; weekends and holidays, winter. Full bar on board.

Santa Barbara Coast

Captain Don's Harbor Cruises (805/969-5217; Stearns Wharf/PO Box 1134, Summerland) 40-minute narrated cruise aboard the *Harbor Queen* up and down Santa Barbara coast. Sails mid-June–Labor Day on the hour between 11–4; rest of year weekends and holidays, weather permitting. Sunset coastal cruises, summer, Sat. 6–8pm. Whale-watching trips during annual migration.

Condor **Sunset Dinner & Cocktail Cruises** (805/963-3564; Sea Landing, Santa Barbara) Guests aboard the 88-ft. motorized *Condor* have option of cocktails only or barbecued fish or tri-tip steak dinner.

Museum of Natural History Island Cruises (805/963-1067; 211 Stearns Wharf, Santa Barbara) All-day boat tours of the Channel Islands in conjunction with the Sea Center. Length of tour depends on the island visited.

Sunset Kidd's (805/962-8222; Breakwater, Santa Barbara) Variety of sail trips (overnight Channel Islands, sunset and hour-long harbor cruises) and private charters.

Sailing Center of Santa Barbara

(805/962-2826; Breakwater, Santa Barbara) The largest sailing school in Southern California features beginning to advanced lessons aboard 42 boats that range in size from 14 ft. to 50 ft. Sail boats and 40-horsepower boats also are available for rent.

CAMPING

Nurtured by enterprising nature lovers and the mighty California State Parks system, the Central Coast could reasonably be viewed as a 300-mile-long campground dotted with a few population centers. Visitors come

Campers in the Central Coast will find quiet sylvan retreats and majestic coastal views.

Kim Reierson

from all over the country — indeed, the world — to spend a few nights outdoors within view of the majestic coastal landscape. The camping possibilities range from plush private campgrounds complete with stores, showers, electricity, and laundry facilities, to beach and backcountry environmental campsites equipped only with table, tent space, and pit toilets. In summer, only the foolhardy would set out without reservations.

Santa Cruz Coast

Henry Cowell Redwoods State Park (408/335-4598, 408/438-2396; 101 North Big Trees Park Rd., Felton) Take the Graham Hill Rd. turnoff from Hwy. 1 at the north edge of Santa Cruz to the main camping area of this enormous park. Magnificent stands of redwood giants share the hilly terrain with towering maples, Douglas fir, and moss-covered bay. Hiking trails lead through shaded areas carpeted with ferns and wildflowers, and up to open meadows. Remains of a 19th-century limekiln are in the Fall Creek area of the park, as are abundant creeks and waterfalls. Steelhead and coho fishing is excellent in the San Lorenzo River here. Cool in summer and popular with extended-stay campers. Tables, stoves, sanitation facilities. Day-use and camping fee.

New Brighton State Beach Park (408/475-4850; 1500 Park Ave., Capitola) Framed by sheltering bluffs thick with eucalyptus groves, this wide, sandy beach offers 115 campsites, some bicycle camping facilities, wheelchair-accessible restrooms, and interpretive nature trails. Fossils from ancient seabeds in the bluffs; driftwood abounds after stormy weather. Entrance fee.

Seacliff State Beach Park (408/688-3222, 408/688-3241; Seacliff exit off Hwy. 1, Aptos) 26 campsites and trailer hookups on the wide white beach from the edge of Rio Del Mar's summer houses to the "cement ship" fishing pier. Walk for miles along this stretch of coastline, though you'll have plenty of company on summer weekends. Wheelchair-accessible restrooms. Camping fee.

Sunset State Beach Park (408/724-1266; 201 Sunset Beach Blvd.) Framed by hills and meadows, this fine vacation setting has 90 campsites, restrooms, picnic grounds, and excellent surf fishing. Only the reckless would attempt the chilly water and hazardous surf, but the 7 miles of broad, white sand beach make for fine walking, beachcombing — look for tiny sand dollars and sea anemone shells — and sunbathing. Camping and day-use fee.

Monterey Coast

Mistix — Campground Reservations

For all State Park campground reservations, call 800/444-7275. Make reservations at least two days but no more than eight weeks before the desired date. State Parks have a one-week stay limit between June 1–September 30 and a 15-day limit the rest of the year.

Andrew Molera State Park (408/667-2315; PO Box A, Big Sur) An array of landscapes and ecozones merge in 5000 acres of forests, shoreline, meadows, and lagoon bordering the ocean and the sycamore-lined Big Sur River. Walk-in campsites are one-third mile from the parking lot; 3-day overnight limit. Fire pits, chemical toilets; campers must carry their own water. No fee for camping.

Big Sur Campground and Cabins (408/667-2322; Hwy. 1, Big Sur) Popular, secluded, and forested, this privately owned landmark along the Big Sur River has reserve-in-advance campsites — each with wood-burning fire pit, table, water outlet, and power hookup. Bathhouses with hot showers, a playground, laundry, grocery store, tent rental.

Limekiln Beach Redwoods Campground (408/667-2403; Hwy. 1, Big Sur) A privately owned campground with 60 campsites on the beach and in the encircling redwoods offers waterfalls and glimpses of historic limekilns. Restrooms, showers, supply store; but no electricity.

Pfeiffer Big Sur State Park Campground (408/667-2315; Hwy. 1, Big Sur) Over 800 redwood-forested acres stretch along the steep hillsides and along the secluded Big Sur River. 218 campsites with a picnic table and stove; many are wheelchair-accessible. The campground offers swimming and fishing, and a prime trailside stopping point at Pfeiffer Falls. Group campsites are available, as well as a store and laundry, guided hikes, and cozy campfire gatherings in the summer.

Ventana Campground (408/667-2331, 408/624-4812; Hwy. 1, 2 mi. S. of Pfeiffer Big Sur State Park, Big Sur) A privately owned campground in a world-class setting. Luxurious restaurant amenities are available just up the hill at the rustically elegant Ventana Inn. No reservations; show up before 6pm to stake your claim. Camping fee.

San Luis Obispo Coast

Montaña de Oro State Park (805/722-2560; 805/528-0513; Pecho Rd., Los Osos) 8000 acres of sage and wildflower bluffs, and enormous eucalyptus groves highlight this coastal sanctuary, where 50 miles of hiking trails lead through steep canyons and down to secluded pocket beaches. A table and stove come with each of the 50 rustic campsites. Restrooms, ample parking, and the illusion of complete isolation. Camping fee.

Morro Bay State Park (805/772-2560; Morro Bay) The park overlooks the extensive mud flats at the mouth of Los Osos Creek, a prime marshland habitat.

Los Padres National Forest

(Main headquarters: 42 Aero Camino St., Goleta, 805/968-1578) Straddling the coast and mountains of the Central Coast from Big Sur to Santa Barbara, this diverse swath of protected natural splendor encompasses close to 2 million acres of rocky shoreline, steep canyons, redwood forests, and dense chaparral rising from sea level up to 6000-ft. peaks. Major rivers originate in the forest's interior, cutting their way through rich wildlife habitats on the way to the Pacific Ocean. Paradise for back-country hikers, Los Padres offers 1700 miles of trails, over 260 trail camps, and 88 campgrounds with 1000 sites. Purists find the wilderness potential of this preserve a refreshing alternative to commercially developed tourist destinations. Reservations are not accepted for campsites, which are limited to 14-day stays. For information about availability, road conditions, and permits for backcountry treks, call 805/683-6711. Worth sending for is the *Trail Guide to the Los Padres National Forest* (Sierra Club, Box 5667, Carmel), with detailed information about the many trails weaving through this mighty resource.

---

135 campsites with picnic tables and stoves; 20 with hookups for electricity and water. Campsites for self-contained RVs, a public golf course, boat ramp, docks. Blue herons nest in the eucalyptus treetops from winter to mid-summer.

Pismo State Beach North Beach Campground (805/489-2684; South Dolliver St., Oceano) Over 100 campsites with picnic tables and stoves lie several hundred yards from the ocean, framed by stands of eucalyptus. Trails to the beach wind along Meadow Creek, passing through one of the favorite haunts of the monarch butterfly. Golfers can play at the public La Sage Golf Course at the south end of the campground.

Pismo State Beach Oceano Campground (805/489-2684; Pier Ave., Oceano) Between Oceano Lagoon and Pismo Beach, these 82 campsites offer trailer hookups, fire pits, and tables. Showers, restrooms, and hiking trails around the lagoon. Take binoculars to view the area's fabled waterfowl population.

San Simeon State Beach (800/444-7275, 805/927-2035; Hwy. 1 bet. San Simeon Creek and Santa Rose Creek) Two campgrounds, one developed (San Simeon Creek), the other primitive (Washburn) include over 200 campsites, and a hiker/bicyclist group site. Paths lead to the splendid beach and creeks. A very popular summer overnight destination, given the proximity to superior coastal scenery and Hearst Castle; reservations are advised.

Santa Barbara Coast

Carpinteria State Beach (805/684-2811; 5361 Sixth St., Carpinteria) 50 acres of dunes and bluffs frame the secluded narrow shoreline — self-proclaimed the safest beach on the Central Coast. Over 100 campsites for tents and trailers; 160 sites for RVs; expansive grassy picnic area. Showers, fire pits, restrooms, ample parking. Legendary surfing action.

El Capitan State Beach (805/968-1411, 805/ 968-3294; south of Hwy. 101, 12 mi. N. of Goleta) Rugged hiking trails skirt the rocky coastline at this 130-acre park, with 142 camping sites, restrooms — some wheelchair-accessible — showers, fire pits, hiking trails, and access to the popular surfing beach.

Gaviota State Park (805/968-3294; Hwy. 101 at Gaviota Beach Rd., Gaviota) Miles of shoreline, thousands of acres of upland terrain, sandy beaches, and a fishing pier attract campers to this popular coastal playground. Store for fishing and outdoor supplies and outdoor-life necessities, 20 tent sites, 36 sites for self-contained RVs, and 40 trailer sites (no hookups), all with picnic tables and fire pits. Wheelchair-accessible restrooms.

Refugio State Beach (805/968-1350, 805/968-3294; Hwy. 101 at Refugio Rd., 15 mi. N. of Goleta) With tide pools and welcoming lifeguarded beaches in summer, this 90-acre beachfront park has a camping area with 85 campsites, and spaces for RVs. Restrooms, showers, fire pits, picnic tables, plus snack bar and depot for purchase of fishing licenses and bait.

FISHING

The joys of Central Coast fishing haven't changed all that much from the days when Native American experts plied the rich Pacific waters for bonito and albacore. In many places up and down the coast, settlements continue to exist supported by fishing industries of varying magnitudes. Still teeming with an abundance of fine sport and eating fish, the Central Coast rewards the fishing trip devotee with outstanding salmon, rock cod, halibut, smelt, sand dabs, bonito, and flounder. Pier and surf fishing at many beaches and state parks also are excellent. A California State Fishing License is required; for license information, call the California Department of Fish and Game's 24-hour recording: 916/739-3571.

Santa Cruz Coast

Huck Finn Sportfishing (415/726-7133; PO Box 1432, El Granada) Open-party and charter trips for salmon and rock fish aboard a 60-ft. boat. Bait, tackle, rental gear. Check in 5:15am, depart 6:15am, return 3pm.

Shamrock Charters (408/476-2648; Santa Cruz Yacht Harbor; 2210 East Cliff Dr., Santa Cruz) Open boats or private charters for salmon, rock cod, and ling-cod fishing in season. Complete tackle shop and deli section. Licenses, bait, rod and skiff rental.

Stagnaro's Fishing Trips (408/427-2334, 423-2010; Santa Cruz Municipal Wharf, PO Box 1340, Santa Cruz) Daily, half-day and evening trips for salmon and bottom fish, bait provided. Fish cleaning and ice packing available. Full service wharf shop, bait, tackle, rentals, snacks, beer.

Monterey Coast

Chris' Fishing Trips (408/375-5951; 48 Fisherman's Wharf No. 1, Monterey) Deep sea fishing, boats chartered by appointment.

Monterey Sports Fishing (408/372-2203; 96 Fisherman's Wharf, Monterey) Half- and full-day fishing charters. Salmon and albacore party trips in season. Bottom fish trips for lingcod and others. Bait provided, licenses, tackle, fish cleaning and freezing services, rod rentals.

Randy's Fishing Trips (408/372-7440; 66 Fisherman's Wharf #1, Monterey) Deep-sea fishing trips for salmon and albacore. Bait provided, tackle for rent; licenses, sack lunches, fish cleaning.

Sam's Fishing Fleet (408/372-0577; 84 Fisherman's Wharf No. 1, Monterey) One 65 ft. and three 55 ft. boats for deep sea fishing. Rod rentals available.

Tom's Sportfishing (408/633-2564; PO Box 647, Moss Landing) Private charters, open parties, nature trips, whale watching, bay cruises.

San Luis Obispo Coast

Bob's Sport Fishing (805/772-3340; 845 Embarcadero, Morro Bay) Offshore rock cod, salmon, and albacore fishing trips by day and half-day (some twilight trips). Tackle rentals, bait included. Private charters.

Paradise Sportfishing and Charters (805/595-7200; Port San Luis, Avila Beach) Charter boats for daily rock cod fishing trips year-round, plus salmon and albacore in season. Live bait, tackle shop, licenses, rental equipment.

Virg's Deep Sea Fish'n Centers (805/772-1222; 1215 Embarcadero, Morro Bay) Half-day, full-day, twilight trips for halibut, albacore. Local trips for rock fish and other bottom species. Two-day trips for lingcod. Tackle rentals.

Santa Barbara Coast

Charter Boat *Condor* (805/963-3564; Breakwater Sea Landing, Santa Barbara) One- and two-day fishing trips on a comfortable 88-ft./46-bunk vessel, with galley service and cocktail lounge. Catch includes rock fish, lingcod, cal-

The sport fishing options in Santa Barbara are plentiful and easily accessible at the main Yacht Harbor.

ico bass, halibut.

Hook, Line & Sinker (805/687-5689; 4010-5 Calle Real, Santa Barbara) This bait-and-tackle shop is the place to go for local fishing information, licenses, fresh- or saltwater gear, custom rods, equipment repair.

Hornet Sportfishing (805/963-3564; Breakwater, Santa Barbara) Call for reservations or private charter. Half-day fishing on 50-ft. vessel. Tackle rental, full galley, beer, one-day fishing licenses, CPR certified crew.

Paradise Sport Fishing & Charter (805/595-7200; PO Box 356, Avila Beach) Rock cod, salmon, albacore, halibut are the catch. Charters, rod rental.

Sea Landing Sport Fishing (805/963-3564; Breakwater, Santa Barbara) Half-day, three-quarter day, all-day coastal and island trips, and twilight trips in season. Live bait, tackle rental.

GOLF

The internationally renowned links that cluster on the rugged Monterey coastline annually fete the gifted and the famous at the U.S. Open. But golf is a way of life throughout the Central Coast, where lush manicured greens merge with the superb natural scenery.

Santa Cruz Coast

Aptos Seascape Golf Course (408/688-3213; 610 Clubhouse Dr., Aptos) Public, 18 holes, 6123 yards, par 72, rated 69.6. Pro shop, restaurant, banquet facility, golf lounge.

De Laveaga Golf Course (408/423-7212, 408/423-7214; Upper Park Rd. & De Laveaga Dr., Santa Cruz) Public, 18 holes, 6010 yards, par 72, rated 70.1. Cart rental, pro shop, restaurant, bar.

Half Moon Bay Golf Links (415/726-4438; 2000 Fairway Drive, Half Moon Bay) Public, 18 holes, 7100 yards, par 72, rated 71. Cart rental, pro shop, restaurant, bar.

Pasatiempo Golf Club (408/459-9155; 18 Clubhouse Rd., Santa Cruz) Semi-private, 18 holes, 6483 yards, par 72, rated 72.9. Pro shop, restaurant, bar.

Monterey Coast

Carmel Valley Ranch Golf Course (408/626-2510; 1 Old Ranch Rd., Carmel) Public, members, and guests; 18 holes, 6055 yards, par 70, rated 67.8. Cart rental, pro shop, restaurant, bar.

Cypress Point Golf Club (408/624-2223; 17 Mile Dr., Pebble Beach) Members and guests, 6332 yards, par 72, rated 72.3. Cart rental.

Laguna Seca Golf Course (408/373-3701; 10520 York Rd., Monterey) Public, 18 holes, 5711 yards, par 71, rated 68.5.

Links at Spanish Bay (408/647-7495, 800/654-9300; 2700 17 Mile Dr., Pebble

In the heart of Carmel Valley, Quail Lodge surrounds its gorgeous golfing greens with a series of ponds and classic California rancho scenery.

Beach) Public and members, 18 holes, 6078 yards, par 72, rated 72.1. Cart rental, pro shop, restaurant, bar.

Monterey Peninsula Country Club (408/373-1556; 3000 Club Rd., Pebble Beach) Members and guests, 36 holes, (Dunes) 6161 yards, 72 par, rated 69.4; (Shore) 6173 yards, par 71, rated 69.7. Cart rental, pro shop, restaurant, bar.

Old Del Monte Golf Course (408.373-2436; 1300 Sylvan Rd., Monterey) Public and guests, 18 holes, 6007 yards, par 72, rated 69.5. Cart rental, pro shop, restaurant, bar.

Pacific Grove Municipal Golf Links (408/648-3177; 77 Asilomar Blvd., Pacific Grove) Public, 18 holes, 5547 yards, par 70, rated 66.3. Lessons, pro shop, lockers, practice range.

Pebble Beach Golf Links (408/624-6611; 17 Mile Dr., Pebble Beach) Public and guests, 18 holes, 6345 yards, par 72, rated 72.7. Cart rental, pro shop, restaurant, bar.

Peter Hays Golf Course (408/625-8518; 17 Mile Dr., Pebble Beach) Public, 9 holes, 819 yards, par 27, unrated.

Poppy Hills Golf Course (408/625-2035; 3200 Lopez Rd., Pebble Beach) Public, members, and guests; 18 holes, 6219 yards, par 72, rated 71.7. Cart rental, pro shop, restaurant, bar.

Quail Lodge (408/624-2770; 8000 Valley Green Dr., Carmel) Members and guests, 18 holes, 6141 yards, par 71, rated 70.2. Cart rental, pro shop, restaurant, bar.

Rancho Cañada Golf Club (408/624-0111; Carmel Valley Rd., Carmel) Public, 36 holes, (east) 5822 yards, par 71, rated 67.3; (west) 6071 yards, par 72, rated 69.6. Cart rental.

Spyglass Hill Golf Course (408/625-8563, 800/654-9300; Stevenson Dr. and Spy Glass Hill, Pebble Beach) Members and guests, 18 holes, 6346 yards, par 72, rated 73. Cart rental, pro shop, restaurant, bar.

San Luis Obispo Coast

Morro Bay Golf Club (805/772-4560; State Park Rd., Morro Bay) Public, 18 holes, 6113 yards, par 71, rated 69.1. Cart and club rental, pro shop, lessons, snack bar.

Pismo State Beach Golf Course (805/481-5215; 9 LeSage Dr., Grover City) Public, 9 holes, 2795 yards, par 54 for 18, unrated. Cart and club rentals, pro shop, clubhouse, locker room, snack bar, restaurant.

San Luis Bay Golf Course (805/595-2307; 2 mi. W. of Hwy. 101 off Avila Dr., San Luis Obispo) Public, 18 holes, 6048 yards, par 71, rated 60. Cart and club rental, pro shop, lessons, cocktail lounge, restaurant

San Luis Obispo Golf & Country Club (805/543-4035; 255 Country Club Dr., San Luis Obispo) Members and guests, 18 holes, 6390 yards, par 72, rated 70. Cart and club rental, lessons, bar and restaurant.

Santa Barbara Coast

Alisal Guest Ranch (805/688-4215; 1054 Alisal Rd., Solvang) Members and guests, 18 holes, 6100 yards, par 72, rated 68.5. Cart rental, pro shop, restaurant, bar, dress code.

Birnan Woods Golf Club (805/969-0919; 2031 Packing House Rd., Santa Barbara) Members and guests, 18 holes, 5890 yards, par 70, rated 68.7. Cart rental.

Montecito Country Club (805/969-0800; 920 Summit Rd., Santa Barbara) Members and guests, 18 holes, 6184 yards, par 71, rated 69.9. Cart rental, pro shop, restaurant, bar.

River Course at the Alisal (805/688-64042, 805/688-2510 fax; 150 Alisal Road, Solvang) Public, 18 holes, 6117 yards, par 72, rated 68.8. Cart rentals, lessons.

Sandpiper Golf Course (805/968-1541; 7925 Hollister Ave., Goleta) Public; 18 holes, 6645 yards, par 72, rated 72.5. Cart rental.

Santa Barbara Golf Club (805/687-7087; 3500 McCaw Ave., Santa Barbara) Public, 18 holes, 5777 yards, par 70, rated 66.1. Club and cart rental, pro shop, snack bar, tournament banquets.

Valley Club of Montecito (805/969-4681; 1901 East Valley Rd., Santa Barbara) Members and guests, 18 holes, 6600 yards, par 72, rated 70. Cart rental, pro shop, restaurant, bar.

Village Country Club (805/733-3537; 4300 Clubhouse Rd., Lompoc) Members and guests, 18 holes, 6269 yards, par 72, rated 69.6. Cart rental.

Zaca Creek Golf Course (805/688-2575; 223 Shadow Mountain Dr., Buellton) Public, 9 holes, 3088 yards, par 58 for 18, rated 50. Pro shop.

HIKING

When visionary naturalist John Muir urged an entire nation to "climb the high mountains and get their glad tidings," Californians took him at his compelling terrain of forests, wetlands, canyons, meadows, and shoreline, unequaled for sheer diversity and ease of access. Beginning with an environmental renaissance in the 1970s, an explosion of hikers has sought out the Central Coast's pristine natural micro-environments. Endless stretches of trails interlace millions of acres of public and State Park lands on this slender border of 5000-foot mountains and restless tides. Much of this wealth is available to those with no more sophisticated equipment than good walking shoes, a daypack, map, water bottle, and healthy sense of wonder. But the accomplished adventurer as well will find ample outdoor challenges for world-class overnight wilderness exploration.

The first State Park in California, Big Basin State Park, north of Santa Cruz, has 80 miles of hiking trails wandering through more than 18,000 acres.

Shmuel Thaler

Santa Cruz Coast

Big Basin State Park (14 mi. N. of Santa Cruz on Hwy. 9, extending to Hwy. 1, 30 mi. N. of Santa Cruz) 80 miles of hiking trails on 18,000 acres of redwood forest stretching down to the rocky Pacific coastline. Founded in 1902, Big Basin was the first State Park in the California system. Its crystal-clear streams, surging waterfalls, wildlife-rich meadows, fern canyons, and old-growth redwoods provide some of the finest hiking on the West Coast. *Berry Creek Falls/Sunset* loop begins at the park headquarters and threads through cathedral stands of redwoods to the 65-ft.-high Berry Creek Falls cascading into a mossy pool in the heart of the forest. For a variety of landscape in a single, all-day trek, follow trails along *Waddell Creek* and *Gazos Creek*. Leading from the park's mountain interior all the way down to the ocean at Hwy. 1, 6 to 8 hour odysseys wind through stands of Douglas fir, madrone and tanbark oak, wild huckleberry, orchids, iris, and western azalea. Maps for trails at the ranger's station at Park Headquarters.

Forest of Nisene Marks (Aptos Creek Rd., via Hwy. 1, Seascape exit) Ablaze with wildflowers during the spring and carpeted with mosses and ferns during the lush winter wet season, 10,000 acres of relatively undeveloped splendor showcase towering second-growth redwoods, vigorously reborn after the intensive logging of the late 19th century. Hiking trails lead into deep canyons and up to bluffs with views of the ocean; the most popular follow Aptos Creek Canyon past the ghost town remnants of mining and logging camps. Quail, possum, and mule deer thrive here and, in spring, the forest floor explodes with exquisite trillium, toothwort, and starflowers. The forest contains the epicenter of the recent 1989 Loma Prieta Earthquake, marked by a sign on the Aptos Creek Trail. Day walks, picnics, horseback riding, bicycling, and overnight camping.

Wilder Ranch State Park (Coast Rd. at Hwy. 1, 5 mi. N. of Santa Cruz) Recently purchased by the state, this former dairy ranch includes authentically restored structures as part of an interpretive site celebrating ranch life on the 19th-century Central Coast. Hiking trails comb the park's 5000 acres, which stretch from plover sanctuaries on the shoreline to heron rookeries, meadows, and redwood bluffs at the 2000-ft. summit. Invigorating views of the ocean from the park's windswept bluffs. The park is open daily from 8am until sunset; call 408/426-0505.

Monterey Coast

Asilomar State Beach (Sunset Dr., Pacific Grove) A challenging stretch of rocky shore offers breathtaking views of boiling white-water tides and wild crashing surf accenting the turquoise Monterey Bay waters. A sandy beach wanders into soft, pillowy dunes filled with native plants and waterfowl habitats. The renowned tide pools fanning out from the bluffs can occupy days of absorbing exploration. Ample parking, restrooms.

Garrapata State Park (Hwy. 1, 2 mi. S. of Malpaso Creek, Big Sur) Hiking the cove and bluffs at this coastal gateway to Big Sur offers spectacular views of the coast from the top of a 1.2 mile trail. The lengthy Sea Otter Game Refuge extends offshore down to the San Luis Obispo county line. Tide pools, too. 408/667-2315.

Julia Pfeiffer Burns State Park (Hwy. 1, 11 mi. S. of Big Sur State Park, Big Sur) Sprawling from the edge of the ocean up through forested ridges filled with creeks and waterfalls, this 2000-acre preserve contains abundant hiking trails. Splendid ocean view overlooks are at McWay Waterfall, which spills 50 feet into the sea. Magnificent sea caves and sharp rock crags rim the soft sand at many of the park's beaches, including Partington Cove, accessible by a trail that cuts across a wooden footbridge and through a 200-foot-long tunnel carved into the cliffs at Partington Creek. The park closes at sunset; day-use fee.

Pfeiffer Beach Trail (Sycamore Canyon Rd. at Hwy. 1, S. of Big Sur State Park entrance) At the Forest Service parking area, follow the sandy trail to the small lagoon where Sycamore Creek meets the beach. A stunning coastal seascape with caves, tortured rock formations, and swirling water. Not for swimming and usually windy, it's well worth the effort to get there. Scenes in the 1965 Liz Taylor/Richard Burton film *The Sandpiper* were filmed here.

Point Lobos (Hwy. 1 at Riley Ranch Rd., Carmel) This 2500-acre preserve encompasses pristine coves with beaches, jagged rocky outcroppings, ancient cypress groves, tide pools, marshlands, and isolated meadows. The diversity of landscape is staggering — especially bountiful are spring wildflower displays, and hundreds of species of other native plants, birds, and wildlife. Interpretive historic displays at the 19th-century *Whaler's Cabin* museum. Admission fee, ample parking. For information and brochures: 408/624-4909.

Shoreline Park (Ocean View Blvd., bet. Point Cabrillo & Lover's Point, Pacific Grove) Stretching along the rocky cliffs and sheltered sandy coves with magnificent views of the Monterey Bay, the park's paths wind steeply down to tiny beaches, where hazardous surf (and chilly water) preclude swimming. A paved pedestrian trail threads the length of the park along a railroad right of way connecting a series of scenic settings with plenty of benches. Street parking, no facilities.

Spanish Bay Pedestrian Trail (Spanish Bay Rd. at 17 Mile Dr., Pebble Beach) The Monterey pine forests of this stretch of cliffs, tide pools, and pounding surf are accessible via many pedestrian and cycling paths looping from Sunset Dr. at 17-Mile Drive. Stroll through the Spanish Bay Hotel toward the dunes for the *Shoreline Trail*. A mile-long stretch of path fans around Point Joe and leads to pocket beaches and prime bird-watching areas at Seal Rock and Bird Rock.

Ventana Wilderness (Hwy. 1 at Big Sur Coast) Much of the Big Sur Coast and Santa Lucia Mountains lie within this 150,000-acre preserve, itself embraced by the 2-million-acre Los Padres National Forest. A magnificently wild terrain of forests and coastal canyons, and stunning views high above the ocean. Between May–Oct., campfire permits required for backpacking excursions (408/385-5434). Trails lead into the wilderness area; maps, permits, information at Palo Colorado Rd., off Hwy. 1, 10 mi. S. of Carmel.

San Luis Obispo Coast

Leffingwell Landing Bluffs (Moonstone Beach Dr. at Hwy. 1, N. of Cambria) This gorgeous stretch of windswept bluffs with cypress groves, coastal lupines, and dense grasses has well-maintained hiking trails, some leading down to tide pools and cove beaches (look for moonstone agates), others to benches set at seascape vista points. Prime sea otter viewing. Parking, restrooms.

Los Osos Oaks State Park (Los Osos Valley Rd. at Palomino Dr., Los Osos) The rare sight of gnarled, primeval coast live oak is yours for the hiking of two well-marked miles of trails in this beautiful preserve. Vistas of the enchanting Los Osos Valley, with its distinctive volcanic plugs (the so-called Seven Sisters, including Morro Rock). Hikers must honor trail markings along this complex and sensitive ecosystem.

Montaña de Oro State Park (end of Pecho Valley Rd., Los Osos) A wild expanse of fields, canyons, bluffs, and cove beaches. Over 50 miles of hiking and equestrian trails are within 8400 acres bordering 3 miles of coastline. The 1.5-mile *Hazard Canyon Trail* winds through forests and shaded slopes; several trails descend from bluff tops down to the beach and others into vast euca-

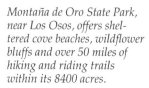

Montaña de Oro State Park, near Los Osos, offers sheltered cove beaches, wildflower bluffs and over 50 miles of hiking and riding trails within its 8400 acres.

Jay Swanson

lyptus groves, one of the state's favored winter nesting spots for the monarch butterfly. The *Montaña de Oro Bluffs Trail* skirts Spooner's Cove and seals lounging near coastal tide pools, offering springtime glimpses of golden poppies and mustard. Restrooms, parking.

Morro Bay Sandspit Trail (Morro Bay at Estero Bay) A 5-mile trail excursion along the sandspit dividing the two bays offers a chance to wander through sand dunes and explore shell mounds left by Chumash ancestors.

Pismo Dunes Preserve (Arroyo Grande Creek off Hwy. 1, Pismo Beach) Protected from vehicle traffic, mountainous sand dunes form a mysterious landscape from the ocean to a mile inland, extending southward for 1.5 miles from Arroyo Grande Creek. A favorite hiking area.

Santa Barbara Coast

Coal Oil Point (Storke Rd., Isla Vista.) Part of the University of California's system of habitats maintained for scientific study, this area offers engaging coastal hiking, especially through the waterfowl sanctuary at Devereaux Lagoon. Use the self-guided walking tour path marked with maps. Observe signs indicating areas off-limits to the public.

Gaviota Hot Springs Trail (Hwy. 101 and Hwy. 1, Gaviota; take Hwy. 1 exit, follow the frontage road until it dead-ends at the trail parking lot; coming from Gaviota State Beach, follow Hwy. 1 N. toward Lompoc) A small hot spring offers a soothing soak in the body-temp mineral water (take off your jewelry first, or it will turn black from the sulphur). It's only one of the hiking experiences in the 2700-acre Gaviota State Park, which also yields over 5 miles of shoreline.

Nipomo Dunes Preserve (end of Main St., Guadalupe) This 26-acre preserve's sensuous dunes are home to intriguing plants and birds, many on California's endangered species list. From the estuary landscape of the Santa Maria River to the windswept beaches extending to rocky Point Sal, you'll find some of the largest dunes in California, including the West Coast's reigning giant, 450-ft. Mussel Rock. Restrooms, visitor center.

Point Sal Trail (Brown and Point Sal Rds., W. of Guadalupe) The dirt and tarmac Point Sal Rd. leads to this steep point, where lead to tiny sandy beaches below. Rugged and truly off the beaten track, the main trail weaves a dizzying course between high, sheer cliffs and the wildlife-filled tide pools and beaches below. Terrific whale-watching at the end of the trail, where the Santa Maria River spills into the sea. Recommended for experienced hikers with nerves of steel.

Refugio State Beach (Hwy. 101 at Refugio Rd., 15 mi. N. of Goleta) 90 acres of hiking, swimming, and fishing, set in a stretch of coast famous for its sand, dramatic cliffs, and tide pools. Walks are enchanting in spring, when the beach is framed by fields of chartreuse mustard. Parking, restrooms; lifeguards in summer.

HORSEBACK RIDING

Blame it on Hollywood, but the very idea of horseback riding along some isolated stretch of beach — at sunset — is the quintessence of romance. And on the Central Coast, some select expanses of flat, tide-lapped sand have become colleagues with nearby stables. The result is what many consider the ultimate riding experience: full gallop, or maybe just a slow canter, through the Pacific surf. And many Central Coast State Park areas offer miles of equestrian trails that can take the rider back to the very dawn of the Old West, through redwood-shaded canyons and along sandstone bluffs overlooking the ocean.

Santa Cruz Coast

Big Basin Stables 408/438-4226; Hwy. 236 off Hwy. 9, Boulder Creek
Sea Horse/Friendly Acres Ranch 415/726-8550; 2159 Hwy. 1, Half Moon Bay

Horseback riders find miles of scenic equestrian trails along the shoreline and canyons of the Central Coast.

Monterey Coast

Cypress Stables 408/372-0511; 550 Aguajito Rd., Carmel
Nasom Ranches 408/625-8664; PO Box 2336, Carmel Valley

San Luis Obispo Coast

Livery Stables Inc. 805/489-8100; 1207 Silver Spur Pl., Oceano
Rocking D Stables 805/595-7407; 555 Avila Beach Dr., Avila Beach
Trail Horse Rentals 805/238-5483; San Luis Obispo

Santa Barbara Coast

Circle Bar B Stables 805/968-9301; 1800 Refugio Rd., Goleta
Gene O'Hagan Riding Stables 805/968/5929; 1900 Refugio Rd., Goleta
Sage Hill Farm 805/683/4454; 1840 N. San Marcos Rd., Santa Barbara
San Ysidro Ranch Stables 805/969-5046; 900 San Ysidro Ln., Montecito

NATURE PRESERVES AND PARKS

Since the days of the first California State Park, almost a century ago, significant stretches of coastal mountains, shoreline, and offshore marine areas beyond have been set aside — often at great political and financial cost — for future generations to cherish and explore. Some of the last great stretches of our natural inheritance flourish free of development and rich with wildlife along the Central Coast. To spend time here is to be renewed in ways that can reward an entire lifetime.

Santa Cruz Coast

Big Basin Redwoods State Park (408/338-6132; Hwy. 9 to Boulder Creek, W. on Hwy. 236) Founded in 1902 as California's first State Park, the vintage redwood preserve encompasses 15,000 acres of redwood and oak terrain, with 80 miles of hiking trails. In summer, rangers offer nature walks and campfire programs with lectures, slide shows, and movies. An extremely popular summer camping site, the park offers a wide variety of overnight facilities, including 36 tent cabins with wood-burning stoves (closed winter), laundry facilities, showers.

Henry Cowell Redwoods State Park (408/335-4598; main entrance 1 mi. S. of Felton on Hwy. 9) 4000 acres of magnificently forested redwood preserve were once the home of Ohlone Indians. Today, miles of trails lead through impressive stands of oak, madrone, digger pine, and chaparral terrain on sunny ridge tops. The ancient heart of this sanctuary is the stand of soaring old-growth redwoods — the oldest and most beautiful remaining on the Central Coast — easily enjoyed via the one-mile Redwood Grove nature trail loop near the main picnic area.

Monterey Coast

Elkhorn Slough National Estuarine Research Reserve (408/728-2822; 1700 Elkhorn Rd. near Dolan Rd., Moss Landing) 5 miles of trails thread this 1400-

---

Año Nuevo Elephant Seal Walks

(MISTIX 800/444-7275; Hwy. 1 at New Years Creek Rd., 19 mi. N. of Santa Cruz) This fascinating peninsula and island contain tide pools filled with sea urchins, hermit crabs, anemones, and other intertidal life forms; shell mounds left by Ohlone residents thousands of years ago still dot its rugged marsh, scrub, and dunes. The Año Nuevo State Reserve protects colonies of northern elephant seals, who populate the sandy reaches of the reserve's million-plus acres during the annual winter breeding season. On guided walks, visitors may observe these enormous creatures at close hand from December–March. Highly popular, the three hour tour requires advance reservations. Dress warmly.

---

acre reserve, with one of the country's largest salt marshes, as well as nutrient-rich tidal flats supporting marine communities. Formed by the confluence of the freshwater Salinas River and saltwater tides, this briny cradle of life is home to more than 250 wildlife species, including golden eagles, herons, egrets, clapper rails, and endangered California brown pelicans. Bring binoculars! The dunes surrounding this fragile ecosystem explode with wildflowers during the spring and, within the watery estuary fingers, astonishing quantities of fish, shrimp, and oysters are spawned. Weekend guided walks at 10am and 1pm. Visitors center (9–5 Weds.–Sun.) provides exhibits, maps, brochures.

Point Lobos State Reserve (408/624-4909; Hwy. 1 at Riley Ranch Rd., Carmel) Widely considered the most beautiful spot on the Central Coast, Point Lobos' 1225 seafront acres (plus 1300 more acquired in mid-1993) comprise a paradise of rocky headlands, cove beaches, transparent waters, and forests of pine and moss-festooned cypress. Trails, many sparkling with crushed abalone shell, lead to panoramic points, through meadows sparkling with water and crowned with wild irises, orchids, lilac, and lupines in the springtime. Where marshes meet tide pools and beaches, blue heron stalk and Bird Rock shimmers black with huge nesting cormorants. Its hidden cove beaches and mysterious sea caves are said to have inspired Robert Louis Stevenson's *Treasure Island*.

Sea Otters

Once hunted to the edge of extinction for its thick, lustrous fur, the playful southern sea otter now thrives in the Central Coast between Santa Cruz and San Luis Obispo. Especially prolific in the kelp beds along the Monterey Bay, the intelligent otter is enamored of shellfish, for which it dives with admirable speed and skill, consuming them by lying on its back and hammering open the shells using rocks. Sea otters forage continuously for the enormous quantity of food — two tons a year — needed to keep up body temperatures in cold waters. Protected by state and federal law, this charming whiskered creature can be spotted by watching for sea gulls who dive for the portions of shellfish it discards.

San Luis Obispo Coast

Montaña de Oro State Park (805/528-0513 (summer), 805/772-2560; 2 mi. S. of Los Osos via Los Osos Valley/Pecho Rd) 8000 unspoiled acres of rugged cliffs, deeply forested canyons, tide pools, and hidden cove beaches provide spectacular vantage points for flora and fauna observation: sea otters and migrating California gray whales; hilltop bluffs filled with California poppies, coreopsis, and lupine. In the winter, monarch butterflies congregate in the extensive eucalyptus forests. Views up and down the coast for 100 miles from the park's highest point, 1300-foot Valencia Peak. Superb hiking, horseback riding, and camping far from the madding crowd.

Poison Oak

As if to even up the score in the stunning Central Coast, Mother Nature liberally populated the hills, fields, and coastline with that three-leafed devil: poison oak. The oils in the leaves and stems of *Rhus diversiloba* are highly toxic to most people, and the allergic rash produced by contact is most uncomfortable. The rash — with its redness, burning, excruciating itching — can last for weeks, though calamine lotion can provide some relief. The best course is to avoid *any* cross-country detours and stick to cleared areas and trails. For example, don't clamber down the bluffs leading from Hwy. 1 to the shoreline below. In the rocky pockets and dense grasses right on the edge of the ocean wait some of the worst stretches of poison oak in the state. Find out what this plant looks like and memorize its shiny, three-leafed outline. It's unmistakable in fall — the leaves turn to a blaze of red and orange glory.

Deceptively beautiful, the three-leafed scourge of the coastal hillsides — poison oak — produces a highly allergic reaction.

Jay Swanson

Morro Bay State Park (805/772-2560; east of Embarcadero via State Park Rd., Morro Bay) A profusion of wildlife is protected within this 2000-acre preserve, famed for the expansive mud flats that attract shorebirds by the tens of thousands. Eucalyptus groves housing the largest blue heron rookery between

San Francisco and Mexico fill with nests beginning in late January. The park also includes the Morro Estuary Natural Preserve, home to ancient moss-draped pygmy oaks and myriad marsh birds, including the Audubon warbler. The Park's Museum of Natural History (805/772-2694) provides guided walks of the area.

Santa Barbara Coast

Channel Islands National Park (805/644-8157, 805/644-8262; Headquarters & Visitor Center, 1901 Spinnaker Dr., Ventura) The 8 islands of this 1252 square nautical miles of the park lie 20 miles off the Santa Barbara coast within the Channel Islands National Marine Sanctuary, created to protect 27 species of whales and dolphins, and myriad fish and seabirds. Campsites are available on Anacapa Island, lying closest to the mainland, and on Santa Barbara Island. Santa Rosa Island still contains undisturbed Chumash Indian archaeological sites, and all the islands are home to a rich diversity of wildlife, including the endangered California brown pelican, sea lions, and elephant seals. Permits are required to land boats on the islands; trips are arranged through the park concessionaire, Island Packers, Inc. (805/642-1393; 1867 Spinnaker Dr.).

Nipomo Dunes Preserve (805/545-9925, 805/546-8378; end of Main St., Guadalupe) 18 miles of coastline and 22,000 acres of isolated natural diversity make up the most extensive sand dunes in California, home to rare plants like the surf thistle, Nipomo lupine, and crisp monardella, and to endangered bird species such as the California least tern. Spectacular giant coreopsis cover many dunes with blankets of golden blossoms. The area still contains shell middens left by Chumash settlers. Open and unspoiled, this dramatic coastal preserve continues to exert its pull on walkers, campers, and swimmers.

Nature Conservancy

Keeping close watch over the rarest natural resources of the Central Coast, the California Nature Conservancy manages protected reserves at Elkhorn Slough in Monterey, Nipomo Dunes in San Luis Obispo/Santa Barbara counties, and Santa Cruz Island off Santa Barbara. For information about the organization and access to its sanctuaries, write or call the California Nature Conservancy, 785 Market St., San Francisco, CA 94103; 415/777-0487.

SURFING

The national sport of Polynesia hit the mainland of the United States at a point just north of the city of Santa Cruz over 100 years ago. In 1887,

The Central Coast is famed for its surfing spots.

Shmuel Thaler

Hawaiian Prince David Kawananakoa and his brother commissioned local woodworkers to shape 15-foot, 100-pound surfboards out of redwood and promptly wowed the locals by riding the obliging waves at Steamers Lane on Monterey Bay. The spot where surfing began in California is today commemorated by a surfing museum and elegant statue of a youthful surfer and his longboard. While the slow, languid rides of longboard surfing still flourish all over the Central Coast, the hang-ten style of surfing has since been joined by the slice and dice gymnastics of a new breed of surf riders with their chopped, shorter fiberglass boards. All year long, an array of regional, national, and international surfing competitions provide prime viewing of one of the most exciting, exhilarating, and — when it's done right — poetic orchestrations of body and wave.

The surf action attracts wannabees as well as pros from around the world. Santa Cruz is legendary for its surf and competitions, while the east-west waves hitting the Santa Barbara coastline have made it one of the top meccas in the state. All along Highway 1, it's easy to spot the best surfing: look for the invariable VW vans with surf racks parked along the road or follow the nearest pack of wetsuited bodies.

Santa Cruz Coast

Año Nuevo (Hwy. 1 near Santa Cruz/San Mateo County line) Sand bottom, mostly rights; strong currents, risky, for the advanced; in the "red triangle" — great white shark attack area.

Capitola Jetty Reef bottom, both rights and lefts; best at low tides, needs a 6–8 foot swell before it works, good beginner spot; lifeguards in summer.

Cowells Beach (near Santa Cruz Boardwalk) Sand bottom, very gentle rights; best at low tides, slow, easy peaks rolling onto a safe beach, perfect spot for beginners; lifeguards in summer.

Four Mile Beach (Hwy. 1, 1 mi. S. of Davenport) Reef break, fun rights; intermediate to advanced spot; cars get broken into a lot; "red triangle" — great white sharks frequent area — not worth the risk to outsiders.

Hook (The) (end of 41st Avenue, S. of Pleasure Point) Reef bottom, rights and lefts; smaller but usually faster waves than Pleasure Point, gets crowded (and angers locals), intermediate to advanced spot; exit from water dangerous at high tides (prepare to paddle half mile south to Capitola Pier)

Inside Pleasure (juncture of East Cliff Dr. & 41st Ave.) Rocky reef bottom, all rights; good for beginners during small swell, needs 6-ft. swell to work for advanced; can be gnarly (dangerous) during large swells, difficult to exit during high tides.

Natural Bridges Outer Reef (N. Santa Cruz) Reef bottom, right break; needs a minus tide and big swell to work, advanced spot; nasty currents when big but nice place for day on the beach.

Pleasure Point Reef bottom, rights and lefts; "Sewer Peak" has big bowls, super steep, for the advanced; 1st peak and 2nd has good longboard waves, works on any swell, intermediate to advanced.

Scott Creek Reef bottom, beach break and a right point break; point break still rideable at 15–20 ft.; unpredictable, lots of kelp; "Red Triangle," sharky.

Shark's Cove Reef bottom, mostly a right, left when it's small; fun, secondary waves that roll through the "Hook" continue wrapping, best at low tide, larger waves line up and close out, beginner to advanced.

Steamers Lane Reef bottom mostly a right, left when it's big; "Outsides" holds any swell, big rights that peel along the cliff line, not a beginner break, advanced; "Middle Peak" lines up nearly 50 yds. from the cliff, holds any swell; a haven for seals and otters, kelp gets thick in some spots at low tide, high tide poses difficulties for exiting the water.

Sunset State Beach Sand bottom, lots of peaks, lefts and rights; beginners spot when small, intermediate to advanced otherwise; can get big rips when there's a swell.

Manresa State Beach Sandy beach break; best on smaller swells, large swells line up and close out, advanced; strong current during heavy surf.

26th Avenue Reef/sand bottom, lefts and rights; under-appreciated spot popular with body surfers, intermediate to advanced.

Monterey Coast

Lover's Point Reef break, lefts off a small point; easy to ride, only breaks on a big swell, intermediate to advanced; really rocky spot.

Marina State Beach Sand bottom, lefts and rights; advanced; bad rips.

Moss Landing State Beach Sand bottom, lefts and rights; breaks like Hawaii Pipeline, swells come from the deep and hit the reef and jack straight up, always bigger than it looks, intermediate to advanced only; has rips and shifty peaks, respect its raw power.

Salinas River Reef bottom, lefts and rights; intermediate to advanced, sharky, rips, lots of debris floating around.

Sand City Beach Sand bottom, lefts and rights; beginner to intermediate; can get small rips.

Zmudowski State Beach Sand bottom, lefts and rights; intermediate to advanced; can get rips.

San Luis Obispo Coast

Hazard Canyon Reef break, lefts and rights; for experienced surfers only; can get rips, cold water, sharks, jagged reef, only for diehards — it's called hazard for a reason, and help is a long way away.

Pismo Beach Pier Northside Sand bottom, lefts and rights; fun spot, breaks all year during any swell, larger swells are too consistent and lined up to make it worth the paddle, beginner to advanced depending on swell size.

Morro Rock Jetty Sand bottom, beach break, lefts and rights; fun beach peaks break all year, smaller surf is clean, larger swells get big and hairy, beginner to advanced; note: warm water emitted from nearby PG&E plant.

Morro Rock Harbor Entrance Small sand bar on the inside of the break walls, all lefts; needs powerful swell but can be super clean, rarely gets above three feet; note: paddling across entrance can be hazardous during tide change — the small opening in the entrance turns into a river.

Santa Barbara Coast

Carpinteria State Beach Tar Pits Sand bottom, beach break lefts and rights; fun spot, never gets too big, good for beginners; lots of tar in the water.

El Capitan Point Reef bottom, mostly left; Channel Islands block out most swells but the ones that get through peel with perfection; intermediate to advanced; does get rips.

Hammonds Beach Reef, rights; gets crowded fast, intermediate to advanced.

Jalama Beach Sand bottom, lefts and rights; wind blows hard either offshore or onshore, unbeatable when the conditions are right, worth the look if you have time, intermediate to advanced; gets rips.

Refugio State Beach Sand/reef bottom, mostly rights, some lefts; rarely breaks but when it does it's a precision point break, real fun, beginner to intermediate.

Rincon Point Reef bottom, right point break; lots of peaks, holds any swell, precision all the way, gets real crowded, beginner to advanced; rocks show at low tide.

Santa Barbara Harbor Outside Breakwater Sand bar begins to fill in the harbor entrance, right; fast and hollow; not for beginners.

Tarantula Point Reef bottom, point break lefts and rights; secluded, gets gnarly; long, long, long walk south of Jalama State Park.

Coal Oil Point Sand bottom, all rights from the point, lefts along the beach; short walk to the point, needs a good swell to really work, main spot for UC Santa Barbara students living in Isla Vista; natural seepage of tar in water and sand.

SWIMMING

See the section on "Beaches" above for ocean swimming locations.

TENNIS

Some Central Coast residents spend every spare minute on the tennis courts, another reward of living in a Mediterranean climate. The region is paved with tennis clubs, most of which welcome guests and provide extra amenities like swimming pools, restaurants, and spa facilities.

Every populated area of the Central Coast offers a selection of well-groomed tennis courts.

Shmuel Thaler

PRIVATE

Santa Cruz Coast

Imperial Courts Tennis Club 408/476-1062; 2505 Cabrillo College Dr., Aptos

Seascape Sports Club 408/688-1993; 1505 Seascape Blvd., Aptos

Tennis Club of Rio del Mar 408/688-1144; 360 Sandalwood Dr., Rio Del Mar

Monterey Coast

Carmel Valley Racquet and Health Club 408/624-2737; 27300 Rancho San Carlos Rd., Carmel

Mission Tennis Ranch 408/624-4335; 26260 Dolores St., Carmel

San Luis Obispo Coast

Avila Bay Club 805/595-7600; PO Box 2149, Avila Beach
San Luis Obispo Golf & Country Club 805/544-9880; 255 Country Club Dr., San Luis Obispo

Santa Barbara Coast

Cathedral Oaks Club 805/964-7762; 5800 Cathedral Oaks Rd., Goleta
Knowlwood Tennis Club 805/969-0558; 1675 East Valley Rd., Montecito
Tennis Club of Santa Barbara 805/682-4722; 2375 Foothill Rd., Santa Barbara

PUBLIC

Santa Cruz Coast

Cabrillo College 408/479-6332; 6500 Soquel Dr., Aptos
Derby Park 408/429-3777; Woodland Way at Natural Bridges School, Santa Cruz
Harbor High School 408/429-3810; 300 La Fonda Ave., Santa Cruz
Highland County Park 408/462-8333; Hwy. 9 & Glen Arbor Rd., Ben Lomond
Jade Street Park 408/475-5935; 4400 Jade St., Capitola
Mike Fox Tennis Park 408/429-3768; Riverside at San Lorenzo Blvd., Santa Cruz
Santa Cruz High School 408/429-3960; 415 Walnut St., Santa Cruz
Soquel High School 408/429-3909; 401 Old San Jose Rd., Soquel

Monterey Coast

Bay Club at Inn at Spanish Bay 805/647-7500; 2700 17 Mile Dr., Pebble Beach
Carmel Valley Racquet Club 408/624-2737; 200 Clocktower Pl., Carmel
Mission Tennis Ranch 408/624-4335; 26260 Dolores St., Carmel
Monterey Tennis Center 408/372-0172; 401 Pearl St., Monterey

San Luis Obispo Coast

Arroyo Grande High School 805/473-4205; 495 Valley Rd., Arroyo Grande
Cuesta College 805/544-5356; Rte. 1, San Luis Obispo
Elm Street Park 805/489-1303; Elm & Ash Streets, Arroyo Grande
Hardie County Park 805/549-5219; Birch Ave. & B St., Cayucos
Monte Young Park South St. & Napa Ave., Morro Bay
Pismo Beach Municipal Courts 805/773-4656; Wadsworth Ave. & Bello St., Pismo Beach
Sinsheimer Park 805/781-7300; Southwood Dr., San Luis Obispo
South Bay Community Park 805/781-5930; Los Osos Valley Rd. & Palisades Ave., Los Osos

Santa Barbara Coast

Las Positas Tennis Courts 805/687-2560; 1002 Las Positas Rd., Santa Barbara
Municipal Tennis Center 805/963-0611; 1414 Park Pl., Santa Barbara
Oak Park Tennis Courts 805/564-5517; 300 West Alamar St., Santa Barbara
Pershing Park 805/564-5517; 100 Castillo St., Santa Barbara
Santa Barbara City College 805/965-0581; 721 Cliff Dr., Santa Barbara
Santa Barbara High School 805/966-9101; 700 East Anapuma St., Santa Barbara

---

Whale-Watching

The California Gray Whale roams the waters of the Pacific coast, migrating annually from Canada down to warm water calving areas in Mexico. During the early winter months, these elegant creatures can be easily viewed from vantage points all along the Central Coast, spouting water high into the air and thrashing their enormous tails. At *Montaña de Oro State Park* near San Luis Obispo, whales can be observed from the cliffs during their annual migration. Other well known spots for leviathan-viewing are *San Simeon Landing, Moonstone Beach* near Cambria in the south, and *Año Nuevo State Reserve, Greyhound Rock*, and *Davenport Landing* from bluffs overlooking the sea in the northern Central Coast. In the Big Sur area, the rocky tip of *Soberanes Point* in Pfeiffer Big Sur State Park is a favorite whale-watching area, as is *Garrapata State Park* and *Point Lobos State Reserve*. A pair of binoculars and patience are all that's required. And the sight of these enormous creatures cruising the coast in pods of up to 20 individuals is awesome. The *Oceanic Society* (415/441-5970; Building E, Fort Mason, San Francisco, CA 94123 and the *American Cetacean Society* (408/646-8743; PO Box HE Pacific Grove) will provide detailed information and tips if contacted by phone or mail.

CHAPTER EIGHT

We Want It All

SHOPPING

The thoroughly California concept of shopping as entertainment is alive and well along the Central Coast, where emporia of regional arts and crafts, exotic imports, fine antiques, funky collectibles, and designer clothing exist side by side with state of the art shopping malls packed with retail giants.

Few can resist the charms of the region's many rustic old towns and restored civic centers from bygone eras, all filled with delightful arrays of small shops, galleries, and cafés. The

Shmuel Thaler

Browsing Bookshop Santa Cruz is a morning-to-night ritual for locals, passionate about bestsellers, regional tomes, and foreign magazines.

past, the present, and a plethora of cultural styles form the backdrop for an inviting network of shopping districts. From Spanish-style arcades to boutiques in Victorian gingerbread homes, the shopping scene is vigorous and plentiful.

Antiques and collectibles from all over the world, housed in old barns, canneries, and sleek adobe shops, repeat the pattern of trade from the eras when most goods were brought in from "back East" or "around the Horn." The hunting is still good for memorabilia from the Central Coast's Wild West days, or for the delicate china and glassware that represented European culture in rough whaling or ranching communities.

From the area's many resident artisans come luxurious contemporary glass, jewelry, pottery, tapestries, and hand-sculpted furniture, sharing the shopping stage with top international designer names in leather, silk, and wool.

ANTIQUES AND COLLECTIBLES

To cruise the Central Coast is to practically trip over opportunities to rummage through memorabilia-packed shrines to yesteryear, proudly showcasing artifacts of a frontier heritage and of immigrants from all over the world who brought with them reminders of distant homelands. While the larger cities are handsomely stocked with shops offering the finest in 18th- and 19th-century European wares — as well as astonishing museum-quality collections of vintage Asian artifacts — it's almost always the very tiny towns that offer the greatest opportunities for browsing through the gleanings of the past. To maximize your searches for the rare and unusual, don't miss the many antiques collectives along the Central Coast, arrangements where many individual collectors band together to offer their specialties under one roof.

Santa Cruz Coast

Mr. Goodie's Antiques (408/427-9997; 1541 Pacific Ave., Santa Cruz) Wonderful stuff from bygone eras, including lavish antique and vintage costume jewelry, Depression glass and Fiesta-ware, classic Hawaiian shirts, and nostalgic prints.

Shen's Gallery (408/425-0525; 1368 Pacific Ave., Santa Cruz) Perfumed by incense, this beautiful shop imports burnished Chinese furniture, jade and coral jewelry, ceramics, carvings, prints, and Hsing tea pots — antiques every one.

Trader's Emporium (408/475-9201; 4940 Soquel Dr., Soquel) A popular browsing spot with local antique and collectible buffs, this gigantic old Quonset hut houses 26 distinct shops offering antique items of every possible description.

Monterey Coast

Antiques International (408/633-3663; Moss Landing Rd., Moss Landing) Tucked into the antique gold coast of this sleepy fishing village, this shop specializes in rare, pre-WWII Meissen porcelain, as well as fine European antiques, furniture, paintings, and sterling silver.

Carmel Valley Antiques & Collectibles (408/624-3414; Valley Hills Shopping Center, Carmel Valley) The focus is on vintage quilts, glassware, antique furniture, jewelry, and accessories.

Moss Landing Antique & Trading Co. (408/633-3988; Moss Landing Rd., Moss Landing) One of the best of a plethora of fine and funky antique stores lining the pier of this fishing village. Strong on turn-of-the-century estate collections.

The Tuck Box (408/624-6365; Dolores bet. Ocean & 7th, Carmel) Famous since 1925 as an utterly quaint tea room, this bit of fairy tale charm also sells petite and precious porcelain gifts, cookbooks, teapots, and preserves. A local landmark.

San Luis Obispo Coast

Antique Center (805/541-4040; 6 Higuera, San Luis Obispo) Thirteen dealers have gathered together to offer a seductive array of early American and country furniture, glassware, lighting, and singular antique jewelry.

The Glass Basket (805/772-4569; 245 Morro Bay Blvd., Morro Bay) The specialty of the house is a glittering array of highly collectible American cut glass and pastel-hued Depression pressed glass tableware. Additional antique and collectible must-haves as well.

Vignette's (805/547-9535; 11246 Garden St., San Luis Obispo) A charming shop in a historic area, offering adorable decorator objets d'art and an abundance of yesteryears' paraphernalia.

Santa Barbara Coast

Antique Market Place (805/966-5655; 26 East Ortega St., Santa Barbara) Oriental rugs, porcelain, furniture, artwork, cut glass, Native American artifacts, paintings, and clocks share this bountiful emporium with American, Asian, and European antiques.

Michael Aaron Antique Center (805/568-1848; 1030 State St., Santa Barbara) A very classy dealer offering imaginative and unique antique accessories, carpets, linens, period lighting fixtures, nostalgic and exquisite oils, as well as distinctive antique furniture.

Peregrine Galleries (805/969-9673; 1133 Coast Village Rd., Montecito) A bountiful blend of Early California and American paintings shares space with vintage jewelry from Bakelite to Taxco and Jensen silver. (Also at 508 Brinkerhoff Ave., Santa Barbara; 805/963-3134.)

Solvang Antique Center (805/968-2322; 486 First St., Solvang) Housed in the historic half-timbered Old Mill Shopps building in the middle of this Danish theme park village, the center offers an array of fine antiques, silver, cut glass, estate jewelry, and American oak from over 50 collections.

Summerland Antique Collective (805/565-3189; 2192 Ortega Hill Rd., Summerland) Twenty-five dealers fill 8000 square feet with a seductive smorgasbord of regional and vintage furniture, jewelry, toys, tableware, quilts, kitsch, and collectibles.

ARTS AND CRAFTS

The California arts and crafts revival of the 1960s — especially in art glass, ceramics, and jewelry — was especially concentrated in the Central Coast region. Eager to escape commercial metropolitan areas, some of the finest designers of handmade art objects and housewares relocated here, filling the studios and galleries with remarkable personal expressions in gold, silver, wood, glass, stone, and clay. Always an import capital, the Central Coast is the place to look for the exotic and unusual in fine blown glass, raku-glazed stoneware, and contemporary jewelry.

The tiny town of **Davenport**, just north of Santa Cruz, boasts not only the art glass virtuosos of Lundberg Studios, but also knife makers, potters, cabinetry experts, and custom boat builders. Just south of Cambria, the micro-village of **Harmony** has turned the ruins of a dairy into a rustic arts and crafts enclave. Here Phoenix Studios produces museum-quality blown glass objects, and art studios, galleries, a pottery works, and clothing and antiques shops all cluster invitingly in a unique combination of upscale hippiedom and 19th-century ambiance.

Many of the designers who relish the privacy and seclusion of coastal lifestyles regularly show and sell in museums and galleries in urban capitals the world over. For the serious collector, however, nothing beats the opportunity to buy here directly from the artist.

Santa Cruz Coast

Annieglass Studio (408/426-5086; 109 Cooper St., Santa Cruz) Studio and price-slashing outlet/showroom for opulent designer glass tableware, serving pieces, and home accessories.

Artisan's (408/423-8183; 1364 Pacific Ave., Santa Cruz) An engaging collection of the very finest in locally produced ceramics, woodwork, hand-loomed textiles, glassware, lamps, innovative toys and games. Walls filled with local paintings and prints distinguish this local treasure.

Gravago (408/427-2667; 1001 Center St., Santa Cruz) Fabulous finds from exotic corners of the Far and Middle East, from tapestries and antique copper and brass to Indonesian carvings and African trade bead jewelry.

Importer extraordinaire, Barbara Horscraft of Gravago in Santa Cruz specializes in exotica from the Far and Middle East.

Paul Schraub

Lundberg Studios (408/423-2532; 123 Old Coast Rd., Davenport) Showrooms for this internationally acclaimed art glass studio offer a world-class selection of Tiffany reproduction lamps, vases, and iridescent lusterware bowls. The fabulous blown-glass paperweights have found their way into the Smithsonian and Louvre Museum catalogs.

New Davenport Cash Store (408/426-4122; Hwy. 1, Davenport) The finest tableware from local Santa Cruz Mountain potters shares floor-to-ceiling displays with Guatemalan hand-loomed textiles, elegant tie-dyed silks, Mexican Day-of-the-Dead figures, antique ivory and amber, as well as stunning contemporary art jewelry.

Pilot Outlet (408/457-8200; 111 Locust St., Santa Cruz) Eclectic global imports, from dazzling hand-carved interior decor from Indonesia to natural fiber hand-screened designer outfits with a tropical flavor, are the specialties of this spacious center for the handiwork of top Southeast Asia designers.

Spanishtown Arts & Crafts Center (415/726-9971; 501 San Mateo Rd. (Rte. 92), Half Moon Bay) A colorful cluster of unique and high quality regional arts and crafts in a dozen shops featuring revolving exhibits (some shops are open during the week, all are open on weekends).

Tenggara (408/423-1177; 1360 Pacific Ave., Santa Cruz) The art of Indonesia fills every nook and cranny of this intriguing shop, including vibrant batik designer clothing, a huge selection of distinctive wood carvings, and quantities of jewelry to suit every taste and credit card limit.

Walter-White Fine Arts (408/476-7001; 107 Capitola Ave., Capitola) Outstanding selection of regional art glass — as well as blown glass, silver, and gold jewelry — creates a dazzling visual experience.

Monterey Coast

Carmel Art Association (408/624-6176; Dolores bet. 5th & 6th, Carmel) Since the 1930s, this respected gallery has showcased the oil paintings, graphics, sculpture, and watercolors of the best California artists.

Coast Galleries (408/624-2002; at The Lodge on 17 Mile Drive, Pebble Beach) A glorious mixed bag of Old Masters and contemporary regional artworks. Of special interest are the collections of original watercolors and prints by former Big Sur resident and literary giant Henry Miller. (Another location is on Hwy. 1, three miles south of Ventana/Nepenthe; 408/667-2301.)

Conway of Asia (408/624-3643; Dolores bet. Ocean & 7th Ave., Carmel) Eye-popping art treasures from Tibet and lands of the East fill this fabulous gallery, including Himalayan altars, ancient Buddhas, silks, brocades, icons, and a sensual array of Oriental rugs.

Gallery Sur (408/626-2615; 2 Northwest Dolores & 6th, Carmel) A new photographic gallery in this hotbed of gallery action showcases breathtaking seascapes of the Central Coast by top local photographers.

Photography West Gallery (408/625-1587; Dolores bet. Ocean & 7th, Carmel) Heavyweights of Carmel's internationally recognized photographic community — Ansel Adams, Edward Weston, Imogen Cunningham, and others — are represented here.

Sun Country (408/625-5907; in the Doud Craft Studios, Ocean & San Carlos Ave., Carmel) Irresistible hand-crafted delicacies include handmade glass marbles, jewelry boxes of exotic and domestic woods, and a significant collection of American kaleidoscopes.

Trotter Galleries (408/373-7166; 309 Forest Ave., Pacific Grove) A fine establishment specializing in rare and undiscovered masterpieces by early California Impressionists.

Village Artistry (408/624-7628; Dolores bet. Ocean & 7th, Carmel) Bold and colorful contemporary blown glass, hand-wrought jewelry, fanciful furniture, and exquisite ceramics jam this bastion of fine local arts and crafts.

Weston Gallery (408/624-4453; 6th near Lincoln Ave., Carmel) Named for Carmel's famous native son, photographer Edward Weston, the gallery features exceptional 19th- and 20th-century photographs, including the work of another local legend, Ansel Adams. (Another location is at Dolores near 7th, Carmel.)

San Luis Obispo

Bali Isle Imports (805/544-7662; 1038 Chorro, San Luis Obispo) A tropical treasure trove of vibrant hand-screened batik textiles, masks, carved wood, and exotic jewelry from Bali .

Hand-carved masks from Indonesia are among the crafts found at Bali Isle Imports in San Luis Obispo.

Paul Schraub

Damaka (805/544-5450; 733 Higuera, San Luis Obispo) An exciting and different assortment of sassy imports — from textiles and jewelry to woodwork and ceramics — with Mexican and Latin American origins. California contemporary items also are featured.

Hands Gallery (805/543-1921; 672 Higuera, San Luis Obispo) Sumptuously glazed and wildly innovative ceramic ware and sculpture are the core of this progressive gallery, which also carries playful wood and metal designs by local artisans.

Harmony Pottery Works (805/927-4293; Old Hwy. 1, Harmony) One-stop shopping for the collector of top quality hand-crafted ceramic and stoneware pottery. This spacious showroom offers a wide range of styles and glazes in ware created by top local ceramists.

Phoenix Studios (805/927-4248; Old Hwy. 1, Harmony) Museum quality art glass is blown and sold on site. The gallery next door showcases the best work of area glass artisans.

Seekers Collection & Gallery (805/927-4352; 4090 Burton Dr., Cambria) A breathtaking selection of museum quality blown glass jewelry, sculpture, and furniture from 200 of the country's top art glass designers. Possibly the best of its kind in the entire state.

Simpson-Heller Gallery (805/927-1800; 2289 Main St., Cambria) A fine collection of regional paintings, sculpture, and mixed media works distinguishes this airy, inviting gallery in the middle of a charming 19th-century village.

Suma Sil Gallery (805/927-5642; 4070 Burton Dr., Cambria) Authentic Native American jewelry, artifacts, rugs, crafts and books — representing regional Chumash Indian work, as well as tribes from across the American West — are available here. Also displayed are rare antique bowls, fetishes, and carvings, many pre-historic and all for sale.

Santa Barbara Coast

Cody Gallery (805/688-5083; 2884 Grand Ave., Los Olivos) Sumptuous oils and bronze sculptures highlight Western regional themes in this gallery smack in the middle of the Santa Ynez wine country.

Donlee Gallery of Fine Art (805/686-1088; 2933 Grand Ave., Los Olivos) Substantial and tasteful collections of Western bronze sculpture and regional oil paintings handsomely displayed for leisurely consideration.

Gallery Los Olivos (805/688-7517; 2920 Grand Ave., Los Olivos) Sunny showrooms filled with fine revolving collections of regional and California-theme artworks, plus exhibitions of local works by Santa Ynez Artist Guild members.

Indigo (805/962-6909; 1323 State St., Santa Barbara) Inviting showroom featuring Central Coast handmade furniture and one-of-a-kind lighting and textiles amidst a handsome collection of Asian antique woodwork and pottery.

Letty Rossbach Fine Arts (805/965-5449; 1324 State St., Santa Barbara) Elegant collections of oil paintings showcasing atmospheric regional landscapes.

Maureen Murphy Fine Arts (805/969-9215; 1187 Coast Village Rd., Montecito) Substantial collections of vintage regional artworks with classic California themes fill this gracious gallery.

Objects (805/565-3335; 1187 Coast Village Rd., Montecito) A quintessential craft gallery resplendent with the best in locally designed blown glass, jewelry, art pottery, and hand-woven wearable art.

Santa Barbara Ceramic Design Studio Outlet Store (805/686-5770; 1645 Copenhagen Dr., Solvang) Art Deco designs dance across the rich array of ceramic clocks, frames, tiles, and vases created by this renowned group of Central Coast artisans. Retail outlets include the Smithsonian and Horchow catalogs, but here you can visit and purchase at significant savings. (Another location is at 428 E. Haley St., Santa Barbara; 805/966-3883.)

BOOKS

Whether they're looking for some long-lost literary favorite or simply catching up on old friendships, residents of the Central Coast are drawn to their bookstores, most of which boast cafés and serve as unofficial town halls and prime people-watching venues. As casual as the local lifestyles, bookstores here encourage browsing, often supplying fireplaces and comfy chairs for all-day lingering. The area's many university towns are especially well-stocked with bookstores of every sort, including myriad used and rare book dealerships, as well as those well-lit establishments bristling with unusual greeting cards and paperback bestsellers. Look for the inevitable shelves stocked with locally authored tomes as a quick and engaging way to get acquainted with the special features of each micro-region along the Central Coast.

Santa Cruz Coast

Bookshop Santa Cruz (408/423-0900; 1520 Pacific Ave., Santa Cruz) Many locals consider this sprawling, inviting store the heart of downtown Santa Cruz. Major news and magazine rack, ample seating for browsing and a lively in-house café make it an all-day event.

Capitola BookCafé (408/462-4415; 1475 41st Ave., Capitola) A major selection of national and international magazines highlights this well-stocked cultural mecca, graced by an in-house espresso and dessert café.

Gateways BookCafé (408/429-9600; 1018 Pacific Ave., Santa Cruz) Metaphysical and New Age offerings of every sort fill this engaging retreat, which also features motivational CDs and cassettes, incense, crystals, and a vegetarian café. Very Santa Cruz.

Herland BookCafé (408/429-6636; 902 Center St., Santa Cruz) Women's bookstore in downtown Santa Cruz offers poetry readings and acoustic music some nights; espresso and vegetarian food café.

Literary Guillotine (408/457-1195; 204 Locust St., Santa Cruz) The unusual and fine in small press and university press literature cram this tiny haunt for inquiring browsers and book lovers.

Logos (408/427-5100; 117 Pacific Ave., Santa Cruz) Two huge floors filled with used and rare books, including major science fiction, gothic paperback, and women's sections. Used CDs, tapes, and collector-quality LPs make this place a hot must-visit spot.

New Society Bookstore (408/423-1626; 515 Broadway, Santa Cruz) In the Resource Center for Nonviolence, this progressive boutique sells music, books, calendars, and gifts of a politically correct persuasion. Guest speakers periodically drop by to cheer the troops. Expect sincere, homey ambiance, lively conversation, and a bit of pamphleteering.

Paper Vision (408/453-1345; 1345 Pacific Ave., Santa Cruz) Fiction, travel, and art books are available, plus the most witty and comprehensive selection of fine greetings cards in the area.

Monterey Coast

The Book Tree (408/373-0228; 118 Webster St., Monterey) Specializing in foreign language books, women's studies classics, and children's literature, this shop also boasts plenty of best sellers.

Bookworks (805/372-2242; 667 Lighthouse Ave., Pacific Grove) A coffee house serves espresso, croissants, and light sandwiches to browsers of endless shelves of regional authors, every newspaper under the sun, foreign language classics, and books for children.

Old Monterey Book Co. (408/372-3111; 136 Bonifacio Place, Monterey) Those on the look out for that rare, unusual, and out-of-print classic will revel in the discerning possibilities tucked away in this popular shop.

Thunderbird Bookshop (408/624-4995; The Barnyard, Hwy. 1 & Carmel Valley Rd., Carmel) This landmark bookstore is packed with a stellar collection of current and classic works and offers an adjoining restaurant for lingering with your latest purchase.

San Luis Obispo Coast

Earthling Bookshop (805/543-7951; 698 Higuera, San Luis Obispo) Boasting its own cozy fireplace, this extremely popular local fixture serves up a huge inventory of popular and classic titles, plus live poetry readings, art shows, and children's storytelling. The annex across the street features discount books and a plethora of greeting cards.

Foul Play (805/927-5277; 2380 Main St., Cambria) Thousands of mystery, suspense, and horror titles await the sleuthfully inclined. Also offers a hefty selection of children's games and gifts.

Phoenix Books (805/543-3591; 990 Monterey St., San Luis Obispo) New, used, and rare books fill this bibliophile's haven, featuring western and local history, anthropology, archaeology, and natural history.

Phoenix Books in San Luis Obispo is a haven of new, used, and rare books on the history of the western United States.

Jay Swanson

Spellbinders (805/927-3385; 4070 Burton Dr., Cambria) This winsome book boutique is completely stocked with stories for youngsters, plus games and cards with a youthful attitude.

Santa Barbara Coast

Chaucer's Books (805/682-6787; Loreto Plaza, 3321 State St., Santa Barbara) A browser's bonanza and best friend to the serious bibliophile, this spacious and substantial store offers the largest selection of titles in the southern Central Coast area.

Earthling Bookshop & Café (805/965-0926; 1137 State St., Santa Barbara) The resident fireplace invites you to linger, read, and browse. The café entices you with fine coffee and homemade desserts. And there are over 100,000 titles of every kind in stock. Unique and welcoming.

A cozy fireplace provides an invitation to linger over the huge inventory of popular Earthling Bookshop, with locations in Santa Barbara and San Luis Obispo.

Jay Swanson

Lost Horizon Bookstore (805/962-4606; 703 Anacapa St., Santa Barbara) Antiquarians and history buffs will find much food for thought here, including a hefty collection of books on antiques, California history, and art.

Pacific Travelers Supply (805/963-4438; 529 State St., Santa Barbara) Huge stock of guidebooks for travel anywhere in the world, and everything else for the traveler, from luggage and backpacks to compasses and topographic maps.

CLOTHING

The huge shopping malls and centers of the Central Coast will provide you with all the national chain shopping — from The Nature Company to Nordstrom, Macy's, and the Emporium — you could desire. But we encourage the fashion-seeking visitor to delve into the downtown shopping districts, the small locally owned shops and boutiques, to get in touch with the style of the area. Residents here are invariably partial to natural fiber clothing, and some of the most appealing shops specialize entirely in cotton, rayon, and silk apparel.

Santa Cruz Coast

Bunny's Shoes (408/423-3824; 1350 Pacific Ave., Santa Cruz) The smart, the trendy, even the avant garde in women's footgear stand by in this appealing boutique for the enlightened foot fetishist.

Cat N' Canary (408/423-8696;1100 Pacific Ave., Santa Cruz) Up-to-the-minute fashions for young men and women make this trendy shop a popular local landmark.

Cruz'n (408/476-2533; 127 Monterey Ave., Capitola) For the young with an outdoor lifestyle attitude, this shop features bold and sassy beachwear and resort apparel.

Innovations (408/688-1744; 8035 Soquel Dr., Aptos) Career outfits and sexy evening wear are the focus of this consistently inviting boutique.

Pacific Trading Company (408/476-6109; 504C Bay Ave., Capitola) Elegant contemporary apparel, plus plenty of jewelry and accessories, have made this company popular with locals for the past decade. (Also at 1338 Pacific Ave., Santa Cruz; 408/423-3349.)

Shandrydan (408/425-8411; 107 Walnut Ave., Santa Cruz) This spacious boutique just off downtown's main street is filled with California easy-living styles, local designer outfits, and a bonanza of contemporary designer jewelry.

Yellow Bird (408/425-0542; 1129 Soquel Ave., Santa Cruz) Contemporary easy-to-wear ensembles, bold beach ensembles, smashing one-of-a-kind scarves, imported and contemporary jewelry — all with a distinctly California coastal attitude.

Monterey Area

American Tin Cannery Factory Outlets (408/372-1442; 125 Ocean View Blvd., Pacific Grove) Just around the corner from the Monterey Bay Aquarium is this shop-till-you-drop island of factory outlets — including Carole Little, Geoffrey Beene, Van Heusen, and Maidenform and restaurants — housed inside one of the area's historic canneries.

Big Sur Handwovens (408/667-2589; Village Shops, Hwy. 1, Big Sur) Lushly textured and naturally dyed homespun and hand-woven textiles fashioned into one-of-a-kind pieces by top local artisans are the specialty of this land's end boutique. In the heart of the majestic Big Sur landscape.

R.K. Shugart (408/624-7748; Dolores bet. 7th & 9th, Carmel) Top quality and deluxe designer women's wear, from exciting contemporary sportswear to elegant evening wear.

Reincarnation Antique Clothing (408/649-0689; 214 17th St., Pacific Grove)

Carrying on the timeless California tradition of vintage fashion, this charming store invokes high fashion nostalgia with its amazing selection of earlier epoch clothing, jewelry, hats, and irresistible accessories.

Sensations (408/625-2943; 6th & San Carlos, Carmel) Contemporary fashions, sportswear, and accessories of the bold and glittering variety for high style fashion statements.

San Luis Obispo Coast

Ambiance (805/541-0988; 716 Higuera, San Luis Obispo) Locally designed and created contemporary clothing for women; exclusively natural fabrics in soft earth tones.

Ann's (805/543-8250; 895 Monterey St., San Luis Obispo) High quality contemporary women's apparel looks especially inviting displayed inside a classy 19th-century downtown building.

Decades (805/546-0901; 697 Higuera, San Luis Obispo) Racks and racks of top condition vintage clothing and flashy accessories distinguish this shop, which also specializes in camp collectibles of all kinds from the '40s, '50s, and '60s.

Gary Paul (805/543-6692; 770 Higuera, San Luis Obispo) Linen, silk, and rayon designer shirts for men abound in this very smart shop of contemporary designs for the man who's not afraid to make a fashion statement.

London Fog Factory Stores (805/773-5755; Pismo Coast Shopping Plaza, Pismo Beach) A vast selection of the fabled rainwear and outerwear, plus timelessly styled slacks, sport shirts, sweaters, and stormy weather accessories, all at substantial savings off the usual retail prices.

Santa Barbara Coast

Antoinette (805/969-1515; 1046 Coast Village Road, Montecito) Charismatic cashmere fashions are specially designed in Italy for this tempting boutique and created by leading international cashmere weavers. Custom order cashmere sweaters also are available.

Classico (805/965-2494; 916 State St., Santa Barbara) Very contemporary styles for men and women, featuring silky rayon day dresses and easy-tailored jackets and pants.

CP Shades (805/963-4003; 809 State St., Santa Barbara) Subtly hand-dyed natural fabric apparel designed in the San Francisco Bay area is as comfortable to wear as it is California in spirit. A full line of linen, cotton, and rayon outfits in colors of the earth and sea.

Firenze (805/965-5723; 419 State St., Santa Barbara) A bountifully stocked outlet store for fabulous contemporary designs in supple leathers and suede, with cocktail wear, ensembles, and a colorful, high fashion inventory of elegant, sporty jackets.

Intimo (805/565-5606; 1046 Coast Village Rd., Montecito) Fantasy lingerie, from the ultra silky and imported to the seductive and outrageous, is the specialty of this undergarment store-to-the-stars.

Wendy Foster (805/565-1502; 516 San Ysidro Rd., Montecito) Casually elegant silk and linen outfits, and luxuriously modish accessories in an upmarket designer boutique, at the multi-faceted Pierre Lafond emporium. (Another location is at 833 State St., Santa Barbara; 805/966-2276.)

JEWELRY

In addition to your friendly neighborhood jeweler, Central Coast communities are well appointed with boutiques offering exciting wearable art fashioned from nature's own treasury, as well as luxurious high fashion jewelry for those to whom money is no object.

Santa Cruz Coast

Eclectix (408/426-8305; 1132 Pacific Ave., Santa Cruz) Crammed to the rafters with exotic and antique jewelry of every description, this shop specializes in American Indian and East Asian pieces.

Latta (408/475-1771; 120 Stockton Ave., Capitola) Contemporary variations on art nouveau themes distinguish the handsome, handmade jewelry created by local goldsmith Jay Latta. Set with polished and faceted gemstones, the rings are of special beauty.

Many Hands Gallery (408/429-8696; 1516 Pacific Ave., Santa Cruz) A visual feast of hand-crafted gold, silver, and cloisonné jewelry from top regional and California artisans, including many created in-house from antique crystal and semiprecious gemstone beads from around the world.

A playful necklace by Jill Henry is only one of the inventive jewelry pieces by top regional designers showcased at Many Hands Gallery in downtown Santa Cruz.

Paul Schraub

Thomas Mantle Designs (408/429-8232; 1001 Center St., Santa Cruz) A talented resident goldsmith and jewelry designer creates luxurious one-of-a-kind contemporary mounted pieces in this engaging studio and showroom.

The Vault (408/426-3349; 1339 Pacific Ave., Santa Cruz) A stunning inventory of imaginative contemporary gold and silver jewelry grouped into opulent display cases according to gemstones make a visit to this shop like a stroll through a museum. In the back, a small boutique trades in exclusive silk blouses, gowns, and sweaters.

Monterey Coast

Fourtané Estate Jewelers (408/624-4684; Pine Inn Shops, Ocean at Lincoln Ave., Carmel) Scrumptious and elegant jewelry, watches, and objets d'art from the 19th and 20th centuries make this splendid treasure trove of vintage estate luxuries a must-visit.

Jewel Boutique (408/625-1016; The Barnyard, Carmel Valley Rd., Carmel) Custom designed and imported jewelry shares this shop with fabulous antique and estate items.

Mark Areias Jewelers (408/624-5621; 5th & San Carlos, Carmel) This authorized Cartier dealer stocks bedazzling adornments both contemporary and antique. (Another location is at 7552 Soquel Ave, Aptos; 408/688-2799.)

Silver Feather Trading Company (408/624-3622; Carmel Plaza, Carmel) A cache of turquoise and silver is featured in this gorgeously stocked dealer in authentic American Indian jewelry and artwork.

San Luis Obispo Coast

Andrews Jewelers (805/543-4543; 720 Higuera, San Luis Obispo) A shimmering array of custom contemporary designs, showcasing fine diamond, gold, and set gemstone work at a friendly boutique.

Casa de Oro/Sheila Hollingshead Jewelry (805/927-5444; 4090 Burton Dr., Cambria) Innovative jewelry designs are featured in this very contemporary jewelry-as-wearable-art emporium.

The Gold Concept (805/544-1088; 740 Higuera, San Luis Obispo) Irresistible contemporary jewelry designs, bold gold work, and unusual gem selections.

Bold contemporary jewelry is the house specialty at San Luis Obispo's Gold Concept.

Jay Swanson

Nature Gallery (805/544-6883; 844 Monterey, San Luis Obispo) From the center of the earth come the breathtaking crystals, minerals, and gem stones fashioned into jewelry (or dramatically unset) that make this shop unique.

Santa Barbara Coast

Boon Mee Collection (805/966-7369; 609 Paseo Nuevo, Santa Barbara) Stunning wearable art is the specialty here, including hand-crafted art glass and cutting edge artisan jewelry, as well as sumptuous jewel boxes and other artistic fashion accessories.

Dellani Jewelers (805/965-2167; 801 State St., in the Paseo Nuevo, Santa Barbara) Bold and expertly crafted custom design jewelry (wearable art, actually) in 14k and 18k gold are showcased at this glittering studio.

Oliver & Espig Jewelers (805/962-8111; #7 1114 State St., Santa Barbara) Spectacular contemporary jewelry and wearable art designs by leading gold and gem designers fill this exceptional shop.

Shells O'Barbara (805/966-5256; 7 West Victoria, Santa Barbara) Regionally specific jewelry stylings featuring lustrous California green abalone shell, sterling silver, and paua jewelry separates this shop from the landlocked. Ear piercing while you wait.

SPECIALTY

From the terrestrial to the celestial, these sometimes wild and weird shops featuring Central-Coastiana may prove as memorable as any other destination on your sojourn. For some of these, set your brain pan on "experimental" before entering.

Santa Cruz Coast

Anubis Warpus (408/423-3208; 803 Pacific Ave., Santa Cruz) An instant hit of Santa Cruz subculture, this on-the-edge shop offers body-piercing paraphernalia, leather, metal, *de rigueur* Doc Martens, banned books, and an in-house tattoo parlor for that ultimate Central Coast souvenir.

Aries Arts (408/476-6655; 201 Capitola Ave., Capitola) The classic '60s hippie shop, perfumed with incense and filled with colorful clothing, crystals, and handmade jewelry.

Atlantis Fantasyworld (408/426-0158; 1020 Cedar St., Santa Cruz) For the hardcore comic book and trading card aficionado: collector's items issues, plus the new and unusual for kids of all ages.

Cunha's General Store (415/726-4071; 448 Main St., Half Moon Bay) The time-trip starts when you enter this atmospheric store packed with cowboy gear, dry goods, deli items, and the tall tales of resident farmers and local fishermen.

Cowboy paraphernalia and an eclectic variety of dry goods await at Half Moon Bay's historic Cunha's General Store.

Stan Cacitti

Imagine (408/427-0240; 107 Locust St., Santa Cruz) Practically a shrine to Beatles and John Lennon paraphernalia, this imaginative shop stocks books, magazines, cards, posters, and videos with a '60s, all-you-need-is-love theme.

Integrand Design (408/426-4717; 1515 Pacific Ave., Santa Cruz) A local landmark for luxurious housewares, culinary accessories, contemporary furniture, and luscious imported bath items, this longtime favorite is housed inside a stately historic bank building in the heart of downtown.

Salz Leather Store (408/423-1480; 1040 River St., Santa Cruz) In a vintage 1860s tannery, this aromatic shop offers lush leather handbags, wallets, and an executive line of briefcases.

Monterey Coast

Golf Arts & Imports (408/625-4488; 6th & Dolores, Carmel) Golf widows and linksmen alike will be fascinated by this whimsical conglomeration of golf art, reproductions, and historical originals. Golf antiques and paraphernalia such as Scottish tartan club covers and golf logo silk ties from Italy are among the treasures.

Owl's Nest (408/624-5509; San Carlos & 7th Ave., Carmel) This shop recaptures the past with a fascinating selection of artist-made dolls and evocative teddy bears and other stuffed animals.

San Luis Obispo Coast

Country Classics (805/549-0844; 849 Monterey, San Luis Obispo) A huge selection of tasteful country-theme gifts, Victorian and French country home furnishings, scented soap, and folk art provide the content here, but the real gem is the old country store itself, the historic Sinsheimer Brothers building, a trip to the past with hardwood floors and 20-foot wooden ceilings.

Farm Supply Company (805/543-3751; 675 Tank Farm Rd., San Luis Obispo) The real thing, this farm supply depot catering to the needs of area ranchers brims with all those quintessential Western accoutrements for riding the range while mending fences — overalls, saddle blankets, feed troughs, and grooming supplies. A surefire thrill for city slickers.

Games People Play (805/541-GAME; 1119-B Garden St., San Luis Obispo) A fascinating, family-friendly haven of gamesmanship, filled with new and vintage comic books, plus board and role-playing games of astonishing variety.

Santa Barbara Coast

Enlightened Sights (805/962-3008; 819 State St., Santa Barbara) One of the very best contemporary greeting card, art postcard, and progressive T-shirt stores in California.

Jedlicka's (805/688-2626; 2883 Grand Ave., Los Olivos) Preparing you to saddle up and ride off into the sunset, this ultimate Western store outfits real ranchers — and those who just want to look like John Wayne — in Tony Lama boots and Stetson hats. Acres of silver belt buckles, saddles, bridles, and bits. It even smells like the Old West. (Another location is at 2605 De La Vina St., Santa Barbara; 805/687-0747.)

Pierre Lafond (805/565-1502; 516 San Ysidro Rd., Santa Barbara) One-stop shopping for those with luxurious taste. Housed in a warren of interlocking rooms on two floors, this complex offers fabulous pastries; a culinary store that's a who's-who of regional condiments, sauces, pastas, and confections; plus a home furnishings, linens, and imported lingerie section stocked with the ultimate in specialty finery.

Stampa Barbara (805/962-4077; 505 Paseo Nuevo, Santa Barbara) This amazing emporium is lined, floor to ceiling, with over 100,000 rubber stamps from 200 separate purveyors. Highlights include hearts, cats, fish, witty sayings, cartoon characters, Victoriana, and everything else you can think of, plus multi-colored stamp pads and inks.

SPORTS

In an area so aggressively devoted to the outdoor life, sports shops enjoy almost cult status, especially those dedicated to one of the region's top spectator attractions: surfing. Wherever you are along the Central Coast, you're never far from a substantial stock of clothing, equipment, gear, maps, and paraphernalia for outfitting your favorite outdoor activity — even if it's simply a stroll on the beach.

Santa Cruz Coast

Outdoor World, Inc. (408/423-9555; 136 River St., Santa Cruz) Everything you'll need to enjoy the great outdoors is here: sunglasses, snorkeling gear, insect repellent, racquets, balls, bathing suits, fins, goggles, canteens, compasses, shoes, and shirts. (Also at 1440 41st Ave., Capitola; 408/479-1501.)

O'Neill's Surf Shop (408/475-4151; 1149 41st Ave., Capitola) Founded by wetsuit inventor Jack O'Neill, this is the Bonzai Pipeline of north Central Coast surf shops with everything from sunglasses and baggies to surfboards.

Santa Cruz Surf Shop (408/464-3233; 753 41st Ave., Santa Cruz) One block from the beach, and just down the road from top surfing conditions at Pleasure Point, this "locally grown" shop features a huge selection of surf and skateboard equipment, top fashion lines, and locally designed Santa Cruz surfboards.

Monterey Coast

On the Beach Surf Shop (408/624-7282; Ocean & Mission Ave., Carmel) Be a surfer — or just dress like one. Everything you need is for sale, from boards and wetsuits to rollerblades, skateboards, and boogie boards. All this shop lacks is immediate proximity to great surfing. (Another location is at 693 Lighthouse Avenue, Monterey; 408/646-WAVE.)

Sweet Shot Golf & Tennis (408/372-2414; 865 Abrego St., Monterey) An exhaustively complete selection of clubs, racquets, bags, shoes, and gear for the discriminating sports aficionado.

San Luis Obispo Coast

Central Coast Surfboards (805/541-1129; 736 Higuera, San Luis Obispo) Boards for all sports — surfboards, sailboards, skateboards, boogie boards — abound in this well-stocked water sports center.

Hind Inc. (805/541-6019; 699 Higuera, San Luis Obispo) This outlet for Hind high performance sportswear is packed with sleek running, swimming, fitness, and cycling wear, including close-out and seconds bargains.

Santa Barbara Coast

Great Pacific Patagonia (805/966-7370; 1118 State St., Santa Barbara) Complete lines of colorful, durable Patagonia adventure sports gear, plus backpacking, hiking, and camping supplies stock this attractive shop.

Morningstar Surf & Sport (805/967-8288; 179 S. Turnpike Rd., Santa Barbara) State-of-the-art surfboard designs by legendary David Puu are among the custom surfboards available at this fully loaded specialty shop. Also featured are all surfing accessories, wetsuits, boogie boards, skates, skateboards, and sports culture shoes.

Roger Dunn Golf Shops (805/964-3484; 3917 State St., Five Point Shopping Center, Santa Barbara) A veritable supermarket for the golfer. Attractions are equipment and accessories, an indoor driving range, putting green, and expert staff ready to custom-fit your clubs.

Underwater Sports (805/962-5400; Breakwater Harbor, Santa Barbara) Before you shoot some curls or hunt for abalone, you'll want to check out the diving and surfing equipment housed in this full-service aquatic hot spot.

Shopping Complexes

Central Coast villages, towns, and cities invariably offer fine shopping districts, clustered tightly around central downtown art, theater, and civic bastions. Monterey's historic *Cannery Row* is lined with antique and wine shops, T-shirt and upscale clothing boutiques, and everything in between. The same can be said of *Pacific Avenue* in Santa Cruz and San Luis Obispo's *Higuera Street*. *The Tin Palace* on Half Moon Bay's Main Street is a former wagon repair shop converted into a tiny regional mall filled with arts, crafts, fine clothing, cards, a coffee shop, and several terrific restaurants.

Those devoted to the huge, generic mall concept will also find ample opportunities to flex their credit cards in brand-name department stores. But this region also features several tastefully organized centers boasting fine and innovative shops offering the best in regional consumerism. *Carmel Crossroads*, on Hwy. 1 just south of Carmel, is one especially inviting conglomeration of upscale bistros, culinary boutiques, and exceptional clothing emporia, all served up with a Western ranch club flavor. In Santa Barbara, where the native Spanish architecture has turned even multi-story parking garages into charming vine-draped haciendas with faux balconies, the *El Paseo* al fresco mall blends old and new in a celebration of Andalusian ambiance. Here visitors will find galleries, curio shops, jewelry, and designer clothing stores encircling a historic old adobe. Across the street is an even more sprawling, newer cluster of fine stores at *Nuevo Paseo*. Quintessentially Central Coast, this gorgeously landscaped façade of Spanish adobe boasts gorgeous tile work, splendid fountains, and ample outdoor seating for leisurely snacking — a setting so seductive that shoppers find it easy to spend an entire day there.

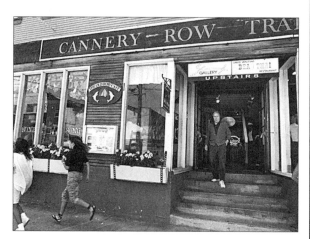

Monterey's historic Cannery Row is a shopper's paradise, lined with a delightful array of stores.

Shmuel Thaler

CHAPTER NINE
Nuts and Bolts
INFORMATION

The big picture: two people can join a pilot for a ride in an open cock-pit antique plane, in a Wings Over Paradise Biplane Tour.

Bob Hill

This chapter is a one-stop Central Coast survival guide. Filled with hard facts, it is compiled with both the local and visitor in mind, providing guidance in the following areas:

AMBULANCE/FIRE/POLICE

Dial (or press) **911** to request an ambulance, report a fire or any situation requiring immediate police response, or to get help for any and all emergency situations anywhere on the Central Coast.

AREA CODES

The Area Code for Santa Cruz, Monterey, Santa Clara, and San Benito counties is **408**, and for San Mateo and San Francisco counties, **415**.

The Area Code for San Luis Obispo, Santa Barbara, and Ventura counties is **805**, and for Los Angeles County **213**.

BABY-SITTING/CHILD CARE

For vacationing parents who need a night out or a day alone together, short-term child care or babysitting services provided by reputable licensed individuals could be the answer: Call for services and fees.

Santa Cruz Coast

Kids' Klub 408/476-8444; 1440 41st Ave., Capitola

Monterey Coast

Peninsula Child Care Services 408/649-8119; PO Box 1924, Monterey

Time Out! Child Care 408/375-9269, 316 Van Buren #10, Monterey

San Luis Obispo Coast

Child Care Company 805/544-5154; PO Box 3921, San Luis Obispo

The Child Care Company in San Luis Obispo accepts young travelers 15 months to 5 years old.

Paul Schraub

Santa Barbara Coast

Grandmothers Only Baby-sitting Service 805/685-4450; PO Box 21402, Santa Barbara

BIBLIOGRAPHY

The Central Coast has long inspired storytellers, historians, and novelists to put pen to paper. Bookstores here usually boast special sections devoted to lore, cuisine, natural history, reminiscence, and fiction written about this fascinating wedge of the Golden State. Public libraries are additional fonts of literature about this land and its people, from the archival diaries of the Spanish explorers to charming tourism guides spanning the past two centuries. Reference librarians specialize in directing newcomers to a wealth of browsing material on everything from tide pools to winemaking.

BOOKS YOU CAN BUY

Autobiography, Biography, Reminiscence

Dunn, Geoffrey. *Santa Cruz is In the Heart*. Capitola Book Company Publishing, 1989. 198 pp., illus., photos, $10.95. Delicious anecdotes, courageous pioneers, and charismatic characters spill from these pages of crisply written memoirs by the scion of a third-generation Italian fishing family.

Boutelle, Sara Holmes. *Julia Morgan, Architect*. Color photos by Richard Barnes. Abbeville Press, 1988. 265 pp., index, illus., photos, $55. A richly told and rewarding biography of the remarkable California architect whose elegantly rustic Arts and Crafts style shaped many landmarks of the northern California coast. Morgan, the first American woman admitted to the Beaux Arts enclave of Paris, is best known for surviving the wild imagination of William Randolph Hearst during the building of his San Simeon castle.

Houston, James D. *Californians: Searching for the Golden State*. Santa Cruz: Otter B Books, 1992. 288 pp., $10.95. Reminiscence, anecdote, environmental puzzling, and historical detective work in a literary treasure hunt for the spirit of the Golden State.

Cultural Studies

Miller, Bruce W. *Chumash*. Los Osos: Sand River Press, 1988. 135 pp., index, photos, $8.95. Knowledgeable, clearly written historical and archaeological account of the fortunes of these early Central Coast natives. Placing the hunter/gatherer peoples in intelligible historical context, the book includes chapters on religion, rock painting, basketry, social customs.

Margolin, Malcolm. *The Ohlone Way*. Illustrated by Michael Harney. Berkeley: Heyday Books, 1978. 168 pp., index, illus., $9.95. A sensitive and sympathetic glimpse into the lives of these gentle hunter/gatherers, recounting their nomadic movements, artistic preoccupations, hunting rituals, and metaphysical beliefs.

Clark, Donald. *Santa Cruz County Place Names*. Santa Cruz: Santa Cruz Historical Society, 1986. 552 pp., illus., maps, $23.95. Oral histories, folklore, and rare archival information in a fascinating encyclopedia of Santa Cruz County places and how they got their names, both official and colloquial.

Clark, Donald. *Monterey County Place Names*. Carmel Valley: Kestrel Press, 1991. 661 pp., index, maps, $21.95. An exploration of the origin of official and unofficial place names of the territory that comprised the most important outpost of Spanish domination in Old California.

Lydon, Sandy. *Chinese Gold*. Capitola Book Company, 1985. 550 pp., illus., photos, $24.95. Eye-opening and brilliantly researched, this work reveals the productivity and enterprise of Chinese immigrants throughout the Central Coast. Written with flourish and confidence, this book bursts with archival photographs and eye-witness accounts.

Monterey Bay historian Sandy Lydon recorded the legacy of the Central Coast's fascinating immigrant past and its many Chinatowns in his award-winning book Chinese Gold.

Shmuel Thaler

Fiction

Haslam, Gerald W., ed. *Many Californias: Literature from the Golden State*. Reno: University of Nevada Press, 1992. 250 pp., index, $14.95. Handy literary tour guide through some of the best minds that ever penned the West. A contemporary sampler filled with excerpts, poems, and stories from Californians including Wallace Stegner, Maxine Hong Kingston, Joan Didion, Raymond Chandler, Toshio Mori, Jack London, Richard Henry Dana, and John Muir.

Jeffers, Robinson. *Cawdor/Medea*. New York: New Directions, 1970. 191 pp., $10.95. A riveting introduction to the moody genius of a Central Coast master. Written in 1928, *Cawdor* is a stormy narrative love poem set on the turbulent Big Sur coast. Jeffers' 1946 verse adaptation of the Greek tragedy *Medea* was created for Dame Judith Anderson.

Steinbeck, John. *Grapes of Wrath*. Penguin Books, 1939. 580 pp., $7. The Salinas-born Nobel Prize-winner crafted this American classic out of the blood, sweat, and tears of Okie immigrants seeking to escape Dust Bowl depression in the relative paradise of Coastal California.

Stegner, Wallace. *Angle of Repose*. Penguin Books, 1971. 568 pp. $14.99. A Pulitzer Prize-winning exploration of the fears, failures, hopes, dreams, and sheer toughness of a California pioneer family, whose energies and accomplishments shaped the landscape of contemporary Central California. One of the best introductions to how the West was really won.

Stevenson, Robert Louis. *The Works of Robert Louis Stevenson*. London: Octopus Pub. Group, 1989. 687 pp., $7.98. Classic tales penned by the author of *Treasure Island*, which was inspired by his visits to the Monterey Coast.

History

McPhee, John. *Assembling California*. New York: Farrar, Straus and Giroux, 1993. 303 pp., $21. Master wordsmith McPhee continues his explorations into the geologic mysteries of the New World by laying down the geology of California layer by layer. With anecdote, poetic spin, parable, wry wit, and salty observation, the narrative traces the imaginary intersection of human and geologic time in the Golden State, from deserts to coastal ranges.

Woodbridge, Sally B. *California Architecture: Historic American Buildings Survey*. San Francisco: Chronicle Books, 1988. 270 pp., index, illus., photos, $25. A richly detailed and scholarly overview of California's architectural history — from Native American to Post Modern — precedes this encyclopedia of important historic landmarks throughout the state.

Starr, Kevin. *Americans and the California Dream: 1850-1915*. New York: Oxford University Press, 1973. 479 pp., index, photos, $15.95. Rich interweaving of the tales of Yankee speculators, explorers, and leading lights who came to find and fabricate their version of the promised land. Vivid portraits, from Luther Burbank and Jack London to Phoebe Hearst and Isadora Duncan.

Hamman, Rick. *California Central Coast Railways*. Boulder, Colorado: Pruett Publishing Company, 1980. 307 pp., index, illus., photos, $45. A copiously illustrated and lovingly documented train buff's guide that tracks the expansion of the Central Coast via rail. The rich saga of the opening of communications lines throughout the Central Coast is the story of men who demonstrated both engineering expertise and sheer courage in blasting iron highways through the coastal mountains.

Nature Guides

LeBoeuf, Burney, and Stephanie Kaza. *The Natural History of Año Nuevo*. Pacific Grove: Boxwood Press, 1981. 414 pp., index, illus., photos, $12.95. Exhaustively detailed, this is the definitive overview of a unique natural sanctuary — from the history of original whaling settlers to detailed reports on weather, tide pools, plants, currents, and shore life.

Bakker, Elna. *An Island Called California*. Berkeley: University of California

Press, 1984, 2nd ed. 455 pp., index, maps, illus., photos, $15. An eye-opening walk through the ecological niches of California, this is a vivid aid to the non-scientist in interpreting the diversity of flora and fauna. Strong sections on seashore, salt marshes, and sea cliff ecology.

Schoenherr, Allan A. *A Natural History of California.* Berkeley: University of California Press, 1992. 768 pp., $38. Ecological awareness distinguishes this expansive exploration of the biological and geological diversity of California. Natural communities and their interactions and origins are elucidated in a highly engaging style.

Photographic Studies

Crouch, Steve. *Fog and Sun, Sea and Stone: the Monterey Coast.* Portland, Oregon: Graphic Arts Center Publishing Co., 1980. 157 pp., photos, $19.95. Text and images convey the natural wonders, elusive and bold, that adorn this vibrant stretch of the Central Coast.

California Coast. Photos by Larry and Donna Ulrich; text by Sandra L. Keith. Portland, Oregon: Graphic Arts Center, 1990. 160 pp., photos, $40. An armchair stroll up and down the state, photographed in all weather and seasons and from breathtaking points of view.

Recreation

California Coastal Commission. *California Coastal Access Guide.* Berkeley: University of California Press, 1991. 295 pp., index, illus., maps., photos, $16. Coastal state parks, facilities, shoreline topography, and access locations for the entire California coastline. An impressive resource.

McKinney, John. *California Coastal Trails. Vol. 1: Mexican Border to Big Sur.* Santa Barbara: Capra Press, 1983. 208 pp., photos, $15. Written by a veteran hiker and nature enthusiast, this book points to off-the-beaten track walks, camping loops, and scenic trails in and around the Central Coast. Contains good descriptions and clear instructions of what to expect, what to bring, and how long it will all take.

BOOKS YOU CAN BORROW

Baer, Morley, et. al. *Adobes in the Sun: Portraits of a Tranquil Era.* San Francisco: Chronicle Books, 1980. 144 pp., illus., photos. Historic adobes of Monterey as captured by a Bay Area master image maker.

Benjamin, William A. and Karen Bridgers. *Santa Barbara: The American Riviera.* Photographs by Austin MacRae. Santa Barbara: Pacific Travelers Press, 1989. 158 pp., illus. Written with a sense of fun, this focus on a privileged slice of the Central Coast offers up historical and cultural tidbits, and detailed takes on various attractions.

Hague, Harlan and David J. Langum. *Thomas O. Larkin: A Life of Patriotism and Profit in Old California.* University of Oklahoma Press, 1990. 294 pp., index, photos. Focusing on the life and times of the wealthy Monterey merchant who helped finesse the Americanization of Spanish California, this book offers historical analysis of the entrepreneurial spirit that civilized the New World's final frontier.

Hoover, Mildred Brooke *et al. Historic Spots in California*, 3rd ed. Stanford University Press, 1966. 597 pp., index, photos. County by county walking tour through the state's hotbeds of history. Detailed entries on Central Coast landmark regions, chronicling the people, politics, settlements, and battles.

Nordhoff, Charles. *California for Travelers and Settlers.* [1872] Centennial Printing, Berkeley: Ten Speed Press, 1973. 255 pp., illus. Utterly mesmerizing first-hand account of the journey West by the columnist for a popular 19th-century East Coast newspaper. Filled with lore and anecdotes of the day and eye-witness analysis of then little-known natural wonders. It so extolled the balmy climate and therapeutic seaside atmosphere that Nordhoff's tales helped launch a Westward migration still in progress today.

Schaffer, Jeffrey P. *Hiking the Big Sur Country*, Berkeley: Wilderness Press, 1988. 165 pp., index, photos. Detailed and in-depth hiker's guide to the trails, vistas, topography, natural history, and swimming holes of this vast natural preserve. The author talks you step-by-step into hidden canyons and along the tops of ridges, discussing campsite possibilities and climate.

Stanger, Frank M. *South from San Francisco: San Mateo County, California, Its History and Heritage.* San Mateo County Historical Association, 1963. 208 pp., index, photos. Captivating chronicles of the wild-eyed dreamers and sturdy folk who logged, ranched, built, parlayed, and cultivated the wild coastal lands surrounding San Francisco.

Winslow, Jr., Carleton M. and Nickola L. Frye. *The Enchanted Hill: the Story of Hearst Castle at San Simeon.* Millbrae: Celestial Arts, 1980. 168 pp., index, illus., photos. With glossy color photos and Hearst family album snapshots, this oversized volume tracks the construction of the amazing Spanish baroque complex that housed the fantasies and celebrity guests of newspaper magnate William Randolph Hearst.

CLIMATE, WEATHER, WHAT TO WEAR

The very expression "Mediterranean climate," which most appropriately describes the prevailing meteorological ambiance of the Central Coast, conjures balmy days filled with sunshine and temperate, frost-free winters. For most of this almost 300-mile-stretch of California, that image is enjoyably accurate. Santa Cruz' summer days average in the mid to high 70s, while further south in Santa Barbara the warmest days tend to add 10 degrees to that figure. This is idyllic beach climate, with summer evenings cooling down pleasantly into the 50 degree range.

Winters in the rainier northern stretch of the Central Coast offer days ranging from 50 degrees, hitting the 70s during the glorious "false spring" of Janu-

The Central Coast boasts sunny mild temperatures all year round, so pack for outdoor activities (but don't forget a sweater or jacket for chilly nights or foggy mornings).

Don Fukuda

ary and February. Along this coast, summer beach weather begins sometime in March and extends through the end of October. The dry season — often without a drop of rain except for the very rare occasional shower — lasts from May through mid-November.

While the summer is by far the most popular touring season, fall and winter offer days mild enough to require only a sweater or light jacket. Free of the summer crowds, the so-called "off" season rewards the traveler with open roads and crowd-free destinations. Locals revel in the luxury of deserted beaches and unencumbered hiking through mountain forests. All Central Coast residents know that the most beautiful months here — especially with warm, bright sunny days and fog-free nights — are May and October.

A word about the famous coastal fog. The moisture-laden low-lying clouds that hug the Central Coast during summer evenings and early mornings are responsible for the area's year-round vegetation, extended growing season, and mighty redwood forests. It can also come as a surprise to those expecting to hit the beaches on summer mornings, only to find the fog obscuring the sun. As locals are fond of telling first-time visitors, the fog inevitably "burns off" by noon, leaving the afternoon absolutely cloud-free and perfect for outdoor activities. In the summer, the fog rolls back in around sunset, so even in the warmest weather, it's important to come prepared with sweater, jacket, and long pants. The Central Coast claims to have invented the "layered look" in deference to the tendency for a single day to run the gamut of weather and temperature changes.

Wherever and whenever you're traveling along the Central Coast, it's a good idea to pack comfortable walking shoes, a warm sweater or down vest, and a bathing suit. Most nightspots and restaurants in this area stress casual dress, so a tie and high heels usually aren't required. Still, it's smart to pack at least one outfit that makes you feel dressed up for exploring some of the upscale evening destinations, especially in downtown Monterey, Carmel, and Santa Barbara.

GUIDED TOURS

If it's worth seeing here, you can bet that someone has organized a guided tour to see it. Many involve motor coaches the size of condominiums. Some follow a knowledgeable leader through primeval wilderness.

Remember that weekends inevitably bring the largest tour groups to top attractions. There will always be plenty of sightseers at the Monterey Bay Aquarium, Hearst Castle, or the Santa Cruz Beach Boardwalk. But, naturally, there are those who prefer to blaze their own trails, and the Central Coast is used to people doing their own thing.

Santa Cruz Coast

Cherie's Walking Tours (415/726-9333; 353 Myrtle St., Half Moon Bay) One and a half hour walks through downtown Half Moon Bay's hidden and forgotten past every Saturday at 10am (any day during summer by appointment). The cost is $12 per person and groups are limited to 10.

Rag Tyme Air Corp. (408/724-0774; 150 Aviation Way Suite 7, Watsonville) Aviator Mike McIntyre serves up a variety of sightseeing flights in his World War II Stearman trainer bi-plane. He calls them "short hop adventures," they last half an hour and cost $90. Hour trips to Big Sur, Half Moon Bay or the San Joaquin Valley cost $165.

Wings Over Paradise Biplane Tours (408/662-9464; PO Box 671, Aptos) Two people can join a pilot for a ride in an open cock-pit antique Travel Air biplane out of Watsonville's intimate airport. A 30 minute Santa Cruz coastline flight costs $95/one, $125/two. The Point Lobos tour lasts an hour and costs $180/one, $240/two and can be expanded into a whale-watching extravaganza for $50 more. A guaranteed spine shaker is the Barnstormer aerobatic tumbler for $110 (one passenger only) — and if you've flown before, you can even take the stick.

Monterey Coast

Alicia Antiques (408/372-1423; 835 Cannery Row, Monterey) As Alicia Harby-De Noon says, she's "one of the real ones." Presently ensconced in the historic Wing Chong Building, Harby-De Noon has created a Steinbeck Room crammed with memorabilia of the legendary author and paraphernalia from the sardine industry that provided a backdrop to two of his novels. A stand-up lecture takes place in her antique shop and includes tales of the Chinese, Native Americans, and Spanish. The cost is $10 per person, and everyone walks away with a gift of a real sardine label that Alicia bought in mass quantities in the '50s. Call ahead.

Cannery Row Walking Tours (408/373-5571; PO Box 82, Pacific Grove) Rohana LoSchiavo leads walking tours of Cannery Row for $12.50 per person (two person minimum, group rate of $90 for maximum of 15). Participants get an earful of the colorful history of the area, including tales of the old Chinatown, analysis of the sardine industry's impact on the waterfront's present-day architecture, and loads of info on Steinbeck and his milieu.

Gourmet Food & Wine Tours of Monterey Bay (408/655-8687; PO Box 3211, Carmel) Helaine Koffler generally works with corporate or convention groups, but will arrange a limo/gourmet tour for one to three couples. The itinerary is dictated by the size, desires, and budget of the participants; half or full day trips.

On the Loose Secret Tours (408/624-3964; PO Box 22113, Carmel) Myrna Brandwein focuses on made-to-order excursions — visits to artists' studios, historic adobes, exclusive gardens, and even private homes for cooking demonstrations by area chefs. The per person cost is between $50 and $100.

Otter-Mobile Tours & Charters (408/625-9782; PO Box 2743, Carmel) Historic and nature tours are Paula DiCarlo's specialty. Two detailed five hour scenic tours at $30 per passenger spotlight the Monterey Peninsula. An all-day Big Sur/Hearst Castle trip costs $60 per person (all admission tickets are included), leaves at 8:30am and returns at 6pm. An all-day Steinbeck Country/wine tasting tour is also $60.

Seacoast Safari (408/372-1288; 1067 Sawmill Gulch, Pebble Beach) Bob Hamaker has three different five hour tours available at $30 per participant: Big Sur sightseeing and art-gallery hopping, Monterey Peninsula tour, and a Wine Country foray. An all-day venture down the Big Sur coast to Hearst Castle costs $60. He also offers personalized tours.

San Luis Obispo Coast

Central Coast Adventures (805/927-4386; PO Box 160, San Simeon) Walt Rolsma's company provides guided tours of San Luis Obispo County, Big Sur, and San Simeon on bikes and in kayaks. Overnights also are available.

Originating in San Luis Obispo, Hearst Castle Transportation offers chartered trips and tours of the San Simeon landmark.

Shmuel Thaler

Hearst Castle Transportation/San Simeon Stages (805/541-4636; San Luis Obispo) This is the only SLO-originating transportation and tour of the San Simeon landmark. Duncan White's outfit will squeeze in small maverick parties on its chartered bus trips as space permits. The cost of $38 per person includes pick up and drop off at your hotel or B&B, narration by driver/guide, and all admission tickets to the castle.

Slo Spokes (805/542-9396; 1319 Kentwood Dr., San Luis Obispo) Larry Souza will customize a bicycling outing according to the capabilities of the participants and their destination desires, including half day, full day, and overnight pedal-fests through the San Luis Obispo countryside for one to eight people. Costs are negotiable.

Santa Barbara Coast

Pathfinder Tours (805/686-1991; PO Box 81, Los Olivos) Dianne Bermant and Renee Chelew offer everything under the Santa Ynez Valley's glorious sun, including basic sightseeing, winery tours, and visits to see thoroughbred horse training centers, miniature horse, ostrich and llama farms, art galleries and museums. Gourmet bicycle and hiking tours, picnic luncheons, Cachuma Lake cocktail parties, and eagle watch parties can also be arranged.

Santa Barbara Courthouse Tours 805/962-6464; 1100 Anacapa St., Santa Barbara) A free docent-led tour of this wonder of Spanish/Moorish architecture, with its rich murals and lavishly appointed interior, sets off for an hour at 2pm each day (except Sunday). An additional tour begins at 10:30am on Wednesday and Friday.

Walking Tours Through History 805/967-9869; 18 San Marcos Trout Club, Santa Barbara) Elias Chiacos leads two hour tours through the historic downtown section of Santa Barbara for $10 per person ($40 minimum for small parties). The emphasis of his walk is on the art, architecture, history, culture, and horticulture of the 18th through 19th centuries. Tours start at the Courthouse, corner of Anacapa and Anapamu streets.

Santa Cruz Island

Day trips to Santa Cruz Island through the Nature Conservancy, which owns 90 percent of the island, are given about three times a month; $49 per person. Tours start at Ventura Harbor and dock at 5:30; bring your own lunch (805/962-9111). Tours through the Santa Barbara Museum of Natural History (805/682-4711) are at Christy Ranch, are given once or twice a month, last two nights/three days, and cost $450 per person, which includes air transportation, lodgings, meals, and tours/lectures by naturalist guides. Day trips are scheduled one or two times a month, cost $160 per person, and last from lift off at Camarillo Airport at 9am until return set down at 5pm (bring your own lunch, or for $10 more a boxed one can be provided).

Santa Barbara Foreign Visitors Language Services

For international business travelers and tourists, this organization conducts walking tours of historic Santa Barbara in German, French, Spanish, Italian, Portuguese, or Japanese. The cost is $35 per person or couple, $75 for groups large or small. Multi-lingual and multi-talented Patricia Borgman also will arrange foreign language guides for tours originating with other companies, and will provide written translations or personalized assistance to visitors in any of 50 languages. Polyglotal operators are standing by: 805/967-6038.

HANDICAPPED SERVICES

Progressive in more than politics and attitudes, Californians have led the way in providing access to all the resources of this region to persons with disabilities. Government facilities of every kind — from libraries to restrooms — are in the process of accommodating that access, which has been mandated by law to be completed in 1995. Under aggressive action on the part of the State Department of Parks and Recreation, many beaches, trails, parks, and forests have been equipped to offer ample enjoyment to all.

Campsites at Pismo State Beach, Morro Bay State Park, Carpinteria State Beach, and Pfeiffer Big Sur State Park have been created for wheelchair access. Many beaches now boast special wheelchairs that enable beachcombing along the surf; at Año Nuevo, a portable wheelchair-friendly trail can be arranged to provide visitors a close-up look at elephant seal rookeries.

Information about lodgings, restaurants, and cultural attractions noting accommodations for persons with disabilities may be obtained by turning to specific sections of this book. City departments of Parks and Recreation — which may be reached through TDD numbers for the hearing-impaired — also will provide detailed and up-to-date information on facilities in each area.

By checking county transit listings in the local telephone directory, visitors can find out about wheelchair-accessible services like **Dial-A-Ride**. And Erick Mitiken's *Wheelchair Rider's Guide* covers natural areas from Half Moon Bay down to Santa Cruz and Goleta Beach in Santa Barbara County. This free guide is available from the **California State Coastal Conservancy** (510/286-1015).

HOSPITALS & EMERGENCY MEDICAL SERVICE

All of the hospitals listed below have emergency rooms that are open 24 hours a day.

Santa Cruz Coast

Dominican Hospital 1555 Soquel Dr., Santa Cruz; 408/462-7710

Watsonville Community Hospital 298 Green Valley Rd., Watsonville; 408/724-4741

Monterey Coast

Community Hospital of the Monterey Peninsula 23625 West Holman Highway, Monterey; 408/625-4900

San Luis Obispo Coast

Arroyo Grande Community Hospital 345 South Halcyon Rd., Arroyo Grande; 805/489-4261

French Hospital Medical Center 1911 Johnson Ave., San Luis Obispo; 805/542-6377

General Hospital 2180 Johnson Ave., San Luis Obispo; 805/781-4800

Sierra Vista Regional Medical Center 1010 Murray Ave., San Luis Obispo; 805/546-7600

Santa Barbara Coast

Lompoc District Hospital 508 East Hickory Ave., Lompoc; 805/735-3351.

Goleta Valley Community Hospital 351 South Patterson Ave., Santa Barbara; 805/967-3411 (Ext. 255)

Santa Barbara Cottage Hospital Pueblo & Bath Sts., Santa Barbara; 805/569-7210

St. Francis Medical Center 601 East Micheltorena St., Santa Barbara; 805/962-7661

Santa Ynez Valley Hospital 700 Alamo Pintado Rd., Solvang; 805/688-6431 (Ext. 231)

REAL ESTATE

It's only natural that a visit to the Central Coast can provoke love at first sight. For some, that first crush creates a longing to own their very own slice of this seductive pie. That longing will not be satisfied cheaply, however, since the landscape here is considered some of the most desirable available anywhere. Since much of the coast is state-, city-, and county-owned, land is at a premium. Prices along the Central Coast of California are among the highest in the country.

While the median price for a single-family dwelling starts at above $200,000 in the most widely sought-after areas, the Central Coast offers varied possibilities, from oceanfront property and ranches to mountain retreats and quiet neighborhood bungalows. Only those in search of subdivision property will be disappointed.

Current information on the Central Coast real estate market is readily available. Statistics and referrals are available from the **Santa Cruz Association of Realtors** (408/464-2000), **Monterey Peninsula Board of Realtors** (408/373-3002), **San Luis Obispo Association of Realtors** (805/541-2282), and **Santa Barbara Association of Realtors** (805/963-3787). These agencies will happily provide names of reputable real estate agents and brokers, most of whom are listed in the Yellow Pages of local telephone directories.

ROAD SERVICE

For members, *AAA/California State Automobile Association* maintains a toll-free 24-hour emergency telephone number: 800/400-4222, as does the. *National Automobile Club*: 800/622-2130.

TOURIST INFORMATION

Most cities and counties on the Central Coast have tourist-friendly visitors' bureaus eager to send potential travelers information packages on their particular area's bountiful charms. In addition to the obligatory sales job, enough good information, hard facts, and suggestions will be provided for a starting place for your own itinerary.

Santa Cruz Coast

Half Moon Bay Coastside Chamber of Commerce 520 Kelly Ave., Half Moon Bay; attn: Suzanne Cardoza; 415/726-8380

Santa Cruz County Conference & Visitors Council 701 Front St., Santa Cruz; 800/833-3494, 408/425-1234

Monterey Coast

Monterey Peninsula Visitors & Convention Bureau and Chamber of Commerce 380 Alvarado St. (PO Box 1770), Monterey; 408/649-1770

San Luis Obispo Coast

Cambria Chamber of Commerce & Visitors Bureau 767 Main St., Cambria. 805/927-3624

Hearst Castle/San Simeon State Park 750 Hearst Castle Rd., San Simeon; attn: John Blades; 805/927-2093

San Luis Obispo County Visitors & Conference Bureau 1041 Chorro St. Suite E, San Luis Obispo; 800/634-1414, 805/541-8000

San Simeon Chamber of Commerce & Visitors Information 9255 Hearst Dr. (PO Box 1), San Simeon; 800/342-5613, 805/927-3500, 805/927-8358 Fax

Santa Barbara Coast

Santa Barbara Conference & Visitors Bureau 510 State St. Suite A, Santa Barbara; 800-676-1266, 800/927-4688, 805/966-9222, 805/966-1728 Fax

Santa Barbara Visitor Information Center 1 Santa Barbara St. (PO Box 299), Santa Barbara; 805/965-3021

Solvang Conference & Visitors Bureau (Solvang Chamber of Commerce) PO Box 70, Solvang; 800/468-6765, 805/688-0701 (Ext. 520)

Fishing and Hunting Regulations

California Department of Fish & Game 3211 S St., Sacramento, CA 95814; information, licenses, and tags 916/227-2244.

ZIP CODES

Aptos: 95003	Grover Beach: 93433	San Gregorio: 94074
Arroyo Grande: 93420	Guadalupe: 93434	San Juan Bautista: 95045
Avila Beach: 93424	Half Moon Bay: 94019	San Luis Obispo: 93401
Ballard: 93463	Harmony: 93435	San Miguel: 93451
Ben Lomond: 95005	Isla Vista: 93117	San Simeon: 93452
Big Sur: 93920	Lompoc: 93436	Santa Barbara: 93103
Boulder Creek: 95006	Los Olivos: 93441	Santa Cruz: 95060
Buellton: 93427	Los Osos: 93402	Santa Maria: 93454
Cambria: 93428	Montecito: 93108	Santa Ynez: 93460
Capitola: 95010	Monterey: 93940	Saratoga: 95070
Carmel Highlands: 93923	Morro Bay: 93442	Scotts Valley: 95066
Carmel Valley: 93924	Moss Landing: 95039	Shell Beach: 93449
Carmel: 93921	Nipomo: 93444	Soledad: 93960
Carpinteria: 93013	Oceano: 93445	Solvang: 93463
Cayucos: 93430	Old Cuyama: 93214	Soquel: 95073
Davenport: 95017	Pacific Grove: 93950	Summerland: 93067
El Granada: 94108	Paso Robles: 93446	Templeton: 93465
Felton: 95018	Pebble Beach: 93953	Ventura: 93001
Goleta: 93117	Pescadero: 94060	Watsonville: 95076
Gonzales: 93926	Pismo Beach: 93449	
Greenfield: 93927	Salinas: 93902	

Index

LODGING BY RATE CATEGORY

Price Codes

Inexpensive	Up to $75
Moderate	$75 to $150
Expensive	$150 to $225
Very Expensive	$225 to more

INEXPENSIVE–MODERATE
Apple Lane Inn
Castle Inn by the Sea
New Davenport B&B Inn

INEXPENSIVE–EXPENSIVE
Blue Quail Inn & Cottages
Zaballa House

INEXPENSIVE–VERY EXPENSIVE
Inn at Morro Bay

MODERATE
Babbling Brook B&B Inn
Beach House B&B Inn
Blue Spruce Inn
Chaminade at Santa Cruz
Chateau Victorian B&B Inn
Cliff Crest B&B Inn
Fogcatcher Inn
Gosby House Inn
J. Patrick House
Mangels House
Olallieberry Inn
Old Thyme Inn
Old Yacht Club Inn
Rancho San Gregorio
Stonehouse Inn

MODERATE–EXPENSIVE
Apple Farm Inn
Bayview Hotel B&B Inn
Blue Whale Inn
Casablanca Inn
Centrella Hotel
Darling House
Garden Street Inn
Gatehouse Inn

Green Gables Inn
Madonna Inn
Mission Ranch Resort
Parsonage B&B
Sandcastle Inn
Sandpiper Inn
Sea & Sand Inn
Sea Venture Hotel
Seven Gables Inn
Spindrift Inn
Villa Rosa Inn

MODERATE–VERY EXPENSIVE
Cheshire Cat Inn
El Encanto Hotel & Garden Villas
La Playa Hotel
Montecito Inn
Monterey Plaza
Robles del Rio Lodge
Simpson House Inn
Tickle Pink Inn
Upham Victorian Hotel & Garden Cottages

EXPENSIVE
Ballard Inn
Inn at Depot Hill
Seascape Resort

EXPENSIVE–VERY EXPENSIVE
Inn on Summer Hill
Los Olivos Grand Hotel
Mill Rose Inn
Quail Lodge Resort & Golf Club
San Ysidro Ranch
Ventana

VERY EXPENSIVE
Alisal Guest Ranch
Four Seasons Biltmore Hotel
Highlands Inn
Inn & Links at Spanish Bay
The Lodge at Pebble Beach
Post Ranch Inn
Stonepine Estate Resort

RESTAURANTS BY PRICE CATEGORY

Price Codes

Inexpensive	Up to $10
Moderate	$10 to $25
Expensive	$25 to $40
Very Expensive	$40 or more

INEXPENSIVE
China Szechwan
Duarte's Tavern
Katy's Cottage
Linnaeas Café
Manuel's
Pacific Grill
Real Thai Kitchen
La Super-Rica Taqueria

INEXPENSIVE–MODERATE
Café Stravaganza
El Palomar
Emi's Korean Restaurant & Bar
Jocko's
Mustache Pete's
Rhythm Café
Robin's
Tarpy's Roadhouse

MODERATE
Acacia
Apple Farm
Black Beach Café
Brophy Brothers Restaurant & Clam
    Bar
Café Bittersweet
Cold Spring Tavern
Crow's Nest
Dorn's Original Breakers Café
El Cocodrilo
Gayle's Bakery & Rosticceria
Linn's Main Bin
Mobo Sushi
Montecito Café
Monterey Joe's
Mousse Odile

Nepenthe
New Davenport Cash Store
O'Mei Restaurant
Old Custom House
Old Harmony Pasta Factory
Oysters
Palapas
Pasta Moon
Ranjeet's
Rio Grill
Ristoranti Avanti
San Benito House
Seafood Mama
Silver Jones
Sow's Ear Café
Steamers
Sukeroku
Terrace Grill

MODERATE–EXPENSIVE
Ballard Store
Bay Club
Bindel's
Brambles
Brigitte's
Café Fina
Café Sparrow
Casanova
Central 159
Chez Renee
Duck Club
F. McClintock's Saloon & Dining
    House
Gardens of Avila
Ian's
India Joze
Mattei's Tavern
Pane e Vino
Pearl Alley Bistro & Wine Bar
Piranha
Sea Cloud Restaurant & Social Club
Shadowbrook
21 Victoria
Verandah
Will's Fargo

RESTAURANTS BY CUISINE

About the Authors

Don Harris

Christina Waters is a fifth-generation Californian who has written about people and places in the Central Coast for the past 15 years. Born in Santa Cruz, she spent her childhood traveling as part of an Air Force family. Armed with an expanded palate and a degree in anthropology, she did her Ph.D. work at the University of California, Davis, and moved back to Santa Cruz, working as a journalist for a variety of regional publications. Currently she is Food Editor for *Metro*, a San Jose weekly, and works as a research analyst in the arts at the University of California, Santa Cruz. In her free time, she enjoys sampling the eclectic and award-winning wines of the Central Coast and is coaxing a travel novel out of her computer.

Paul Schraub

Buz Bezore is a fourth-generation Californian and an award-winning editor of myriad newspapers and magazines in the Monterey Bay area. He grew up in the sleepy little town of Santa Clara, which ballooned into the epicenter of Silicon Valley shortly after he left to get a degree in film and anthropology at the University of California, Santa Cruz. Over the past 20 years, he has developed and launched a dozen weekly papers and magazines, and he is presently the editor of *Taste*, a Central Coast food and wine monthly published by San Jose's *Metro*, and also the editor and ringmaster of *Metro Santa Cruz*, which hits the streets in early 1994. In his free time, he enjoys baseball, beer, bodysurfing, and cooking trans-cultural meals.

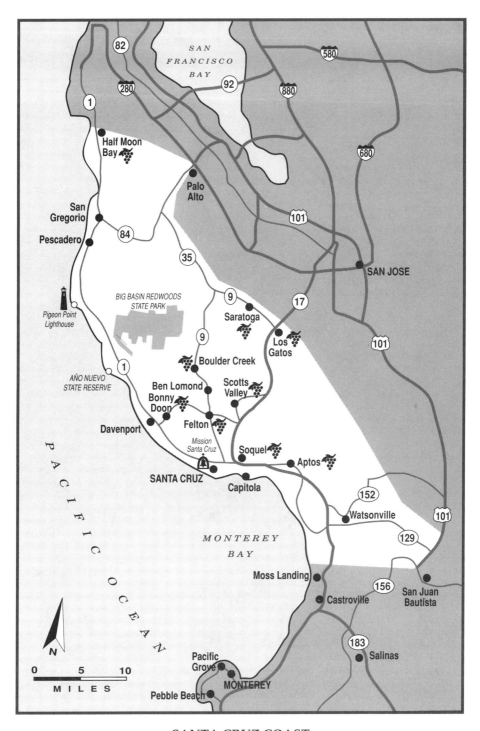

SANTA CRUZ COAST

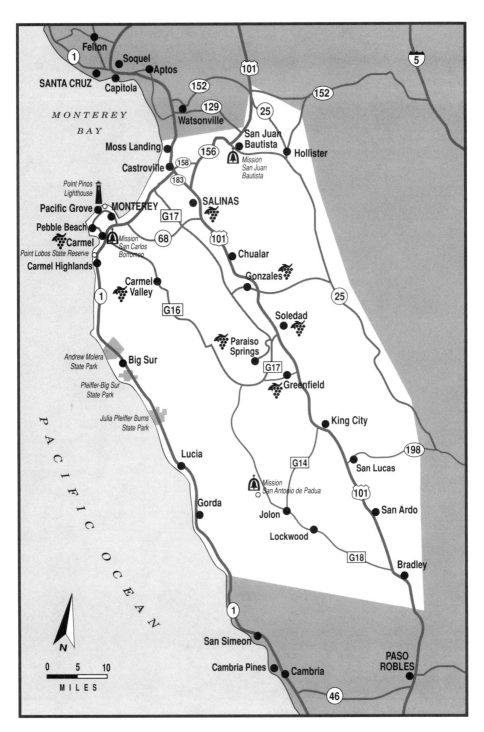

MONTEREY COAST

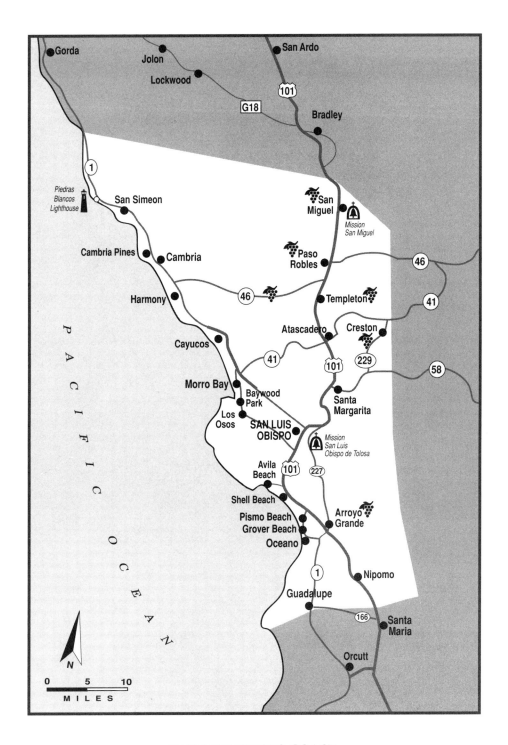

SAN LUIS OBISPO COAST

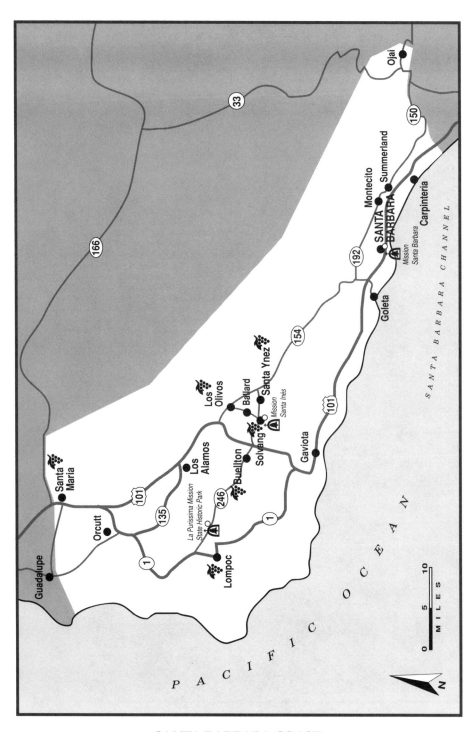

SANTA BARBARA COAST

NOTES

NOTES